Fodor's 2001

KU-488-532

Cape Cod

The complete guide, thoroughly up-to-date

Packed with details that will make your trip

The must-see sights, off and on the beaten path

What to see, what to skip

Mix-and-match vacation itineraries

City strolls, countryside adventures

Smart lodging and dining options

Essential local do's and taboos

Transportation tips, distances, and directions

Key contacts, savvy travel tips

When to go, what to pack

Clear, accurate, easy-to-use maps

Books to read, background essays

Fodor's Cape Cod 2001

EDITORS: Christine Cipriani, Bree Scott

Editorial Contributors: Carolyn Heller, Karl Luntta, Laura V. Scheel
Editorial Production: Ira-Neil Dittersdorf, Rebecca Zeiler Wintle
Maps: David Lindroth, *cartographer*; Rebecca Baer and Bob Blake, *map editors*
Design: Fabrizio La Rocca, *creative director*; Guido Caroti, *art director*; Jolie Novak, *senior picture editor*; Melanie Marin, *photo editor*
Cover Design: Pentagram
Production/Manufacturing: Robert B. Shields
Cover Photo: William H. Johnson

Copyright

ISBN 0–679–00608–7

ISSN 1093–7986

Special Sales

Fodor's Travel Publications are available at special discounts for bulk purchases for sales promotions or premiums. Special editions, including personalized covers, excerpts of existing guides, and corporate imprints, can be created in large quantities for special needs. For more information, contact your local bookseller or write to Special Markets, Fodor's Travel Publications, 280 Park Avenue, New York, NY 10017. Inquiries from Canada should be directed to your local Canadian bookseller or sent to Random House of Canada, Ltd., Marketing Department, 2775 Matheson Boulevard East, Mississauga, Ontario L4W 4P7. Inquiries from the United Kingdom should be sent to Fodor's Travel Publications, 20 Vauxhall Bridge Road, London SW1V 2SA, England.

PRINTED IN THE UNITED STATES OF AMERICA

10 9 8 7 6 5 4 3 2 1

Important Tip

Although all prices, opening times, and other details in this book are based on information supplied to us at press time, changes occur all the time in the travel world, and Fodor's cannot accept responsibility for facts that become outdated or for inadvertent errors or omissions. So **always confirm information when it matters,** especially if you're making a detour to visit a specific place.

CONTENTS

Maps

ON THE ROAD WITH FODOR'S

EVERY VACATION IS IMPORTANT. So here at Fodor's, we've pulled out all stops in preparing *Cape Cod 2001*. To guide you in putting together your Cape experience, we've created multiday itineraries and neighborhood walks. And to direct you to the places that are truly worth your time and money, we've rallied the team of endearingly picky know-it-alls we're pleased to call our writers. Having seen all corners of the Cape, they're real experts. If you knew them, you'd poll them for tips yourself.

One of **Carolyn Heller**'s early memories is of digging in the tide pools along Cape Cod Bay, and she's now introducing her own daughters to the Cape's beaches. A travel writer based in Cambridge, Carolyn tracks the area's dining and arts scenes as Boston bureau chief of the online business-travel site *ontheroad.com*. Her writing has appeared in the *Boston Globe*, the *Los Angeles Times*, the *Philadelphia Inquirer*, the *Miami Herald*, *Family Fun* magazine, and several other Fodor's guidebooks, including *Boston*.

Karl Luntta has lived on Cape Cod for more than 10 years and covered the Cape and islands for such publications as the *Cape Cod Travel Guide*, *Cape Cod Life*, and the *Cape Cod Times*. Along with hav-

ing published his own travel guides to Jamaica, St. Lucia, the Virgin Islands, and the Caribbean region, Karl is also a frequent contributor to Fodor's *Caribbean*.

Yet another Cape Cod transplant, **Laura V. Scheel** was attracted to both the area's natural splendor and unique way of life. A freelance writer and editor based in Wellfleet, she has written on travel and the arts for *Cape Cod Life*, the *Cape Cod Travel Guide*, the *Cape Codder*, the *Provincetown Banner*, and *On the Water*. She is also the editor of *A-Plus*, a local monthly on arts and antiques.

Don't Forget to Write

Keeping a travel guide fresh and up-to-date is a big job. So we love your feedback—positive and negative—and follow up on all suggestions. Contact the Cape Cod editor at editors@fodors.com or c/o Fodor's, 280 Park Avenue, New York, New York 10017. And have a wonderful trip!

Karen Cure

Karen Cure
Editorial Director

Cape Cod *(Boxes Refer to Detail Maps)*

TO BOSTON

Rac

June - Oct.

Duxbury

Plymouth Bay

Plymouth

■ Plimoth Plantation

White Horse Beach

Cape Cod Bay

Manomet

3A

3

Myles Standish State Forest

Great Herring Pond

Sagamore Beach

Scusset Beach State Reservation

Shawme-Crowell State Forest

Town Neck Beach

Sandy Neck Beach

Sandy Neck

25

Buzzards Bay

Canal

Sandwich

West Barnstable

Barnstable

H

Barnstable

US 6

Wareham

Onset

Cape

Bourne

Cod

Sagamore

6

■ **Heritage Plantation**

6A

132

Monument Beach

28

Massachusetts Military Reservation

149

Wequaquet Lake

Pocasset

28A

Mashpee-Wakeby Ponds

Marstons Mills

Centerville

Hya

Buzzards Bay

130

Mashpee

28

Osterville

Hyannis Port

North Falmouth

151

Ashumet Pond

■ **Ashumet Holly and Wildlife Sanctuary**

Santuit

Craigville Beach

Old Silver Beach

Coonamessett Pond

Cotuit

West Falmouth

Waquoit

Poppponesset Bay

Sippewissett

Long Pond

East Falmouth

28

■ **Waquoit Bay Reserve**

Falmouth

New Seabury

May - Oct.

TO MARTHA'S VINEYARD

Woods Hole

■ **Nobska Light**

TO MARTHA'S VINEYARD

South Cape Beach

TO MARTHA'S VINEYARD

Upper Cape

Nobska Pt.

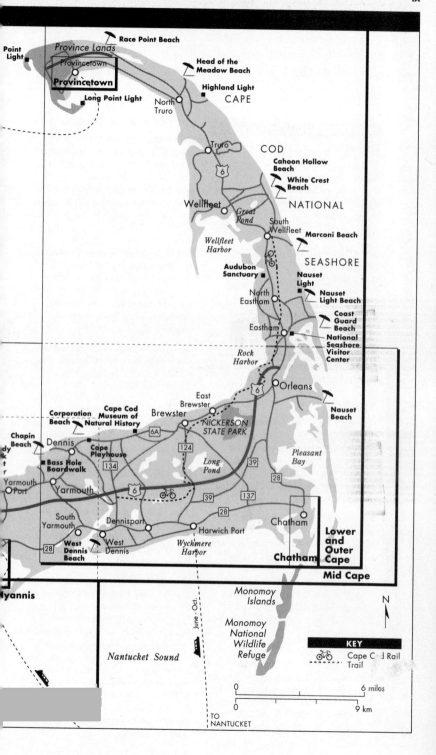

SMART TRAVEL TIPS A TO Z

Basic Information on Traveling on Cape Cod, Savvy Tips to Make Your Trip a Breeze, and Companies and Organizations to Contact

AIR TRAVEL

BOOKING

When you book **look for nonstop flights** and **remember that "direct" flights stop at least once.** Try to avoid connecting flights, which require a change of plane.

CARRIERS

The major U.S. airlines provide service to Boston, the nearest gateway city to Cape Cod. Providence, Rhode Island also served by the major carriers, is an easy drive from the Cape. Airline service to Cape Cod is extremely unpredictable, however, because of the seasonal nature of travel—carriers come and go, while others juggle their routes. Barnstable Municipal Airport will always know which carriers are currently operating.

➤ MAJOR AIRLINES: **American** (☎ 800/433–7300). **Continental** (☎ 800/525–0280). **Delta** (☎ 800/ 221–1212). **Northwest** (☎ 800/225– 2525). **TWA** (☎ 800/221–2000). **US Airways** (☎ 800/428–4322). **United** (☎ 800/241–6522).

➤ SMALLER AIRLINES: **Cape Air/Nantucket Airlines** (☎ 508/771–6944 or 800/352–0714) flies between Boston and Hyannis. **US Airways Express/ Colgan Air** (☎ 800/428–4322) flies to Hyannis from Boston and New York (La Guardia Airport). **Island Airlines** (☎ 508/228–7575 or 800/ 248–7779) flies between Hyannis and Nantucket.

➤ CHARTERS: **Direct Flight** (☎ 508/ 693–6688) is based on Martha's Vineyard and provides charter service off-island. **Westchester Air** (☎ 914/ 761–3000 or 800/759–2929) serves Cape Cod, Martha's Vineyard, and Nantucket from White Plains, New York.

CHECK-IN & BOARDING

Assuming that not everyone with a ticket will show up, airlines routinely overbook planes. When everyone does appear, airlines ask for volunteers to give up their seats. In return, these volunteers usually get a certificate for a free flight and are rebooked on the next flight out. If there are not enough volunteers, the airline must choose who will be denied boarding. The first to get bumped are passengers who checked in late and those flying on discounted tickets, so **get to the gate and check in as early as possible,** especially during peak periods.

Always **bring a government-issued photo ID to the airport.** You may be asked to show it before you are allowed to check in.

CUTTING COSTS

The least expensive airfares to Cape Cod must usually be purchased in advance and are nonrefundable. It's smart to **call a number of airlines, and when you are quoted a good price, book it on the spot**—the same fare may not be available the next day. Always **check different routings** and look into using different airports. Travel agents, especially low-fare specialists (☞ Discounts & Deals, *below*), are helpful.

Consolidators are another good source. They buy tickets for scheduled international flights at reduced rates from the airlines, then sell them at prices that beat the best fare available directly from the airlines, usually without restrictions. Sometimes you can even get your money back if you need to return the ticket. Carefully read the fine print detailing penalties for changes and cancellations, and **confirm your consolidator reservation with the airline.**

➤ CONSOLIDATORS: **Cheap Tickets** (☎ 800/377–1000). **Discount Airline**

Ticket Service (☎ 800/576–1600). Unitravel (☎ 800/325–2222). Up & Away Travel (☎ 212/889–2345). World Travel Network (☎ 800/409–6753).

ENJOYING THE FLIGHT

For more legroom **request an emergency-aisle seat.** Don't sit in the row in front of the emergency aisle or in front of a bulkhead, where seats may not recline. If you have special dietary needs, such as vegetarian, low-cholesterol, or kosher food, **ask for special meals when booking.** To help fight jet lag on long flights, try to maintain a normal routine: **get some sleep** at night, and by day **eat light meals, drink water** (not alcohol), and **move around the cabin** to stretch your legs.

FLYING TIMES

Flying time is 1 hour from New York, 2½ hours from Chicago, 6 hours from Los Angeles, and 3½ hours from Dallas.

HOW TO COMPLAIN

If your baggage goes astray or your flight goes awry, complain right away. Most carriers require that you **file a claim immediately.**

➤ AIRLINE COMPLAINTS: U.S. Department of Transportation **Aviation Consumer Protection Division** (✉ C-75, Room 4107, Washington, DC 20590, ☎ 202/366–2220, airconsumer@ost.dot.gov, www.dot.gov/airconsumer). **Federal Aviation Administration Consumer Hotline** (☎ 800/322–7873).

AIRPORTS

The major gateway to Cape Cod is Boston's Logan International Airport. The expanded T. F. Green Airport in Providence, Rhode Island, served by the low-cost carrier Southwest Airlines and other major carriers, is an alternative. Smaller airports include the Barnstable and Provincetown municipal airports. For more information *see* Arriving and Departing *in* the A to Z section of the appropriate chapter.

➤ AIRPORT INFORMATION: Boston: **Logan International Airport** (☎ 617/561–1806 or 800/235–6426). Providence: **T. F. Green Airport** (☎ 401/737–8222 or 888/268–7222). Hyannis: **Barnstable Municipal Airport** (☎ 508/775–2020). Provincetown: **Provincetown Municipal Airport** (☎ 508/487–0241).

BEACHES

In season you have to pay for parking at public beaches. Parking at "restricted" beaches is available only to residents and to visitors with permits. If you're renting a house, you can purchase a weekly beach permit; contact the town chamber of commerce for details (☞ Visitor Information *in* the A to Z sections of the appropriate chapters). Walkers and cyclists do not need permits to use restricted beaches. The official season generally begins the last weekend in June and ends on Labor Day. Note that even at resident beaches in season, the lots are often thrown open to all early in the morning (before 8) and late in the afternoon (after 4 or 5).

BIKE TRAVEL

Biking is very popular on Cape Cod—some trails are as busy as the roads in summer. Note that Massachusetts law requires children under 13 to wear protective helmets while riding a bike, even as a passenger. For information on trails, maps, and rentals in your area, *see* Getting Around *in* the A to Z section of the appropriate chapter, as well as listings for your specific town.

BIKES IN FLIGHT

Most airlines accommodate bikes as luggage, provided they are dismantled and boxed. For bike boxes, often free at bike shops, you'll pay about $5 from airlines (at least $100 for bike bags). International travelers can sometimes substitute a bike for a piece of checked luggage at no charge; otherwise, the cost is about $100. Domestic and Canadian airlines charge $25–$50.

BUS TRAVEL

Greyhound serves Boston from all over the country; from there you can connect to a local carrier, such as Bonanza Bus Lines, which serves Bourne, Falmouth, and Woods Hole on the Cape, plus nearby Fall River and New Bedford. The Plymouth &

Brockton Street Railway buses travel all the way to Provincetown from Boston and Logan Airport, with stops en route.

The Cape Cod Regional Transit Authority operates several buses within the Cape, all of them wheel-chair-accessible and equipped with bike racks. The SeaLine runs along Route 28 Monday–Saturday between Hyannis and Woods Hole (one-way fare $3.50, from Hyannis to Woods Hole; shorter trips are less), with stops including Mashpee Commons, Falmouth, and the Woods Hole Steamship Authority docks. The SeaLine connects in Hyannis with the Plymouth & Brockton line as well as the Villager, another bus line that runs along Route 132 between Hyannis and Barnstable Harbor, serving the Cape Cod Mall. The driver will stop when signaled along the route.

The b-bus is composed of a fleet of minivans that will transport passengers door to door between any towns on the Cape. Service runs seven days a week, year-round, though reservations must be made in advance. The cost is $2 per ride plus 10¢ per mile.

The H2O Line offers daily regularly scheduled service year-round between Hyannis and Orleans along Route 28. The Hyannis–Orleans fare is $3.50; shorter trips are less. Buses connect in Hyannis with the SeaLine, the Villager, and Plymouth & Brockton lines.

➤ BUS INFORMATION: **Bonanza** (☎ 508/548–7588 or 800/556–3815, www.bonanzabus.com). **Cape Cod Regional Transit Authority** (☎ 508/385–8326, 800/352–7155 in MA; www.capecodtransit.org). **Greyhound** (☎ 800/231–2222, www.greyhound.com). **Plymouth & Brockton Street Railway** (☎ 508/746–0378, www.p-b.com).

BUSINESS HOURS

MUSEUMS & SIGHTS

Hours for sights on the Cape vary widely from place to place and from season to season. Some places are staffed by volunteers and have limited hours (open just a few hours a day several days a week), even in summer, although major museums and attrac-tions will be open daily in summer. Always check the hours of a place you plan to visit, and if you'll be traveling some distance to a sight, call ahead to confirm that it will be open.

SHOPS

Shop hours are generally from 9 or 10 to 5, though in high season many tourist-oriented stores stay open until 10 PM or later. Except in the main tourist areas, shops are often closed on Sunday.

CAMERAS & PHOTOGRAPHY

➤ PHOTO HELP: **Kodak Information Center** (☎ 800/242–2424). *Kodak Guide to Shooting Great Travel Pictures,* available in bookstores or from Fodor's Travel Publications (☎ 800/533–6478; $18 plus $5.50 shipping).

EQUIPMENT PRECAUTIONS

Always **keep your film and tape out of the sun.** Carry an extra supply of batteries, and **be prepared to turn on your camera or camcorder** to prove to security personnel that the device is real. Always **ask for hand inspection of film,** which becomes clouded after repeated exposure to airport X-ray machines, and **keep videotapes away from metal detectors.**

CAR RENTAL

Rates in Boston begin at $35–$40 a day and $150–$179 a week for an economy car with air-conditioning, an automatic transmission, and unlimited mileage. Rates in Hyannis range from $30 to $45 a day and from $169 to $235 a week. These rates do not include tax on car rentals, which is 5%.

For details on reaching and navigating Cape Cod by car, *see* Driving, *below.*

➤ MAJOR AGENCIES: **Alamo** (☎ 800/327–9633, 020/8759–6200 in U.K.). **Avis** (☎ 800/331–1212, 800/331–1084 in Canada, 02/9353–9000 in Australia, 09/525–1982 in New Zealand, 0870/606–0100 in U.K.). **Budget** (☎ 800/527–0700; 0144/227–6266 in U.K.). **Dollar** (☎ 800/800–4000; 0124/622–0111 in U.K.,where it is known as Sixt; 02/9223–1444 in Australia). **Hertz** (☎ 800/654–3131, 800/263–0600 in

Canada, 020/8897–2072 in U.K., 02/ 9669–2444 in Australia, 09/256– 8690 in New Zealand). **National Car Rental** (☎ 800/227–7368; 0845/722– 2525 in U.K., where it is known as National Europe).

➤ LIMOUSINE AGENCIES: **Aristocrat Limousine** (☎ 508/420–5466 or 800/ 992–6163) provides service from the Boston or Providence airports to the Cape; **Avlamar, Inc.** (☎ 508/430– 0666 or 888/404–5663) and **Black Tie Limousine** (☎ 508/775–1780) provide service Cape-wide.

CUTTING COSTS

To get the best deal, **book through a travel agent who will shop around.** Also **price local car-rental companies,** although the service and maintenance may not be as good as those of a major player. Remember to ask about required deposits, cancellation penalties, and drop-off charges if you're planning to pick up the car in one city and leave it in another. If you're traveling during a holiday period, also make sure that a confirmed reservation guarantees you a car.

Do **look into wholesalers,** companies that do not own fleets but rent in bulk from those that do and often offer better rates than traditional car-rental operations.

➤ WHOLESALERS: **Kemwel Holiday Autos** (☎ 800/678–0678, FAX 914/ 825–3160, www.kemwel.com).

INSURANCE

When driving a rented car, you are generally responsible for any damage to or loss of the vehicle as well as for any property damage or personal injury that you may cause. Before you rent, see what coverage your personal auto-insurance policy and credit cards already provide.

For about $15–$20 per day, rental companies sell protection, known as a collision-damage or loss-damage waiver (CDW or LDW), that eliminates your liability for damage to the car.

In Massachusetts the car-rental company must pay for damage to third parties up to a preset legal limit, beyond which your own liability insurance kicks in. So be sure to **make sure you have enough coverage to pay for the car.** If you do not have auto insurance or an umbrella policy that covers damage to third parties, purchasing liability insurance and a CDW or LDW are highly recommended.

REQUIREMENTS & RESTRICTIONS

In Massachusetts you must be 21 to rent a car, and rates may be higher if you're under 25. You'll pay extra for child seats (about $3 per day), which are compulsory for children under five, and for additional drivers (about $2 per day). When picking up a car, non–U.S. residents will need a reservation voucher (for prepaid reservations made in the traveler's home country), a passport, a driver's license, and a travel policy that covers each driver.

SURCHARGES

Before you pick up a car in one city and leave it in another, **ask about drop-off charges or one-way service fees,** which can be substantial. Note, too, that some rental agencies charge extra if you return the car before the time specified in your contract. To avoid a hefty refueling fee, **fill the tank just before you turn in the car,** but be aware that gas stations near the rental outlet may overcharge.

CHILDREN ON CAPE COD

Cape Cod is extremely family-oriented—every imaginable diversion is available for children, including lodgings and restaurants that cater specifically to them and that are affordable for families on a budget. Cottages and condominiums are popular with families, offering privacy, room, kitchens, and sometimes laundry facilities. Often cottage or condo communities have play yards and pools, sometimes even a full range of children's programs.

For local resources consult the A to Z section of the appropriate chapter. For other child-friendly events, *see* Festivals and Seasonal Events *in* Chapter 1.

If you are renting a car, don't forget to **arrange for a car seat** when you reserve.

SMART TRAVEL TIPS A TO Z

► LOCAL INFORMATION: The Bristol County Convention & Visitors Bureau (✉ 70 N. 2nd St., Box 976, New Bedford, MA 02741, ☎ 508/997–1250 or 800/288–6263) has a calendar that lists family-oriented events along south-coastal New England in its "Southern Coastal New England Americana Trail Guide."

FLYING

If your children are two or older, **ask about children's airfares.** As a general rule, infants under two not occupying a seat fly at greatly reduced fares or even for free.

Experts agree it's a good idea to use safety seats aloft for children weighing less than 40 pounds. Airlines set their own policies: U.S. carriers usually require that the child be ticketed, even if he or she is young enough to ride free, since the seats must be strapped into regular seats. Do **check your airline's policy about using safety seats during takeoff and landing.** And since safety seats are not allowed everywhere in the plane, get your seat assignments early.

When reserving, **request children's meals or a freestanding bassinet** if you need them. But note that bulkhead seats, where you must sit to use the bassinet, may lack an overhead bin or storage space on the floor.

LODGING

Most hotels on Cape Cod allow children under a certain age to stay in their parents' room at no extra charge, but others will charge children as extra adults; be sure to **find out the cutoff age for children's discounts.**

If you're planning to stay at a bed-and-breakfast, be sure to **ask the owners in advance** whether the B&B welcomes children. Some establishments are filled with fragile antiques, and owners may not accept families with children of a certain age.

SIGHTS & ATTRACTIONS

Places that are especially appealing to children are indicated by a rubber duckie icon in the margin.

CONSUMER PROTECTION

Whenever shopping or buying travel services on Cape Cod, **pay with a major credit card** so you can cancel payment or get reimbursed if there's a problem. If you're doing business with a particular company for the first time, **contact your local Better Business Bureau and the attorney general's offices** in your own state and the company's home state, as well. Have any complaints been filed? Finally, if you're buying a package or tour, always **consider travel insurance** that includes default coverage (☞ Insurance, *below*).

► BBBs: **Council of Better Business Bureaus** (✉ 4200 Wilson Blvd., Suite 800, Arlington, VA 22203, ☎ 703/276–0100, FAX 703/525–8277 www.bbb.org).

DINING

The restaurants we list are the cream of the crop in each price category. Properties indicated by an ✕☰ are lodging establishments whose restaurant warrants a special trip.

CATEGORY	COST*
$$$$	over $40
$$$	$25–$40
$$	$15–$25
$	under $15

per person for a three-course meal, excluding drinks, service, and 5% sales tax

RESERVATIONS & DRESS

Reservations are always a good idea: we mention them only when they're essential or not accepted. Book as far ahead as you can, and reconfirm as soon as you arrive. We mention dress only when men are required to wear a jacket or a jacket and tie.

DISABILITIES & ACCESSIBILITY

► LOCAL RESOURCES: **Cape Organization for Rights of the Disabled** (CORD; ☎ 508/775–8300, 800/541–0282 in MA) will supply information on accessibility of restaurants, hotels, beaches, and other tourist facilities on Cape Cod. **Sight Loss Services** (☎ 508/394–3904, 800/427–6842 in MA) provides information on accessibility and other needs and referrals for people with vision impairments. The **Cape Cod National Seashore** (✉ South Wellfleet 02663, ☎ 508/349–3785) has facilities, services, and programs accessible to visitors with disabilities. Write for information on what is available. You can ask at the **Cape Cod National Seashore visitor centers** (☎ 508/255–3421 in Eastham, 508/487–1256 in Provincetown; ☞ Web Sites, *below,* for site). For information about accessibility in Massachusetts state parks and beaches, contact the **Massachusetts Department of Environmental Management** (☞ Visitor Information, *below*).

RESERVATIONS

When discussing accessibility with an operator or reservations agent, **ask hard questions.** Are there any stairs, inside *or* out? Are there grab bars next to the toilet *and* in the shower/tub? How wide is the doorway to the room? To the bathroom? For the most extensive facilities meeting the latest legal specifications, **opt for newer accommodations.**

➤ COMPLAINTS: **Disability Rights Section** (✉ U.S. Department of Justice, Civil Rights Division, Box 66738, Washington, DC 20035-6738, ☎ 202/514–0301 or 800/514–0301; 202/514–0383 TTY; 800/514–0383 TTY, ℻ 202/307–1198, www.usdoj.gov/crt/ada/adahom1.htm) for general complaints. **Aviation Consumer Protection Division** (☞ Air Travel, *above*) for airline-related problems. **Civil Rights Office** (✉ U.S. Department of Transportation, Departmental Office of Civil Rights, S-30, 400 7th St. SW, Room 10215, Washington, DC 20590, ☎ 202/366–4648, ℻ 202/366–9371) for problems with surface transportation.

TRAVEL AGENCIES

In the United States the Americans with Disabilities Act requires that travel firms serve the needs of all travelers. Some agencies specialize in working with people with disabilities.

➤ TRAVELERS WITH MOBILITY PROBLEMS: **Access Adventures** (✉ 206 Chestnut Ridge Rd., Scottsville, NY 14624, ☎ 716/889–9096, dltravel@prodigy.net), run by a former physi-

cal-rehabilitation counselor. **Accessible Vans of America** (✉ 9 Spielman Rd., Fairfield, NJ 07004, ☎ 888/282–8267, ℻ 303/781–2329, www.accessiblevans.com). **CareVacations** (✉ 5-5110 50th Ave., Leduc, Alberta T9E 6V4, ☎ 780/986–6404 or 877/478–7827, ℻ 780/986–8332, www.carevacations.com), for group tours and cruise vacations. **Flying Wheels Travel** (✉ 143 W. Bridge St., Box 382, Owatonna, MN 55060, ☎ 507/451–5005 or 800/535–6790, ℻ 507/451–1685, thq@ll.net, www.flyingwheels.com).

➤ TRAVELERS WITH DEVELOPMENTAL DISABILITIES: **Sprout** (✉ 893 Amsterdam Ave., New York, NY 10025, ☎ 212/222–9575 or 888/222–9575, ℻ 212/222–9768, vacations@gosprout.org, www.gosprout.org).

DISCOUNTS & DEALS

Be a smart shopper and **compare all your options** before making decisions. A plane ticket bought with a promotional coupon from travel clubs, coupon books, and direct-mail offers may not be cheaper than the least expensive fare from a discount ticket agency. And always keep in mind that what you get is just as important as what you save.

DISCOUNT RESERVATIONS

To save money, **look into discount reservations services** with toll-free numbers, which use their buying power to get a better price on hotels, airline tickets, even car rentals. When booking a room, always **call the hotel's local toll-free number** (if one is available) rather than the central reservations number—you'll often get a better price. Always ask about special packages or corporate rates.

➤ AIRLINE TICKETS: ☎ **800/FLY–ASAP.**

➤ HOTEL ROOMS: **RMC Travel** (☎ 800/245–5738, www.rmcwebtravel.com). **Turbotrip.com** (☎ 800/473–7829, www.turbotrip.com).

PACKAGE DEALS

Don't confuse packages and guided tours. When you buy a package, you travel on your own, just as though you had planned the trip yourself.

SMART TRAVEL TIPS A TO Z

Fly/drive packages, which combine airfare and car rental, are often a good deal.

DRIVING

To reach Cape Cod from Boston (60 mi), take Route I–93 south, then Route 3 south, and cross the Sagamore Bridge. After finding your way out of a rotary, you'll be on U.S. 6, the Cape's main artery, leading toward Hyannis and Provincetown. From western Massachusetts, northern Connecticut, and northern New York State, take I–84 East to the Massachusetts Turnpike (I–90E) and take I–495 to the Bourne Bridge. From New York City, New Jersey, Philadelphia, Washington, D.C., and all other points south and west, take I–95 north toward Providence, where you'll pick up I–195 east (toward Fall River/New Bedford) to Route 25 east to the Bourne Bridge. From the Bourne Bridge you can take Route 28 south to Falmouth and Woods Hole (about 15 mi), or follow signs to U.S. 6 if you're headed east.

Driving times can vary widely depending on traffic. In good driving conditions you can reach the Sagamore Bridge from Boston in about 1¼ or 1½ hours, the Bourne Bridge from New York City in about 4½ or 5 hours.

On summer weekends, when more than 100,000 cars a day cross each bridge, **make every effort to avoid arriving in late afternoon,** especially on holidays. U.S. 6 and Route 28 are heavily congested eastbound on Friday evening, westbound on Sunday afternoon, and in both directions on Saturday (when rental homes change hands). On the north shore, the Old King's Highway—Route 6A—parallels U.S. 6 and is a scenic country road passing through occasional towns. When you're in no hurry, use back roads—you won't get there any faster, but they're less frustrating and much more rewarding.

AUTO CLUBS

➤ IN AUSTRALIA: **Australian Automobile Association** (☎ 02/6247–7311).

➤ IN CANADA: **Canadian Automobile Association** (CAA; ☎ 613/247–0117).

➤ IN NEW ZEALAND: **New Zealand Automobile Association** (☎ 09/377–4660).

➤ IN THE U.K.: **Automobile Association** (AA; ☎ 0990/500600). **Royal Automobile Club** (RAC; ☎ 0990/722722 for membership, 0345/121345 for insurance).

➤ IN THE U.S.: **American Automobile Association** (☎ 800/564–6222).

RULES OF THE ROAD

Massachusetts permits a right turn on a red light (after a stop) unless a sign says otherwise. Also, when you approach one of the Cape's numerous rotaries (traffic circles), note that the vehicles already in the rotary have the right of way and that those vehicles entering the rotary must yield. Be careful: some drivers forget this principle.

In Massachusetts highway speed limits are 55 mph near urban areas, 60 or 65 mph elsewhere. Speed limits on U.S. 6 on the Cape vary as it changes from four lanes to two lanes.

FERRY TRAVEL

In season, ferries connect Boston and Plymouth with Provincetown.

Ferries to Martha's Vineyard leave Woods Hole year-round. In summer you can also catch Vineyard ferries in Falmouth and Hyannis. All provide parking lots where you can leave your car overnight ($6–$10 per night). A number of parking lots in Falmouth hold the overflow of cars when the Woods Hole lot is filled, and free shuttle buses take passengers to the ferry, about 15 minutes away. Signs along Route 28 heading south from the Bourne Bridge direct you to open parking lots, as does AM radio station 1610, which you can pick up within 5 mi of Falmouth.

Ferries to Nantucket leave Hyannis year-round. In season, a passenger ferry connects Nantucket with Martha's Vineyard, and a cruise from Hyannis makes a day trip with stops at both islands.

From New Bedford you can take a ferry to Martha's Vineyard from mid-May to mid-October and to Cuttyhunk Island year-round (although between mid-October and mid-April, service is very limited).

➤ FERRIES TO MARTHA'S VINEYARD: The **Steamship Authority** runs the only car ferries, which make the 45-minute trip to Vineyard Haven year-round and to Oak Bluffs from late May through September. During the summer and on autumn weekends, you *must* have a reservation if you want to bring your car (passenger reservations are never necessary). You should make car reservations as far ahead as possible; in season call weekdays from 5 AM to 9:55 PM for faster service. Standby car reservations to the Vineyard are only available Tuesday–Thursday. Those with confirmed car reservations must be at the terminal 30 minutes (45 minutes in season) before sailing time. ☎ 508/477–8600 *for information and car reservations; 508/693–9130 on the Vineyard; 508/540–1394 TTY for information and car reservations; 508/548–3788 for day-of-sailing information.* 🚢 *Passengers one-way year-round $5, bicycles $3. Cars one-way in season (mid-May–mid-Oct.) $52 per car (not including passengers). Call for off-season rates.*

Hy-Line makes the 1¾-hour run from Hyannis to Oak Bluffs May–October. From June to mid-September the Around the Sound cruise makes a one-day round-trip from Hyannis with stops at Nantucket and Martha's Vineyard ($37.50). The parking lot fills up in summer, so call to reserve a space in high season. ☒ *Ocean St. dock,* ☎ *508/778–2600 or 888/778–1132; 508/778–2602 for reservations; 508/693–0112 in Oak Bluffs.* 🚢 *One-way $12.50, bicycles $5.*

The *Island Queen* makes the 35-minute trip to Oak Bluffs from late May through Columbus Day. ☒ *Falmouth Harbor,* ☎ *508/548–4800.* 🚢 *Round-trip $10, bicycles $6; one-way $6, bicycles $3.*

Patriot Boats (☎ 508/548–2626) allows passengers ($6 one-way) on its Falmouth Harbor–Oak Bluffs mail runs (mornings only, daily in-season, more frequently during off-season) and operates a year-round 24-hour water taxi. You can also charter a

boat—with rates starting at $125 per hour.

The 600-passenger ferry *Schamonchi* travels several times a day from New Bedford to Vineyard Haven from mid-May to mid-October. The trips takes about 1½ hours. ☒ *Billy Wood's Wharf, Rodney French Blvd., New Bedford,* ☎ *508/997–1688.* 🚢 *Same-day round-trip $17, one-way $9.50, bicycles $2.50.*

➤ FERRIES TO NANTUCKET: For details on ferries from Harwich Port, *see* The Lower Cape A to Z *in* Chapter 5.

The **Steamship Authority** runs car-and-passenger ferries from Hyannis to Nantucket year-round, a 2¼-hour trip. A faster passenger ferry only takes an hour. All of the ferries have snack bars. For policies *see* Ferries to Martha's Vineyard, *above*. Note that there are no standby car reservations on ferries to Nantucket. ☒ *South St. dock,* ☎ *508/477–8600; 508/228–3274 on Nantucket for reservations; 508/228–0262 for information; 508/540–1394 TTD. One-way $12, bicycles $5. Cars one-way mid-May–mid-Oct. $158; mid-Oct.–mid-May $97. High-speed passenger ferry one-way $23, bicycles $5.*

Hy-Line's high-end, high-speed *Grey Lady II* ferries between Hyannis and Nantucket year-round in just under an hour. Such speed has its downside in rough seas—lots of bucking and rolling that some find literally nauseating. Seating ranges from benches on the upper deck to airlinelike seats in side rows of the cabin to café-style tables and chairs in the cabin front. There's a snack bar on board. ☒ *Ocean St. dock,* ☎ *508/778–0404 or 888/778–1132; 508/228–3949 on Nantucket.* 🚢 *One-way $31, bicycles $5.*

Hy-Line's slower **ferry** makes the roughly two-hour trip from Hyannis between early May and late October. The M.V. *Great Point* offers a first-class section ($21 one-way) with a private lounge, rest rooms, upholstered seats, carpeting, complimentary Continental breakfast or afternoon cheese and crackers, a bar, and a snack bar. ☒ *Ocean St. dock,* ☎ *508/778–2602 for reservations; 508/778–*

2600 for information or 888/778–1132; 508/228–3949 on Nantucket. 🚢 One-way $11, bicycles $5.

➤ FERRIES TO CUTTYHUNK ISLAND: The M/V *Alert II* travels between New Bedford and Cuttyhunk Island. The trip takes about one hour. The ferry runs daily mid-June–mid-September, several times a week from mid-April to mid-June and from mid-September to mid-October, and once a week the rest of the year. ⊠ Fisherman's Wharf/Pier 3, New Bedford, ☎ 508/992–1432. 🚢 Same-day round-trip $17, One-way $12, bicycles $2.50.

GAY & LESBIAN TRAVEL

Provincetown, at the tip of the Cape, is one of the East Coast's leading lesbian and gay seaside destinations and also has a large year-round lesbian and gay community. Dozens of P-town establishments, from B&Bs to bars, cater specifically to lesbian and gay visitors, and most of the town's restaurants are gay-friendly; several are gay-owned and -operated. Hyannis has Cape Cod's sole gay bar outside P-town.

➤ BOOKS: *Fodor's Gay Guide to the USA,* available in bookstores or from Fodor's Travel Publications (☎ 800/533–6478; $19.50 plus $4 shipping), has a chapter on Provincetown.

➤ GAY- & LESBIAN-FRIENDLY TOUR OPERATORS: **New England Vacation Tours** (⊠ Box 560, West Dover, VT 05356, ☎ 802/464–2076 or 800/742–7669, FAX 802/464–2629) offers vacation packages to Cape Cod.

➤ GAY- & LESBIAN-FRIENDLY TRAVEL AGENCIES: **Different Roads Travel** (⊠ 8383 Wilshire Blvd., Suite 902, Beverly Hills, CA 90211, ☎ 323/651–5557 or 800/429–8747, FAX 323/651–3678, leigh@west.tzell.com). **Kennedy Travel** (⊠ 314 Jericho Turnpike, Floral Park, NY 11001, ☎ 516/352–4888 or 800/237–7433, FAX 516/354–8849, kennedytravel1@yahoo.com, www.kennedytravel.com). **Now Voyager** (⊠ 4406 18th St., San Francisco, CA 94114, ☎ 415/626–1169 or 800/255–6951, FAX 415/626–8626, www.nowvoyager.com). **Skylink Travel and Tour** (⊠ 1006 Mendocino Ave., Santa Rosa, CA 95401, ☎ 707/546–9888 or 800/225–5759, FAX 707/546–9891, skylinktvl@aol.com, www.skylinktravel.com), serving lesbian travelers.

HEALTH

Most Cape Cod pharmacies will refill an out-of-town prescription if you provide the prescribing doctor's phone number for verification. Most pharmacies post emergency numbers on their doors.

A common problem on the East Coast is Lyme disease (named after Lyme, Connecticut, where it was first diagnosed). This bacterial infection is transmitted by deer ticks and can be very serious, leading to chronic arthritis and worse if left untreated. Pregnant women are advised to **avoid areas of possible deer tick infestation**; if contracted during early pregnancy, Lyme disease can harm a fetus.

Deer ticks are most prevalent April–October but can be found year-round. They are about the size of a pinhead. Wear light-color clothing, which makes it easier to spot any ticks that might have attached themselves to you. Anyone planning to explore wooded areas or places with tall grasses (including dunes) should **wear long pants, socks drawn up over pant cuffs, and a long-sleeve shirt with a close-fitting collar**; boots are also recommended. The National Centers for Disease Control recommends that DEET repellent be applied to skin (not face!) and that permethrin be applied to clothing directly before entering infested areas; **use repellents very carefully** and conservatively with small children. Ticks also attach themselves to pets.

Recent research suggests that if ticks are removed within 12 hours of attachment to the body, the infectious bacteria is not likely to enter the bloodstream. That makes evenings a good opportunity to check yourself for ticks—look at the warm spots and hairlines on the body that attract ticks.

To remove a tick, apply tweezers to where it is attached to the skin and pull on the mouth parts. Try not to squeeze the body of the tick, which can send the body fluids containing the bacteria into the bloodstream. (Heating the tip of the tweezers before grasping the tick will cause the bug to release its bite, allowing for removal of the entire tick, including the sometimes-embedded head.) Disinfect the bite with alcohol and save the tick in a closed jar in case symptoms of the disease develop.

The first symptom of Lyme disease may be a ringlike rash or flulike symptoms, such as general feelings of malaise, fever, chills, and joint or facial pains. If diagnosed early, it can be treated with antibiotics. If you suspect your symptoms may be due to a tick bite, inform your doctor and ask to be tested.

Also **ask your physician about Ly-merix, the new Lyme disease vaccine**; it takes three shots and 12 months to be 80% effective but is worth considering. Brochures on the disease are available at many tourist information areas.

Poison ivy is a pervasive vinelike plant, recognizable by its leaf pattern: three shiny green leaves together. In spring new poison ivy leaves are red; likewise, they can take on a reddish tint as fall approaches. The oil from these leaves produces an itchy skin rash that spreads with scratching. If you think you may have touched some leaves, **wash as soon as you can** with soap and cool water.

➤ LYME DISEASE INFO: **Centers for Disease Control** (☎ 404/332–4555) or the **Massachusetts Department of Public Health** (✉ Southeast Office, 109 Rhode Island Rd., Lakeville, MA 02347, ☎ 508/947–1231).

HOLIDAYS

Major national holidays include New Year's Day (Jan. 1); Martin Luther King, Jr., Day (3rd Mon. in Jan.); President's Day (3rd Mon. in Feb.); Memorial Day (last Mon. in May); Independence Day (July 4); Labor Day (1st Mon. in Sept.); Thanksgiving Day (4th Thurs. in Nov.); Christmas Eve and Christmas Day (Dec. 24 and 25); and New Year's Eve (Dec. 31). Patriot's Day (3rd Mon. in Apr.) is a Massachusetts state holiday.

INSURANCE

The most useful travel-insurance plan is a comprehensive policy that includes coverage for trip cancellation and interruption, default, trip delay, and medical expenses (with a waiver for preexisting conditions).

Without insurance you will lose all or most of your money if you cancel your trip, regardless of the reason. Default insurance covers you if your tour operator, airline, or cruise line goes out of business. Trip-delay covers expenses that arise because of bad weather or mechanical delays. Study the fine print when comparing policies.

Always **buy travel policies directly from the insurance company**; if you buy them from a cruise line, airline, or tour operator that goes out of business, you probably will not be covered for the agency or operator's default, a major risk. Before making any purchase, **review your existing health and home-owner's policies** to find what they cover away from home.

➤ TRAVEL INSURERS: In the U.S.: **Access America** (✉ 6600 W. Broad St., Richmond, VA 23230, ☎ 804/285–3300 or 800/284–8300, FAX 804/673–1586, www.previewtravel.com), **Travel Guard International** (✉ 1145 Clark St., Stevens Point, WI 54481, ☎ 715/345–0505 or 800/826–1300, FAX 800/955–8785, www.noelgroup.com).

FOR INTERNATIONAL TRAVELERS

CAR TRAVEL

At press time, gasoline cost $1.49–$1.79 per gallon. Gas stations are plentiful, and most stay open late (24 hours along large highways and in big cities) except in rural areas, where Sunday hours are limited, and you may drive long stretches without a refueling opportunity. Highways are well paved. Interstate highways—limited-access multilane highways whose numbers are prefixed by "I–"—are the fastest routes. Interstates with three-digit numbers encircle urban areas, which may have other limited-access expressways, freeways, and parkways as well. Tolls may be levied on limited-access highways. So-called U.S. highways and state highways are not necessarily limited-access but may have several lanes.

Along larger highways, roadside stops with rest rooms, fast-food restaurants, and sundries stores are well spaced. State police and tow trucks patrol major highways and lend assistance. If your car breaks down on an interstate, pull onto the shoulder and wait for help, or have your passengers wait while you walk to an emergency phone. If you carry a cell phone, dial *55, noting your location on the small green roadside mileage markers.

Driving in the United States is on the right. Do **obey speed limits** posted along roads and highways. Watch for lower limits in small towns and on back roads. Massachusetts requires front-seat passengers to wear seat belts. On weekdays between 6 and 10 and again between 4 and 7, **expect heavy traffic.** To encourage carpooling, some freeways have special lanes for so-called high-occupancy vehicles (HOVs—cars carrying more than one passenger).

Book stores, gas stations, convenience stores, and rest stops sell maps (about $3) and multiregion road atlases (about $10).

CURRENCY

The dollar is the basic unit of U.S. currency. It has 100 cents. Coins include the copper penny (1¢); the silvery nickel (5¢), dime (10¢), quarter (25¢), and half-dollar (50¢); and the golden $1 coin, replacing a now-rare silver dollar. Bills are denominated $1, $5, $10, $20, $50, and $100, all green and identical in size; designs vary. The exchange rate at press time was $1.45 per British pound, 66¢ per Canadian dollar, 52¢ per Australian dollar, and 39¢ per New Zealand dollar.

CUSTOMS & DUTIES

Australian residents who are 18 or older may bring home $A400 worth of souvenirs and gifts (including jewelry), 250 cigarettes or 250 grams of tobacco, and 1,125 milliliters of alcohol (including wine, beer, and spirits). Residents under 18 may bring back $A200 worth of goods. Prohibited items include meat products. Seeds, plants, and fruits need to be declared upon arrival.

Canadian residents who have been out of Canada for at least seven days may bring home C$500 worth of goods duty-free. If you've been away less than seven days but more than 48 hours, the duty-free allowance drops to C$200; if your trip lasts 24–48 hours, the allowance is C$50. You may not pool allowances with family members. Goods claimed under the C$500 exemption may follow you by mail; those claimed under the lesser exemptions must accompany you. Alcohol and tobacco products may be included in the seven-day and 48-hour exemptions but not in the 24-hour exemption. If you meet the age requirements of the province or territory through which you reenter Canada, you may bring in, duty-free, 1.14 liters (40 imperial ounces) of wine or liquor or 24 12-ounce cans or bottles of beer or ale. If you are 16 or older, you may bring in, duty-free, 200 cigarettes and 50 cigars. Check ahead of time with Revenue Canada or the Department of Agriculture for policies regarding meat products, seeds, plants, and fruits. You may send an unlimited number of gifts worth up to C$60 each duty-free to Canada. Label the package UNSOLICITED GIFT—VALUE UNDER $60. Alcohol and tobacco are excluded.

Homeward-bound New Zealand residents 17 or older may bring back NZ$700 worth of souvenirs and gifts. Your duty-free allowance also includes 4.5 liters of wine or beer; one 1,125-milliliter bottle of spirits; and either 200 cigarettes, 250 grams of tobacco, 50 cigars, or a combination of the three up to 250 grams. Prohibited items include meat products, seeds, plants, and fruits.

From countries outside the European Union, including the United States, residents of the United Kingdom may bring home, duty-free, 200 cigarettes or 50 cigars; 1 liter of spirits or 2 liters of fortified or sparkling wine or liqueurs; 2 liters of still table wine; 60

milliliters of perfume; 250 milliters of toilet water; plus £136 worth of other goods, including gifts and souvenirs. If returning from outside the EU, prohibited items include meat products, seeds, plants, and fruits.

➤ IN AUSTRALIA: **Australian Customs Service** (Regional Director, ✉ Box 8, Sydney, NSW 2001, Australia, ☎ 02/9213–2000, FAX 02/9213–4000, www.customs.gov.au).

➤ IN CANADA: **Revenue Canada** (✉ 2265 St. Laurent Blvd. S, Ottawa, Ontario K1G 4K3, ☎ 613/993–0534; 800/461–9999 in Canada, FAX 613/991–4126, www.ccra-adrc.gc.ca).

➤ IN NEW ZEALAND: **New Zealand Customs** (Custom House, ✉ 50 Anzac Ave., Box 29, Auckland, ☎ 09/300–5399, FAX 09/359–6730), www.customs.govt.nz.

➤ IN THE U.K.: **HM Customs and Excise** (✉ Dorset House, Stamford St., Bromley, Kent BR1 1XX,, ☎ 020/7202–4227, www.hmce.gov.uk).

ELECTRICITY

The U.S. standard is AC, 110 volts/60 cycles. Plugs have two flat pins set parallel to each other.

EMERGENCIES

For police, fire, or ambulance, **dial 911** (0 in rural areas).

INSURANCE

Britons and Australians need extra medical coverage when traveling overseas.

➤ INSURANCE INFORMATION: In the U.K.: **Association of British Insurers** (✉ 51–55 Gresham St., London EC2V 7HQ, ☎ 020/7600–3333, FAX 020/7696–8999, info@abi.org.uk, www.abi.org.uk). In Australia: **Insurance Council of Australia** (☎ 03/9614–1077, FAX 03/9614–7924). In Canada: **Voyager Insurance** (✉ 44 Peel Center Dr., Brampton, Ontario L6T 4M8, ☎ 905/791–8700, 800/668–4342 in Canada). In New Zealand: **Insurance Council of New Zealand** (✉ Box 474, Wellington, ☎ 04/472–5230, FAX 04/473–3011, www.icnz.org.nz).

MAIL & SHIPPING

You can buy stamps and aerograms and send letters and parcels in post offices. In addition, stamp-dispensing machines can be found in some airports, bus and train stations, office buildings, drugstores, and the like. You can also deposit mail in the stout, dark blue steel bins at strategic locations everywhere and in the mail chutes commonly found in large buildings; pickup schedules are posted.

For mail sent within the United States, you need a 33¢ stamp for first-class letters weighing up to 1 ounce (22¢ for each additional ounce) and 20¢ for domestic postcards. For overseas mail you pay 60¢ for ½-ounce airmail letters, 50¢ for airmail postcards, and 35¢ for surface-rate postcards. For Canada you need a 52¢ stamp for a 1-ounce letter and 40¢ for a postcard. For 50¢ you can buy an aerogram—a single sheet of lightweight blue paper that folds into its own envelope, stamped for overseas airmail.

To receive mail on the road, have it sent c/o General Delivery at your destination's main post office (use the correct five-digit zip code). You must pick up mail in person within 30 days and show a driver's license or passport.

PASSPORTS & VISAS

When traveling internationally, **carry your passport** even if you don't need one (it's always the best form of ID) and **make two photocopies of the data page** (one for someone at home and another for you, carried separately from your passport). If you lose your passport, promptly call the nearest embassy or consulate and the local police.

Visitor visas are not necessary for Canadian citizens or for citizens of Australia, New Zealand, and the United Kingdom staying fewer than 90 days.

➤ AUSTRALIAN CITIZENS: **Australian Passport Office** (☎ 131–232). **U.S. Office of Australia Affairs** (✉ MLC Centre, 19-29 Martin Pl., 59th floor, Sydney NSW 2000,).

➤ CANADIAN CITIZENS: **Passport Office** (☎ 819/994–3500; 800/567–6868 in Canada).

➤ NEW ZEALAND CITIZENS: **New Zealand Passport Office** (☎ 04/494–0700 for application procedures; 0800/225–050 in New Zealand for application-status updates). **U.S. Office of New Zealand Affairs** (✉ 29 Fitzherbert Terr., Thorndon, Wellington).

➤ U.K. CITIZENS: **London Passport Office** (☎ 0870/521–0410) for application procedures and emergency passports. **U.S. Embassy Visa Information Line** (☎ 01891/200–290). **U.S. Embassy Visa Branch** (✉ 5 Upper Grosvenor Sq., London W1A 1AE); send a self-addressed, stamped envelope. **U.S. Consulate General** (✉ Queen's House, Queen St., Belfast BTI 6EO, Northern Ireland).

TELEPHONES

All U.S. telephone numbers consist of a three-digit area code and a seven-digit local number. Normally, you dial only the seven-digit number when calling locally. At press time, however, eastern Massachusetts was planning to switch to a 10-digit dialing system in April 2001. Assuming this happens, you'll have to **dial the area code plus the seven-digit number for all local calls.** (New area codes are being created.) To call another region, as always, dial "1," then all 10 digits; the same goes for calls to numbers prefixed by "800," "888," and "877"—all toll-free. For calls to numbers preceded by "900" you must pay—usually dearly.

For international calls dial "011" followed by the country code and the local number. For help dial "0" and ask for an overseas operator. Country codes: 44 for the United Kingdom, 61 for Australia, 64 for New Zealand. (Calling Canada is the same as calling within the United States.) Most local phone books list country codes and U.S. area codes. The country code for the United States is 1.

For operator assistance, dial "0." To obtain someone's phone number, call directory assistance, 555–1212 or occasionally 411 (free at public phones). To have the person you're calling foot the bill, phone collect; dial "0" instead of "1" before the 10-digit number.

At pay phones, instructions are usually posted. Usually you insert coins in a slot (10¢–35¢ for local calls) and wait for a steady tone before dialing. When you call long-distance, the operator will tell you how much to insert; prepaid phone cards, widely available in various denominations, are easier. Call the number on the back, punch in the card's personal identification number when prompted, then dial your number.

LODGING

Accommodations on the Cape range from campsites to B&Bs to luxurious self-contained resorts offering all kinds of sporting facilities, restaurants, entertainment, services (including business services and children's programs), and all the assistance you'll ever need in making vacation arrangements.

Single-night lodgings for those just passing through can be found at countless tacky but cheap and conveniently located little roadside motels, as well as at others that are spotless and cheery yet still inexpensive, or at chain hotels at all price levels; these places often have a pool, TVs, or other amenities to keep children entertained in the evening.

Families may want to **consider condominiums, cottages, and efficiencies,** which offer more space; living areas; kitchens; and sometimes laundry facilities, children's play areas, or children's programs.

The lodgings we list are the cream of the crop in each price category. We always list the facilities that are available—but we don't specify whether they cost extra: when pricing accommodations, always ask what's included and what costs extra. Properties indicated by an ✕▥ are lodging establishments whose restaurant warrants a special trip even if you are not staying at that establishment.

CATEGORY	COST*
$$$$	over $200
$$$	$150–$200
$$	$100–$150
$	under $100

All prices are for a standard double room in high season, excluding 5.7% state tax and gratuities. Some inns add a 15% service charge.

Assume that hotels operate on the **European Plan** (EP, with no meals included) unless we specify that they use the **Continental Plan** (CP, with a Continental breakfast), **Breakfast Plan** (BP, with a full breakfast), **Modified American Plan** (MAP, with breakfast and dinner), or the **Full American Plan** (FAP, with all meals).

CONDO & HOUSE RENTALS

If you want a home base that's roomy enough for a family and comes with cooking facilities, **consider a furnished rental.** Many visitors to the Cape rent a house if they are going to stay for a week or longer, rather than stay at a B&B or hotel. These can save you money; however, some rentals are luxury properties, economical only when your party is large. Many local real-estate agencies deal with rentals, and most specialize in a specific area. If you do decide to rent, be sure to book a property well in advance of your trip, as many properties are rented out to the same families or groups year after year. Rental opportunities are often greater in the smaller, quieter towns, such as Yarmouth, Chatham, Wellfleet, and Truro. For the names of regional agencies, *see* the A to Z section of the appropriate chapter in this book, consult the local chamber of commerce guide, and if you can, get hold of the local yellow pages. *See* Home, Sweet Rental Home *in* Chapter 7 for tips on arranging a rental.

Home-exchange directories (☞ Home Exchanges, *below*) list rentals (often second homes owned by prospective house swappers), and some services search for a house or apartment for you (even a castle, if that's your fancy) and handle the paperwork. Some send an illustrated catalog; others send photographs only of specific properties, sometimes at a charge. Up-front registration fees may apply.

➤ INTERNATIONAL AGENTS: **Hideaways International** (✉ 767 Islington St., Portsmouth, NH 03801, ☎ 603/430–4433 or 800/843–4433, FAX 603/430–4444 info@hideaways.com www.hideaways.com; membership $99).

➤ CAPE-WIDE RENTAL AGENT: **Waterfront Rentals** (✉ 20 Pilgrim Rd., West Yarmouth, 02673, ☎ 508/778–1818, FAX 508/771–3563, www.waterfrontrentalsinc.com) covers Bourne to Truro, listing everything from one-bedroom condos to multibedroom beachfront estates.

B&BS

Bed-and-breakfast inns are also very popular on Cape Cod. Many are housed in interesting old sea captains' homes and other 17th-, 18th-, and 19th-century buildings; others are in newer homes in which a few rooms and bathrooms have been set aside for rent. In many cases, B&Bs are not appropriate for families—noise travels easily, rooms are often small, and the furnishings are often fragile; so be sure to ask. Most B&Bs do not provide phones or TVs in guest rooms, many are not air-conditioned, and more and more prohibit smoking.

In summer you must reserve lodgings as far in advance as possible—several months for the most popular inns. Assistance with last-minute reservations is available at the Cape Cod Chamber of Commerce information booths and through the chamber of commerce's Web site (☞ Web Sites, *below*). Off season, rates are much reduced, and service may be more personalized.

Numerous B&B reservation agencies can aid you in choosing an inn. For more information get a free B&B guide from the Massachusetts Office of Travel & Tourism (☞ Visitor Information, *below*). The Cape Cod Chamber of Commerce (☞ Visitor Information, *below*) also publishes a free B&B guide.

➤ RESERVATION SERVICES: **Bed and Breakfast Cape Cod** (✉ Box 1312, Orleans 02653, ☎ 508/255–3824 or 800/541–6226, FAX 508/240–0599, www.bedandbreakfastcapecod.com).

SMART TRAVEL TIPS A TO Z

DestINNations (✉ 29 Bassett La., Hyannis 02601, ☎ 508/790–0577 or 800/333–4667, FAX 508/771–8107, www.destinnations.com) handles a limited number of upscale inns, resorts, and B&Bs on the Cape.

CAMPING

There are many private and state-park camping areas on Cape Cod. Write to the Massachusetts Office of Travel & Tourism and the Cape Cod Chamber of Commerce (☞ Visitor Information, *below*). For details on camping in specific areas, look for the ⚠ icon in that area's Dining and Lodging section and consult the A to Z section of that chapter.

HOME EXCHANGES

If you would like to exchange your home for someone else's, **join a home-exchange organization,** which will send you its updated listings of available exchanges for a year and will include your own listing in at least one of them. It's up to you to make specific arrangements.

➤ EXCHANGE CLUBS: **HomeLink International** (✉ Box 650, Key West, FL 33041, ☎ 305/294–7766 or 800/638–3841, FAX 305/294–1448, usa@homelink.org, www.homelink. org; $98 per year). **Intervac U.S.** (✉ Box 590504, San Francisco, CA 94159, ☎ 800/756–4663, FAX 415/435–7440, intervacus@aol.com, www.intervacus.com; $93 per year includes two catalogs).

HOSTELS

No matter what your age, you can **save on lodging costs by staying at hostels.** In some 5,000 locations in more than 70 countries around the world, Hostelling International (HI), the umbrella group for a number of national youth-hostel associations, offers single-sex, dorm-style beds and, at many hostels, rooms for couples and family accommodations. Membership in any HI national hostel association, open to travelers of all ages, allows you to stay in HI-affiliated hostels at member rates; one-year membership is about $25 for adults (C$26.75 in Canada, £9.30 in the U.K., $30 in Australia, and $30 in New Zealand); hostels run about

$10–$25 per night. Members have priority if the hostel is full; they're also eligible for discounts around the world, even on rail and bus travel in some countries.

Cape Cod has some excellent hostels. In season, when all other rates are jacked up beyond belief, hostels are often the only budget-accommodation option, but you must plan ahead to reserve space. You may luck out on last-minute cancellations, but it would be unwise to rely on them. *See* the lodging listings *in* the appropriate chapters for specific information.

➤ ORGANIZATIONS: **Hostelling International—American Youth Hostels** (✉ 733 15th St. NW, Suite 840, Washington, DC 20005, ☎ 202/783–6161, FAX 202/783–6171, hiayhserv@hiayh.org, www.hiayh.org). **Hostelling International—Canada** (✉ 400–205 Catherine St., Ottawa, Ontario K2P 1C3, ☎ 613/237–7884, FAX 613/237–7868, info@hostellingintl.ca, www.hostellingintl.ca). **Youth Hostel Association of England and Wales** (✉ Trevelyan House, 8 St. Stephen's Hill, St. Albans, Hertfordshire AL1 2DY, U.K., ☎ 0870/8708808, FAX 01727/844126, customerservices@yha. org.uk, www.yha.org.uk). **Australian Youth Hostel Association** (✉ 10 Mallett St., Camperdown, NSW 2050, ☎ 02/9565–1699, FAX 02/9565–1325, www.yha.com.au). **Youth Hostels Association of New Zealand** (✉ Box 436, Christchurch, ☎ 03/379–9970, FAX 03/365–4476, info@yha.org.nz, www.yha.org.nz).

HOTELS

All hotels listed have private bath unless otherwise noted.

➤ TOLL-FREE NUMBERS: **Best Western** (☎ 800/528–1234, www.bestwestern. com). **Choice** (☎ 800/221–2222, www.hotelchoice.com). **Comfort** (☎ 800/228–5150, www.comfortinn. com). **Days Inn** (☎ 800/325–2525, www.daysinn.com). **Holiday Inn** (☎ 800/465–4329, www.basshotels. com). **Radisson** (☎ 800/333–3333, www.radisson.com). **Ramada** (☎ 800/228–2828, www.ramada.com). **Sheraton** (☎ 800/325–3535, www.starwood.com).

MEDIA

NEWSPAPERS & MAGAZINES

Glossy regional magazines include *Cape Cod Life,* with feature articles about Cape people and places; *Provincetown Arts,* which focuses on Provincetown artists, performers, and writers, and also publishes essays, fiction, interviews, and poetry; and *CapeWomen,* in which articles feature profiles of Cape-based women and address issues of interest to women; the magazine also publishes the annual *P'TownWomen.*

The *Cape Cod Times* is a daily newspaper, with current news from the around the Cape and elsewhere. *A-Plus,* available free in galleries and as several newspaper supplements, has arts listings. In Provincetown look for the *Banner* and *Provincetown Magazine,* both weeklies, for art and entertainment listings.

MONEY MATTERS

Prices throughout this guide are given for adults. Substantially reduced fees are almost always available for children, students, and senior citizens. For information on taxes, *see* Taxes, *below.*

ATMS

Cape Cod has no lack of ATM machines.

➤ ATM LOCATIONS: **Cirrus** (☎ 800/424–7787). **Plus** (☎ 800/843–7587) for locations in the United States and Canada, or visit your local bank.

CREDIT CARDS

Throughout this guide, the following abbreviations are used: **AE,** American Express; **D,** Discover; **DC,** Diner's Club; **MC,** MasterCard; and **V,** Visa.

➤ REPORTING LOST CARDS: To report lost or stolen credit cards, call the following toll-free numbers: **American Express** (☎ 800/327–2177); **Discover Card** (☎ 800/347–2683); **Diners Club** (☎ 800/234–6377); **MasterCard** (☎ 800/307–7309); and **Visa** (☎ 800/847–2911).

NATIONAL PARKS

Look into discount passes to save money on park entrance fees. The National Parks Pass ($50) gets you and your companions free admission to all parks for one year (camping and parking are extra). A percentage of the proceeds from sales of the pass will fund National Parks projects. Both the Golden Age Passport ($10), for those 62 and older, and the Golden Access Passport (free), for travelers with disabilities, entitle holders to free entry to all national parks, plus 50% off fees for the use of many park facilities and services. You must show proof of age and of U.S. citizenship or permanent residency (such as a U.S. passport, driver's license, or birth certificate) and, if requesting Golden Access, proof of disability. The Golden Age and Golden Access passes are available at all national parks wherever entrance fees are charged. The National Parks Pass and Golden Access passes are available by mail or at their Web site.

➤ PASSES BY MAIL: **National Park Service** (✉ National Park Service/Department of Interior, 1849 C St. NW, Washington, DC 20240-0001, ☎ 202/208–4747, www.nps.gov).

National Parks Pass (✉ 27540 Mentry Ave., Valencia, CA 91355, ☎ 888/467–2757, www.nationalparks.org).

OUTDOORS & SPORTS

For details on enjoying the outdoors in your chosen vacation spot, including water sports, *see* the appropriate regional chapter.

FISHING

Charter boats and party boats (per-head fees, rather than the charters' group rates) fish in season for bluefish, tuna, marlin, and mako and blue sharks. Throughout the year there's bottom fishing for flounder, tautog, scup, fluke, cod, and pollack.

The Cape Cod Chamber of Commerce's *Sportsman's Guide* provides fishing regulations, surf-fishing access locations, a map of boat-launching facilities, and more. The state Division of Fisheries and Wildlife has a book with dozens of maps of Cape ponds. Remember, you'll need a license for freshwater fishing, available for a nominal fee at bait-and-tackle shops.

Molly Benjamin's fishing column in the Friday *Cape Cod Times* gives the latest information about fishing on the Cape—what's being caught and where.

GOLF

The Cape Cod Chamber of Commerce has a "Golf Map of Cape Cod," locating dozens of courses on the Cape. Summer greens fees range from $25 to $50.

PACKING

Only a few Cape Cod restaurants require formal dress, as do some dinner cruises. The area prides itself on informality. Do **pack a sweater or jacket, even in summer,** for nights can be cool.For suggested clothing to minimize bites from deer ticks and to prevent Lyme disease, *see* Health, *above.*

In your carry-on luggage, **pack an extra pair of eyeglasses or contact lenses** and **enough of any medication you take** to last the entire trip. You may also ask your doctor to write a spare prescription using the drug's generic name, since brand names may vary from country to country. In luggage to be checked, **never pack prescription drugs or valuables.** To avoid customs delays, carry medications in their original packaging. And don't forget to carry with you the addresses of offices that handle refunds of lost traveler's checks.

Perhaps most important of all, **don't forget a swimsuit** (or two).

CHECKING LUGGAGE

How many carry-on bags you can bring with you is up to the airline. Most allow two, but not always, so make sure that everything you carry aboard will fit under your seat or in the overhead bin, and get to the gate early. Note that if you have a seat at the back of the plane, you'll probably board first, while the overhead bins are still empty.

If you are flying internationally, note that baggage allowances may be determined not by piece but by weight—generally 88 pounds (40 kilograms) in first class, 66 pounds (30 kilograms) in business class, and 44 pounds (20 kilograms) in economy.

Airline liability for baggage is limited to $1,250 per person on flights within the United States. On international flights it amounts to $9.07 per pound or $20 per kilogram for checked baggage (roughly $640 per 70-pound bag) and $400 per passenger for unchecked baggage. You can buy additional coverage at check-in for about $10 per $1,000 of coverage, but it excludes a rather extensive list of items, shown on your airline ticket.

Before departure, **itemize your bags' contents** and their worth, and label the bags with your name, address, and phone number. (If you use your home address, cover it so potential thieves can't see it readily.) Inside each bag, **pack a copy of your itinerary.** At check-in, **make sure that each bag is correctly tagged** with the destination airport's three-letter code. If your bags arrive damaged or fail to arrive at all, file a written report with the airline before leaving the airport.

SENIOR-CITIZEN TRAVEL

To qualify for age-related discounts, **mention your senior-citizen status up front** when booking hotel reservations (not when checking out) and before you're seated in restaurants (not when paying the bill). When renting a car, ask about promotional car-rental discounts, which can be cheaper than senior-citizen rates.

➤ EDUCATIONAL PROGRAMS: Elderhostel (✉ 75 Federal St., 3rd floor, Boston, MA 02110, ☎ 877/426–8056, ℻ 877/426–2166, www. elderhostel.org).

SHOPPING

For an overview of some of the local specialties, *see* Pleasures and Pastimes *in* Chapter 1. Because of the Cape's large year-round population, shops tend to remain open, though most Provincetown and Wellfleet shops and galleries do close.

Provincetown and Wellfleet are the main centers for art, and their gallery associations have pamphlets on local galleries. For a directory of area antiques dealers and auctions, contact the Cape Cod Antique Dealers Association. For a listing of crafts shops on the Cape, write to the Artisans'

Guild of Cape Cod, Cape Cod Potters, or the Society of Cape Cod Craftsmen.

Throughout the Cape, shop owners respond to both the flow of tourists and their own inclinations. Especially off season, it's best to **phone a shop before going out of your way to visit.**

➤ LOCAL RESOURCES: **Cape Cod Antique Dealers Association** (send business-size self-addressed, stamped envelope to ⊠ Box 191, Yarmouth Port 02675). **Provincetown Gallery Guild** (⊠ Box 242, Provincetown 02657). **Wellfleet Art Galleries Association** (⊠ Box 916, Wellfleet 02667).

Artisans' Guild of Cape Cod (send business-size self-addressed, stamped envelope to ⊠ 46 Debs Hill Rd., Yarmouth 02675). **Cape Cod Potters** (⊠ Box 76, Chatham 02633). **Society of Cape Cod Craftsmen** (⊠ Box 1709, Wellfleet 02667-1709).

STUDENTS ON CAPE COD

➤ IDs & SERVICES: **Council Travel** (CIEE; ⊠ 205 E. 42nd St., 14th floor, New York, NY 10017, ☎ 212/822–2700 or 888/268–6245, FAX 212/822–2699, info@councilexchanges.org, www.councilexchanges.org) for mail orders only, in the United States. **Travel Cuts** (⊠ 187 College St., Toronto, Ontario M5T 1P7, Canada, ☎ 416/979–2406 or 800/667–2887 in Canada, www.travelcuts.com).

TAXES

SALES TAX

Massachusetts state sales tax is 5%.

TIME

Cape Cod is in the Eastern Standard time zone.

TIPPING

At restaurants a 15% tip is standard for waiters; up to 20% may be expected at more expensive establishments. The same goes for taxi drivers, bartenders, and hairdressers. Coat-check operators usually expect $1 per coat; bellhops and porters should get 50¢ to $1 per bag; hotel maids in upscale hotels should get about $1.50 per day of your stay. On package tours, conductors and drivers usually get $10 per day from the group as a whole; check whether this has already been figured into your cost. For local sightseeing tours you may individually tip the driver-guide $1–$5, depending on the length of the tour and the number of people in your party, if he or she has been helpful or informative. Ushers in theaters do not expect tips.

TOURS & PACKAGES

Because everything is prearranged on a prepackaged tour or independent vacation, you'll spend less time planning—and often get it all at a good price.

BOOKING WITH AN AGENT

Travel agents are excellent resources. But it's a good idea to collect brochures from several agencies as some agents' suggestions may be influenced by relationships with tour and package firms that reward them for volume sales. If you have a special interest, **find an agent with expertise in that area;** ASTA (☞ Travel Agencies, *below*) has a database of specialists worldwide.

Make sure your travel agent knows the accommodations and other services of the recommended place. Ask about the hotel's location; room size; beds; and whether it has a pool, room service, or programs for children, if you care about these. Has your agent been there in person or sent others whom you can contact?

Do some homework on your own, too: local tourism boards can provide information about lesser-known and small-niche operators, some of which may sell only direct.

BUYER BEWARE

Each year consumers are stranded or lose their money when tour operators—even large ones with excellent reputations—go out of business. So **check out the operator.** Ask several travel agents about its reputation and try to **book with a company that has a consumer-protection program** (look for information in the company's brochure). In the United States, members of the National Tour Association and the United States Tour Operators Association are required to set aside funds to cover your payments and travel arrangements in the event the company defaults. It's also a good idea to choose a company that participates in the American Society of Travel Agents' Tour Operator Program (TOP); ASTA will act as mediator in any disputes between you and your tour operator.

Remember that the more your package or tour includes, the better you can predict the ultimate cost of your vacation. Make sure you know exactly what is covered, and **beware of hidden costs.** Are taxes, tips, and transfers included? Entertainment and excursions? These can add up.

➤ TOUR-OPERATOR RECOMMENDATIONS: **American Society of Travel Agents** (☞ Travel Agencies, *below*). **National Tour Association** (NTA; ✉ 546 E. Main St., Lexington, KY 40508, ☎ 859/226–4444 or 800/682–8886, www.ntaonline.com). **United States Tour Operators Association** (USTOA; ✉ 342 Madison Ave., Suite 1522, New York, NY 10173, ☎ 212/599–6599 or 800/468–7862, FAX 212/599–6744, ustoa@aol.com, www.ustoa.com).

TRAIN TRAVEL

Because of continuing financial difficulties, Amtrak service to the Cape was suspended in 1998; it is not currently scheduled to resume, but call for an update.

➤ TRAIN INFORMATION: **Amtrak** (☎ 800/872–7245).

TRANSPORTATION ON CAPE COD

A good general resource for information about getting around the Cape is the free **Smart Guide,** published by the Cape Cod Chamber of Commerce; it's available from the Chamber (*see* Visitor Information, *below*) or online at www.smartguide.org. Also *see* Getting Around *in* the A to Z sections of the appropriate chapters.

TRAVEL AGENCIES

A good travel agent puts your needs first. Look for an agency that has been in business at least five years, emphasizes customer service, and has someone on staff who specializes in your destination. In addition, **make sure**

the agency belongs to a professional trade organization. The American Society of Travel Agents (ASTA), with 27,000 agents in some 170 countries, is the largest and most influential in the field. Operating under the motto "Integrity in Travel," it maintains and enforces a strict code of ethics and will step in to help mediate any agent-client disputes if necessary. ASTA also maintains a Web site that includes a directory of agents. (If a travel agency is also acting as your tour operator, *see* Buyer Beware *in* Tours & Packages, *above*.)

➤ LOCAL AGENT REFERRALS: **American Society of Travel Agents** (ASTA; ☎ 800/965–2782 24-hr hot line, FAX 703/684–8319, www.astanet.com). **Association of British Travel Agents** (✉ 68–71 Newman St., London W1P 4AH, ☎ 020/7637–2444, FAX 020/7637–0713, information@abta.co.uk, www.abtanet.com). **Association of Canadian Travel Agents** (✉ 1729 Bank St., Suite 201, Ottawa, Ontario K1V 7Z5, ☎ 613/237–3657, FAX 613/521–0805, acta.ntl@sympatico.ca). **Australian Federation of Travel Agents** (✉ Level 3, 309 Pitt St., Sydney 2000, Australia, ☎ 02/9264–3299, FAX 02/9264–1085, www.afta.com.au). **Travel Agents' Association of New Zealand** (✉ Box 1888, Wellington 10033, New Zealand, ☎ 04/499–0104, FAX 04/499–0827, taanz@tiasnet.co.nz).

VISITOR INFORMATION

Before you go, contact the state's office of tourism and the area's chambers of commerce for general information, seasonal events, and brochures. For specific information on Cape Cod's state forests and parks, the area's farmers' markets and fairs, or wildlife, contact the special-interest government offices below. You can also check Web sites on the Internet (☞ Web Sites, *below*). When you arrive, you can pay a visit to the local chamber of commerce for additional information.

➤ CHAMBERS OF COMMERCE: **Cape Cod Chamber of Commerce** (✉ Junction of Rtes. 6 and 132, Hyannis 02601, ☎ 508/862–0700 or 888/332–2732, FAX 508/862–0727). For a list of local Cape Cod and nearby chambers of commerce that can also provide information, *see* Visitor Information *in* the A to Z sections of the appropriate chapters.

➤ STATE: **Massachusetts Office of Travel & Tourism** (✉ 10 Park Plaza, Suite 4510, Boston 02116, ☎ 800/ 227–6277; 800/447–6277 for brochures; FAX 617/973–8525).

➤ SPECIAL INTERESTS: **Army Corps of Engineers** has a 24-hour hot line (☎ 508/759–5991) for canal-area events and tidal and fishing information. **Department of Environmental Management** (✉ Division of Forests and Parks, 251 Causeway St., Suite 600, Boston 02114, ☎ 617/973– 8700, FAX 617/973–8798). **Department of Food and Agriculture** (✉ 251 Causeway St., Suite 500, Boston 02114, ☎ 617/626–1700, FAX 617/626–1850). **Division of Fisheries and Wildlife** (✉ Field Headquarters, 1 Rabbit Hill Rd., Westborough 01581, ☎ 508/792–7270, FAX 508/ 792–7275).

WEB SITES

Do check out the World Wide Web when you're planning. You'll find everything from current weather forecasts to virtual tours of famous cities. Fodor's Web site, www.fodors.com, is a great place to start your online travels. When you see a 🕸 in this book, go to www.fodors.com/urls for an up-to-date link to that destination's site.

➤ GENERAL INFORMATION: **Bristol County Convention and Visitors Bureau** (www.bristol-county.org). **Cape Cod Chamber of Commerce** (www.capecodchamber.org). **Cape Cod National Seashore** (www.nps. gov/caco). **Destination Plymouth** (www.visit-plymouth.com). Other general sites include the **Cape Cod Information Center** (www.allcapecod. com); **Cape Cod Online** (www. capecodonline.com), which has links to the *Cape Cod Times* and other local publications; **Massachusetts Office of Travel & Tourism** (www.massvacation.com).

➤ TRANSPORTATION: **Smart Traveler** (www.smarttraveler.com) provides real-time updates on traffic conditions on Cape Cod. You can look at live Web cam pictures of the Bourne and Sagamore bridges at the **Cape Cod USA** site (www.capecodusa.com).

For Cape Cod bus and trolley schedules, check with the **Cape Cod Regional Transit Authority** (www. capecodtransit.org). The transportation information site of the **Cape Cod Commission** (www.gocapecod. org) has links to transportation providers, updates on transportation-related construction projects, and information on bicycling and walking, including updates on the Cape Cod Rail Trail. The **Massachusetts Bicycle Coalition** (www.massbike. org) has information for bicyclists. **Rails-to-Trails Conservancy** (www.railtrails.org) provides general information about rail trails, such as the Cape Cod Rail Trail.

Island ferry information and schedules are available online from the **Steamship Authority** (www.islandferry. com) and from **Hy-Line** (www. hy-linecruises.com). From New Bedford you can travel to Vineyard Haven on the ferry *Schamonchi* (www.mvferry.com) and to Cuttyhunk Island on the *M/V Alert II* (www. cuttyhunk.com).

➤ DISABILITY ACCESS: **Directory of Accessible Facilities** lists accessible recreational facilities in Massachusetts (www.state.ma.us/dem/access. htm). **Cape Cod Disability Access Directory** (www.capecod.net/ccdad/).

WHEN TO GO

Memorial Day through Labor Day (or, in some cases, Columbus Day) is high season on Cape Cod. This is summer with a capital *S*, a time for barbecues, beach bumming, swimming, and water sports. During summer everything is open for business on the Cape, but you can also expect high-season evils: high prices, crowds, and traffic.

The Cape, however, is increasingly a year-round destination. *See* The Cape's Six Seasons *in* Chapter 7 for some highlights of the off-season.

CLIMATE

Although there are plenty of idyllic beach days to go around on the Cape, rain or fog is not an uncommon part of even an August vacation here. Visitors who do not learn to appreciate the beauty of the land and sea in mist and rain may find themselves mighty cranky.

Temperatures in winter and summer are milder on the Cape than on the mainland, due in part to the warming influence of the Gulf Stream and the moderating ocean breezes. As a rule (some years are dramatically anomalous, 1994 and 1999 in particular), the Cape gets much less snow than the mainland, and what falls generally does not last. Still, winter can bring bone-chilling dampness.

The following are average daily maximum and minimum temperatures for Hyannis; it's likely to be 2–3 degrees cooler on the coast.

➤ FORECASTS: **Weather Channel Connection** (☎ 900/932–8437), 95¢ per minute from a Touch-Tone phone. For local Cape weather, coastal marine forecasts, and today's tide times, call the weather line of **WQRC** (☎ 508/771–5522) in Hyannis.

Climate

Jan.	40F	+4C	May	62F	17C	Sept.	70F	21C
	25	–4		48	+9		56	13
Feb.	41F	+5C	June	71F	22C	Oct.	59F	15C
	26	–3		56	13		47	8
Mar.	42F	+6C	July	78F	26C	Nov.	49F	9C
	28	–2		63	17		37	3
Apr.	53F	12C	Aug.	76F	24C	Dec.	40F	4C
	40	+4		61	16		26	–3

1 DESTINATION: CAPE COD

THE SEASONS OF AMERICA PAST AND PRESENT

HE WORLD TO-DAY is sick to its thin blood for lack of elemental things," wrote Henry Beston in his 1928 Cape Cod classic, *The Outermost House,* "for fire before the hands, for water welling from the earth, for air, for the dear earth itself underfoot." It is this that Cape Cod most has to offer an increasingly complex and artificial world: the chance to reconnect with elemental things. Walking along the shore poking at the washed-up sea life or watching birds fish in the surf, listening to the rhythm of the waves, experiencing the tranquillity of night on the beach or the power of a storm on water—all this is somehow life affirming and satisfyingly real.

Shaped continually by ocean currents, this windswept land of sandy beaches and dunes has an amazing natural beauty. Everyone comes for the seaside, yet Cape Cod's crimson cranberry bogs, birch and beech forests, grassy meadows, freshwater ponds, and marshlands are just as splendid. Local history is fascinating; whale-watching offers an exhilarating encounter with the natural world; bike trails lace the landscape; shops display everything from antiques to fashions to kitsch; and restaurants cook up seafood as fresh as it comes, as well as fine international cuisine.

Separated from the Massachusetts mainland by two heavily trafficked bridges over the Cape Cod Canal (17½ mi long and, at 480 ft wide, the world's widest sea-level canal), the Cape is always likened in shape to an outstretched human arm bent at the elbow, its Provincetown fist turned back toward the mainland. Writer Philip Hamburger, a Wellfleet habitué, has said the Cape "winds around to face itself"; Cape Cod Bay rests within the arm's embrace. The open Atlantic Ocean pounds the Cape's eastern coast, and Nantucket Sound washes the southern shore.

Cape Cod is only about 60 mi southeast of Boston and 70 mi from end to end, so you could make a cursory circuit of it in two or three days, but this is a place to relax—to swim and sun, to fish, boat, and golf, to hunt for antiques and wander through art galleries, to attend summer theater, to buy lobster and fish fresh off the boat, or just to take leisurely walks, bike rides, and drives along pretty country roads that happily hold out against modernity.

HE CRAGGY ARM has modest geologic origins: it started as debris deposited by a retreating glacier in the last Ice Age. The peninsula's moderate coastal climate and diverse terrain foster an equally diverse assortment of plant and animal life, some of which exist nowhere else in northern climes. Barrier beaches (sandbars that protect an inner harbor from the battering of the ocean) such as Monomoy, near Chatham, are breeding and nesting grounds for a stunning variety of shore and sea birds, and the Cape's marshes and ponds are rich in waterfowl. Stellwagen Bank, just north of Provincetown, is a prime feeding ground for whales and dolphins, and shallow sandbars are favorite playgrounds for harbor and gray seals. Among the flotsam and jetsam along the shores, beachcombers find horseshoe crabs, starfish, sea urchins, sponges, jellyfish, and a plethora of shells—white quahogs, elegant scallops, blue mussels, long, straight razor clams, spiraling periwinkles, pointy turret shells, smooth, round moon snails, conical whelks, and rough-ridged oysters.

Life on Cape Cod has always been linked to the sea. The Cape got its current name from English explorer Bartholomew Gosnold, who first anchored off what is now Provincetown in 1602 and named the area for the "great store of codfish" his crew took aboard. The importance of whaling to the area—in the early to mid-19th century Nantucket was the world's premier whaling port, and mainland New Bedford was a prosperous whaling city—is reflected in local museums, where the travels of the area's whaling and packet-schooner seamen and captains are illustrated with antique nautical equipment, harpoons, charts, maps, journals, scrimshaw (created in the seamen's copious spare time), and gifts from faraway ports for wives who had waited so patiently. Of course, not all wives waited; some chose to go along with their husbands for the ride. For today's vacationer, the maritime environment also yields plenty of recreational activities, including water sports, fishing charters, and even Jeep safaris to isolated beaches for surf casting.

Happily, much of the Cape's land is protected from development. Nature preserves encompassing pine forests, marshes, swamps, cranberry bogs, and other topographical features are patterned with well-marked walking and cycling trails. Thanks to the establishment of the Cape Cod National Seashore in 1961, in low season you can walk for almost 30 mi along the Atlantic beach and rarely see a trace of human habitation, other than the lighthouses that stand watch over the Cape's dangerous shoals and a few old shacks in the dunes of Provincetown. Across dunes anchored by poverty grass sprawl beach plums, pink salt-spray roses, and purple beach peas.

Through the creation of National Historic districts, in which change is kept to a minimum to preserve the area's historic integrity, similar protection has been extended to the Cape's oldest and loveliest man-made additions. One of the most important and eye-pleasing districts is the Old King's Highway (Route 6A), on the Cape's north shore, where some of the Cape's first towns were incorporated in the mid-1600s. Lining this tree-shaded country road are simple saltboxes from the earliest days, fancier houses built later by prosperous sea captains, and traditional Cape cottages, shingles weathered to a silvery gray, with soft pink roses spilling across them. Here, too, are the Cape's windmills, as well as the white-steepled churches, the taverns, and the village greens so redolent of early New England. The city of Provincetown is a historic district as well, preserving for posterity its cheerful mix of tiny waterfront shops (former fish shacks) and captains' mansions, among them a 1746 Cape house and a mansarded French Second Empire building.

The Cape also preserves its past in a wealth of small museums—nearly every town has one—where exhibits often hark back to the days when Native Americans were the sole inhabitants (in 1620, when the Pilgrims first anchored at Provincetown before heading on to Plymouth, an estimated 30,000 Wampanoags lived on what is now Cape Cod). Often set in historic homes, these museums provide a visual history of the lives of the English settlers and their descendants, including their economic pursuits: from farming to harvesting salt, salt hay, and cranberries (first cultivated commercially in Dennis in the early 1800s and still an important local crop) to fishing and whaling to tourism, which first took hold in the late 19th century.

THE CAPE is rightly noted for its shopping, especially for art, crafts, and antiques. Although there's no shortage of touristy souvenirs, Cape Cod has a long tradition of serious galleries, most featuring the works of local artists. Provincetown, in particular, has been known as an art colony for more than 100 years. In 1899 Charles W. Hawthorne opened the Cape Cod School of Art, attracting students and fellow artists to the tip of the Cape in droves; by 1916 five additional art schools had been established, and more than 300 artists lived and worked in Provincetown. The prominence of artists and art schools continued through the 20th century, and the Cape Cod School of Art, Hawthorne School of Art, Provincetown Art Association and Museum School, and Provincetown Fine Arts Work Center still serve hundreds of students each year.

Theater groups, too, are well established. The oldest professional summer theater in the county is Dennis's Cape Playhouse, founded in 1927. Eugene O'Neill's first play was produced in Provincetown even earlier, in 1916. Both professional troupes and small community theaters carry on the tradition each summer.

If you come here in summer, you'll soon see that the Cape is highly family oriented. The endless child-friendly amusements range from miniature golf to nature walks, from canoe trips to the Cape Cod Baseball League and the ever-beckoning beach. Typical New England diversions include chowder suppers and clambakes, outdoor band concerts, and, of course, ice cream.

The "season" used to be strictly bounded by Memorial Day and Labor Day, but these lines have blurred; many properties now open as early as April and close as late as November, and a core remain open year-round. Unfortunately, most historic sites and museums, staffed mainly by volunteers, must adhere to the traditional dates, making them inaccessible in the off season. In summer you have your choice of plunking yourself down on or near a beach and never moving; filling your schedule with shopping, historic sites, and active exploration; or combining the two.

In fall the water might be warm enough for swimming as late as October, the crowds are gone, and prices are lower. Changing foliage, though no match for the dramatic displays farther north, is an enjoyable addition to a fall visit. The moors turn to purple and gold and rust; bushes along roadsides burn a brilliant red. Cranberries ripen to a bright burgundy hue and are harvested by a method fascinating to watch. The trees around freshwater marshes, ponds, and swamps tend to color brighter and earlier, particularly the red-maple swamps, Provincetown's Beech Forest, and all of Route 6A from Sandwich to Orleans. Fall and winter are oyster and scallop season, so those restaurants that remain open serve a wide selection of dishes made with these fresh delicacies. Winter is a quiet time, when many facilities and activities shut down, but prices don't get any lower, and you can often walk the beaches in total solitude. For quiet or romantic weekend getaways, country inns offer cozy rooms with canopy beds, where you can curl up before the fireplace after a leisurely candlelight dinner.

Spring is a wee bit wet. Once the daffodils burst up from the roadsides, everything starts to turn green. By April seasonal shops and restaurants begin to open their doors, and the locals open their arms to yet another summer.

NEW AND NOTEWORTHY

Mashpee's **Wampanoag Indian Museum** plans to reopen in 2001 after a lengthy renovation, which has expanded its exhibits on the history and culture of this tribe.

The **Cape & Islands Chamber Music Festival** (☎ 508/945–8060 or 800/229–5739), an annual three-week summer concert se-

ries, launched an off-season schedule in 2000: during the 2000–2001 and 2001–2002 seasons, the Borromeo String Quartet will present six all-Beethoven programs. Call for dates and locations.

In Dennis, the **Cape Museum of Fine Arts** embarked on a major expansion in January 2000, with two new galleries scheduled to open early in 2001.

Provincetown's annual **Portuguese Week** has evolved into quite an event, with ethnic foods and crafts, bands playing in the streets, a children's fishing derby, traditional dances, and a parade with people in traditional Portuguese dress. Honoring the history of the Portuguese in Provincetown and their role in the fishing industry, the festival ends with a Sunday procession from St. Peter's Church to MacMillan Wharf, where the bishop blesses the town's fishing vessels.

The Cape Cod Chamber of Commerce has expanded its "Smart Map" of transportation into a more detailed **"Smart Guide,"** which includes bus, ferry, train, trolley, and flight services; bicycling and walking information; and sources for traffic reports. (The guide is designed to encourage visitors to take advantage of local transportation, thus easing the severe summertime traffic.) Pick up a copy at any chamber of commerce office, at many shops and attractions, or on the World Wide Web (🖱).

WHAT'S WHERE

Cape Cod has 15 towns, each broken up into villages. Things can get complicated: the "town" of Barnstable, for example, consists of Barnstable, West Barnstable, Cotuit, Marstons Mills, Osterville, Centerville, and Hyannis. Likewise, the terms *Upper Cape* and *Lower Cape*, derived from a sailing viewpoint, can be confusing; they were named based on their relations to the latitudes, which increase as you sail south. The **Upper Cape**—think "upper arm"—encompasses Bourne, Falmouth, Mashpee, and Sandwich. The **Mid Cape** includes Barnstable, Yarmouth, and Dennis. The **Lower Cape** covers Brewster, Harwich, Chatham, Orleans, Eastham, Wellfleet,

Truro, and Provincetown. The **Outer Cape,** as in "outer reaches," is the end of the Lower Cape; technically it includes only Wellfleet, Truro, and Provincetown.

There are three major roads on the Cape. U.S. 6 is the fastest way to get from the mainland to Orleans or to most points along the way. Route 6A winds more slowly along the north shore through scenic towns, while Route 28 runs south through some overdeveloped sections. Past Orleans, on the way out to Provincetown, the roadside clutter of much of U.S. 6 belies the beauty of what actually surrounds it.

Approaching the Cape

Heading for the Cape from either Boston or Providence, you'll pass southeastern Massachusetts towns that range from intriguing historic villages to gritty industrial cities to bucolic seaside communities with as much charm—and far fewer crowds—than the Cape itself. Along Boston's South Shore, historic **Plymouth** takes visitors back to the 1600s, while the shorefront suburbs of **Scituate** and **Duxbury** offer beach stops and more modern pleasures. If you're approaching from the south and west, **Fall River** and **New Bedford** provide a dose of history from the country's whaling days and early industrial era (as well as plenty of outlet shopping). Along the southeastern coast and onward to the Cape, the communities of **Westport, South Dartmouth, Fairhaven, Marion,** and **Mattapoisett** are seafront destinations that hark back to the old-time New England pleasures of seafood, summertime, and the shore.

The Upper Cape

The sprawling region nearest the bridges is perhaps the Cape's most historic area and its most contemporary area rolled into one. Along the northern bay side lie the Cape's oldest towns—**Sandwich** was settled back in 1637. Nearby **Mashpee,** where more than 600 residents are descended from the original Wampanoags, is one of two Massachusetts towns with Native American–governed areas. The west coast from **Bourne** through **North and West Falmouth** mixes residential suburbs with hidden coves and beaches lining the bay, while **Falmouth** proper is an established year-round community with all the suburban amenities you'd expect.

The Mid Cape

Like the Upper Cape, the Mid Cape region has a northern shore lined with quiet, historic villages, in this case, **Barnstable, Yarmouth,** and **Dennis.** There's more hubbub—some would say honky-tonk eyesores—along the southern coast. **Hyannis,** the Cape's geographic center and transportation hub, is popular with those who like to be in the thick of things; dining and entertainment options are many. Still, even amid the south-shore bustle, there are plenty of quiet attractions in the villages of **Cotuit, Osterville,** and **West Dennis.**

The Lower Cape

The Lower Cape towns of **Brewster, Harwich, Chatham, Orleans,** and **Eastham** make good bases for exploring the Cape. A fine area for nature lovers, the Lower Cape is home to the peaceful Monomoy National Wildlife Refuge, the popular Nickerson State Park, and a plentiful assortment of beaches and ponds. The area also has plenty of fine restaurants and attractive shops.

The Outer Cape

The narrow "forearm" of the Cape, at spots less than 2 mi wide between Cape Cod Bay and the Atlantic Ocean, includes many of the Cape's least-developed areas, particularly in **Wellfleet** and **Truro.** This is the Cape of dunes and beach grasses, of crashing surf and scrubby pines—the Cape that most attracts seekers of solitude. But there's action here, too, at the Cape's "fist," in popular **Provincetown,** where the dunes give way to a summer scene packed with nightlife, art, food, and fun.

PLEASURES AND PASTIMES

Beaches

Cape Cod has more than 150 ocean and freshwater beaches, with something for just about every taste. Bay-side beaches generally have more temperate waters and gentle waves. South-side beaches, on Nantucket Sound, have rolling surf and are warmed by the Gulf Stream. The inland areas of the Cape are dotted with numerous freshwater ponds, many with warm water and sandy beaches that are ideal for young children. Ocean beaches on the Cape Cod National Seashore have cold water, serious surf, and are, by and large, superior—wide, long, sandy, and dune backed, with great views. They're also contiguous: you can walk from Eastham to Provincetown practically without leaving sand. This almost always ensures privacy, if you stroll far enough away from crowds. From late July through August, Outer Cape beaches are sometimes troubled with red algae in the water, which, while harmless, can be annoying; check with the Cape Cod National Seashore about conditions. To mitigate the crowd factor, arrive either early in the morning or later in the afternoon. Parking lots tend to fill up by 10 AM in summer.

In season you'll have to pay for parking at public beaches; parking at restricted beaches is open to residents and visitors with permits (☞ Beaches *in* Smart Travel Tips A to Z). Walkers and bicyclists can enter these restricted beaches without permits, however. From the last June weekend ending before July 1 through Labor Day is the latest official take on what constitutes the season's boundaries. Although parking is usually free in the off-season, you'll probably also find snack bars closed and lifeguards nowhere to be found.

Biking

Biking on the Cape will satisfy avid and occasional cyclists alike. There are plenty of flat back roads, as well as a number of well-developed bike trails. The Cape's top bike path, the Cape Cod Rail Trail, offers a scenic ride through the area. Following the paved right-of-way of the old Penn Central Railroad, it's about 25 mi long, stretching from South Dennis to South Wellfleet (☞ Close-Up: Riding the Rail Trail *in* Chapter 4). The Cape Cod National Seashore maintains three bicycle trails. Head of the Meadow Trail is 2 mi of easy cycling between dunes and salt marshes from High Head Road, off Route 6A in North Truro, to the Head of the Meadow Beach parking lot. Province Lands Trail is a 5¼-mi loop off the Beech Forest parking lot on Race Point Road in Provincetown, with spurs to the Herring Cove and Race Point beaches and to Bennett Pond. The paths wind up and down hills amid dunes, marshes, woods, and ponds and offer spectacular views—on an exceptionally clear day, you can see the Boston skyline. There's a picnic grove at Pilgrim Spring. Nickerson State Park in Brewster has 8 mi of trails through forest.

Conservation Areas

Bustle and noise may seem unavoidable on a Cape vacation, but you'll find a surefire escape at one of the numerous nature refuges. There you can delight in seeing an osprey nest, the slow-motion stalking of a great blue heron, the head of a river otter coursing through the water, great shorebird colonies, a meadow in late summer, or that stray berry-studded blueberry bush. This is simply the best way to experience the vitality and diversity of the region.

Flora and fauna of local interest are beach-plum bushes, which bloom in late May and bear fruit in the fall; the spring-blooming, white-flowered shadbush and its red-purple June berries; shade- and moisture-loving cinnamon ferns; June-blooming pasture rose and the lovely Rugosa roses, which bloom throughout the summer; the brilliant orange butterfly weed, so named for the affinity monarch butterflies have for the nectar of its summer flowers; the fragrant midsummer blooms of the sweet pepper bush; blueberry and huckleberry bushes; the low-slung, waxy-leaved, dark-green teaberry, with its early fall red berries; fall-flowering seaside goldenrod and sea lavender; caribou moss, also near the sea; the plentiful beach grass (which you should avoid treading on in order to keep it plentiful); oval-leaf bayberry bushes, whose scent is a wintertime household delight; and tupelo, sassafras, pygmy beech, cottonwood, Norway spruce, red cedar, pitch pine, tamarack, and numerous other trees. Unfortunately, you need to watch out for poison ivy, that invasive spoiler of human comfort (its berries are a great boon to birds, however).

As for wildlife, there are hawks and harriers, ospreys, pheasants, quail, numerous ducks and geese, terns, bobwhites, meadowlarks, catbirds, towhees, swallows, orioles, goldfinches, yellowthroats, a great variety of warblers, and more spring and fall migrants than can be mentioned; a kingdom of mollusks and sea creatures—horseshoe, hermit, fiddler, and blue crabs; oysters; scallops; quahogs; and so on; and rabbits, raccoons, otter, muskrats, mice, and deer. From beach to marsh to meadow to salt-sprayed sand plains, the variety of habitats is tremendous.

Note: Along with the poison ivy alert, check yourself for deer ticks after a day's walk or hike in the outdoors (☞ Health *in* Smart Travel Tips A to Z).

Dining

Cape Cod received its name from the thickness of the schools of cod that early explorers found around its shores. These days the ominous local joke is that the peninsula should be renamed, except there is no alternative species certain to be around for the next few generations. But don't give up hope and expect to eat steaks. Plenty of great seafood can still be had, and here's one encouraging little secret: largely because of strict federal regulations, codfish have been making a quiet but remarkable comeback in the past few years. You'll see more and more cod on the menus, and it will be fresh.

The other interesting new development is that many Cape fisherfolk took a look at the offshore problems and decided to become less hunter and more farmer. Many have moved into aquaculture, staking grants along the tidal flats of Cape Cod Bay and planting quahogs or oysters. These shellfish are not fed any artificial food, and they aren't laced with any chemicals. They are simply planted in one area, protected from predators, and harvested when they reach market size. As a result, fresh shellfish is a great bet at restaurants and markets. If you buy some littlenecks or quahogs, turn the shell over and see if there are little rays or lines of lighter color radiating from the base of the shell. If so, you've gotten a cultured clam, known by scientists as a "notata." They're as sweet to eat as their wild cousins.

Traditionally, Cape restaurants have not favored fancy sauces or sophisticated cooking techniques. Now there is a new, younger generation of Cape Cod chefs who aren't afraid to bring more ingredients and international influence to the table, who know that if they keep everything else on the plate as fresh as the fish, the results can be truly memorable. This new approach has tended to drive the price of dinner ever higher. Prices have not reached chic New York levels by a long shot, but good Cape restaurants are charging as much as many good Boston restaurants—and delivering equally impressive quality. The emerging cuisine speaks to a new confidence among chefs; they are willing to mix and match, to grab something from Italy and something from Thailand, and to marry ingredients and techniques to the fish from Cape Cod Bay. That confidence is matched by a shift in their audience, who have come to appreciate the culinarily adventurous and experimental.

The other emerging trend at many Cape restaurants is toward a menu that runs up and down the price ladder. Except for at the fanciest spots, it is common to find both expensive full dinners and fancy burgers and eclectic pizzas side by side. This can help hold down the price of an evening out.

That said, there's a—you name it—Lobster Pot/Trap/Claw/Bowl/Net in every town. These restaurants are still authentic and the best place to go with a family, although there is no place left where good seafood could be called inexpensive. You don't need to be a stodgy traditionalist to agree that the fry-o-lators in many homestyle seafood restaurants and clam shacks impart the real lusciousness to classic Cape Cod cooking. For a quintessential summertime Cape experience, nothing beats simple standbys. The standard summer lunch is a lobster roll—a very light lobster salad with practically no mayonnaise on a plain white frankfurter roll. One of the best meals you may ever have on the Cape might just consist of nothing more than a catch-of-the-day dinner and a drive to a sunset beach: a plate of local steamers or mussels, a six-pack of Sam Adams, and a special someone.

At dinnertime dress is largely casual. One older Cape Codder takes this edict so seriously that he chops off any ties he sees and adorns his cabin in Chatham with the remains. But in certain rooms—such as Chillingsworth or the Dan'l Webster Inn or Chatham Bars Inn—a sports coat is virtually mandatory. Another recent and important development: an increasing number of restaurants are remaining open year-round, even if they scale back in winter.

Finally, note that several towns on the Cape, notably Orleans and Chatham, do not allow smoking inside any restaurant or bar. Several more (Eastham and Brewster) are on the verge of doing the same. This is strictly enforced, so if you see some people standing outside your restaurant of choice in one of these towns, they may not be in line for a table but may be taking a puff in the open air.

For price ranges *see* Dining *in* Smart Travel Tips A to Z.

Lodging

With a tourism-based economy, the Cape naturally abounds in lodgings, including self-contained luxury resorts, grand old oceanfront hotels, chain hotels, mom-and-pop motels, antiques-filled bed-and-breakfasts, cottages, condominiums, and apartments. If you're planning to stay a week or longer, renting a house is another popular option (☞ Contacts and Resources *and* Close-Up: Home, Sweet Rental Home *in* Chapter 7).

Choosing where you want to stay will depend on the kind of vacation you have in mind. If you love the beach, think about whether you'd rather stay near the dune-backed national seashore, where waters are coldest, or near the warmer south-shore waters. The national seashore is less developed and great for walking, while the Mid Cape and Falmouth beaches most often are more circumscribed and more crowded with families.

Sandwich and other towns along the north-shore Route 6A Historic District have quiet, traditional villages with old-Cape atmosphere and charming B&Bs. If you want more action, head for the Mid Cape. Hyannis is the center of it all, with a busy Main Street, active nightlife, and some fine warm-water beaches.

For the austere Cape of dunes and sea, try the beach cottages of the sparsely developed Lower Cape between Wellfleet and Provincetown. P-town itself is something completely different: in summer a frantic wall-to-wall jumble of shops and houses bursting with a large contingent of lesbians and gay men, along with a hopping nighttime scene. Staying in town makes getting to everything by foot or bike possible.

For price ranges *see* Lodging *in* Smart Travel Tips A to Z.

Nightlife and the Arts

Since the early 1900s creative people have been drawn to Cape Cod summers, and their legacy and ongoing contribution is a thriving arts scene. In addition to professional theater, which offers top-name talent in season, almost every town has a community theater that provides quality entertainment—often mixing local players with visiting pros—throughout the year. The Cape also gets its share of music stars, from pop to classical, along with local groups ranging from barbershop quartets to Bach chorales to classical music or chamber ensembles, often playing at school auditoriums or town halls.

In 1999 Provincetown celebrated its centennial as America's oldest art colony, a tradition that still thrives today. Its many galleries exhibit Cape and non-Cape artists, and the Fine Arts Work Center has launched the careers of many well-known award-winning authors. Wellfleet and Orleans have emerged as vibrant art centers. Both towns have attracted craftspeople who sell through a number of unique and sophisticated shops.

Nighttime on Cape Cod can be very special in many ways. In less developed areas, the stars are amazingly bright and make beach walks even more wondrous. Lighthouse beacons cutting shafts through the night sky have a fascination impossible to resist. If you're up *really* late, or really early, head for Chatham Light or a National Seashore beach to catch a terrific sunrise.

Another Cape twist on nightlife is that many daytime activities, such as fishing, take on a completely different aspect at night. Scuba enthusiasts might consider night diving: colors are more vivid by flashlight, much sea life is phosphorescent or bioluminescent, and nocturnal species come out to play. It's important to know the tides and safe locations—check with a dive shop.

Shopping

Art galleries and crafts shops abound on Cape Cod, a reflection of the long attraction the area has held for artists and craftspeople. Throughout the Cape you'll find weavers, candle makers, glassblowers, papermakers, and potters, as well as an inordinate number of shops specializing in country crafts from straw dolls to handmade Christmas ornaments—and, of course, plenty of tourist schlock. The region is also popular for antiquing, which means that both the genuine articles and the kitschy wanna-bes are in ready supply. Coastal environments and a seafaring past account for the proliferation of sea-related crafts (as well as marine-antiques dealers) on the Cape. A craft form that originated on the years-long voyages to whaling grounds is scrimshaw, the etching of finely detailed designs of sailing ships and sea creatures onto a hard surface. In the beginning, the bones or teeth of whales were used; today's ecologically minded (and legally constrained) scrimshanders use a synthetic substitute such as Corian, a Du Pont countertop material.

Cranberry glass, a light ruby glass made by fusing gold with glass or crystal, is sold in gift shops all over the Cape. It was once made by the Sandwich Glass company (among others) but now retains only the association with Cape Cod, as it is made elsewhere in the United States and in Europe.

For great vacation reading, the Cape has a number of highly browsable bookstores, some specializing in secondhand titles. Many have large selections of books about Cape Cod, from fiction to nautical matters to the great outdoors.

Auctions, held on the Cape all year long, range from country-barn types to the internationally known Eldred's Auctions. Though the high-end auctions deal in very fine antiques, they also include some lower-price merchandise and often yield interesting Cape pieces, such as old sea chests, at good prices.

Sports and the Outdoors

The Cape is a top American destination for swimming, surfing, windsurfing, sailing, and indulging in virtually all other water sports. Shipwrecks make for interesting dive sites, but don't expect a tropical underwater landscape. On the water, canoeing and sea kayaking are great around the bay's marshy inlets. The Cape is also one of the world's finest whale-watching spots; a whale breaching alongside your boat is an awe-inspiring sight (☞ Outdoor Activities and Sports *in* Provincetown, *below*).

Fishing on the Cape is both a profession and a pastime. Hundreds of freshwater ponds are good for perch, pickerel, and trout; surf casting off beaches and deep-sea fishing for blues, bass, and flounder is also popular. You'll need a license for freshwater fishing, available for a nominal fee at most bait-and-tackle shops.

Golfers will find a number of excellent courses, including championship layouts; most stay open nearly year-round. Bicycling is a joy on the mostly level roads, along paved and scenic bike paths, and through the many nature preserves. Bird-watchers

have many habitats from which to choose, often in a single nature preserve. The Cape Cod National Seashore has nine walking trails through varied terrain, and there are paths through conservation areas and nature preserves Cape-wide. In winter, ponds and shallow flooded cranberry bogs sometimes freeze hard enough for skating. Check conditions with the local fire department before venturing onto unfamiliar territory.

Spectators can choose from a plethora of bike and running races, golf competitions, horse shows, sailboat races, and the well-attended Cape Cod Baseball League games, breeding ground of champions (☞ Close-Up: The Cape Cod Baseball League *in* Chapter 5).

Theater

In 1916 a young aspiring writer arrived in Provincetown to try his hand at writing plays. In July of that year, Eugene O'Neill's first play, *Bound East for Cardiff*, made its debut in a waterfront fish house to tremendous success. More than 80 years later theater continues to thrive on the Cape. The country's most renowned summer theater, the Cape Playhouse, in Dennis—where Bette Davis got her start, first as an usher, then as an actress (in 1928, in *Mr. Pim Passes By*)—tops the list for the best and brightest stage fare. The Wellfleet Harbor Actors Theater has staged many important New England and world premieres. The Cape Cod Theatre Project, in Falmouth and Woods Hole, presents staged readings of new works by leading playwrights, followed by an audience discussion with the author.

Then there's the newest kid on the creative block: Provincetown Repertory Theatre (PRT). Founded in 1995 by Ken Hoyt, PRT brought legendary director Jose Quintero out of retirement in the summer of 1996 to direct two one-act O'Neill plays. In 1997 three-time Pulitzer Prize–winning playwright Edward Albee appeared at a benefit reading to help raise money for PRT's new theater on the grounds of the Pilgrim Monument and Provincetown Museum.

Community theater abounds as well, most notably at the Academy Playhouse in Orleans, the Cape Cod Repertory Theatre Co. in Brewster, and the Harwich Junior Theatre.

Town-Band Concerts

Traditional New England town-band concerts are held weekly each summer in many Cape towns—take along chairs, blankets, sweaters, and a picnic supper if you like and go early to get a good spot.

FODOR'S CHOICE

No two people will agree on what makes a perfect vacation, but it's fun and helpful to know what others think. We hope you'll have a chance to experience some of Fodor's Choices yourself while visiting Cape Cod. For detailed information about each, refer to the appropriate chapter.

Old New England

★ The town of **Sandwich,** with its salt marsh, cemetery, museums, abundance of old houses, and lovely setting on Shawme Pond, is unsurpassed for regional charm.

★ **Bright crimson cranberries** floating on flooded bogs just before the fall harvest are a perfect reminder of the handwork that was one of the joys of the seasonal roundup.

★ At **Hallet's century-old drugstore** in Yarmouth Port, life can be sweet, especially when you're sipping an ice cream soda while swiveling on a stool at a marble bar.

Natural Phenomena

★ If you crave a little rejuvenation or just want to commune with nature, spend an afternoon observing life on the salt marsh at **Bass Hole Boardwalk** in Yarmouth Port or taking a walk onto the tidal flats when the water is out.

★ From Chatham Light, looking out at the **Chatham Break** in the sandbar is a reminder of the power of the sea and a fascinating display of the process of geological change.

★ **Seeing harbor seals off Race Point** in Provincetown in winter is one of the pleasures of the seaside Cape at a time when you feel like you have the place to yourself.

★ **Sunset over Cape Cod Bay** on any bay beach from Eastham to Provincetown is an unforgettable delight at any time of year.

★ **Whales breaching** alongside your whale-watch boat will fill you with a sense of wonder unlike any you've ever felt. It's also quite a treat to see dolphins jumping in and out of the boat's bow waves or in its wake.

Beaches and Conservation Areas

★ The **Massachusetts Audubon Wellfleet Bay Wildlife Sanctuary** in South Wellfleet, with its numerous adult and children's programs and its beautiful salt-marsh setting, is a favorite migration stop for Cape vacationers year-round.

★ **Nauset Light, Coast Guard, Marconi, and Race Point beaches** stretch majestically along the length of the Cape Cod National Seashore. Backed by dunes, they are *the* classic Cape beaches.

★ **Walking along the beach,** any beach, particularly in the peaceful early morning or late afternoon, is a great reminder of what the Cape is all about.

Shopping

★ **Sandwich Auction House** has been holding weekly auctions for more than two decades, with periodic theme sales of toys, silver, paperweights, and collectibles.

★ The **weekly flea market** (Wednesday, Thursday, and weekends in summer; weekends all other seasons) at the Wellfleet Drive-In Theater is one big browse, whether or not you take anything home with you.

★ **Herridge Books** in Wellfleet reflects the town's longtime appeal to vacationing writers, with an outstanding collection of interesting reading. A book lover could easily take a day or more to do justice to what's on the shelves in this store.

★ **Farm stands,** (often roadside) throughout the Cape, provide one of the best ways to get close to the land and the rhythm of rural life.

Dining

★ **Front Street, Provincetown.** In a town that consistently continues to raise the level of the Cape's cuisine, this small, unassuming venue serves nothing short of superb, original food, offered by a marvelous staff. You couldn't ask for much more at Cape's end. $$$

★ **Inaho, Yarmouth Port.** To recommend a Japanese restaurant on Cape Cod is only superficially surprising. Inaho uses the great Cape fresh seafood to maximum effect, and the setting and presentation, from lighting to service, perfectly celebrate a remarkably conscious kitchen. $$-$$$

★ **Sagamore Inn, Sagamore.** Rustic, roomy, family run, not pretentious or expensive—this is the kind of place you might stop in for lunch on a rainy day and then for dinner the following night. $$

★ **Mojo's, Provincetown.** If every hole-in-the-wall were as inventive and cared as much about its menu as this one, the world would be a cheaper, better place. You'll find everything from fried clams and steak subs to veggie burgers and salads here. $

Lodging

★ **Brass Key, Provincetown.** This elegant complex encompasses several fully restored structures that unite Victorian splendor and modern luxury. $$$$

★ **Captain's House Inn, Chatham.** Friendly and professional service, colonial atmosphere, and wonderful old buildings make this one of the Cape's most pleasant B&Bs. $$-$$$$

★ **Augustus Snow House, Harwich Port.** This elegant Victorian inn takes you back to another era, with a tearoom where you can savor afternoon tea on weekends. $$$

★ **Heaven on High, West Barnstable.** Perfectly named, perfectly decorated, and perfectly comfortable, Heaven on High is such a blessed hilltop haven you might never want to leave to explore the town's nearby sights and sounds. $$-$$$

Children's Activities

★ Sandwich has the **Thornton W. Burgess Museum,** namesake of the creator of Peter Rabbit and great for children; **Heritage Plantation,** with superb old cars, a working 1912 carousel, and grounds perfect for running around; and the **Green Briar Nature Center and Jam Kitchen,** with walking trails, the Smiling Pool pond, natural-history exhibits, and Peter Rabbit's great-great-grandchildren.

★ The **Cape Cod Museum of Natural History** in Brewster offers a great variety of bay, marsh, and estuary cruises with naturalists who haul up traps so children can observe aquatic creatures up close. There are also field walks, exhibits, and a pond- and sea-life room with live specimens.

★ **Pirate's Cove** in South Yarmouth far outdoes the average miniature golf course, architecturally speaking. Give in and pick up a putter at least once—you may have a good time even if your children aren't alongside you.

★ **Whale watches** out of Provincetown can be a tremendous thrill—genuinely exciting and pleasantly educational.

FESTIVALS AND SEASONAL EVENTS

The Massachusetts Office of Travel & Tourism (☞ Visitor Information *in* Smart Travel Tips A to Z) offers events listings and a whale-watch guide for the entire state. Also see the events calendar in "CapeWeek," an arts-and-entertainment supplement published every Friday in the *Cape Cod Times.*

EARLY DEC.:➤ Many Cape towns do up the Christmas season in grand style. To take in the best-known celebration, plan an excursion to the nearby island of Nantucket for the annual **Christmas Stroll** (☎ 508/228–1700), which takes place the first weekend of the month. Carolers and musicians entertain strollers as they walk the festive cobblestone streets and sample shops' wares and seasonal refreshments. Activities include theatrical performances, art exhibitions, crafts sales, and a tour of historic homes. To avoid the throngs, though, visit on one of the surrounding weekends (festivities begin the day after Thanksgiving and last through New Year's Eve).

Various Cape towns also have **holiday strolls**; call the Cape Cod Chamber of Commerce for a free brochure (☎ 508/862–0700).

Falmouth's **Christmas by the Sea** (☎ 508/548–8500 or 800/526–8532), the first full weekend of December, includes lighting ceremonies at the Village Green, caroling at Nobska Light in Woods Hole, a house tour, church fairs, and a parade.

DEC.:➤ Chatham's **Christmas by the Sea** weekend (☎ 508/945–5199) includes caroling, a book-and-author tea, and a dinner dance at the grand Chatham Bars Inn. The events are part of a monthlong celebration beginning just after Thanksgiving and ending with a lavish First Night celebration, with fireworks over Oyster Pond on New Year's Eve.

LATE APR.:➤ The weekend-long **Brewster in Bloom** (☎ 508/896–3500 or 508/896–2670) greets the spring season with a daffodil fest each year during the last weekend in April. Geared to promote small-town life, the festival includes arts-and-crafts shows, a parade, tours of historic homes and inns, a golf tournament, and a giant antiques and collectibles market.

APR. 1 AND MAY 5:➤ On April 1 **Opera New England of Cape Cod** (☎ 508/771–3600) will perform a concert version of Verdi's *Aida* at Cape Cod Community College in Hyannis (✉ Rte. 132). On May 5, at the same location, you can catch Verdi's *Rigoletto.*

MID-MAY:➤ In Hyannis, **Cape Cod Maritime Week** (☎ 508/362–3828) celebrates Cape Cod's maritime history with events including lighthouse tours, guided shorefront walks, and special exhibits.

The Green Briar Nature Center and Jam Kitchen in Sandwich holds its annual **Green Briar Herb Festival** (☎ 508/888–6870), where you can pick up perennials, wildflowers dug out of their garden, and dozens of herb varieties.

JUNE–AUG.:➤ **Summer theater, town-band concerts,** and **arts-and-crafts fairs** enliven most every Cape town.

EARLY JUNE:➤ The **Cape Cod Antique Dealers Association Annual Antiques Show** at Sandwich's Heritage Plantation (☎ 508/888–3300) is attended by 50 dealers of fine 18th- and 19th-century English and American furniture, folk art, Sandwich glass, jewelry, paintings, and quilts.

MID- TO LATE JUNE:➤ **Cape Heritage '01** (☎ 508/862–0700) is a weeklong celebration of the Cape's history and culture hosted by museums, historical societies, theater groups, libraries, and the Cape Cod National Seashore.

The **Blessing of the Fleet** (☎ 508/487–3424) in

Provincetown is the culmination of a weekend of festivities, including a banquet and dance. On the last Sunday of the month a parade ends at the wharf, where fishermen and their families and friends pile onto their boats and form a procession. The bishop stands on the dock and blesses the boats with holy water as they pass by.

The **Portuguese Festival** coincides with the Blessing of the Fleet (☞ *above*), with traditional foods, dances, games, fireworks, and events honoring the Portuguese heritage in Provincetown.

JUNE 16–29:➤ Falmouth welcomes the **Soundfest Chamber Music Festival** (☎ 508/548–2290), including the Colorado Quartet and guest artists. Daily events during the two-week festival include student performances, concerts, master classes, and lectures.

JULY 4 WEEKEND:➤ The **Mashpee Powwow** (☎ 508/477–0208) brings together Wampanoags from North and South America for three days of dance contests, drumming, a fireball game, and a clambake, plus the crowning of the Mashpee Wampanoag Indian princess on the final night.

Fireworks displays are a part of July 4 celebrations in several Cape towns.

MID-JULY:➤ In East Sandwich, the **Cape Cod Antiquarian Book Fair** (☎ 508/888–2331) welcomes more than 50 dealers in old and rare books. The night before the book fair,

the Greenbriar Nature Center hosts an auction of books by and items related to Thornton W. Burgess.

LATE JULY:➤ The Cape Cod Symphony Orchestra sets up at the Mashpee Commons for the first of two annual **Sounds of Summer Pops Concerts** (☎ 508/362–1111).

The **Barnstable County Fair** (☎ 508/563–3200) in East Falmouth, begun in 1844, is Cape Cod's biggest event. The nine-day affair features livestock and food judging; horse, pony, and oxen pulls and shows; arts-and-crafts demonstrations; carnival rides; lots of food; and appearances by the formerly famous bent on comebacks.

Billed as a gala event the Great Gatsby and his counterparts would never have missed, the annual **Lawn Cotillion** (☎ 508/896–9000), held on the grounds of Brewster's grand Ocean Edge resort, is indeed quite the affair. Participants are encouraged to dress in the whites of the 1920s era for the Celebrity Croquet Tournament. Other activities include a fashion show and fine-art auction.

AUG.:➤ The **Cape & Islands Chamber Music Festival** (☎ 508/945–8060 or 800/229–5739) is three weeks of top-caliber performances, including a jazz night, at various locations in August. In 2000 the festival also launched an off-season concert series; call for schedule.

EARLY AUG.:➤ The Boston Pops Esplanade Orchestra

wows the crowds with its annual **Pops by the Sea** concert (☎ 508/362–0066), held at the Hyannis Village Green at 5 PM. Each year a guest conductor strikes up the band.

MID-AUG.:➤ The **Falmouth Road Race** (✉ Box 732, Falmouth 02541, ☎ 508/540–7000) is a world-class race covering the coast from Woods Hole to Falmouth Heights; to participate, apply by mail the fall or winter prior to the race.

Sails Around Cape Cod (☎ 508/430–1165) is a two-day, 140-nautical-mi race that circumnavigates the Cape, starting at the west end of Cape Cod Canal and ending at the east end. The event was canceled in 2000 and may not happen in 2001; call to confirm.

AUG. 25–26:➤ The Otis Air Base near Falmouth holds a free two-day **open house and air show** (☎ 508/968–4090) with exhibitions that may include precision flying by teams of the air force's Thunderbirds or the navy's Blue Angels.

LATE AUG.:➤ The Cape Cod Symphony Orchestra comes to Eldridge Field Park in Orleans for its **Sounds of Summer Pops Concert** (☎ 508/362–1111).

The annual **New England Jazz Festival** (☎ 508/477–2580), produced by the Boch Center for the Performing Arts, takes place at Mashpee Commons.

The Osterville Historical Society holds its annual **antiques show** (☎ 508/428–5861) on the third or fourth Thursday in August.

SEPT.:➤ The 32nd **Annual Bourne Scallop Fest** (☎ 508/759–6000), the weekend after Labor Day, attracts thousands of people to Buzzards Bay for three days of music; parades; carnival rides; and, of course, fried scallops.

The **Harwich Cranberry Festival** (☎ 508/430–2811) features an arts-and-crafts show, a carnival, fireworks, pancake breakfasts, an antique-car show, and much more.

MID-OCT.:➤ **Seafest,** an annual tribute to the maritime industry, marks one of the few times that Chatham Light (☎ 508/945–5199) is open to the public.

LATE OCT.:➤ **Fall foliage.** The leaf season usually peaks around the end of October. Colors might flame a few weeks earlier or later, however, depending on the weather in the preceding months.

OCT. 28:➤ For its annual fall production, **Opera New England of Cape Cod** (☎ 508/771–3600) will perform Johann Strauss's *Die Fledermaus* at the Tilden Art Center at Cape Cod Community College in Hyannis.

THANKSGIVING EVE:➤ **Provincetown Festival of Lights** (☎ 508/487–3424), commemorating the Pilgrims' landing, begins with the lighting of 5,000 white and gold bulbs draped over the Pilgrim Monument. The lights are lighted nightly until Little Christmas (January 6). A performance of Handel's *Hallelujah Chorus* accompanies the lighting, and the monument museum offers an open house and tours. Other events include a reenactment of the first landing of the Pilgrims on Provincetown shores, dramatic readings of the Mayflower Compact (which was signed in Provincetown Harbor), fireworks, and an abundance of Thanksgiving dinner celebrations.

2 APPROACHING THE CAPE

PLYMOUTH, FALL RIVER, WESTPORT, SOUTH DARTMOUTH, NEW BEDFORD

If you're driving to the Cape, make the journey half the fun—explore a little *before* you reach the bridges. Southeastern Massachusetts is a time warp, and Plimoth Plantation meticulously re-creates New England's first settlement as it appeared in 1627. Approaching Cape Cod from the west, you'll pass through Fall River, with its bizarre history of Lizzie Borden, and New Bedford, a 19th-century whaling center. Along the way are some lovely seaside villages where a stop for fresh fish or a walk on the beach will help get you into that Cape state of mind.

Revised by
Carolyn Heller

M ANY LESSER-KNOWN SITES in southeastern Massachusetts make enjoyable stops en route to Cape Cod. If you're a history buff or want to give your children an educational experience they won't soon forget, don't miss Plymouth, the community locals proudly call America's Hometown: here you can see that monument you've heard about since childhood, Plymouth Rock, and walk the decks of the *Mayflower II*. A few miles down the road is Plimoth Plantation, a re-created 17th-century Puritan village where trained staff members vividly dramatize the everyday lives of the first English settlers. Watch them make cheese, forge nails, and explain where and when they bathe (hint: not often).

If you're coming from the south or west, consider stopping in the seafaring towns of New Bedford and Fall River. In Fall River, history took a macabre turn with the Trial of the Century—the 19th century, that is. Fall River was the hometown of Lizzie Borden, who was accused, and acquitted, of dispatching her parents with "40 whacks" of an axe. Borden history has become a cottage industry here, yet there's more to Fall River than the Borden saga; the town is home to Battleship Cove, a floating museum complex, and serves as a regional center for outlet shopping.

Nearby New Bedford was a major whaling port in the 19th century and now holds the nation's largest museum on the history of whaling. Exhibits include the world's largest model ship and a rare skeleton of a 66-ft blue whale.

Along the coves of Buzzards Bay, southeastern Massachusetts is dotted with seaside towns and sandy beaches, the best known of which is Horseneck Beach in Westport. The pretty villages of South Dartmouth are also worth a stop. Last but not least, a sustained roll through this part of the state reveals some high-quality restaurants and charming bed-and-breakfasts.

Pleasures and Pastimes

The Sea

With a coastline that meanders in and out of Buzzards Bay, southeastern Massachusetts has plenty of choice seaside areas. Westport's Horseneck Beach is a long stretch of sand that's hugely popular on weekends. Plymouth, too, has several popular beaches, from Plymouth Beach near town to the long crescent of sand at White Horse Beach to the south. But there are smaller beaches and coves where you can enjoy the shore in relative quiet—in Fairhaven, for example, and other small towns that dot the area.

If you're more interested in being on the water than in it, try a cruise from Onset Harbor or take a whale-watching trip. Several companies run excursions from Plymouth between May and October; they usually last three to four hours.

Dining

Like other Massachusetts shorefront towns, the communities approaching the Cape have plenty of seafood restaurants. You'll find everything from clam shacks to more upscale dining options—Westport and South Dartmouth both have restaurants that are worth a detour. In New Bedford and Fall River, which have large Portuguese populations, you can sample dishes made with spicy *linguica* (sausage) or *bacalau* (salt cod), and pick up some soft, doughy Portuguese sweet bread to sustain you as you explore. For price ranges *see* Dining *in* Smart Travel Tips A to Z.

Lodging

Plymouth's numerous lodging options include quaint B&Bs and large motels. Choices on the coast are more limited, although the area does have several recommendable small inns and B&Bs. If you're traveling with children, be sure to ask whether they are welcome at smaller properties; some are not set up for youngsters. For price ranges *see* Lodging *in* Smart Travel Tips A to Z.

Numbers in the margin correspond to points of interest on the Approaching the Cape map.

Plymouth

❶ *40 mi southeast of Boston.*

On December 26, 1620, 102 weary British men, women, and children disembarked from the *Mayflower* to found the first permanent European settlement north of Virginia. (Virginia was their intended destination, but storms pushed the ship off course.) Of the settlers, now known as the Pilgrims, a third were members of a Puritan sect of religious reformers known as the Separatists, so called because they wanted to establish their own church separate from the national Church of England. This separation was considered treasonous, so the group first fled to the city of Leiden in the Netherlands seeking religious freedom. After more than 10 years there, the group joined with other emigrants to start a new life in the New World.

Before coming ashore, the expedition's leaders drew up the Mayflower Compact, a historic agreement binding the group to the law of the majority. This compact became the basis for the colony's government. After a rough start (half the original settlers died during the first winter), the colony stabilized and grew under the leadership of Governor William Bradford. Two other founding fathers—military leader Myles Standish and John Alden—acquired mythical status via a poem by Longfellow, *The Courtship of Miles Standish*.

Forty miles south of Boston, Plymouth today is characterized by narrow streets, clapboard mansions, shops, and antiques stores. Some commercial names would make the Pilgrims shudder: The John Alden Gift Shop, Mayflower Seafoods, and, incongruously, Pocahontas Gifts, Sportswear and Sundries (Pocahontas lived in Virginia). But it's easy to overlook these and admire the picturesque waterfront. The town also holds a parade, historic-house tours, and other activities to mark Thanksgiving.

Plymouth is dotted with historic statues, including depictions of William Bradford on Water Street, a Pilgrim maiden in Brewster Gardens, and Massasoit (chief of the local Wampanoag tribe) on Carver Street. The largest freestanding granite statue in the country, the **National Monument to the Forefathers** stands high on a grassy hill. Designed by Hammet Billings of Boston in 1854 and dedicated in 1889, it depicts Faith, surrounded by Liberty, Morality, Justice, Law, and Education and includes scenes from the Pilgrims' early days in Plymouth. ⊠ *Allerton St.*

Several historic houses are also open for visits, including the 1640 **Sparrow House,** Plymouth's oldest structure. ⊠ *42 Summer St.,* ☎ *508/747–1240.* 🎫 *$2.* ☉ *Apr.–Dec., Thurs.–Tues. 10–5, Sat. 10–8 (or until dark).*

The 1749 **Spooner House,** home to the same family for 200 years, has guided tours and a garden. ⊠ *27 North St.,* ☎ *508/746–0012.* 🎫 *$4.* ☉ *June–early Oct., Thurs.–Sat. 10–4.*

Approaching the Cape

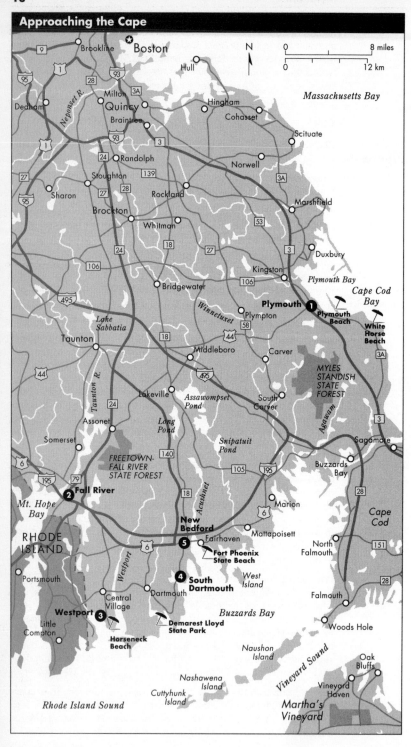

N

0   8 miles
0   12 km

Brookline
Boston
Hull
95 **1** **28** **93** **9**
Milton
Dedham
Quincy **3A**
Braintree
Hingham
Cohasset
93
Scituate
Randolph **3**
Stoughton **24** **139**
Sharon **27** **28**
Rockland
Brockton
Whitman
53
Marshfield
3A
24 **18** **27**
106
Kingston
495
Bridgewater
106
Plymouth **1**
Winnetuxet
Plympton
Plymouth Beach
Cape Cod Bay
Plymouth Bay
White Horse Beach
Taunton
Lake Sabbatia
18
58
44
Middleboro
Carver
3A
44
18
495
MYLES STANDISH STATE FOREST
Lakeville
Assawompset Pond
South Carver
Agawam
3
Assonet
Long Pond
Snipatuit Pond
Sagamore
Somerset
140
FREETOWN-FALL RIVER STATE FOREST
105
195
Buzzards Bay
6
195
79
Fall River **2**
18
Acushnet
Marion
28
Cape Cod
Mt. Hope Bay
New Bedford **5**
Fairhaven
Mattapoisett
6
North Falmouth
RHODE ISLAND
6
Fort Phoenix State Beach
West Island
151
Portsmouth
Westport
Central Village
Dartmouth
South Dartmouth **4**
Buzzards Bay
Falmouth
28
Westport **3**
Demarest Lloyd State Park
Woods Hole
Little Compton
Horseneck Beach
Naushon Island
Vineyard Sound
Oak Bluffs
Nashawena Island
Vineyard Haven
Cuttyhunk Island
Rhode Island Sound
Martha's Vineyard

Massachusetts Bay

Neponset R.

Taunton R.

Westport R.

Like Plimoth Plantation (☞ *below*), the **Mayflower II,** a replica of the 1620 *Mayflower,* is manned by staff in period dress. The ship was built in England through research and a bit of guesswork, and then it sailed across the Atlantic in 1957. ⊠ *State Pier,* ☎ *508/746–1622.* ☎ *$7; free with Plimoth Plantation ticket.* ◷ *Apr.–Nov., daily 9–5.*

A few dozen yards from the *Mayflower II* is **Plymouth Rock,** popularly believed to have been the Pilgrims' stepping-stone when they left the ship. Given the stone's unimpressive appearance—it's little more than a boulder—and dubious authenticity (as explained on a nearby plaque), the grand canopy overhead seems a trifle ostentatious.

Across the street from Plymouth Rock is **Cole's Hill,** where the company buried its dead—at night, so the local Native Americans could not count the dwindling numbers of survivors. Just past the hill, on what was once called 1st Street, is the site of the original settlement; in 1834 the street was renamed Leyden Street in honor of the Dutch city that sheltered the Pilgrims. Look for plaques designating the locations of the original lots.

For a more traditional view of the Pilgrims, visit the **Plymouth National Wax Museum,** on top of Cole's Hill. It contains 26 scenes with 180 life-size models that tell the settlers' story. ⊠ *16 Carver St.,* ☎ *508/ 746–6468.* ☎ *$6.* ◷ *Mar.–May and Nov., daily 9–5; June and Sept.– Oct., daily 9–7; July–Aug., daily 9–9.*

From the waterfront sights it's a short walk to one of the country's oldest public museums. The **Pilgrim Hall Museum,** established in 1824, transports you back to the time just before the Pilgrims' landing, with items carried by those weary travelers to the New World. Included are a carved chest, a remarkably well preserved wicker cradle, Myles Standish's sword, John Alden's Bible, Native American artifacts, and the remains of the *Sparrow Hawk,* a sailing ship that was wrecked in 1626. ⊠ *75 Court St. (Rte. 3A),* ☎ *508/746–1620.* ☎ *$5.* ◷ *Feb.–Dec., daily 9:30–4:30.*

Imagine an entire museum devoted to a Thanksgiving side dish. But the Ocean Spray–operated **Cranberry World** is amazingly popular. For one thing, it's free. After viewing details of how the state's local crop is grown, harvested, and processed, you can sip juices and sample products made from *Vaccinium macrocarpon* (the Latin name for cranberries). ⊠ *158 Water St.,* ☎ *508/747–2350.* ☎ *Free.* ◷ *May–Nov., daily 9:30–5.*

....

NEED A BREAK?　　Sample some cranberry wine—it's oddly refreshing, and free—at the **Plymouth Bay Winery** (⊠ 114 Water St., ☎ 508/746–2100), open March–December. For more substantive fare, the **Lobster Hut** (☎ 508/ 746–2270), open year-round (except January) on Town Wharf at the waterfront, offers seafood in the classic breaded-and-fried style, plus sandwiches and luncheon specials.

....

★ ☾　Above the entrance of the **Plimoth Plantation** is the caution: you are now entering 1627. Believe it. Against the backdrop of the Atlantic Ocean, a Pilgrim village has been painstakingly re-created, from the thatch roofs, cramped quarters, and open fireplaces to the long-horned livestock. Throw away your preconception of white collars and funny hats; through ongoing research, the Plimoth staff has developed a portrait of the Pilgrims that's more complex than the dour folk pictured in elementary-school textbooks. Listen to the accents of the "residents," who never break out of character. You might see them plucking ducks, cooking rabbit stew, or tending garden. Feel free to engage them in conversation about their life, but expect only curious looks if you ask about anything that happened later than 1627.

Elsewhere on the plantation is **Hobbamock's Homestead,** where descendants of the Wampanoag Indians re-create the life of a Native American who chose to live near the newcomers. In the **Carriage House Craft Center** you'll see items created using the techniques of 17th-century English craftsmanship—that is, what the Pilgrims might have imported (you can also buy samples). At the **Nye Barn** you can see descendants of 17th-century goats, cows, pigs, and chickens, bred to represent animals raised in the original plantation. The visitor center has gift shops, a cafeteria, and multimedia presentations. Dress for the weather since many exhibits are outdoors. Admission tickets are good for two consecutive days; if you have time, you may want to spread out your plantation visit to take in all the sights. ⊠ *Warren Ave. (Rte. 3A),* ☎ *508/ 746–1622.* ☞ *$16; $19 including entry to Mayflower II.* ☉ *Apr.–Nov., daily 9–5.* 🕭

Dining and Lodging

$$–$$$ ✕ **Bert's Cove.** This local landmark, just off the entrance to Plymouth Beach, has great ocean views and a menu encompassing veal medallions, sirloin steak, risotto, and fresh seafood. ⊠ *140 Warren Ave., Rte. 3A,* ☎ *508/746–3330. AE, D, MC, V. Closed Mon. Nov.–Apr.*

$–$$ ✕ **Iguana's.** A good choice for both lunch and late-night dining, Iguana's serves fajitas, burritos, and other Mexican-Southwestern fare, plus burgers; sandwiches; and chicken, steak, and rib dishes. You'll find a bar, a patio, ocean views—and a live iguana. ⊠ *Village Landing Marketplace, 170 Water St.,* ☎ *508/747–4000. AE, DC, MC, V.*

$ ✕ **The All-American Diner.** The look is nostalgia—red, white, and blue with movie posters. The specialty is beloved American foods—omelets and pancakes for breakfast; burgers, salads, and soups for lunch. ⊠ *60 Court St.,* ☎ *508/747–4763. AE, DC, MC, V. No dinner.*

$$–$$$ ✕🏠 **John Carver Inn.** This three-story Colonial-style redbrick building with a massive pillared facade is just a few steps from Plymouth's main attractions. The public rooms and dining rooms are lavish, with period furnishings and stylish drapes. The guest rooms are more matter-of-fact, but ask for one of the six environmentally sensitive rooms, which have filtered air and water and four-poster beds. The two-room suites have fireplaces and whirlpool baths. The indoor pool has a *Mayflower* ship model and a water slide. At its Hearth 'n Kettle Restaurant, a huge menu of American favorites, including hearty sandwiches and many types of seafood, is served by a staff dressed in Colonial attire. ⊠ *25 Summer St., 02360,* ☎ *508/746–7100 or 800/274–1620,* ℻ *508/746–8299. 79 rooms, 6 suites. Restaurant, bar, pool, exercise room, meeting rooms. AE, D, DC, MC, V.* 🕭

$$ 🏠 **Governor Bradford on the Harbour.** The waterfront location here (directly across from the *Mayflower II*) is a big plus. Rooms are motel-basic, each with two double beds, a small refrigerator, and free HBO. ⊠ *98 Water St., 02360,* ☎ *508/746–6200 or 800/332–1620,* ℻ *508/ 747–3032. 94 rooms. No-smoking rooms, refrigerators, pool. AE, D, DC, MC, V.* 🕭

$–$$ 🏠 **Beach House Oceanfront B&B.** At the end of a rutted dirt road, this contemporary gray-shingle home overlooking the Atlantic makes a perfect hideaway. Although only about 10 minutes south of Plymouth center, the house feels a world apart. The deck, screened porch, and living room/dining room with floor-to-ceiling windows all face the wide expanse of the ocean, and steps lead down the cliff to a small private beach. Inside, the theme is white—from the leather sofas to the lace curtains and quilts. ⊠ *45 Black Pond La. (mailing address: 429 Center Hill*

Rd.), 02360, ☎ 508/224–3517 or 888/262–2543. 2 rooms, 1 2-bed-
room suite. Beach. No smoking. MC, V. BP. 🐾

Outdoor Activities and Sports

BEACHES

Plymouth Beach (✉ Warren Ave. [Rte. 3A]), south of town near Bert's
Cove restaurant, has rest rooms, showers, and lifeguards (in season).
Daily parking fees are $7 weekdays, $10 weekends.

White Horse Beach (✉ Taylor Ave.) is a popular long, sandy beach in
a neighborhood of summer cottages, off Rte. 3A south of Plimoth Plantation. Parking is very limited.

STATE PARKS

Myles Standish State Forest (✉ Cranberry Rd., South Carver, Exit 5
off Rte. 3, ☎ 508/866–2526) has more than 16,000 acres for hiking,
biking, swimming, picnicking, and canoeing.

OFF THE
BEATEN PATH

DUXBURY – Settled in 1628 by Pilgrim colonists Myles Standish and
John Alden, among others, Duxbury is now a suburban community
about 10 mi north of Plymouth that's home to the **John Alden House
Museum**, the only standing structure in which original Pilgrims are
known to have lived. John Alden, who served as assistant governor of
Plymouth colony, his wife, Priscilla, and eight or nine of their children occupied the house, which was built in 1653. One bedroom has a "seven-
day dresser" with a drawer for each day of the week; the Sunday
drawer, which held formal church wear, is the largest. ✉ 105 Alden St.,
Duxbury, ☎ 781/934–9092. 🎫 Guided tours $2.50. ☉ Mid-May–
mid-Oct., Mon.–Sat. 10–5, Sun. noon–5.

Fall River

❷ 54 mi southeast of Boston.

It's a famous rhyme of woe: "Lizzie Borden took an axe / And gave
her mother forty whacks. / When she saw what she had done, / She
gave her father forty-one." And yet Lizzie, the maiden daughter of the
town's prominent banker, was found innocent of the 1892 bludgeon-
ing deaths of her father and stepmother in the most sensational trial
of its time. She went on to spend the rest of her life quietly in Fall River,
today a fading port and factory town.

In the 1800s Fall River became a major textile milling area, but by the
1920s much of the textile industry had moved to southern states.
Many former mills now house factory outlets that attract bargain
hunters, and the Borden tragedy continues to draw the curious.

The best place to learn about the Borden case is the **Fall River Historical Society,** which has the world's largest collection of Borden artifacts,
including courtroom evidence, photographs, and the handleless hatchet
suspected of being the murder weapon. The 1835 Greek Revival–style
mansion also has a wealth of information about the region, display-
ing memorabilia from the Fall River steamship line and artifacts related to Fall River's days as home of the world's largest cotton cloth
manufacturer. Another exhibit illustrates 19th-century mourning practices, including elaborate decorations woven from human hair. One-
hour tours are available on the hour (weekdays 9–3, no tour at noon;
weekends 1–4). ✉ 451 Rock St., at Maple St., ☎ 508/679–1071. 🎫
Guided tours $5. ☉ Apr.–May and Oct.–Nov., Tues.–Fri. 9–4:30;
June–Sept. and Dec., Tues.–Fri. 9–4:30, weekends 1–5.

If you're strong of heart and stomach, you may also want to take in the **Lizzie Borden Bed & Breakfast Museum** (☞ *Lodging, below*). In 1996 the Borden home, the site of the murders, was transformed into a B&B. Even if you don't spend the night here, you can stop in to see the display of Lizzie-related items. ⊠ *92 2nd St.,* ☎ *508/675–7333.* ⊠ *Guided tours $7.50.* ۩ *Memorial Day–Labor Day, daily 11–3; early Apr.–Memorial Day and Labor Day–Oct., weekends 11–3; tours every ½ hr, last tour at 2:30.*

Another Lizzie highlight is the **Borden burial plot** in the Oak Grove Cemetery on Prospect Street. Lizzie's home after her acquittal was at **306 French Street** (a private residence), where she lived until her death in 1927.

A visit to Fall River can skirt Lizzie Borden's sad saga entirely. The town's industrial docks and enormous factories recall the city's past as a major textile center in the 19th and early 20th centuries. Fall River also served as a port; today the most interesting nautical site is **Battleship Cove,** a "floating" museum complex docked on the Taunton River. The cove is home to the 35,000-ton battleship USS *Massachusetts;* the destroyer USS *Joseph P. Kennedy, Jr.;* a World War II attack sub, the USS *Lionfish;* two PT boats from World War II; and a Cold War–era Russian-built warship. ⊠ *5 Water St., at Davol St., off Rte. 79,* ☎ *508/ 678–1100 or 800/533–3194.* ⊠ *$9.* ۩ *Late Apr.–June and Sept.–late Oct., daily 9–5; July–Aug., daily 9–6; late Oct.–late Apr., daily 9–4:30.*

From May through October the **HMS Bounty,** built for the 1962 film *Mutiny on the Bounty,* is docked adjacent to Battleship Cove. Visitors can participate in sails organized by the Tall Ship Bounty Foundation; call for details. ☎ *508/673–3886.* ⊠ *$5.* ۩ *Daily 10–6; call ahead, as ship is often on sail.*

The **Fall River Carousel,** built in the 1920s, was rescued from the defunct Lincoln Amusement Park in 1992 and moved to Battleship Cove. The glorious restoration is now housed dockside. ⊠ *Battleship Cove,* ☎ *508/324–4300.* ⊠ *Rides $1.* ۩ *Generally June–Labor Day, Tues.– Sun. 11–7; mid-Apr.–May, reduced hrs., call to confirm.*

The riverside **Fall River Heritage State Park** tells the story of Fall River's industrial past, focusing on the city's textile mills and their workers. The park has a visitor center, exhibits, and a summer concert series. ⊠ *200 Davol St. W,* ☎ *508/675–5759.* ⊠ *Free.* ۩ *July–Aug., daily 10–6; Sept.–June, daily 10–4.*

Two blocks from Battleship Cove, the **Marine Museum at Fall River** celebrates the age of sail and steamship travel, especially the lavishly fitted ships of the Old Fall River Line, which operated until 1937 between New England and New York City. The museum also contains the 28-ft-long, 1-ton model of the *Titanic* used in the 1952 movie. ⊠ *70 Water St.,* ☎ *508/674–3533.* ⊠ *$4.* ۩ *Weekdays 9–5, Sat. noon–5, Sun. noon–4.*

Dining and Lodging

$–$$ ✕ **Waterstreet Café.** This casually sophisticated café, with exposed brick and sponge-painted walls, serves hummus and tabbouleh roll-ups, falafel, and other Middle Eastern–inspired salads and sandwiches. Other specialties are "something fresh in a shell over linguine" (pasta with clams or mussels) and Greek Island Shrimp, sautéed with artichoke hearts and feta cheese. It's across the street from the Marine Museum. ⊠ *36 Water St.,* ☎ *508/672–8748. AE, MC, V. Closed Mon. No dinner Sun.–Wed.*

$$$ ☷ **Lizzie Borden Bed & Breakfast Museum.** Could you stand to sleep in the same house where Lizzie Borden's father and stepmother met a

bloody end? Choose from one of the four original bedrooms, two of which are suites, or two rooms converted from attic space. A full breakfast and a house tour are included. Guests can also watch videos about the Borden case. Nonguests may tour the place between 11 and 3. Overnight guests must be 12 or older. ⊠ *92 2nd St., 02721,* ☎ 𝗙𝗔𝗫 *508/675–7333. 4 rooms, 2 suites. No smoking. AE, D, MC, V. BP.*

Shopping

Fall River is home to more than 70 brand-name factory-outlet stores, clustered at Exit 8A from I–195 and housed in original granite mills that once turned out cotton. The largest of the outlet centers is **Quality Factory Outlets** (⊠ 638 Quequechan St., ☎ 508/677–4949).

Westport

❸ *12 mi southeast of Fall River.*

As you venture south and east of Fall River, the urban landscape gives way to farm country. You'll pass rows of corn, old stone walls, and pastures of cows and horses. About 12 mi from Fall River, Westport has a mix of farmland and summer homes in a small village and scattered throughout the countryside, as well as one of the area's nicest beaches.

Although grapes may not come immediately to mind as a Massachusetts crop, the **Westport Rivers Vineyard and Winery** grows grapes and has been selling its wines since 1991. Its sparkling wines are particularly well regarded. Visitors can sample the wines, and there's a small art gallery above the store with changing exhibits. Free winery tours are offered on weekends. ⊠ *417 Hixbridge Rd., off Rte. 88,* ☎ *508/636–3423.* ☉ *Tasting room, shop, and gallery: daily 11–5; tours: weekends 11–4:30.*

Dining and Lodging

$$$ ✕ **The Back Eddy.** Owner Chris Schlesinger has earned raves for his East
★ Coast Grill in Cambridge, and he's translated the same formula from Boston to the Westport waterfront. The menu emphasizes fish preparations ranging from straightforward (steamers, oysters on the half shell) to worldly (grilled peppered tuna with Asian spinach salad, roasted clams over linguine). The casual, wood-floor dining room is boisterous, with a lively bar scene, and most of the large windows overlook the harbor, ideal at sunset. Expect to wait for a table; reservations are accepted only for parties of six or more. ⊠ *1 Bridge Rd.,* ☎ *508/636–6500. AE, D, MC, V. Memorial Day–Labor Day, no lunch Mon.–Tues.; Labor Day–Memorial Day, closed Mon.–Tues.; no lunch Wed.–Fri.*

$–$$ 🏠 **Paquachuck Inn.** Built in 1827 as a supply house for whaling ships, this wood-shingle building on Westport Point is now a modest, comfortable inn. The wood-floored rooms with exposed beams aren't large, but several have four-poster beds, and all offer at least a glimpse of the water. Unfortunately, none has a private bath, although one shared bath does have a whirlpool tub, and there's an outdoor shower, too. The large sunny breakfast room with comfy couches leads to a patio and yard—note the three whale vertebrae that are now a garden sculpture. ⊠ *2056 Main Rd., 02791,* ☎ 𝗙𝗔𝗫 *508/636–4398. 9 rooms share 3 baths. Breakfast room, dock. No smoking. MC, V. CP.*

Outdoor Activities and Sports

BEACHES

One of the nicest beaches in this part of the state, **Horseneck Beach State Reservation** (⊠ Rte. 88, ☎ 508/636–8816) draws summer crowds to its 2 mi of sand. There are rest rooms with showers, and lifeguards in season. Parking (in summer) is $2.

South Dartmouth

❹ *4 mi east of Westport.*

As in nearby Westport, the South Dartmouth countryside is dotted with farms and summer homes; but since it's only a few miles south of New Bedford, residents who work in the New Bedford area also make their homes here year-round. One of the prettiest spots is Padanarum Village, where Gulf Road and Dartmouth Road meet—built around the sailboat-filled harbor, Padanarum is a little oasis of shops, galleries, cafés, and restaurants. Nearby, the village of Russells Mills houses one of the region's oldest general stores and a pottery studio.

Dining and Lodging

$$–$$$ ✕ **Bridge Street Café.** With greenhouse windows, an upstairs terrace, and a cherry-wood bar, this comfortable restaurant serves a changing menu of contemporary fare. The white tablecloths and floral napkins mean you could dress up a bit, but many patrons turn up in shorts or khakis. Entrées range from hoisin-grilled salmon on crispy noodles to swordfish with fruit salsa to grilled filet mignon. There's a good selection of creative salads, too. The crisp soft-shell crabs with red-pepper mayonnaise make a fine lunch. ⊠ *10 Bridge St., Padanarum Village,* ☎ *508/994–7200. AE, MC, V. No lunch Sun.–Mon. Oct.–May, generally closed Mon.–Tues.*

$ ⊟ **Saltworks Bed & Breakfast.** This large 1840 Greek Revival house on the edge of Padanarum Village has only two guest rooms, but they're lovely. Both are actually suites, with a fireplace in the large bedroom—one has a striking brass bed—and a smaller bedroom/sitting room attached. The walls are decorated with artwork by owner Sandra Hall, who runs the inn with her husband, David. Downstairs are a comfortable common room and a wraparound porch, with views out to the harbor. ⊠ *115 Elm St., Padanarum Village 02748,* ☎ *508/991–5491,* ⅏ *508/979–8470. 2 suites. No smoking. AE, MC, V. Closed mid-Dec.–mid-Jan. CP.*

Outdoor Activities and Sports

BEACHES

Demarest Lloyd State Park (⊠ Barney's Joy Rd., ☎ 508/636–8816) may be hard to find, but it's worth seeking out for its long beach of soft, white sand on a sheltered Buzzards Bay cove. Behind the beach is a wooded area with picnic tables and barbecue grills. The bathhouse has rest rooms and showers. In season there are lifeguards, and parking is $2 a day.

Shopping

Davoll's General Store (⊠ 1228 Russells Mills Rd., ☎ 508/636–4530), established in 1793, sells antiques and collectibles, as well as clothing, deli sandwiches, and a small selection of groceries.

Salt Marsh Pottery (⊠ 1167 Russells Mills Rd., ☎ 508/636–4813 or 800/859–5028) makes platters, bowls, and other unique ceramic pieces decorated with wildflowers.

New Bedford

❺ *15 mi east of Fall River, 50 mi south of Boston.*

In 1652 colonists from Plymouth settled in the area that now includes the city of New Bedford. The city has a long maritime tradition, beginning as a shipbuilding center and small whaling port in the late 1700s. By the mid-1800s the city had developed into a center of North American whaling.

Today New Bedford is home to the largest fishing fleet on the East Coast, and although much of the town is industrial, the restored historic district near the water is a delight. It was here that Herman Melville set his masterpiece, *Moby-Dick,* a novel ostensibly about whaling. The city's whaling tradition is commemorated in the **New Bedford Whaling National Historical Park,** encompassing 13 blocks of the waterfront historic district. The park visitor center, housed in an 1853 Greek Revival former bank, provides maps and information about whaling-related sites. ⊠ *33 William St.,* ☎ *508/996–4095.* ☉ *Daily 9–4.*

The **New Bedford Whaling Museum,** established in 1903, is the world's largest museum devoted to the history of whaling. A highlight is the skeleton of a 66-ft blue whale, one of only three on view anywhere in the world. An interactive exhibit lets you listen to the underwater sounds of whales, dolphins, and other sea life, plus the sounds of a thunderstorm and a whale-watching boat—all as a whale might hear them. You can also peruse the collection of scrimshaw, visit exhibits on regional history, and climb aboard an 89-ft half-scale model of the 1826 whaling ship *Lagoda*—the world's largest ship model. ⊠ *18 Johnny Cake Hill,* ☎ *508/997–0046.* 🖭 *$6.* ☉ *Late May–early Sept., Fri.–Wed. 9–5, Thurs. 9–8; early Sept.–late May, daily 9–5.*

Seaman's Bethel, the small chapel described in *Moby-Dick,* is across the street from the whaling museum. ⊠ *15 Johnny Cake Hill,* ☎ *508/ 992–3295.*

The **New Bedford Art Museum,** a compact gallery space housed in the 1918 Vault Building (a former bank), showcases the work of area artists. Included are paintings by 19th- and early 20th-century New Bedford artists Albert Bierstadt, William Bradford, and Charles Henry Gifford. ⊠ *608 Pleasant St.,* ☎ *508/961–3072.* 🖭 *$3.* ☉ *June–Aug., Mon–Wed. and Fri.–Sat. 10–5, Thurs. 10–7, Sun. noon–5; Sept.–May, Wed. and Fri.–Sun. noon–5, Thurs. noon–7.*

For a glimpse of upper-class life during New Bedford's whaling heyday, head ½-mi south of downtown to the **Rotch-Jones-Duff House and Garden Museum.** This 1834 Greek Revival mansion, set amid a full city block of gardens, was home to three prominent families in the 1800s and is filled with elegant furnishings from the era, including a mahogany piano, a massive marble-top sideboard, and portraits of the house's occupants. A self-guided audio tour is available. ⊠ *396 County St.,* ☎ *508/997–1401.* 🖭 *$4.* ☉ *June–Dec., Mon.–Sat. 10–4, Sun. 12:30–4; Jan.–May, Tues.–Sat. 10–4, Sun 12:30–4.*

Dining and Lodging

$$$ ✕ **Davy's Locker.** A huge seafood menu is the main draw at this spot overlooking Buzzards Bay. Choose from more than a dozen shrimp preparations or a Healthy Choice entrée—dishes prepared with olive oil, vegetables, garlic, and herbs. For landlubbers, chicken, steak, ribs, and the like are also served. ⊠ *1480 E. Rodney French Blvd.,* ☎ *508/ 992–7359. AE, D, MC, V.*

$–$$ ✕ **Antonio's.** If you'd like to sample the traditional fare of New Bedford's large Portuguese population, friendly unadorned Antonio's serves up hearty portions of pork and shellfish stew, *bacalau* (salt cod), and grilled sardines, often on plates piled high with crispy fried potatoes and rice. ⊠ *267 Coggeshall St. (near intersection of I–195 and Rte. 18),* ☎ *508/990–3636. No credit cards.*

$–$$ ✕ **Freestone's City Grill.** Conveniently located in an 1877 former bank in the historic district, Freestone's serves soups and chowders, sandwiches and salads, plus fish, steaks, and vegetarian dishes. Decor blends traditional details—mahogany paneling, marble floors, brass

CUTTYHUNK ISLAND

IF CAPE COD AND OTHER MASSACHU-setts seaside towns seem too crowded with sun-and-surf seekers, hop on the ferry from New Bedford to Cuttyhunk Island. One of the Elizabeth Islands, a chain that extends along Buzzards Bay 16 mi southwest of Woods Hole, Cuttyhunk has a year-round population of about 20 (although more people do turn up in the summer). It's a New England island the way New England islands used to be—with tall beach grass swaying in the breeze, rocky shores, a handful of sailboats cruising into the harbor, and few people.

There are some cars on Cuttyhunk, but not many. The island is only 2 mi long and 1 mi wide, and most people get around by foot or golf cart; you'll see lots of aging golf vehicles putt-putting around the island. There's a road that circles the island, although it withers to a dirt path as it heads out toward Gosnold Pond and the Cuttyhunk lighthouse. Near the center of the island, you can climb up Lookout Hill for views of the other Elizabeth Islands and across the sound to Martha's Vineyard. Nearby, there's a small village with a general store, a one-room schoolhouse, a church, a library, at least one seasonal café, and a B&B.

If you want to stay over, contact the Cuttyhunk Fishing Club B&B (☎ 508/992–5585), which rents eight rooms, plus a three-bedroom apartment. Pete's Place Rentals (☎ 508/992–5131) has a small number of homes and apartments available for weekly rentals from mid-June to Labor Day; from Memorial Day to mid-June and from Labor Day to Columbus Day, their properties can be rented with a two-night minimum.

English explorer Bartholomew Gosnold (1572–1607), who is credited with giving Cape Cod its name, landed on Cuttyhunk in 1602. He and his crew reportedly stayed for about three weeks on the island before continuing his journey and eventually returning to England.

Today Cuttyhunk is the only one of the Elizabeth Islands accessible by regular ferry service (you'll need a private boat to visit the others). The M/V Alert II ferry (☎ 508/992–1432, www.cuttyhunk.com) makes the one-hour trip from New Bedford's Fisherman's Wharf (Pier 3) to Cuttyhunk daily June–Labor Day and several days a week in the spring and fall; between mid-October and mid-April regular service runs only once a week. The ferry generally leaves New Bedford in the morning and returns from Cuttyhunk in the midafternoon (with additional trips on Friday, Saturday, and Sunday); same-day round-trip fares are $17.

You can also visit Cuttyhunk as a day trip from Falmouth Harbor. On Sunday from mid-July to mid-October, the Ashumet Holly and Wildlife Sanctuary (☞ East Falmouth and Waquoit in Chapter 3) runs a sailing trip from Falmouth to Cuttyhunk. Also departing from Falmouth, Patriot Boats (☞ Upper Cape A to Z in Chapter 3) offers summer weekday excursions to Cuttyhunk, with a guided walk around the island.

If you're looking for nightlife, crowds, or organized activities, don't come to Cuttyhunk. There's not a lot to do here besides walk, swim, and stare out to sea. But after the hustle and bustle of mainland life, that's the way most visitors like it.

— By Carolyn Heller

rails—with contemporary art. ✉ *41 William St.,* ☎ *508/993–7477. AE, DC, MC, V. Closed Sun.*

$–$$ ⊡ **Edgewater Bed & Breakfast.** One of the most pleasant places to stay in New Bedford is just across the Acushnet River in Fairhaven, a residential suburb. The Edgewater's slogan is "So close to the water, you'll think you're on a boat," and it's true—this casual shingle house, built in 1760 and expanded in the 1880s, has water views from three sides. All the rooms are simply and traditionally furnished; the window-lined Captain's Suite, with a working fireplace and a king-size bed, has the best views. Guests can curl up by the fireplace on the living room's comfy couches or look out over the water from the deck. Owner Kathy Reed, who has run the B&B since the early 1980s, has plenty of ideas for things to see and do. ✉ *2 Oxford St., Fairhaven 02719,* ☎ *508/997–5512,* 𝔽𝔸𝕏 *508/997–5784. 3 rooms, 1 suite, 1 apartment. Breakfast room. No smoking. MC, V. CP* ✎

Outdoor Activities and Sports

BEACHES

Fort Phoenix State Beach Reservation (✉ Green St., Fairhaven, off Rte. 6, ☎ 508/992–4524), the site of the Revolutionary War's first naval battle, has a small sandy beach. Parking is free, and there are rest rooms with showers.

En Route   As you head east toward Cape Cod, a wet and wild adventure for the ↻   children awaits at the **Water Wizz Water Park,** with a 50-ft-high water slide complete with tunnels and dips, a wave pool, a river ride, three tube rides, two enclosed water-mat slides, a children's slide, a pool, miniature golf, and food. The enclosed Black Wizard water slide descends 75 ft in darkness. ✉ *U.S. 6 and Rte. 28, Wareham, 2 mi west of Bourne Bridge,* ☎ *508/295–3255.* ✍ *$25.* ☉ *Memorial Day–mid-June, weekends 11–4; mid-June–Labor Day, daily 10–6:30.*

APPROACHING THE CAPE A TO Z

Arriving and Departing

By Bus

American Eagle Motorcoach Inc. (☎ 800/453–5040) offers service from Boston to New Bedford. **Bonanza Bus Lines** (☎ 508/548–7588 or 800/556–3815) runs frequent direct service between Boston and Fall River, as well as service to both Fall River and New Bedford from Providence. From Fall River and New Bedford to the Cape, Bonanza provides service to Bourne, Falmouth, Woods Hole, and Hyannis. **Plymouth & Brockton Street Railway** (☎ 508/746–0378) buses stop in Plymouth en route to the Cape from Boston. From the Plymouth bus depot take the **Plymouth Area Link** buses (☎ 508/746–0378) to the town center or to Plimoth Plantation.

By Car

To get to **Plymouth** from Boston, take the Southeast Expressway I–93 south to Route 3 toward Cape Cod; Exits 6 and 4 lead to downtown Plymouth and Plimoth Plantation, respectively. To reach **Fall River** from Boston, take I–93 to Route 24 south to I–195; from Providence just follow I–195 east. To get to **New Bedford** from Fall River, continue east on I–195 from Fall River, or if you're coming from Boston, follow I–93 to Route 24 south to Route 140 south, and continue to I–195 east. Allow about one hour from Boston to any of these three cities, about one hour from Plymouth to either Fall River or New Bedford, and about 15–20 minutes between New Bedford and Fall River. From Providence you can reach Fall River in about 20–25 minutes.

To reach **Westport** from Fall River, take I–195 east to Route 88 south, and continue on Route 88. For **South Dartmouth** take I–195 east to the Faunce Corner Mall Road exit, or take Dartmouth Road south from New Bedford, toward Padanarum Village.

By Plane

Boston and Providence are the major air gateways for the region approaching Cape Cod (☞ Airports *in* Smart Travel Tips A to Z).

By Train

With the exception of Plymouth, southeastern Massachusetts is not well served by trains. **MBTA** (☎ 617/222–3200) commuter rail service is available from Boston to Plymouth. Travel time is about one hour. From the station take the **Plymouth Area Link** buses (☞ By Bus, *above*) to the historic attractions.

Contacts and Resources

Emergencies

Police (☎ 911 or dial township station).

CVS Pharmacy (✉ 2100 Acushnet Ave., New Bedford, ☎ 508/995–2653) is open until 10 weeknights and 9 weekends. **CVS Pharmacy** (✉ 317 State Rd., Manomet [Plymouth], ☎ 508/224–3312) is open until 9 Monday through Saturday and until 6 on Sunday.

St. Luke's Hospital (✉ 101 Page St., New Bedford, ☎ 508/997–1515). **Jordan Hospital** (✉ 275 Sandwich St., Plymouth, ☎ 508/746–2000).

Guided Tours

Cape Cod Canal Cruises (two or three hours, narrated) leave from Onset, just northwest of the Bourne Bridge. A Sunday jazz cruise, sunset cocktail cruises, and Friday and Saturday dance cruises are available. Children 12 and under cruise free on Family Discount Cruises, Monday through Saturday at 4. ✉ *Onset Bay Town Pier, Onset,* ☎ *508/295–3883.* 🎟 *$10–$13.*

Colonial Lantern Tours (✉ 35 North St., Plymouth 02360, ☎ 508/747–4161 or 800/698–5636) offers guided evening tours April through November of the original Plymouth plantation site and historic district, as well as the nightly Blood, Gore, and Ghosts tour highlighting Plymouth's more macabre history.

Plymouth Amphibious Tours are one-hour tours of Plymouth and its waterfront, half on land and half in the water, in restored World War II amphibious "duck boats." ✉ *Harbor Pl. (off Water St.), Plymouth,* ☎ *508/747–7658 or 800/225–4000.* 🎟 *$17.* ☉ *Apr.–Oct.*

WHALE-WATCHING

Capt. John Boats (☎ 508/746–2643) offers several daily whale-watch cruises from Plymouth Town Wharf, April to November. **Andy Lynn Boats** (☎ 508/746–7776), at Plymouth Town Wharf, runs trips June through September; call for schedule.

Visitor Information

Bristol County Convention and Visitors Bureau (✉ 70 N. 2nd St., Box 976, New Bedford 02741, ☎ 508/997–1250 or 800/288–6263). **Destination Plymouth** (✉ 170 Water St., Suite 10C, Plymouth 02360, ☎ 800/872–1620). **Fall River Chamber of Commerce** (✉ 200 Pocasset St., Fall River 02721, ☎ 508/676–8226). **New Bedford Office of Tourism** (✉ Waterfront Visitors Center, Pier 3, New Bedford 02740, ☎ 508/979–1745 or 800/508–5353). **Plymouth Waterfront Visitor Information Center** (✉ 130 Water St. [at Rte. 44], Plymouth 02360, ☎ 508/747–7525).

3 THE UPPER CAPE

As thick as a slab of its namesake fish, upper Cape Cod is the peninsula's most varied region and has its largest year-round population. Sandwich, the oldest town on the Cape, hugs the north shore, while the Buzzards Bay coast is a wooded mix of upscale vacation homes, small beaches, and inland countryside. The historic core of Falmouth is surrounded by modern development; to the south, the lively village of Woods Hole gives way to the beaches of Nantucket Sound. Farther east, in Mashpee, Native American traditions are very much part of the present, as is one of the Cape's finest shopping centers.

Revised by
Carolyn Heller

THE CLOSEST PART OF THE CAPE to the mainland, the Upper Cape has none of the briny, otherworldly breeziness of the Outer Cape and little of the resort feel of Chatham. Instead, many year-round residents make their homes here, the beaches are intimate, and more attractions—freshwater ponds, conservation areas, and small museums— are inland. There's plenty of history here: Sandwich is the oldest town on the Cape, and Bourne was the Pilgrims' first Cape Cod settlement and an important trading area. The first Native American reservation in the United States was established in Mashpee, which still maintains a large Wampanoag population and a tribal council governing body.

Being able to find peace and quiet so close to the mainland and the traffic-clogged bridges is a nice Upper Cape surprise. Sandwich, its village streets lined with historic houses and museums, is preserved like a stage set. Heading east, Route 6A meanders past antiques shops, bed-and-breakfasts, and salt marshes. Falmouth, to the south, is an active year-round community, more suburban than seaside, though its easy-to-reach beaches are popular with families. In the villages of North and West Falmouth, along Buzzards Bay, tree-lined country lanes lead to sandy coves, while in East Falmouth and Waquoit, narrow spits of land jut into marshy inlets, and plenty of secluded sites for hiking and walking are yours for the taking.

To make the most of this convenient mix, take an early morning hike through a nature reserve, or sit on a beach overlooking the sound and Martha's Vineyard. Pack a picnic, with fresh-from-the-farm-stand fruits or home-baked breads, and eat on the banks of a freshwater pond. Ride your bike along a shaded country road, or stretch out in the sand to watch the sailboats bobbing in the harbor and the sun sinking low over Buzzards Bay. You'll still have time to head back into town for that lobster roll or plate of fried clams.

Pleasures and Pastimes

Beaches

The Upper Cape is surrounded by water on three sides, giving beach lovers plenty of options. The south-side beaches, on Nantucket Sound, have rolling surf and are warmed by the Gulf Stream. Along Buzzards Bay, many small coves are home to sandy stretches (although most restrict parking to residents or permit holders in season). To the north, on Cape Cod Bay, the beaches generally have more temperate waters and gentle waves, but watch out for pebbles mixed in with the sand, particularly in the Sandwich area. Remember that you can even swim inland—the Upper Cape has many child-friendly freshwater ponds with sandy beaches and calm waters.

Biking

Several short bike trails, including the Shining Sea Trail between Falmouth and Woods Hole and the Cape Cod Canal Trail, which follows both sides of the canal, make the Upper Cape a good place for easy day rides. Many of the less-traveled roads in Bourne, West and North Falmouth, and in the interior between Sandwich and Falmouth are also good biking areas. And the beaches of Buzzards Bay, their parking restricted to those with resident stickers, make excellent destinations for bike rides.

Dining

Like other parts of Cape Cod, the Upper Cape's dining scene includes basic seafood shacks, contemporary restaurants that draw inspiration from the far corners of the globe and everything in between. Overall, the restaurant options tend toward the traditional, with fried clams, baked scrod, and boiled lobster gracing the most popular menus. Restaurants are more widely scattered in the Upper Cape towns—there are few "restaurant rows"—but if you like to wander and check out your dining options, try Mashpee Commons or Water Street in Woods Hole.

For price ranges *see* Dining *in* Smart Travel Tips A to Z.

Lodging
Sandwich and other towns along the north-shore Route 6A historic district have quiet, traditional villages with old-Cape atmosphere and charming B&Bs. Along Route 6A you can also find family-friendly motels, ranging from the modest to the more well equipped. In Falmouth the center of town is filled with historic B&Bs, while other small inns line the shore and neighboring streets of Falmouth Heights. Lodging options are fewer on the Buzzards Bay side (Bourne and West and North Falmouth), but several small B&Bs hidden away on country lanes provide glimpses of old New England. In Mashpee's New Seabury community, modern town houses and condominiums—with extensive resort amenities—are available to rent.

For price ranges *see* Lodging *in* Smart Travel Tips A to Z.

Nightlife and the Arts
There's plenty of entertainment in the Upper Cape, especially in season; choices range from the summer concerts at Sandwich's Heritage Plantation to the staged readings at the Cape Cod Theatre Project (in Falmouth and Woods Hole) to the year-round concerts sponsored by Mashpee's Boch Center for the Performing Arts. Bourne, Sandwich, and Falmouth all host summer town-band concerts, and there are festivals with entertainment throughout the year. If you're looking for art galleries and crafts shows, explore the Falmouth downtown area, Route 6A in East Sandwich, and Mashpee Commons.

Outdoor Activities and Sports
Hikers and walkers will find plenty of places to wander on the Upper Cape. Several recreation areas line the Cape Cod Canal, and trails crisscross the region's wildlife sanctuaries and nature reserves, including the Ashumet Holly sanctuary, Waquoit Bay Reserve, and the Mashpee River Woodlands. Canoeing and kayaking are great around the marshy inlets of both Cape Cod Bay and Buzzards Bay and on the Upper Cape's many freshwater ponds. In addition, the ponds, as well as the banks of the canal, are popular fishing sites.

Shopping
With its large year-round population, the Upper Cape houses many of the same shops you'd find anywhere in suburban America—the Gap, Starbucks, and Banana Republic are all here. Route 28 in Falmouth is lined with strip malls, although by far the nicest mall in this part of the Cape is the villagelike Mashpee Commons. Like any good tourist destination, the Upper Cape has plenty of T-shirt and souvenir shops almost everywhere you turn, and just over the bridges are several meccas for outlet shoppers, including the Cape Cod Factory Outlet Mall and the Tanger Outlet Center. But the real charms of this part of the Cape are in its small boutiques and tucked-away galleries, where you can find that one-of-a-kind sweater or a watercolor inspired by the sun setting over the bay.

Exploring the Upper Cape

On the north shore, **Sandwich,** gracious and lovely, is the Cape's oldest town. Centered inland, **Mashpee** is a long-standing Native American township whose Native-owned land is governed by local Wampanoags. **Fal-**

mouth, the Cape's second-most-populous town, is still green and historic, if seemingly overrun with strip malls. **Woods Hole,** one port from which to ferry over to Martha's Vineyard, is an international center of marine and biological research. Along the west coast, in parts of **Bourne** and **West and North Falmouth,** you'll find wooded areas ending in secluded coves; the south coast has long-established resort communities.

Numbers in the text correspond to numbers in the margin and on the Upper Cape map.

Great Itineraries

It's astonishing that, so close to the mainland, the lovely old town of **Sandwich** ①, stands as one of the best examples of the Cape of yesteryear. Visit the Hoxie House, the Sandwich Glass Museum, or **Heritage Plantation**'s ② beautiful grounds and collection of old cars; have a picnic lunch on the banks of Shawme Pond; or spend the afternoon at the old-timey Green Briar Nature Center and Jam Kitchen walking the nature trails and picking out homemade jam to take with you. Here and all along the bay shore, you can explore salt marshes, so full of sea and bird life. If history's your thing, take a step back and start your Upper Cape trip at **Plimoth Plantation** (☞ Chapter 2), about 22 mi northwest of the Sagamore Bridge on Route 3A. The reconstructed settlement, where actors dress in period clothing and carry out the activities typical of earlier days, relates a very tangible sense of the Cape's history.

To reach the Upper Cape's south shore, take Route 28A south through some lovely little towns, with detours to beautiful white-sand beaches. This is the way to Falmouth and to **Woods Hole** ⑥, the center for international marine research and the year-round ferry port for Martha's Vineyard. A small aquarium in town has regional sea-life exhibits, and there are several shops and museums. On the way out of town, the view from Nobska Light is breathtaking. In **Falmouth** ④ stroll around the village green, look into some of the historic houses, and stop at the Waquoit Bay National Estuarine Research Reserve for a walk along the estuary and barrier beach. Inland, on the eastern extent of the Upper Cape, the Wampanoag township of **Mashpee** ⑧ is one of the best places to learn about the Cape's Native American heritage.

Sagamore

60 mi southeast of Boston and 30 mi northeast of New Bedford.

The village of Sagamore straddles the Cape Cod Canal and is perhaps best known for the bridge, completed in 1935, that bears its name. Primarily a small suburban community, the town has several stores for those interested in bargain hunting or gift shopping.

At **Pairpoint Crystal,** you can watch richly colored lead crystal being hand-blown in the factory as it has been since 1837. The shop sells candlesticks, vases, stemware, sun catchers, ornamental cup plates (used to hold the cup in the days when tea was poured into saucers to drink), and reproductions of original Boston and Sandwich glass pieces. ⊠ *851 Sandwich Rd. (Rte. 6A),* ☎ *508/888–2344 or 800/899–0953.* ☜ *Free.* ☉ *Showroom weekdays 9–6, Sat. 10–6, Sun. 11–6; demonstrations weekdays 9–4.*

Dining and Lodging

$$ ✕ **Sagamore Inn.** This local favorite—owned by the Pagliarani fam-
★ ily since 1963—keeps old Cape Cod traditions alive. Pressed-tin walls and ceilings, fans, old wooden booths and tables, lace curtains, and white linen add up to a dining room so casual you almost overlook its elegance. All the food here is homemade (except the stuffed quahogs),

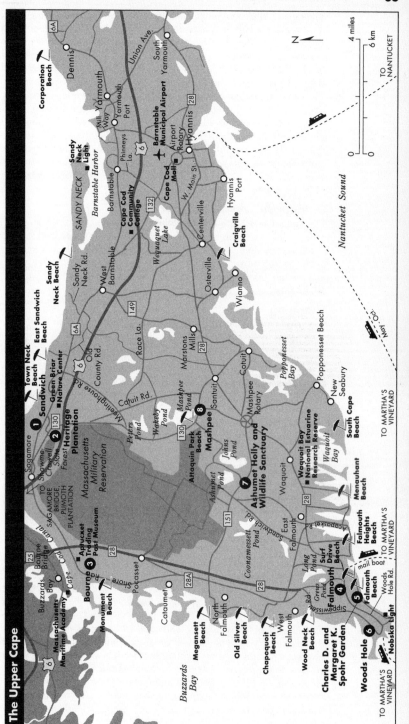

The Upper Cape

Corporation Beach

Dennis

South Yarmouth

6A

Union Ave.

Yarmouth

Yarmouth Port

Barnstable Municipal Airport

28

Mill Way

Phinneys La.

Airport Rotary

Hyannis

Sandy Neck Light

6

Sandy Neck Harbor

Cape Cod Mall

Hyannis Port

SANDY NECK

Barnstable

Cape Cod Community College

W. Main St

Sandy Neck Beach

Barnstable Harbor

132

Wequaquet Lake

Centerville

Craigville Beach

East Sandwich Beach

West Barnstable

Sandy Neck Rd.

Osterville

Wianno

Sandy Neck Beach

6A

149

Town Neck Beach

Sandwich

Green Briar Nature Center

Old County Rd.

Marstons Mills

28

Popponesset Beach

1

Crowell Store

Shawme-Crowell State Forest

2

130

Heritage Plantation

Meetinghouse Rd.

Race La.

Cotuit Rd.

Cotuit

Popponesset Bay

Popponesset Beach

Saggamore

TO SAGAMORE BRIDGE, PLIMOTH PLANTATION

Massachusetts Military Reservation

Peters Pond

Wakeby Pond

Mashpee Pond

Santuit

8

Mashpee Rotary

Mashpee

New Seabury

South Cape Beach

TO MARTHA'S VINEYARD

Cape Cod Canal

Bourne Bridge

25

Buzzards Bay

Massachusetts Maritime Academy

Aptucxet Trading Post Museum

3

Bourne

28

Pocasset

Ashumet Pond

Attaquin Park Beach

130

Johns Pond

Ashumet Holly and Wildlife Sanctuary

7

Waquoit

151

Waquoit Bay National Estuarine Research Reserve

Waquoit Bay

Menauhant Beach

Monument Beach

Cape Cod Rd.

28A

Coonamessett Pond

East Falmouth

28

Sandwich Rd.

Acapesket Rd.

28

Falmouth Heights Beach

TO MARTHA'S VINEYARD

Catamet

North Falmouth

28

Long Pond

Surf Drive Beach

Megansett Beach

Shore Rd.

West Falmouth

Green Pond

4

Falmouth

Falmouth Heights Beach

5

Woods Hole Rd.

mail boat

Old Silver Beach

Chapoquoit Beach

Wood Neck Beach

Siders Pond

Charles D. and Margaret K. Spohr Garden

Woods Hole

6

Nobska Light

TO MARTHA'S VINEYARD

Buzzards Bay

Cape Cod Bay

Nantucket Sound

TO NANTUCKET

N

4 miles

6 km

0

0

TO NANTUCKET

very good yet traditional at the same time. The seafood platter is a knock-out, the chicken potpie substantial, and the prime rib huge. Luncheon specials attract regulars from all over town, and the service is as friendly as family. A cozy, handsome old bar is under the same roof. ⊠ *1131 Rte. 6A,* ☎ *508/888–9707. Reservations not accepted. AE, MC, V. Closed Tues. and Dec.–Mar.*

$ ⚓ **Scusset Beach State Reservation.** This park (☞ Outdoor Activities and Sports, *below*), which encompasses 490 acres near the Cape Cod Canal, with a cold-water beach on the bay, has 98 RV sites plus five tent sites, some wooded. Three sites are accessible to people with disabilities. There are cold showers on the beach and hot showers in the campground. ⊠ *140 Scusset Beach Rd., off Rte. 3 at Sagamore Bridge rotary, 02532,* ☎ *877/422–6762 for campsite reservations; 508/888–0859 for general information. 103 sites. Beach. MC, V.*

Outdoor Activities and Sports

The **Scusset Beach State Reservation** is a pleasant place for a swim, walk, or bike ride near the mainland side of the Sagamore Bridge. The beach sweeps along Cape Cod Bay, although the view inland is marred by the nearby power plant. Its pier is popular for fishing; other activities include hiking, picnicking, and camping (☞ *above*). ⌑ *Parking $2.* ☉ *Daily 8–8.*

Shopping

Cape Cod Factory Outlet Mall (⊠ Factory Outlet Rd., Exit 1 off U.S. 6, ☎ 508/888–8417) has more than 20 outlets, including Corning/Revere, Carter's, Bass, Bugle Boy, Van Heusen, Izod, London Fog, and Reebok.

Chocolate House Fudge and Gift Shop (⊠ 11 Cranberry Hwy. [Rte. 6A], ☎ 508/888–7065), just over the Sagamore Bridge on the Cape side, sells creamy fudge in 12 flavors, hand-dipped chocolates and truffles, saltwater taffy, and penny candy. The gift shop has cranberry glass and other Cape items.

Christmas Tree Shops (⊠ Cranberry Hwy. [Rte. 6A], Exit 1 off U.S. 6, ☎ 508/888–7010; other locations at Falmouth, Hyannis, Yarmouth Port, West Yarmouth, West Dennis, and Orleans) sell everything from furniture to clothes to kitchen goods.

Sandwich

★ ❶ *3 mi east of Sagamore Bridge, 11 mi west of Barnstable.*

The oldest town on Cape Cod, Sandwich was established in 1637 by some of the Plymouth Pilgrims and incorporated on March 6, 1638. Today it is a well-preserved quintessential New England village that wears its history proudly. Driving through town past the white-column town hall, the gristmill on Shawme Pond, the spindlelike spire of the First Church of Christ, and the 18th- and 19th-century homes that line the streets is like driving back in time—you'll feel as if you should be holding a horse's reins rather than the steering wheel of a car. When you reach Main Street, park the car and get out for a stroll. Look at old houses on Main Street, stop at a museum or two, and work your way to the delightful Shawme Pond. While you walk, look for etched Sandwich glass from the old factory on front doors—there probably aren't two identical glass panels in town.

Unlike other Cape towns, whose deepwater ports opened the doors to prosperity in the whaling days, Sandwich was an industrial town for much of the 19th century. The main industry was the production of vividly colored glass, called Sandwich glass, which is now sought by collectors.

The glass was made in the Boston and Sandwich Glass Company's factory here from 1825 until 1888, when competition with glassmakers in the Midwest—and finally a union strike—closed it.

The **Sandwich Glass Museum** holds information about the history of the company, including a diorama showing how the factory looked in its heyday, and an outstanding collection of blown and pressed glass in many shapes and shimmering hues. Large glass lamps, vases, and pitchers are impressive, but so are the hundreds of small saucers on display. Glassmaking demonstrations are held in the summer. A few galleries contain relics of the town's early history. The gift shop sells some handsome reproductions, including some made by local artisans. ⊠ *129 Main St.,* ☎ *508/888-0251.* 🖼 *$3.50.* ⊙ *Apr.–Dec., daily 9:30–5; Feb.–Mar., Wed.–Sun. 9:30–4.*

A lovely place for a stroll or a picnic is the park around **Shawme Pond** (⊠ Water and Grove Sts.), a favorite fishing site for children. The ducks and swans love to be fed, though posted signs warn you not to indulge them. Across the way—a perfect backdrop for this setting—is the spired, white 1848 First Church of Christ, inspired by a design by British architect Christopher Wren.

Where Shawme Pond drains over its dam, a little wooden bridge leads over a watercourse to the waterwheel-powered **Dexter Gristmill,** built in 1654. In season the miller demonstrates and talks about the mill's operation and sells its ground corn. ⊠ *Water and Grove Sts.,* ☎ *508/888-4910.* 🖼 *$1.50; combination ticket with Hoxie House (☞ below), $2.50.* ⊙ *Late May, Sat. 10–4:45; June–Labor Day, Mon.–Sat. 10–4:45, Sun. 1–4:45; Labor Day–mid-Oct., Tues.–Sat. 10–4:45.*

NEED A BREAK? | Stop in at the delightful **Dunbar Tea Shop** (⊠ 1 Water St. [Rte. 130], ☎ 508/833-2485), a former billiards room–carriage house now converted into a country cottage with paneled walls, a beamed ceiling, and assorted antiques and kitschy doodads. Lunch—everything from a smoked-fish platter with salad to quiche or a salmon tart—English cream tea, and tasty sweets are served from 11 to 5 daily, July through October (till 4:30 the rest of the year). A gift shop sells British tea, specialty foods, and home decorating items.

☾ The **Thornton W. Burgess Museum** is dedicated to the Sandwich native whose tales of Peter Cottontail, Reddy Fox, and a host of other creatures of the Old Briar Patch have been part of children's bedtimes for decades. Thornton Burgess (1874–1965), an avid conservationist, made his characters behave true to their species to educate children as he entertained them. A storytelling session, often featuring the live animal that the Burgess story is about, is held regularly in July and August. The many displays crowded into the small old house include some of Burgess's 170 books (although children are welcome, the exhibits are of the don't-touch variety). The small gift shop carries puppets, Burgess books, and Pairpoint Crystal cup plates decorated with Burgess characters. ⊠ *4 Water St. [Rte. 130],* ☎ *508/888-4668.* 🖼 *$2 suggested donation.* ⊙ *Apr.–Oct., Mon.–Sat. 10–4, Sun. 1–4; 1st 2 wks in Dec., Sat. 10–4, Sun. 1–4.*

Overlooking Shawme Pond is the **Hoxie House,** a remarkable old saltbox virtually unaltered since it was built in 1675. Even though people lived in it until the 1950s, the house was never modernized with electricity or plumbing. It has been furnished to reflect daily life in the colonial period, with some pieces on loan from the Museum of Fine Arts in Boston. Highlights are diamond-shape lead-glass windows and a collection of antique textile machines. ⊠ *18 Water St. [Rte. 130],* ☎ *508/*

888–1173. ✉ $1.50; combination ticket with Dexter Gristmill (☞ above) $2.50. ⊙ *Mid-June–mid-Oct., Mon.–Sat. 10–5, Sun. 1–5.*

The **Old Town Cemetery** (✉ Grove St.), on the opposite side of Shawme Pond (☞ *above*) from Hoxie House, is a classic, undulating New England graveyard. Stop in for a peaceful moment and trace the genealogy of old Sandwich.

★ ☾ On 76 beautifully landscaped acres overlooking the upper end of
❷ Shawme Pond is the **Heritage Plantation,** an impressive complex of museum buildings and gardens and a café. In 1967 pharmaceuticals magnate Josiah K. Lilly III purchased the estate and turned it into a nonprofit museum. The Shaker Round Barn showcases classic and historic cars—including a 1930 yellow-and-green Duesenberg built for Gary Cooper, a 1919 Pierce-Arrow, and a 1911 Stanley Steamer—as well as art exhibitions. The military museum houses antique firearms, a collection of 2,000 hand-painted miniature soldiers, military uniforms, and Native American arts. The art museum has an extensive Currier & Ives collection, Americana (including a mechanical-bank collection), antique toys such as a 1920 Hubley Royal Circus, and a working 1912 Coney Island–style carousel.

The grounds are crisscrossed by paths and include gardens planted with daylily, hosta, heather, herb, fruit-tree, and other gardens. Rhododendron enthusiasts will recognize the name of onetime estate owner and hybridizer Charles O. Dexter; the rhododendrons are in full glory from mid-May through mid-June. Daylilies reach their peak from mid-July through early August. Families visiting with youngsters should ask at the ticket office for the Family Funpacks with children's activities, or the Clue tours, scavenger-hunt games for exploring the grounds. In summer concerts are held in the gardens, often on Saturday evening and Sunday afternoon. The center of the complex is about ¾ mi on foot from the in-town end of Shawme Pond. ✉ *Grove and Pine Sts.,* ☎ *508/ 888–3300.* ✉ *$9.* ⊙ *Mid-May–mid-Oct., daily 10–5.* ✎

For a view of the bay, you can walk to Town Neck Beach on the **Sandwich Boardwalk,** built over a salt marsh, creek, and low dunes. In 1991 Hurricane Bob and an October nor'easter destroyed the previous boardwalk. Individuals and businesses donated planks to rebuild it, which volunteers then installed. The donors' names; jokes (GET OFF OUR BOARD); thoughts (SIMPLIFY/THOREAU); and memorials to lovers, grandparents, and boats are inscribed on the planks. The long sweep of Cape Cod Bay stretches out around the beach at the end of the walk, where a platform provides fine views, especially at sunset. Stone jetties, dunes and waving grasses, and the entrance to the canal are in the foreground, and you can look out toward Sandy Neck, Wellfleet, and Provincetown or toward the white cliffs beyond Sagamore. The sandy strip on this mostly rocky beach is near the rugosa rose–patch dunes; the flowers have a delicious fragrance, and it's a good place for birding. If you have a canoe, the creeks running through the salt marsh make for great paddling. From the town center it's about a mile to the boardwalk; cross Route 6A on Jarves Street and at its end turn left, then right, and continue to the boardwalk parking lot.

☾ At the **Sandwich Fish Hatchery** you'll see more than 200,000 brook, brown, and rainbow trout at various stages of development; they are being raised to stock the state's ponds. The mesh over the raceways is to keep kingfishers and herons from a free lunch. You can buy feed for 25¢ and watch the fish jump for it. ✉ *164 Rte. 6A,* ☎ *508/888– 0008.* ✉ *Free.* ⊙ *Daily 9–3.*

OFF THE
BEATEN PATH

GREEN BRIAR NATURE CENTER AND JAM KITCHEN – Is it the soothing pond-side setting or its simple earthiness—who's to say? Whatever the reason, Green Briar Nature Center and Jam Kitchen, owned and operated by the Thornton Burgess Society, is as solid a symbol of the old Cape as you'll find. You'll pass a wildflower garden on your way in, and the Smiling Pool sparkles out back. Birds flit about the grounds, and great smells waft from vintage stoves in the Jam Kitchen, where you can watch as jams and pickles are made according to Ida Putnam's recipes, used here since 1903 (sun-cooked fruit preserves are especially superb). Come weekdays mid-April through mid-December to see jam being made in the Jam Kitchen; you can even take a jam-making class some evenings or Saturdays. The nature center has classes for adults and children, as well as walks, lectures, and a May herb festival, where you can take home herbs, wildflowers, and perennials. The Briar Patch Conservation Area behind the building has nature trails to explore—take a walk and visit the real live animals that inspired Peter Cottontail, Grandfather Frog, and other beloved Thornton Burgess characters. ⊠ *6 Discovery Hill Rd., off Rte. 6A east of Sandwich Center,* ☎ *508/888-6870.* ◫ *$1 suggested donation.* ◷ *Apr.–Dec., Mon.–Sat. 10–4, Sun. 1–4; Jan.–Mar., Tues.–Sat. 10–4.*

Dining and Lodging

$$–$$$ ✕ **Aqua Grille.** At this smart-casual bistro by the marina, offerings range from Cape basics (clam chowder, fried seafood, boiled lobsters) to more creative contemporary fare. The Grille's excellent version of lobster salad, for example, is a hearty serving of greens, tomatoes, avocados, baby green beans, and big meaty lobster chunks. The far-ranging menu and lively atmosphere make this a good spot to bring a crowd; sandwiches (salmon burgers, turkey wraps), grilled seafood, pastas, and steaks are all available. ⊠ *14 Gallo Rd.,* ☎ *508/888–8889. AE, MC, V. Closed mid-Oct.–Mar.*

$–$$ ✕ **Bee-Hive Tavern.** This informal and friendly colonial-style tavern hasn't been here since Revolutionary times (it opened in 1992), but the cozy dark-wood booths and wide-board floors look the part. The food is solid American fare and includes burgers and sandwiches, fried seafood, Yankee pot roast, ribs, and steaks. If you're craving some veggies, there's a good selection of dinner-size salads, too. ⊠ *406 Rte. 6A, East Sandwich,* ☎ *508/833–1184. MC, V.*

$ ✕ **Marshland Restaurant and Bakery.** This tiny coffee shop tucked onto a parking lot is Sandwich's version of down-home. For breakfast try an Italian omelet, a rich mix of Italian sausage, fresh vegetables, and cheese. The lunch specials—a grilled chicken club sandwich, lobster salad, a turkey Reuben, a daily quiche, and the like—are the best choices midday, and for dinner the prime rib does not quit. ⊠ *109 Rte. 6A,* ☎ *508/888–9824. No credit cards. No lunch or dinner Sun., no dinner Mon.*

$ ✕ **Seafood Sam's.** Across from the Coast Guard station, in the shadow of the canal power plant and a stone's throw from the Cape Cod Canal, Sam's is all about fried seafood. You order from the counter, get a number, and sit in an airy dining room where the sound of lobsters cracking open is accompanied by the munch of fried clams. It's casual enough that it needs a sign near the entrance to remind you that shirt and shoes are required. Sam's has gotten around, with branches in Harwich, Falmouth, and South Yarmouth. ⊠ *6 Coast Guard Rd.,* ☎ *508/888–4629. D, MC, V. Closed Nov.–Mar.*

$$$–$$$$ ✕▥ **Dan'l Webster Inn.** Built in 1971 on the site of a 17th-century inn, the Dan'l Webster is essentially a contemporary hotel with old New England friendliness and hospitality. In the more formal restaurant, the menu and wine list are interesting and up-to-date; some hydroponic vegetables and fish come from the local, family-run D. W. Aquafarm. Stand-

out dishes include striped bass encrusted with cashews and macadamia nuts, accompanied by mango sauce. (If you don't feel like a starched-napkin meal, there's also a casual tavern serving pizzas, burgers, and salads.) Guest rooms, in the main inn and wings or in two nearby historic houses with four suites each, have floral fabrics and fine reproduction mahogany and cherry furnishings, including some canopy beds. The eight rooms on the second floor of the Jarves Wing, which were added in 1999, are particularly spacious and have fireplaces and whirlpool tubs, as do some of the suites; one suite even has a baby grand piano. Guests have access to nearby golf courses and a local health club. ✉ *149 Main St., 02563,* ☎ *508/888–3622 or 800/444–3566,* FAX *508/888–5156. 45 rooms, 9 suites. 2 restaurants, air-conditioning, no-smoking rooms, room service, pool. AE, D, DC, MC, V. MAP available.* 🏖

$$$–$$$$ 🏨 **Bay Beach.** Oceanfront accommodations are few in this part of the Cape, but if you want to wake to broad vistas of the bay, this B&B in two adjacent contemporary houses is a fine choice. The seven rooms are appointed like a well-turned-out suburban home, with lots of wicker, floral comforters, CD players, refrigerators, and, best of all, picture windows facing the water or the adjacent marshes. Four rooms have whirlpool tubs, three have gas fireplaces, and several have private decks. Breakfast is a buffet in the casual dining room, with floor-to-ceiling windows for still more bay views; a boardwalk leads to a private beach. ✉ *1–3 Bay Beach La., 02563,* ☎ *508/888–8813 or 800/475–6398,* FAX *508/ 888–5416. 7 rooms. Air-conditioning, exercise room, beach. MC, V. Closed Nov.–Apr. BP.* 🏖

$$–$$$ 🏨 **Belfry Inne & Bistro.** If you've ever wanted to sleep in a church (not to mention live in luxury), here's your chance. In a 1902 former church and an adjacent painted-lady Victorian house that served as the church rectory, owner Christopher Wilson has created a one-of-a-kind inn and restaurant. The six spacious rooms in the Abbey retain many original features of the church—an arch here, a massive stained-glass window there—along with a stylish mix of antique and more modern furnishings; the rooms have sitting areas, whirlpool tubs, and gas fireplaces, too. In the Drew House next door, the nine rooms are decorated with iron, spool, or sleigh beds and a whimsical blend of Laura Ashley prints and pastel-painted furnishings for a look that's fresh but traditional. The bistro, a dramatic space in the former sanctuary, serves contemporary fare: grilled salmon with warm lemon vinaigrette, filet mignon with garlic mashed potatoes, or duck breast with wild mushroom risotto. ✉ *8 Jarves St., 02563,* ☎ *508/888–8550 or 800/844–4542,* FAX *508/888–3922. 14 rooms. Restaurant, bar. AE, D, DC, MC, V. BP.* 🏖

$$–$$$ 🏨 **Sandwich Lodge & Resort.** Set amid 10 rolling acres, this glorified motel—emphasis on glorified—offers a variety of rooms, all nicely decorated in soft mauve and navy. Suites (the deluxe are the newest), like efficiencies, are equipped with gleaming kitchens with refrigerators and two-burner stoves or microwave ovens; two even have two-person whirlpool tubs. The grounds include private volleyball and shuffleboard courts, game rooms, a hot tub, and two of the cleanest pools on the Cape. The on-site restaurant serves lunch and dinner (ample portions, great prices) in a homey atmosphere. With advance notice, pets are allowed for a $15 fee. ✉ *54 Rte. 6A, Box 1038, 02563,* ☎ *508/888–2275 or 800/ 282–5353,* FAX *508/888–8102. 24 rooms, 36 suites, 4 efficiencies. Restaurant, bar, no-smoking rooms, indoor-outdoor pool, hot tub, Ping-Pong, coin laundry. AE, D, MC, V. CP.* 🏖

$$ 🏨 **Captain Ezra Nye House.** Elaine and Harry Dickson's 1829 house in the heart of town once belonged to one of the old local families. The cozy, country-style rooms aren't crammed with period pieces, but the house is brimming with the Dicksons' hospitality—they cook a full breakfast and readily offer suggestions for day- or nighttime activities. ✉ *152 Main St.,*

02563, ☎ *508/888–6142 or 800/388–2278,* FAX *508/833–2897. 5 rooms, 1 suite. No smoking. Air-conditioning. AE, D, MC, V. BP.* 🐾

$$ 🏠 **Inn at Sandwich Center.** This house directly across from the Sandwich Glass Museum is listed on the National Register of Historic Places. Each of the Victorian-style rooms is named after a former owner or occupant of the house, although one, Miss Charlotte's Room, also takes its name from the house cat; the bed is topped with a cat-pattern comforter, and a wallpaper border, decorated with cats, circles the room. The pretty Lottie Chipman Room has an antique four-poster bed and a nicely restored rocker, while the spacious Robert Morse Room has a nautical theme, as well as a private deck overlooking the lush gardens. Breakfast is served in the antiques-furnished keeping room, which has a fireplace and the original 1750 beehive oven. ⊠ *118 Tupper Rd., 02563,* ☎ *508/888– 6958 or 800/249–6949,* FAX *508/888–2746. 5 rooms. Air-conditioning. No smoking. AE, D, MC, V. BP.* 🐾

$$ 🏠 **Wingscorton Farm.** This is, perhaps, the Upper Cape's best-kept se-
★ cret: an enchanting working farm with ducks, chickens (you can help gather eggs), sheep, a donkey, and a pair of llamas. Built in 1763, the main house, once a stop on the Underground Railroad, has a dining room with one of the largest fireplaces in New England—the hearth alone is 9-ft long. Oriental rugs, wing chairs, and a TV are in the paneled library-den. The main house has two second-floor suites, each with a fireplace, Oriental rugs topping the wide-plank floor, wainscoting, and, adjoining the main guest room, a smaller bedroom (these were once the house's "birthing rooms") with twin beds. The property also includes a detached cottage. A stone carriage house offers a fully equipped kitchen, a living room with a pullout queen-size sofa and a wood-burning stove; a spiral staircase leads to a loft (with a queen-size bed) and an oversize sundeck. Traditional clambakes are prepared year-round (for large groups) by visiting members of Martha's Vineyard's Wampanoag tribe, and a private bay beach is a five-minute walk. ⊠ *11 Wing Blvd., off Rte. 6A, about 4½ mi east of Sandwich Center, East Sandwich 02537,* ☎ *508/ 888–0534,* FAX *508/888–0545. 2 suites, 1 carriage house, 1 2-bedroom cottage. Beach, library. AE, MC, V. BP.*

$–$$ 🏠 **Earl of Sandwich Motor Manor.** Single-story Tudor-style buildings are arranged in a U around a duck pond and wooded lawn set with lawn chairs. Rooms in the main building (1966) and the newer buildings (1981–83) have rather somber decor, with dark exposed beams on white ceilings, dark paneled walls, quarry-tile floors with Oriental throw rugs, and chenille bedspreads, but they are of good size and have large windows. Pets are permitted with advance notice. ⊠ *378 Rte. 6A, East Sandwich 02537,* ☎ *508/888–1415 or 800/442–3275,* FAX *508/ 833–1039. 24 rooms. Air-conditioning, no-smoking rooms, refrigerators, pool. AE, D, DC, MC, V. CP.* 🐾

$–$$ 🏠 **Spring Garden Inn Motel.** From the road the Spring Garden looks like yet another roadside motel, albeit a nice, well-maintained gray-shingle one. But walk around back, and you'll step into another world—a wide green lawn overlooking a broad, peaceful expanse of marsh. Sink into a hammock, an Adirondack chair, or a swing, and relax. If you want to barbecue, there are grills and picnic tables available for guest use. Inside, the simple knotty-pine-wall rooms have two double beds topped with floral comforters; all have small refrigerators, and two are efficiencies with kitchenettes. For the best marsh views, choose one of the second-floor rooms with a balcony. ⊠ *578 Rte. 6A, East Sandwich 02537,* ☎ *508/888–0710 or 800/303–1751,* FAX *508/ 833–2849. 8 rooms, 2 efficiencies, 1 suite. Picnic area, air-conditioning, refrigerators, pool. AE, D, MC, V. Closed Dec.–mid-Apr. CP.* 🐾

$ 🏕 **Shawme-Crowell State Forest.** Less than a mile from the Cape Cod Canal, this 742-acre state forest is a good base for local biking and hiking, and campers get free day use of Scusset Beach. Open-air camp-fires are allowed at the wooded tent and RV (no hookups) campsites. There are also heated bathroom and shower facilities—a blessing on chilly mornings. ⊠ *Rte. 130, 02563,* ☎ *508/888–0351, 877/422–6762 for reservations. 285 sites. MC, V.*

Nightlife and the Arts

THE ARTS

Heritage Plantation (☞ *above*) sponsors summer jazz and other con-certs in its gardens from June to mid-September; bring chairs or blan-kets. Most concerts are free with admission to the complex.

Town-band concerts (⊠ Bandstand, Henry T. Wing Elementary School, Rte. 130 and Beale Ave., ☎ 508/888–5144) are held Thursday evening from July through late August starting at 7:30.

NIGHTLIFE

Bobby Byrne's Pub (⊠ 65 Rte. 6A, ☎ 508/888–6088) offers a com-fortable pub atmosphere, a jukebox, and good light and full menus.

Outdoor Activities and Sports

BEACHES

Town Neck Beach, off Town Neck Road, is a long dune-backed bay beach with a mix of sand and pebbles. You'll need a resident parking sticker to leave your car in the large parking area between 8 AM and 4 PM in season. There are rest rooms and a snack bar.

East Sandwich Beach, on North Shore Road, is hidden behind the grass-covered dunes beyond a row of gray-shingle beach cottages. It's a long stretch of sand, but nearby parking is very limited (and restricted to residents between 8 AM and 4 PM in season). From Route 6A follow Ploughed Neck Road to North Shore Road.

Shopping

The sign in front of the **Bee-Hive General Store** (⊠ 385 Rte. 6A, East Sandwich, ☎ 508/833–4907) boasts, WICKED NEAT STUFF. Inside is a hodgepodge of clever and kitsch—candles, door knockers, lawn or-naments, jam, 5¢ candy, fish platters, toys. It's an entertaining place to forage for gifts or souvenirs.

Brown Jug (⊠ 155 Main St., at Jarves St., ☎ 508/833–1088) special-izes in antique glass, such as Sandwich glass and Tiffany iridescent glass-ware, as well as Staffordshire china.

The **Giving Tree** (⊠ 550 Rte. 6A, East Sandwich, ☎ 508/888–5446), an art gallery and sculpture garden, shows contemporary crafts, jew-elry, ceramics, and prints. It has walking paths through a peaceful bam-boo grove, along the marsh, and over a narrow wooden suspension bridge. A café serves coffee and pastries.

Horsefeathers (⊠ 454 Rte. 6A, East Sandwich, ☎ 508/888–5298) sells antique linens, lace, vintage baby and children's clothing, and Victo-riana such as valentines.

Joe's Fish Market (⊠ Cape Cod Canal, ☎ 508/888–2971), opposite Seafood Sam's and the Coast Guard station, sells fresh-from-the-tank lobsters. Call ahead, and they'll boil your crustaceans to order—a great idea for an easy dinner at your cottage or hotel or for a picnic overlooking the canal. If you're doing your own cooking, Joe's sells many varieties of fresh fish.

Sandwich Auction House (⊠ 15 Tupper Rd., ☎ 508/888–1926) is a great place to spend part of a Wednesday night (Saturday in the off-season); come after 2 to preview the items for sale. It's a local institution, with weekly sales; in addition, there are specialty sales every four to six weeks that present the cream of the crop of antiques received in that period. Specialty sales are also held for collections of modern rugs, silver, or toys.

Titcomb's Bookshop (⊠ 432 Rte. 6A, East Sandwich, ☎ 508/888–2331) has used, rare, and new books, including a large collection of Cape and nautical titles and Americana, as well as an extensive selection of new children's books.

En Route **Route 6A** heads east from Sandwich, passing through the oldest settlements on the Cape. It's part of the Old King's Highway historic district and is therefore protected from development. Classic inns and enticing antiques shops alternate with traditional gray-shingle homes on this tree-lined route, and the woods periodically give way to broad vistas across the marshes. In autumn the foliage along the road is bright; maples with their feet wet in ponds and marshes put on a good display. Along Route 6A just east of Sandwich center, you can stop to watch cranberries being harvested in flooded bogs. If you're heading to Orleans and you're not in a hurry, this is a lovely route to take.

Bourne

❸ *6 mi southwest of Sandwich.*

The town of Bourne includes nine villages—Bourne Village, Bournedale, Buzzards Bay, Cataumet, Gray Gables, Monument Beach, Pocasset, Sagamore (☞ *above*), and Sagamore Beach—along Buzzards Bay and both sides of the Cape Cod Canal. The villages range from honky-tonk commercial districts to bucolic waterfront suburbs.

The Pilgrims established their first Cape Cod settlement in Bourne in 1627, but back then it was still part of Sandwich; Bourne didn't become a separate town until 1884. By that time it had grown into a popular summer colony whose part-time residents included President Grover Cleveland and *Boston Globe* publisher Charles Taylor.

Present-day Bourne's maritime orientation was created by the Cape Cod Canal, which opened in 1914. The 17½-mi canal cut the distance for shipping traffic between Boston and New York by 75 mi and eliminated the often-treacherous journey around the Cape. The Army Corps of Engineers took over the canal's operation in the late 1920s and embarked on a project to widen it; the current Bourne and Sagamore bridges were built in the 1930s as part of this project. With a mix of year-round and summer residents, the Bourne area today includes places for learning about the region's marine life and early commercial history, as well as several attractive recreation areas, established and maintained by the Corps of Engineers, for biking, hiking, and fishing along the canal.

Ⓒ The **National Marine Life Center,** on the mainland near the Chamber of Commerce office, has a small exhibit area devoted to whales, dolphins, seals, and other marine life. In summer there are weekly story hours for preschoolers, marine-life educational programs for older children, and evening lectures about the ocean environment for adults. The center hopes to break ground on an expanded facility for rehabilitating stranded marine animals that will include a marine animal hospital and nursery, rehabilitation pools, and additional exhibit space. ⊠ *120 Main St., Buzzards Bay,* ☎ *508/759–8722.* ☜ *Free.* ☉ *Memorial Day–Labor Day, Mon.–Sat. 10–6, Sun. noon–6.*

On the mainland side, the **Massachusetts Maritime Academy,** founded in 1891, is the oldest such academy in the country. Future members of the Merchant Marines receive their training at its 55-acre campus in Buzzards Bay. The library has nautical paintings and scale models of ships from the 18th century to the present and is open to the public at no charge (hours are extensive but vary widely depending on whether school is in session; call ahead, ☎ 508/830–5000, ext. 1201). For a 30- to 60-minute tour of the academy weekdays at 10 and 2, call 48 hours in advance (ext. 1102). The tours are designed for prospective students and their families but are open to all. ⊠ *Taylor's Point, Buzzards Bay.*

A monument to the birth of commerce in the New World, the **Aptucxet Trading Post Museum** was erected on the foundation of the original post archaeologically excavated in the 1920s. Here, in 1627, Plimoth Plantation leaders established a way station between the Native American encampment at Great Herring Pond, 3 mi to the northeast; Dutch colonists in New Amsterdam (New York), to the south; and English colonists on Cape Cod Bay. Before the canal was built, the Manomet River connected Herring Pond with Buzzards Bay (no, scavengers don't frequent it—it was misnamed for the migrating osprey that do), and a short portage connected the pond to Scusset River, which met Cape Cod Bay. The Native Americans traded furs; the Dutch traded linen cloth, metal tools, glass beads, sugar, and other staples; and the Pilgrims traded wool cloth, clay beads, sassafras, and tobacco (which they imported from Virginia). Wampum was the medium of exchange.

Inside the post are 17th-century cooking utensils hanging from the original brick hearth, beaver and otter skins, furniture, and other artifacts such as arrowheads, tools, and tomahawks. Also on the grounds are a gift shop in a Dutch-style windmill, a saltworks, herb and wildflower gardens, a picnic area overlooking the canal, and a small Victorian railroad station built for the sole use of President Grover Cleveland, who had a summer home in Bourne. To get here, cross the Bourne Bridge, then take the first right from the Bourne Bridge rotary onto Trowbridge Road and follow the signs. Note that the site is also open on holiday Mondays in season. ⊠ *24 Aptucxet Rd.,* ☎ *508/759–9487.* 🎫 *$3.50.* 🕑 *May–June and Sept.–Columbus Day, Tues.–Sat. 10–5, Sun. 2–5; July–Aug., Mon.–Sat. 10–5, Sun. 2–5.*

🐾 A break for energetic children pent up in a car for too many miles, **Adventure Isle** has minibikes, a giant slide, a Ferris wheel, children's rides, an arcade, bumper boats, batting cages, a double gyroscope (for those with strong stomachs), a miniature golf course, and laser tag. ⊠ *Rte. 28, 2 mi south of Bourne Bridge,* ☎ *508/759–2636 or 800/535–2787.* 🎫 *$1.75–$3.75 per ride or $9.95 per day for unlimited rides ($11.95 for unlimited rides plus laser tag).* 🕑 *Mid-Mar.–Nov., daily 10 am–11 pm.*

Dining

$$–$$$ ✕ **Chart Room.** Tucked away in the marina, in a former cargo barge, this traditional bay-side spot has been serving up seafood classics and fine harbor views since 1966. Clam chowder, broiled scrod, seafood Newburg, baked stuffed shrimp—they're all here, as are sirloin steak, broiled lamb chops, and even grilled cheese-and-tomato sandwiches. At lunch you can try the Chart Room's version of surf and turf—a stuffed quahog and a hot dog!—but most people opt for the fresh (and overflowing) lobster salad sandwich. ⊠ *1 Shore Rd., at Kingman Marine, Cataumet,* ☎ *508/563–5350. AE, DC, MC, V. Closed Columbus Day–Memorial Day and weekdays Memorial Day–late June and Labor Day–Columbus Day.*

$$ ✕ **Stir Crazy.** One of just a few authentic Asian restaurants on the Cape—owner Bopha Samms hails from Cambodia—Stir Crazy fits the bill when you reach your inevitable limit of seafood and Yankee cooking. Over-

look the anonymous location (beside self-storage lockers, in a building that also houses a real estate office), because the real spice is where it belongs: in the food. Dishes blur the ethnic line with lively Cambodian, Thai, and Vietnamese influences. Look for *nhem shross* (an appetizer of vegetables and shrimp) and beef *lock lack* (sirloin tips on a bed of watercress). ⊠ *626 MacArthur Blvd. (Rte. 28 S), Pocasset,* ☎ *508/564–6464. Reservations not accepted. MC, V. No smoking. Closed Mon. No lunch Sat.–Thurs.*

$ ✕ **My Tinman.** "The family diner with a heart" is one of the only real diners (architecturally speaking) left on the Cape. The outside is covered in silver aluminum; inside, the pink booths share space with *Wizard of Oz* photos and paraphernalia. As you'd expect, it's diner food all the way, and it's all good, especially the meat loaf. Most dishes are named after the film: Lionhearted sandwiches, Scarecrow Garden Salad, and so on. Breakfast is served all day; the diner is open from 5 AM to 2 PM. ⊠ *MacArthur Blvd. (Rte. 28 S), near Massachusetts Military Reservation rotary, Pocasset,* ☎ *no phone. Reservations not accepted. No credit cards. No dinner.*

Nightlife and the Arts

The **Army Corps of Engineers** (☎ 508/759–4431), which maintains the Cape Cod Canal via a field office in Buzzards Bay, offers free daily programs in summer, including slide shows about the canal, sing-alongs, night walks, and storytelling around campfires at the Bourne Scenic Park and Scusset Beach State Park. Call for program details and locations.

In Bourne, **town-band concerts** are held Thursday evening in July and August starting at 7 in Buzzards Bay Park (⊠ Main St., ☎ 508/759–6000).

Outdoor Activities and Sports

BASEBALL

The **Bourne Braves** (☎ 508/432–6909) of the collegiate Cape Cod Baseball League play home games at Coady School (⊠ Trowbridge Rd., Bourne) from mid-June to mid-August.

BEACHES

Monument Beach off Shore Rd. is a small but pretty crescent of sand adjacent to the town harbor, facing Buzzards Bay just south of Bourne Bridge. The beach has a snack bar, rest rooms, and a parking lot, restricted in season to those with resident permits. From Shore Road, turn right onto Emmons Road just past the old train depot.

BIKING

An easy, straight trail stretches on either side of the **Cape Cod Canal,** 6½ mi on the south side, 7 mi on the north, with views of the bridges and ship traffic on the canal. Directly across the street from the canal bike path on the mainland (near the Massachusetts Maritime Academy), **P & M Cycles** (⊠ 29 Main St., Buzzards Bay, ☎ 508/759–2830) rents a large selection of mountain and hybrid bikes at reasonable rates.

FISHING

The Cape Cod Canal is a good place to fish—from the service road on either side—for blues, flounder, herring, mackerel, and striped bass seasonally making their way through the passage (April–November).

HIKING AND WALKING

The Army Corps of Engineers sponsors guided walks, bike trips, and hikes. Outside its **Herring Run Visitor Center,** on a bank of the canal with an excellent view, are picnic tables (note they're close to noisy U.S. 6), access to the canal bike path, a herring run through which the fish travel on their spawning run in May, and short self-guided walking trails through woodland. The visitor center is on the mainland side of the canal on U.S. 6 in Bournedale, between the bridges. ✉ *U.S. 6,* ☎ *508/ 759–4431; 508/759–5991 for tides, weather, and special events.*

On the Cape side of the canal, the Army Corps of Engineers manages the **Tidal Flats Recreation Area** (✉ Shore Rd., ☎ 508/759–4431), a small but peaceful canal-side park near the Cape railroad bridge. It's a pleasant site for picnicking or fishing, with a great view of the canal's ship traffic; there's access to the canal bike path, too. In the late afternoon, generally sometime between 5 and 6, you can watch the bridge lower to allow a train to cross the canal. To reach the recreation area, cross the Bourne Bridge and follow Trowbridge Road to Shore Road.

ICE-SKATING

John Gallo Ice Arena (✉ 231 Sandwich Rd., ☎ 508/759–8904) is the place to go for ice-skating year-round (except May). Hours vary widely; call for details.

SCUBA DIVING

Rentals, instruction, group dives, and information are available through **Aquarius Diving Center** (✉ 3239 Cranberry Hwy., Buzzards Bay, ☎ 508/759–3483), across the Bourne Bridge on the mainland.

Shopping

Tanger Outlet Center (✉ U.S. 6 at Buzzards Bay rotary, Bourne, ☎ 800/ 406–8435) sells women's, men's, and children's apparel from designers such as Izod, Nine West, Levi's, and Liz Claiborne.

West and North Falmouth

9 mi south of Bourne.

Wooded country lanes that lead to secluded coves, small harbors dotted with sailboats, and farm stands selling sweet corn and fresh berries—the villages along Route 28 between Bourne and Falmouth proper offer up a glimpse of the old Cape Cod. Native American names serve as reminders of the true first settlers here, and houses that date from the 18th century (as well as more modern summer retreats) line the roads.

Although Route 28 from the Bourne Bridge south to Falmouth is overly commercial in many areas, Route 28A between Pocasset and West Falmouth is more scenic, with side roads leading to attractive beaches, particularly Old Silver Beach (☞ Outdoor Activities and Sports, *below*), and small harbors. If you've brought your bicycle, the less-traveled lanes here make for good biking; many of the beaches along the bay restrict parking to residents, but bicyclists and walkers are free to explore.

NEED A
BREAK?   **Peach Tree Circle Farm** (✉ 881 Old Palmer Ave., West Falmouth, ☎ 508/548–4006) includes a bakery, a farm stand, and a cheery tearoom. Inexpensive lunches of soups, sandwiches, salads, and a few entrées such as quiche and chicken potpie are served year-round amid the smells of baking bread and herbs hung to dry.

Lodging

$$$–$$$$ 🏨 **Inn at West Falmouth.** This luxurious 1898 estate-house inn is in a secluded area of an exclusive village. A mixture of contemporary and antique furnishings and polished hardwood floors sets an elegant but relaxed mood. Guest rooms have king- or queen-size beds (some with canopies), Italian marble bathrooms with whirlpool tubs, phones, hair dryers, and wall safes; some have fireplaces and private decks. Beyond the French doors, off the pale pink-and-green sunroom, a patio spilling over with lush potted plants and trees overlooks woods, gardens, and

a tennis court and leads to the small pool and deck. ⊠ *Off Blacksmith Shop Rd., Box 1208, West Falmouth 02574,* ☎ *508/540–7696 or 800/ 397–7696,* ℻ *508/540–9977. 8 rooms. Pool, tennis court. No smoking. MC, V. CP.* ❧

$$$–$$$$ 🏨 **Sea Crest Resort.** Location and amenities are strong draws at this conference center and resort, whose eight buildings sprawl along one end of beautiful Old Silver Beach. Rooms are crisp and clean, done in dark blues and pastels. Many rooms have ocean views, and some have gas-log fireplaces. A number of lodging packages are available. ⊠ *350 Quaker Rd., North Falmouth 02556,* ☎ *508/540–9400 or 800/225– 3110,* ℻ *508/548–0556. 258 rooms, 8 suites. Restaurant, deli, piano bar, room service, indoor-outdoor pool, hot tub, sauna, putting green, 2 tennis courts, health club, shuffleboard, video games, children's programs (ages 3–12). AE, D, DC, MC, V.* ❧

$–$$ 🏨 **Ideal Spot Motel.** This neat-as-a-pin gray-shingle motel feels quiet and a bit old-fashioned, but the simple, family-friendly rooms are all good-size. Twelve of the units are efficiencies—each has a queen-size bed or two doubles, plus a kitchen and a sitting area with a sofa bed; two are large motel rooms with refrigerators. If you need a pool, this motel may not be ideal (there isn't one), but it's only a mile to Chapoquoit Beach. ⊠ *Rte. 28A at Old Dock Rd., West Falmouth 02574,* ☎ *508/548–2257 or 800/269–6910. 14 rooms. Air-conditioning. D, MC, V. Closed Nov.–Mar.* ❧

$–$$ 🏨 **Sjöholm Inn.** This rambling 1863 farmhouse on a country lane is comfortable and homey, like staying with a favorite aunt and uncle. The rooms—some in the main inn, some in the adjacent cottage house— are not fancy, but they're a pleasant mix of 1940s colonial-style furniture, hand-me-downs, and the occasional antique. One of the loveliest rooms (though it lacks a private bath) is the airy window-lined Sleeping Porch—perfect for a summer respite. Unlike many B&Bs, the Sjöholm (pronounced *shewr*-holm) welcomes families. Even if you haven't brought yours along, you'll feel like part of the family at breakfast, served at long tables in the cheery breakfast room. There's also a cozy sunporch and a large yard with an outdoor shower. A separate two-bedroom cottage rents by the week. ⊠ *17 Chase Rd., off Rte. 28A, West Falmouth 02574,* ☎ *508/540–5706 or 800/498–5706. 15 rooms, 7 with bath, 1 cottage. Breakfast room, croquet, bicycles. No smoking. MC, V. BP.* ❧

Nightlife and the Arts

Sea Crest Resort (⊠ 350 Quaker Rd., North Falmouth, ☎ 508/540– 9400; ☞ Dining and Lodging, *above*) has a summer and holiday-weekend schedule of nightly entertainment on the outdoor terrace, including dancing to country, Top 40, reggae, and jazz bands and a big-band DJ, as well as karaoke and comedy.

Outdoor Activities and Sports

BEACHES

Chapoquoit Beach (Chapoquoit Rd., West Falmouth), a narrow stretch of white sand, lines a peninsula that juts dramatically into the bay. Resident parking stickers are required at the beach lot in season, but the surrounding roads are popular with bicyclists. The beach has lifeguards and portable toilets.

Megansett Beach, hidden in a residential neighborhood at the end of County Road in North Falmouth, is a small, family-friendly location. Weathered gray-shingle homes line the cove, while boats moored at the adjacent yacht club bob in the bay. The beach has lifeguards and a portable toilet, but no other services. Resident parking stickers are required at the beach lot in season.

Old Silver Beach, off Quaker Road in North Falmouth, is a long, beautiful crescent of soft white sand, with the Sea Crest Resort (☞ *above*) at one end. It is especially good for small children because a sandbar keeps it shallow at one end and creates tidal pools full of crabs and minnows. The beach has lifeguards, rest rooms, showers, and a snack bar. There's a $10 fee for parking in summer.

Wood Neck Beach, on Wood Neck Road in the Sippewisset area of West Falmouth, is a sandy bayside beach backed by grass-covered dunes. At high tide the beach is very narrow, but when the tide is out, sandbars and shallow tide pools make this a good place for children. Resident parking stickers are required in season.

HORSEBACK RIDING

Haland Stables (✉ 878 Rte. 28A, West Falmouth, ☎ 508/540–2552) offers lessons and trail rides by reservation Monday–Saturday.

TENNIS

Ballymeade Country Club (✉ 125 Falmouth Woods Rd., off Rte. 151, North Falmouth, ☎ 508/457–7620) has six Har-Tru and four hard courts, a grass tennis court, lessons, clinics, ball machines, and a pro shop (☎ 508/457–7620) that accepts court-time reservations from mid-June through mid-October.

Shopping

Open Door Gallery (✉ 544 W. Falmouth Hwy., at Chapoquoit Rd., West Falmouth, ☎ 508/540–8484), a lovely place to browse, specializes in high-quality craft works. You may find intricately carved wooden bowls, humorous prints, creative sculpture, nature photographs, and handmade jewelry, as well as garden art. There's also a nice collection of cards and moderately priced gift items.

Summerhouse Gallery (✉ 646 W. Falmouth Hwy., West Falmouth, ☎ 508/548–3593) is a tiny cottage-turned-gallery showing photographs and other works by Cape and New England artists. There's a small snack bar, too.

Falmouth

❹ *2 mi south of West Falmouth, 15 mi south of Bourne Bridge, 4 mi north of Woods Hole.*

The Cape's second-largest town, Falmouth was settled in 1660 by Congregationalists from Barnstable who had been ostracized by their church and deprived of voting privileges and other civil rights for being sympathizers with the Quakers (then the victims of severe repression). The town was incorporated in 1686 and named for Falmouth, England. The Falmouth area, sprawling over 44 square mi, includes eight villages: Falmouth, North Falmouth, West Falmouth (☞ *above*), Hatchville, Teaticket, East Falmouth, Waquoit (☞ *below*), and Woods Hole (☞ *below*).

Much of Falmouth today is suburban, with a mix of old and new developments and a large year-round population. Many residents commute to other towns on the Cape, to southeastern Massachusetts, and even to Boston. The town has a quaint village center, with a typically old New England village green and a shop-lined Main Street. South of town center, Falmouth faces Nantucket Sound and has several often-crowded beaches popular with families. To the east, the Falmouth Heights neighborhood mixes inns, B&Bs, and private homes, nestled close together on residential streets leading to the sea. Bustling Grand Avenue, the main drag in Falmouth Heights, hugs the shore and the beach. The town is also dotted with parks and ponds; one of the nicest, Grews Pond (☞

Outdoor Activities and Sports, *below*) in Goodwill Park, is north of the town center—it's a lovely site for a picnic on a summer afternoon.

The **Village Green,** added to the National Register of Historic Places in 1996, was used as a militia training field in the 18th century and a grazing ground for horses in the early 19th. Today it is flanked by attractive old homes, some built by sea captains, and the 1856 **Congregational Church,** built on the timbers of its 1796 predecessor, with a bell made by Paul Revere. The bell's cheery inscription reads: THE LIVING TO THE CHURCH I CALL, AND TO THE GRAVE I SUMMON ALL.

The **Falmouth Historical Society** maintains two museums that represent life in colonial Cape Cod. The 1790 **Julia Wood House** retains wonderful architectural details—a widow's walk, wide-board floors, lead-glass windows, and a colonial kitchen with wide hearth. It's filled with antique embroideries, baby shoes and clothes, toys and dolls, portraits, furniture, and the trappings of an authentically equipped doctor's office, all from the house's onetime owner. Out back, the Hallett Barn Museum displays antique farm implements, a 19th-century horse-drawn sleigh, and other interesting items. The smaller **Conant House** next door is a 1794 half-Cape (an asymmetrical 1½-story building). Inside are military memorabilia, whaling items, scrimshaw, sailors' valentines, and a genealogical and historical research library. There's also a collection of books, portraits, and things relating to Katharine Lee Bates, the native daughter who wrote "America the Beautiful." Guides give tours of the museums, and a pretty formal garden with a gazebo and flagstone paths is adjacent. Free walking tours of the town are available Tuesday at 4 in July and August, as are historical trolley tours; call for prices and times. ⊠ *Village Green, off Palmer Ave.,* ☎ *508/548–4857.* 🖾 *$3.* ☉ *Mid-June–mid-Sept., Mon.–Thurs. 10–4, Sun. 1–4; mid-Sept.–mid-Nov., weekends 1–4.*

The 1812 white Cape house at 16 Main Street marks the **birthplace of Katharine Lee Bates.** Now owned by the Falmouth Historical Society (☞ *above*), it is no longer open to the public, but a plaque out front commemorates Bates's birth, in 1859.

❺ The **Charles D. and Margaret K. Spohr Garden,** 3 planted acres on Oyster Pond, is a pretty, peaceful, privately owned place. The springtime explosion of more than 700,000 daffodils gives way in turn to the tulips, azaleas, magnolias, flowering crabapples, rhododendrons, lilies, and climbing hydrangeas that inspire garden goers in summer. A collection of old millstones, bronze church bells, and ships' anchors decorates the landscape. ⊠ *Fells Rd. off Oyster Pond Rd.* 🖾 *Free.* ☉ *Daily sunrise–sunset.*

☺ A good place for children on a rainy day, the **Leary Family Amusement Center** (⊠ 23 Town Hall Sq., off Rte. 28, ☎ 508/540–4877) has video-game rooms and candlepin bowling.

Dining and Lodging

$$$–$$$$ ✕ **Regatta of Falmouth-by-the-Sea.** One of the Cape's nicest dining rooms
★ offers beautiful views of Nantucket Sound and Martha's Vineyard and a menu that evolves constantly, responding to culinary innovations while maintaining a traditional appeal. The dining room is modern and subdued, with soft colors, lamplight, and an intimate, romantic ambience. Continental and Asian cuisines have been mingling on the menu, resulting in dishes such as the sautéed shellfish sampler: scallops, mussels, lobster, and shrimp with a sensational curried lobster sauce over Asian greens. In addition to the regular menu, there's a three-course early dinner menu. The Regatta of Cotuit (☞ Chapter 4) is a sibling. ⊠ *End*

of Scranton Ave., Falmouth Harbor, ☎ *508/548–5400. AE, MC, V. Closed Mon. and Oct.–Memorial Day. No lunch.*

$$ ✕ **Quarterdeck Restaurant.** Part bar, part restaurant—but all Cape Cod—this spot is across the street from Falmouth's town hall, so the lunch talk tends to focus on local politics. The stained glass is not old and authentic, but the huge whaling harpoons certainly are. Low ceilings and rough-hewn beams seem a good match for the menu, which features hearty sandwiches such as Reubens and grilled chorizo at lunch and then specials at night. The swordfish kebab, skewered with mushrooms, onion, and green pepper and served over jasmine rice, is especially good. ⊠ *164 Main St. (Rte. 28),* ☎ *508/548–9900. AE, D, DC, MC, V.*

$–$$ ✕ **Betsy's Diner.** An authentic-looking American treasure, Betsy's is a shiny, happy, busy place with a reassuring pink neon sign urging you to EAT HEAVY. The generous dining room, gleaming counter, and stools and booths by the big windows are all done in pretty pastel mauve-and-cream tones. Memorabilia and neon grace the walls. A classic diner menu with pancakes, waffles, and omelets is served all day, and dinner is meat loaf and mashed potatoes, knockwurst and sauerkraut, charbroiled pork chops—those kinds of things. ⊠ *457 Main St. (Rte. 28),* ☎ *508/540–4446. Reservations not accepted. MC, V.*

$ ✕ **The Clam Shack.** Next door to the Regatta of Falmouth-by-the-Sea (☞ *above*) and with the same harbor views, this no-frills seafood joint serves—what else?—fried clams. The clams are crisp and fresh tasting; the meaty lobster roll and the fish-and-chips platter are good choices, too. Place your order at the counter; then take your tray to the picnic tables on the roof deck for the best views. There are more tables on the dock in back, or you can squeeze into the tiny dining room. Just don't plan on a late night here—the Shack closes most evenings around 7:30. ⊠ *227 Clinton Ave., Falmouth Harbor,* ☎ *508/540–7758. No credit cards. Closed Labor Day–Memorial Day.*

$ ✕ **Maryellen's Portuguese Bakery.** It's easy to drive right past this friendly, no-frills breakfast-and-lunch spot, hidden behind a Dairy Queen. Take a seat at the counter or at one of the few tables; call, "Good morning" to Maryellen, who will likely be bustling about the room; then order up breakfast with a Portuguese twist. You can get spicy *linguica* sausage with your eggs, or French toast made with Portuguese bread. Try the savory Portuguese omelet, filled with linguica, parsley, onions, and cheese. The lunch menu starts with BLTs and burgers but quickly moves on to kale soup and *cacoilha* (marinated pork). You can also pick up some Portuguese sweet bread or *malasadas* (fried dough) to go. ⊠ *829 Main St., near Falmouth Heights Rd.,* ☎ *508/540–9696. No credit cards. No dinner.*

$ ✕ **McMenamy's.** For more than 25 years fried seafood has been the reason to eat at McMenamy's. The clams, scallops, and fish are all fried up good and crispy; the onion rings will delight lovers of the pungent bulb. There's no view here—the otherwise pleasant outdoor deck faces the parking lot—and the dining room is done in basic Formica, but there's plenty of seating, so you can bring the family. ⊠ *70 Davis Straits (Rte. 28),* ☎ *508/540–2115. AE, D, MC, V.*

$$–$$$ ✕🔝 **Coonamessett Inn.** Delightfully sunk in the past, this is one of the
★ best—and oldest (since 1953)—of the many quaint inn-restaurants on the Cape. The main dining room is lovely, and the Cape Cod Room looks out over a pond and garden. The menu, not surprisingly, is also traditional, maybe too much so for adventuresome palates; the many seafood choices include charbroiled swordfish with grilled vegetable vinaigrette, steamed or baked and stuffed lobster, and baked scrod. Five buildings of one- or two-bedroom suites range around a broad landscaped lawn that spills down to a scenic wooded pond; several suites directly overlook the pond. Rooms are casually decorated, with bleached wood or

pine paneling and New England antiques or reproductions. There's also a one-bedroom cottage with a full kitchen. A large collection of Cape artist Ralph Cahoon's work is displayed throughout the inn. ✉ *311 Gifford St., at Jones Rd., 02540, ☎ 508/548–2300, ℻ 508/540–9831, www.capecodrestaurants.org/coonamessett. 28 suites, 1 cottage. Restaurant, bar, no-smoking rooms. AE, MC, V. CP.*

$$$–$$$$ 🖫 **La Maison Cappellari at Mostly Hall.** In a landscaped park far back
★ from the street and separated from it by tall bushes, trees, and a wrought-iron fence, this elegant inn with a wraparound porch looks very much like a private estate. (The house got its name when a young turn-of-the-20th-century visitor is said to have exclaimed to his mother, "Look! It's mostly hall!") In 2000 new owners Bogdan and Christina Simcic renovated the imposing 1849 house in an upscale European style. Several bedrooms have intriguing wall murals; in the Tuscan Room the walls are painted to suggest an intimate garden in Tuscany, while in the Corsica Room the murals recall the sunny island shores of Napoléon's birthplace. Three rooms are more traditionally decorated, with floral wallpaper, canopy beds, and other antique pieces. Breakfast is served in the huge living room with its marble fireplace or outside on the veranda. Although the inn is only steps from the town center, you can lounge in the lush gardens behind the house and feel a world away. ✉ *27 Main St. (Rte. 28), 02540, ☎ 508/548–3786 or 800/682–0565, ℻ 508/548–5778. 6 rooms. Air-conditioning, bicycles, library. No smoking. AE, D, MC, V. Closed mid-Dec.–mid-Mar. BP.* ❧

$$–$$$$ 🖫 **Inn on the Sound.** Although far from secluded, this inn, perched on a bluff overlooking Vineyard Sound and offering glimpses of the island itself, is blissfully quiet. The living room and 9 of the 10 guest rooms (all named for various Falmouth area landmarks) face the water. Guest rooms have queen-size beds and unfussy contemporary furnishings such as natural oak tables, unbleached cottons, and ceiling fans; four rooms have private decks. Common areas include the art-laden living room, with its oversize boulder fireplace, oversize windows, and modern white couches; a bistrolike breakfast room; and a large porch with even more stunning water views. ✉ *313 Grand Ave., Falmouth Heights 02540, ☎ 508/457–9666 or 800/564–9668, ℻ 508/457–9631. 10 rooms. Beach. No smoking. AE, D, MC, V. BP.* ❧

$$$ 🖫 **The Beach House.** If your idea of a perfect beach house is a rainbow of sunny colors, hand-painted furniture, and a deck that looks out toward the ocean—all just a two-block walk to the beach, the Beach House will fulfill your expectations. The walls of each guest room in this crisp and contemporary gray-shingle house are painted with a theme—in the small but cheery Sunflower Room, a garden of flowers dances across the wall, while in the Fish Room the bed (with a headboard inspired by the waves) is surrounded by, yes, fish. In the vaulted-ceiling suite, you can lounge in bed and look up at the (painted) clouds. Breakfast is served either in the kitchen, where the walls are painted like a summer garden, or next to the backyard pool. ✉ *10 Worcester Ct., Falmouth Heights 02540, ☎ 508/457–0310 or 800/351–3426, ℻ 508/548–7895. 7 rooms, 1 suite. Pool. No smoking. MC, V. Closed Nov.–Mar. CP.* ❧

$$$ 🖫 **Capt. Tom Lawrence House.** Steps from downtown yet set back from the street enough to feel secluded, this pretty white house with a cupola and black shutters is surrounded by a lawn shaded by old maple trees. Built in 1861 for a whaling captain, this intimate B&B has romantic rooms with antique and painted furniture, French country wallpaper, soft colors, thick carpeting, cable TV, and refrigerators. The beds, all queen size (several with canopies) or king size, have firm mattresses, Laura Ashley or Ralph Lauren linens, and down comforters in winter. A family-friendly efficiency apartment is bright and

spacious, with a fully equipped eat-in kitchen and a private entrance. The large common room has a fireplace. The full breakfast is lavish and delicious. ⊠ *75 Locust St., 02540,* ☎ *508/540–1445 or 800/ 266–8139,* 𝖥𝖠𝖷 *508/457–1790. 6 rooms, 1 efficiency. Air-conditioning. No smoking. AE, MC, V. Closed Jan.–Feb. BP.*

$$$ ⊡ **Holiday Inn.** This chain link is a dependable option for families. The tried-and-true comfort formula has been applied here: large rooms with contemporary pastel decor, suites with king-size beds, and a large pool area surrounded by patio furniture and greenery. The restaurant is open for breakfast and dinner year-round. The hotel is across from a pond ½ mi outside Falmouth center. ⊠ *291 Jones Rd., 02540,* ☎ *508/540– 2000 or 800/465–4329,* 𝖥𝖠𝖷 *508/548–2712. 93 rooms, 5 suites. Restaurant, no-smoking rooms, room service, indoor pool, exercise room, video games. AE, D, DC, MC, V.* ✎

$$$ ⊡ **Wildflower Inn.** You'll find many instances of what innkeepers Phil
★   and Donna Stone call their "old made new again" decorating style: tables are constructed from early 1900s pedal-sewing-machine bases, and the sideboard in the living room/breakfast area was once a '20s Hotpoint electric stove. Each of the inn's five rooms (two with whirlpool tubs) is also innovatively decorated. The bed in the romantic Moonflower Room, tucked under the eaves, is draped in netting and has a skylight above for moon watching, while the bright and cheerful Geranium Room, with baskets of fresh geraniums, has a white-iron bed topped with a geranium-print comforter. The Loft Cottage, once a stable, has a spiral staircase that winds up to the bedroom. Donna whips up delicious concoctions using the edible wildflowers she grows out back (her floral feasts have been featured on the PBS series *Country Inn Cooking).* The wraparound porch serves as the summer's breakfast nook; one morning the five-course breakfast might include sunflower crepes; the next, calendula corn muffins. ⊠ *167 Palmer Ave., 02540,* ☎ 𝖥𝖠𝖷 *508/548–9524 or 800/294– 5459. 5 rooms, 1 cottage. Air-conditioning. No smoking. AE, MC, V. Closed Jan.–Feb. BP.* ✎

$$–$$$ ⊡ **Admiralty Inn.** This large roadside motel outside Falmouth center has a wide range of rooms and suites, and its child-friendly facilities make it a good bet for families. Standard rooms have two queen-size beds or one queen-size and one Murphy bed. King Jacuzzi rooms have king-size beds and whirlpool tubs in the bedroom. Town-house suites have cathedral ceilings with skylights, two baths (one with whirlpool), a loft with a king-size bed, a living room with a sofa bed, and a queen- or king-size bed. Children under 12 stay free. ⊠ *51 Teaticket Hwy. (Rte. 28), 02540,* ☎ *508/548–4240 or 800/341–5700,* 𝖥𝖠𝖷 *508/457– 0535. 70 rooms, 28 suites. Restaurant, bar, 2 pools, hot tub. AE, D, DC, MC, V.* ✎

$$–$$$ ⊡ **Palmer House Inn.** This turn-of-the-20th-century Queen Anne home is set on a tree-lined street in the historic heart of Falmouth, just a short stroll past the village green. The Victorian interior may seem slightly suffocating—dark hardwoods, heavy period furniture, endless lace, and ornate stained-glass windows. Each room has an antique, wicker, or four-poster bed and a ceiling fan. One good bet is the third-floor Tower Room, with a view across the treetops into Woods Hole and beyond. The large rooms in the 1910 carriage house are also airier, with more tailored appointments. The inn added four rooms, all with whirlpool baths, in 1999; three have king-size beds, and all have traditional but less ornate decor. There's a private cottage, set off in the backyard, with a whirlpool tub. A candlelight breakfast is served and afternoon refreshments are available. ⊠ *81 Palmer Ave., 02540,* ☎ *508/548–1230 or 800/472– 2632,* 𝖥𝖠𝖷 *508/540–1878, www.palmerhouseinn.com. 16 rooms, 1 cottage. Air-conditioning, bicycles. No smoking. AE, D, DC, MC, V. BP.*

Nightlife and the Arts

The **College Light Opera Company** (⊠ Highfield Theatre, off Depot Ave., ☎ 508/548–0668), founded in 1969, presents nine musicals or operettas for one week each, the results of a summer program involving music and theater majors from Oberlin and other colleges. The company includes more than 30 singers and an 18-piece orchestra. Be forewarned: when the shows are good, they're mildly enjoyable; when they're bad—and it does happen—they're dreadful.

The **Cape Cod Theatre Project** (☎ 508/457–4242) was established in 1994 to help develop new American plays through a series of staged readings. Each summer the project stages three or four readings, which are followed by audience discussion with the playwright. Recent productions have included *One Under,* by Gloucester Stage Company director Israel Horovitz, and works by Pulitzer Prize winners Lanford Wilson and Paula Vogel. Performances are held in the Woods Hole Community Hall (⊠ Water St., Woods Hole) or at Falmouth Academy (⊠ 7 Highfield Dr., off Depot Ave., Falmouth).

Falmouth's **town-band concerts** are held on Thursday evening starting at 8 in summer (⊠ Marina Park, Scranton Ave., ☎ 508/548–8500 or 800/526–8532).

Coonamessett Inn (⊠ 311 Gifford St., ☎ 508/548–2300) has dancing to soft piano, jazz trios, or other music in its lounge on weekends year-round.

Nimrod Inn (⊠ 100 Dillingham Ave., ☎ 508/540–4132) offers jazz and contemporary music at least six nights a week, including the big band and jazz sounds of Stage Door Canteen, one of the Cape's best bands, every Thursday evening from September through June.

Outdoor Activities and Sports

The **Falmouth Commodores** (☎ 508/432–6909) of the collegiate Cape Cod Baseball League play home games at Guv Fuller Field (⊠ 790 E. Main St. [Rte. 28]) from mid-June to mid-August.

Some Falmouth hotels and motels will sell daily resident parking permits to guests, so if you're planning to drive to the beach, be sure to inquire.

A bit removed from the hubbub of town, with swaying beach grass and a salt pond behind, the narrow **Falmouth Beach,** on Surf Drive, faces Nantucket Sound and Martha's Vineyard. Lifeguards watch the beach in season, and there are portable toilets. A resident parking sticker is required to park in the beach lot in season.

Falmouth Heights Beach, on Grand Avenue, is an often-crowded crescent of sand on Nantucket Sound, backed by a row of inns and B&Bs. The beach has lifeguards (in summer) and portable toilets. Public parking is available; in summer the daily parking fees are $8 weekdays, $10 weekends. There's also a small strip of metered parking on Grand Avenue between Walden Avenue and Crescent Park Avenue.

Grews Pond, in Goodwill Park, a pretty tree-lined freshwater pond with a sandy beach and lifeguarded swimming area, is popular with local families. There are several sites for picnicking, along with rest rooms, and a volleyball net; there's also a playground nearby. You can enter the park from Route 28 just north of Jones Road or from Gifford Street opposite St. Joseph's Cemetery. Parking is free.

Surf Drive Beach, a family-friendly sandy cove on Surf Drive, faces Nantucket Sound with views out toward the Vineyard. There are rest rooms and showers, as well as lifeguards, and public parking is available; in summer the daily parking fee is $8 weekdays, $10 weekends.

BIKING

The **Shining Sea Trail** is an easy 3½-mi route between Locust Street, Falmouth, and the Woods Hole ferry parking lot. It follows the coast, providing views of Vineyard Sound and dipping into oak and pine woods; a detour onto Church Street takes you to Nobska Light. A brochure is available at the trailheads. If you're going to Martha's Vineyard with your bike, you can park your car in one of Falmouth's Steamship Authority lots and ride the Shining Sea Trail to the ferry. (The free shuttle buses between the Falmouth lots and the Woods Hole ferry docks also have bike carriers; ☞ Ferries *in* Smart Travel Tips).

Corner Cycle (✉ 115 Palmer Ave., Falmouth, ☎ 508/540–4195) rents tandem and trail bikes by the hour, day, or week. It also does on-site repairs. The shop is just two blocks from the Shining Sea Trail. **Holiday Cycles** (✉ 465 Grand Ave., Falmouth Heights, ☎ 508/540–3549) has surrey, tandem, and other unusual bikes.

FISHING

Freshwater ponds are good for perch, pickerel, trout, and more; the required license (along with rental gear) is available at tackle shops, such as **Eastman's Sport & Tackle** (✉ 150 Main St. [Rte. 28], Falmouth, ☎ 508/548–6900).

Patriot Boats (✉ 227 Clinton Ave., Falmouth Harbor, ☎ 508/548–2626; 800/734–0088 in MA) has deep-sea fishing from party or charter boats. Midweek you can often get a place on the party boat without reservations, although advance bookings are recommended; reserve ahead for weekend trips.

ICE-SKATING

Fall through spring, ice-skating is available at the **Falmouth Ice Arena** (✉ 9 Skating La., off Palmer Ave., ☎ 508/548–9083). You'll need to bring your own skates, though; rentals are not available.

TENNIS AND RACQUETBALL

Falmouth Sports Center (✉ 33 Highfield Dr., ☎ 508/548–7433) is a huge facility with three outdoor and six indoor tennis courts, and three racquetball-handball courts, as well as steam rooms and saunas, free weights, and physical and massage therapist services. Day and short-term rates are available.

Shopping

Bean & Cod (✉ 140 Main St. [Rte. 28], ☎ 508/548–8840 or 800/558–8840), a specialty food shop, carries cheeses, breads, and gourmet picnic fixings, along with pastas, coffees and teas, and unusual condiments. The store also packs and ships gift baskets.

Eight Cousins Children's Books (✉ 189 Main St. [Rte. 28], ☎ 508/548–5548) is the place to find reading material for toddlers through young adults. The well-stocked shop, which has nice sections on oceans and marine life, Native American peoples, and other Cape topics, also carries audiotapes and games.

Howlingbird (✉ 91 Palmer Ave., ☎ 508/540–3787) carries detailed hand-silk-screened marine-theme T-shirts and sweatshirts, plus hand-painted cards and silk-screened hats and handbags.

Maxwell & Co. (✉ 200 Main St. [Rte. 28[, ☎ 508/540–8752) has traditional men's and women's clothing with flair from European and American designers, handmade French shoes and boots, and leather goods and accessories.

Rosie Cheeks (✉ 233 Main St. [Rte. 28], ☎ 508/548–4572), whose name was inspired by the owner's daughter, stocks creative women's clothing and jewelry, with a particularly nice selection of hand-knit sweaters.

Woods Hole

❻ *4 mi southwest of Falmouth, 19 mi south of the Bourne Bridge.*

The village of Woods Hole, which dangles at the Cape's southwestern tip, has a unique personality shaped by its substantial intellectual community. As the departure point for ferries to Martha's Vineyard, it draws crowds of through traffic in season.

Well known as a center for international marine research, Woods Hole is home to several major scientific institutions. The National Marine Fisheries Service was here first, established in 1871 to study fish management and conservation. In 1888 the Marine Biological Laboratory (MBL), a center for research and education in marine biology, moved in across the street. Then in 1930 the Woods Hole Oceanographic Institution (WHOI) arrived, and the U.S. Geological Survey's Branch of Marine Geology followed suit in the 1960s.

Most of the year Woods Hole is a peaceful community of intellectuals quietly going about their work. In summer, however, the basically one-street village overflows with the thousands of scientists and graduate students who come from around the globe either to participate in summer studies at MBL, WHOI, or the National Academy of Sciences conference center or to work on independent research projects. A handful of waterside cafés and shops along Water Street competes for the most bicycles stacked up at the door. Parking, limited to a relatively small number of metered spots on the street, can be nearly impossible. If you're coming from Falmouth to wander here, either ride your bicycle down the straight and flat Shining Sea Trail (☞ Falmouth, *above*) or take the Cape Cod Regional Transit Authority's WHOOSH trolley (☞ Getting Around *in* Upper Cape A to Z, *below*).

What accounts for this incredible concentration of scientific minds is, in part, the variety and abundance of marine life in Woods Hole's unpolluted waters, and the natural deepwater port. In addition, there is the opportunity for an easy interchange of ideas and information and the stimulation of daily lectures and discussions (many open to the public) by important scientists. The pooling of resources among the various institutions makes for economies of scale that benefit each while allowing all access to highly sophisticated equipment.

A good example of the joining of scientific forces in Woods Hole is the **Marine Biological Laboratory–Woods Hole Oceanographic Institution Library** (✉ 7 Marine Biological Laboratory St., off Water St.), one of the best collections of biological, ecological, and oceanographic literature in the world. On top of its access to more than 200 computer databases and the Internet, the library subscribes to more than 5,000 scientific journals in 40 languages, with complete collections of most from their first issues. During World War II the librarian arranged with a German subscription agency to have German periodicals sent to neutral Switzerland to be stored until the end of the war. Thus the library's German collections are uninterrupted, where even those of many

German institutions are incomplete. All journals are always accessible because they cannot be checked out and because the library is open 24 hours a day. The Rare Books Room contains photographs, monographs, and prints, as well as journal collections that date from 1665.

Unless you are a scientific researcher, the only way you'll get to see the library is by taking the **Marine Biological Laboratory tour** (☎ 508/289–7623; call for reservations and meeting instructions at least a week in advance if possible). The 1½-hour tours are led by retired scientists (mid-June–mid-September, weekdays at 1, 2, and 3) and include an introductory slide show, as well as stops at the library, the Marine Resources Center (where living sea creatures collected each day are kept), and one of the many working research labs.

The **Woods Hole Oceanographic Institution** is the largest independent, private oceanographic laboratory in the world. Several buildings in the village of Woods Hole house its shore-based facilities; others are on a 200-acre campus nearby. During World War II its research focused on underwater explosives, submarine detection, and the development of antifouling paint. Today its $93 million annual budget helps operate many specialized laboratories with state-of-the-art equipment. A graduate program is offered jointly with MIT. WHOI's several research vessels roam the world's waters. Its staff led the successful U.S.–French search for the *Titanic* (found about 400 mi off Newfoundland) in 1985.

The institution itself is open to the public only on guided tours, but you can learn about it at the small **WHOI Exhibit Center,** with videos and exhibits on the institution and its various projects, including research vessels. One-hour walking tours of the institution and its piers are offered in July and August, weekdays at 10:30 and 1:30; tours begin at the WHOI Information Office at 93 Water Street and are free, but reservations are required (☎ 508/289–2252). ⊠ *15 School St., ☎ 508/289–2663. ☜ $2 suggested donation. ☉ Late May–early Sept., Mon.–Sat. 10–4:30, Sun. noon–4:30; Apr. and Nov.–Dec., Fri.–Sat. 10–4:30, Sun. noon–4:30; early-May–mid-May, mid-Sept.–late Sept., and Oct., Tues.–Sat. 10–4:30, Sun. noon–4:30.*

ⓒ The **National Marine Fisheries Service Aquarium** displays 16 tanks of regional fish and shellfish. There are magnifying glasses and a dissecting scope to examine marine life, along with several hands-on pools with banded lobsters, crabs, snails, starfish, and other creatures. The top attraction is two harbor seals, which can be seen in the outdoor pool near the entrance in summer; you can watch their feedings daily at 11 and 4. The exhibits aren't sophisticated, and the facility could be better maintained, but this popular place is definitely child-friendly. ⊠ *Corner of Albatross and Water Sts., ☎ 508/495–2267; 508/495–2001 for recorded information. ☜ Free. ☉ Mid-June–mid-Sept., daily 10–4; mid-Sept.–mid-June, weekdays 10–4.*

| NEED A BREAK? | **Pie in the Sky** (⊠ 10 Water St., ☎ 508/540–5475), a small bakery with tables inside and out, sells cookies, pastries, and coffees, as well as a small selection of sandwiches. The Oreo cookie bars are truly decadent. |

A three-building complex, the **Woods Hole Historical Museum** (formerly known as the Bradley House Museum) displays paintings, a restored Woods Hole Spritsail boat, boat models, and a model of the town as it looked in the 1890s. One room is filled with elegant ladies' clothing from the late 1800s. In the archives of the historical collection you'll find old ships' logs, postcards, newspaper articles, maps, diaries and photographs; more than 200 tapes of oral history provided by local residents; and a 100-volume library on maritime history. Free guided walking tours of the village are available Tuesday at 4 in July and August; tours depart from the museum, which is across from the Martha's Vineyard ferry parking lot. ⊠ *573 Woods Hole Rd.,* ☎ *508/548–7270.* 🖾 *Donations accepted.* ⊙ *Museum mid-June–late Sept., Tues.–Sat. 10–4. Archives year-round, Tues. and Thurs. 10–2.*

The 1888 **Episcopal Church of the Messiah,** a stone church with a conical steeple and a small medicinal herb garden in the shape of a Celtic cross, is a good place for some quiet time. The garden is enclosed by a holly hedge and has a bench for meditation. Inscriptions on either side of the carved gate read ENTER IN HOPE and DEPART IN PEACE. ⊠ *22 Church St.,* ☎ *508/548–2145.* 🖾 *Free.* ⊙ *Daily sunrise–sunset.*

Nobska Light (⊠ Church St.) is an impressive sight, as are the spectacular views from its base of the nearby Elizabeth Islands and of Martha's Vineyard, across Vineyard Sound. The 42-ft cast-iron tower, lined with brick, was built in 1876 with a stationary light. It either shines red to indicate dangerous waters or white for safe passage. Since the light was automated in 1985, the adjacent keeper's quarters have been the headquarters of the Coast Guard group commander—a fitting passing of the torch from one safeguarder of ships to another. The lighthouse is not open to the public except during special tours.

Dining and Lodging

$$$ ✕ **The Dome.** An astonishing, somewhat ominous period piece, the Dome is a great half-sphere designed in 1953 by Buckminster Fuller himself. The canopied ceiling holds a large, flashy chandelier that truly defines the taste of the era. The dining room is a bit like a cruise-ship ballroom, and a band plays several nights a week in summer (☞ Nightlife and the Arts, *below*). The Dome menu is classic with few surprises: scallops Provençale, baked shrimp with a sherried lobster stuffing, and four styles of prime rib. The wine list is fine, and a board lists nightly specials. The Dome has been revived after a period of dormancy but still looks a little past its prime. Then again, maybe the '60s never die. ⊠ *539 Woods Hole Rd.,* ☎ *508/548–0800. AE, D, MC, V. Closed Mon.–Tues. and early Oct.–late-May. No lunch.*

$$–$$$ ✕ **Fish Monger's Café.** To say this is the best restaurant in Woods Hole
★   sounds like faint praise in the scheme of Cape restaurants, but the menu is ambitious—particularly the inventive daily specials that take a new look at traditional seafood. The fried calamari is light and perfectly fried and served with a hot pepper sauce, and the hearty *bruschetta* (broiled bread slices) with ricotta, fresh herbs, basil leaves, and olives is a treat. Many grilled seafood dishes come with tropical fruit sauces or glazes; mango and cilantro sauce over grilled salmon is particularly delectable. Vegetarians have lots of choices here, too. The main dining room overlooks the water, and there's a handsome wood bar. Breakfast and lunch are also served. ⊠ *56 Water St.,* ☎ *508/540–5376. Reservations not accepted. AE, MC, V. Closed mid-Dec.–mid-Feb. and Tues. Nov.–Mar.*

$$–$$$ ✕ **Shuckers.** Some of the harborside tables at this casual, nautical-theme restaurant are so close to the dock that you almost feel like you're sitting in the bobbing sailboats. The menu wanders from jerk chicken to pasta primavera to lobster ravioli, but it's best to stick with the grilled fish and other simple seafood dishes. The "world-famous" lobster boil—a boiled lobster, steamed clams and mussels, and an ear of corn—is justifiably popular. ⊠ *91-A Water St.,* ☎ *508/540–3850. AE, D, MC, V. Closed mid-Oct.–Apr.*

$$–$$$ 🏨 **The Marlborough.** This gem is somewhat hard to find, but look for the white fence and colonial-style black-and-white sign. A classic Cape house built in 1942, it has five rooms in the main house, each with pri-

vate bath and each named for its predominant color. Whether you choose the Green Room or its Yellow, Rose, Blue, or Pink counterparts, expect to find the same basic touches: wicker or brass beds, lace curtains, hooked rugs, fresh flowers, and floral print bed-coverings and pillows. A small cottage is out back, next to the kidney-shape in-ground pool; it has redbrick floors, a queen-size bed, and a sitting room. ⊠ *320 Woods Hole Rd., 02543, ☎ 508/548–6218 or 800/320–2322, FAX 508/ 457–7519. 5 rooms, 1 cottage. Pool. No smoking. MC, V. BP.*

$$ 🏠 **Woods Hole Passage.** Here, a century-old carriage house and barn have been tastefully converted into a romantic showcase. The large rose-hued common room radiates comfort, with lace curtains, overstuffed furniture, and a yellow pine floor. There are five rooms, all with queen-size beds; one (the smallest) is in the main house, the others in the restored barn. In good weather you can have breakfast on the flagstone patio. The inn is near the Martha's Vineyard ferry stop, and owner Deb Pruitt sells ferry tickets at cost so you can avoid lines at the dock. Early risers can request "breakfast-in-a-bag" to take on the road. ⊠ *186 Woods Hole Rd., 02540, ☎ 508/548–9575 or 800/790–8976, FAX 508/540– 4771. 5 rooms. Air-conditioning, croquet, horseshoes, bicycles. No smoking. AE, D, DC, MC, V. BP.* 🐾

Nightlife and the Arts

THE ARTS

The **Cape Cod Theatre Project** (☎ 508/457–4242; ☞ Falmouth, *above*) helps develop new American plays through a series of three or four staged readings each summer. Performances are held in the Woods Hole Community Hall (⊠ Water St., Woods Hole) or at Falmouth Academy (⊠ 7 Highfield Dr., off Depot Ave., Falmouth).

The **Woods Hole Folk Music Society** (⊠ Community Hall, Water St., ☎ 508/540–0320) presents professional and local folk and blues in a no-smoking, no-alcohol environment, with refreshments available during intermission. There are concerts of nationally known performers the first and third Sundays of the month from October to April, as well as on the first Sunday of May.

Woods Hole Theater Company (⊠ Community Hall, Water St., ☎ 508/ 540–6525), the community's resident theater group since 1974, presents several productions each year, generally between late spring and early fall.

NIGHTLIFE

The **Dome** (⊠ 539 Woods Hole Rd., ☎ 508/548–0800) has easy-listening piano on Friday and Saturday in season in its lounge, under an authentic Bucky Fuller geodesic dome.

Shopping

Handworks (⊠ 68 Water St.,, ☎ 508/540–5291), tucked in the back of the Community Hall building next to the drawbridge, is a cooperative arts and crafts gallery showcasing the work of local artists.

East Falmouth and Waquoit

5 mi northeast of Woods Hole.

These bucolic villages (well, bucolic once you leave Route 28 and its strip malls) have much to offer to nature lovers. With narrow fingers of land poking out toward Nantucket Sound, the water is never far away—it's not the crashing surf of the open ocean here, but quiet inlets and marshy bays. The residential neighborhoods here, with both seasonal and year-round homes, often end in dirt lanes that lead to the water. The nicest beach in these towns, Menauhant Beach (☞ Outdoor Activities and Sports, *below*) sits on a thin sliver of land with the sound on one side and a grass-lined cove on the other. Inland, the land is more rural, with a number of farms (and farm stands) still operating.

Note that as you head east from Falmouth center on Route 28, the street signs change names as you travel through different areas. The road is Main Street until you pass Falmouth Heights Rd., when Route 28 becomes Davis Straits. Farther east it becomes Teaticket Highway, then East Falmouth Highway, and then Waquoit Highway.

❼ Overseen by the Massachusetts Audubon Society, **Ashumet Holly and Wildlife Sanctuary** is true to its name and its original plantsman, Wilfred Wheeler, with its 1,000-plus holly trees and shrubs composed of 65 American, Asian, and European varieties. Like Heritage Plantation in Sandwich, this 45-acre tract of woodland, shady groves, meadows, and hiking trails was purchased and donated by Josiah K. Lilly III to preserve local land. Grassy Pond is home to numerous turtles and frogs, and in summer 35 nesting pairs of barn swallows live in the open rafters of the barn. Tours to nearby Cuttyhunk Island (on a 50-ft sailing vessel) leave Falmouth Harbor every Sunday from mid-July to mid-October. Maps for self-guided tours are available. ⊠ *286 Ashumet Rd., East Falmouth,* ☎ *508/362–1426.* 🖃 *$3.* ☉ *Trails daily sunrise–sunset.*

☼ **Waquoit Bay National Estuarine Research Reserve** encompasses 2,500 acres of estuary and barrier beach around the bay, making it a good birding site. **South Cape Beach** is part of the reserve; you can lie out on the sand or join one of the interpretive walks. **Flat Pond Trail** runs through a variety of habitats, including fresh- and saltwater marshes. **Washburn Island** is accessible by boat (your own) or by Saturday-morning tours (call to reserve); it offers 330 acres of pine barrens and trails, swimming, and 11 wilderness campsites (permit required; ☎ 877/422–6762). At the **reserve headquarters,** a 23-acre estate, an exhibit center that opened in 1999 includes displays about the bay's plants and animals, the Cape Cod watershed, and local Wampanoag culture. An interactive exhibit, outside on the lawn, allows you to trace the path of a raindrop; pick up a ball (the pseudo-raindrop) and follow its journey from cloud to land to river and on through the water cycle. In July and August the center schedules various daily nature programs for children and families. A Tuesday-evening series is held midsummer (bring picnics) on environmental, historical, and artistic subjects; call for program updates. ⊠ *Rte. 28, 3 mi west of Mashpee rotary, Waquoit,* ☎ *508/457–0495.* ☉ *Exhibit center: mid-June–Labor Day, Mon.– Sat. 10–4; Labor Day–mid-June, weekdays 10–4.*

Tony Andrews Farm and Produce Stand has pick-your-own strawberries (June), peas and beans (June–July), herbs (July–August), and tomatoes (August), as well as other produce on the stand. Hayrides are available in summer and fall, and there's a haunted house set up in October. You can pick your own pumpkins in fall and choose your Christmas tree in December. ⊠ *394 Old Meeting House Rd., East Falmouth,* ☎ *508/548–4717.* ☉ *June–Oct.; call for hrs. and for information about special events.*

Coonamessett Farm operates a farm store, where you can assemble your own gift baskets or purchase produce and specialty foods, as well as a small café serving soups, salads, baked goods, and beverages. You can tour the greenhouses and fields, learn about hydroponic growing systems, and examine a crayfish-culture research project. Members of the farm's Pick-Your-Own club ($15-per-year membership) can pick strawberries, lettuces, herbs, rhubarb, and other fruits and vegetables. The farm also rents canoes for use on the adjacent Coonamessett Pond. ⊠ *277 Hatchville Rd., East Falmouth,* ☎ *508/563–2560.* ☉ *Call for seasonal hrs.*

Rows and rows of grapevines, 8,000 in all, line the fields of the **Cape Cod Winery.** Kristina and Antonio Lazzari established their winery in 1994. They now produce five wines, and in 1998 their Nobska red won a bronze medal at the International Eastern Wine Competition. ☒ *681 Sandwich Rd., East Falmouth,* ☎ *508/457–5592.* ☽ *July–Aug., tastings Wed.–Sun. noon–5, tours weekends at 2; Memorial Day–June and Sept.–Thanksgiving, tastings weekends noon–4.*

Dining and Lodging

$ ✕ **McGann's of Falmouth Pub and Restaurant.** A discovery to everyone but the local crowd, McGann's calls itself "a touch of Ireland on Cape Cod." The McGann family should know because they also have a pub in the town of Doolin, County Galway, Ireland. The place does have the slightly frayed grit of a true Irish country tavern, with its worn floorboards and dusty ceramic poteen jugs lined up on a high, gloomy shelf. McGann's offers typical bar food, but with an Irish twist: Irish-style fish-and-chips; Gaelic chicken in an Irish whiskey and bacon sauce; garlic mussels over pasta; and a genuine full Irish breakfast with eggs, sausage, and blood pudding, served all day long. Though Guinness reigns, the bar claims 200 beers on draft. There's music every night but Tuesday, and Wednesday is karaoke night. The air-conditioning is like the Irish Arctic. ☒ *734 Teaticket Hwy. (Rte. 28), East Falmouth,* ☎ *508/540–6656. Reservations not accepted. AE, D, MC, V.*

$ ✕ **Moonakis Café.** This cheery café, on Route 28 between Falmouth and Mashpee, gets high marks for its popular breakfast. You'll find all the standards and then some—eggs, pancakes, fruit salad—all nicely done. The chunky hash browns are fried with just the right amount of onions, and if the omelet with roasted tomatoes, olives, and goat cheese is on the menu, it's an excellent choice. Also recommended (if you're not on a diet) are the decadent Belgian waffles buried under strawberries, bananas, and whipped cream. ☒ *460 Waquoit Hwy. (Rte. 28), Waquoit,* ☎ *508/457–9630. No credit cards. No dinner.*

$$ ▥ **Green Harbor Waterfront Lodging.** Although the modest motel rooms here are clean and adequate, it's the friendly, summer camp–like setting that makes the Green Harbor great for families. There are old-fashioned lawn swings, a swimming pool (plus a good-size kiddie pool), umbrella-topped picnic tables, barbecue grills, and the main attraction—the waterfront. It's not the open ocean here, but a peaceful tree-lined inlet, with rowboats and pedal boats for guests' use. Some of the no-frills rooms in the 1960s-vintage motel have microwaves and small refrigerators; others have kitchenettes. ☒ *134 Acapesket Rd., East Falmouth, 02536,* ☎ *508/548–4747 or 800/548–5556. 36 rooms, 1 cottage. Picnic area, kitchenettes, pool, wading pool, volleyball, boating, coin laundry. No smoking. AE, D, DC, MC, V. Closed Nov.–Apr.* ☙

$–$$ ▥ **Cape Wind.** If you're traveling with children who need space to run, the Cape Wind is a good choice. All the rooms in this gray-shingle motel face a broad green lawn that slopes down to the bay. The grass is dotted with lawn chairs and picnic tables, as well as a pool. Rowboats and pedal boats are available, too, if you want to take to the water. The rooms are decidedly basic, with standard motel furnishings and more hand-me-down pieces; some have been updated more recently than others—so ask before you reserve. All have microwaves, refrigerators, and coffeemakers, while some have kitchenettes. The spacious one-bedroom apartment has a pretty private terrace, but its half-basement location makes the interior rather dark. Early spring and late fall rates here are an excellent value—as low as $40 a night midweek. ☒ *34 Maravista Extension, Teaticket (East Falmouth) 02536,* ☎ *508/548–3400 or 800/267–3401,* FAX *508/495–0316. 31 rooms, 1 apartment. No smoking rooms, kitchenettes, pool, boating. D, MC, V. Closed Dec.–Feb.* ☙

Outdoor Activities and Sports
BEACHES
Menauhant Beach, on Menauhant Road in East Falmouth, is a long, narrow stretch of sand, with a pond behind, in a quiet residential neighborhood. Its slightly more secluded location means it can be a bit less crowded than the beaches near Falmouth center. The beach has lifeguards, rest rooms, outdoor showers, and a small snack bar. Public parking is available; in season the fee is $8 per day on weekdays, $10 on weekends.

Mashpee

❽ *7 mi east of East Falmouth, 10 mi south of Sandwich.*

Mashpee is one of two Massachusetts towns (the other is Aquinnah, formerly known as Gay Head, on Martha's Vineyard) that have both municipally governed and Native American–governed areas. In 1660 the missionary Reverend Richard Bourne gave a 16-square-mi parcel of land to the Wampanoags (what irony—an outsider "giving" Native people their own land). Known as the Mashpee Plantation and governed by two local sachems, it was the first Native American reservation in the United States. In 1870 Mashpee was founded as a town. In 1974 the Mashpee Wampanoag Tribal Council was formed to continue its government with a chief, a supreme sachem, a medicine man, and clan mothers. More than 600 residents are descended from the original Wampanoags, and some continue to observe their ancient traditions.

More recently, several resort-residential communities have developed in the Mashpee area; the largest, New Seabury, is a full-fledged resort with apartment units available to visitors (☞ Lodging, *below*). Mashpee, with its villagelike Mashpee Commons mall, has also become a popular shopping destination. Yet away from the stores, Mashpee retains a more rural character, with wooded roads, inland ponds, and reminders of the area's original settlers.

Housed in a 1793 half-Cape, the **Wampanoag Indian Museum** is a small museum on the history and culture of the tribe. Exhibits include baskets, weapons, hunting and fishing tools, clothing, arrowheads, and a small diorama depicting a scene from an early settlement. If you're curious, don't hesitate to ask questions of the Wampanoag staff. There is also a herring run on site, a small tidal stream that runs from the ocean into a pond. In spring, thick schools of herring swim to the calm safety of the pond to spawn. The tribe noticed this cycle and would net great numbers of herring as the fish made their way back to the sea. At press time the museum was renovating but expected to be fully operational by early 2001. ⊠ *416 Rte. 130, near Great Neck Rd. N,* ☎ *508/477–1536.* 🎟 *Donations accepted.* ◷ *Call for hrs.*

The **Old Indian Meeting House** was originally built on Santuit Pond in 1684 and was later moved to its present site on Route 28. The oldest standing church on Cape Cod, the meeting house is still used by the Mashpee tribe for worship and meetings. In summer, memorials and religious events are held, some incorporating traditional Wampanoag practices. At press time the hours for 2001 were not yet confirmed; call before visiting. ⊠ *Meeting House Rd. off Rte. 28,* ☎ *508/477–0208.* ◷ *Jun.–Sept., Wed. and Fri. 10–2 (call to confirm before visiting), and by appointment.*

The **Old Indian Burial Ground,** near the meeting house on Meeting House Road, is an 18th-century cemetery with interesting headstones typical of the period carved with scenes and symbols and inscribed with witty sayings.

☺ In a cavernous former church building, the **Cape Cod Children's Museum** welcomes children with interactive play, science exhibits, a 30-ft pirate play ship, a portable planetarium, and other playtime activities. The museum is best suited for preschoolers and children in the early elementary grades. ✉ *577 Great Neck Rd. S,* ☎ *508/539–8788.* ✉ *$3.50.* ☺ *Mon.–Sat. 10–5, Sun. noon–5.*

A perfect place for bird-watching, fishing, or canoeing, the **Mashpee River Woodlands** comprises 391 acres of conservation land along the Mashpee River. More than 8 mi of trails meander through the marshlands and pine forests. Park on Quinaquisset Avenue, River Road, or Mashpee Neck Road (where there's a public landing for canoe access). Trail maps are available at the Mashpee Chamber of Commerce (☞ Visitor Information *in* The Upper Cape A to Z, *below*). The trails are open daily, dawn to dusk.

Golfers, take note: the resort-residential community of **New Seabury** (☞ Lodging, *below*), a division of Mashpee, has one of the best golf courses on the Cape.

Dining and Lodging

$$$ ✕ **Popponesset Inn.** You'll see a wedding or two at the Popponesset Inn every weekend in summer, and for good reason. The food may not be exceptional—traditional offerings include baked stuffed lobster, grilled swordfish, and steak—but the atmosphere is. The site is a gem, with old Cape Cod saltbox houses, lovely Nantucket Sound in the background, and perfect evening light. The restaurant has a lounge, Poppy's, and a number of small dining rooms, some with skylights and others looking over the water through glass walls. Best of all is to sit outside, either under the tent or at one of the umbrella tables. There's dancing to a band on some weekends. The Popponesset is in the New Seabury Resort (☞ *below*). ✉ *Shore Dr.,* ☎ *508/477–1100. AE, DC, MC, V. Closed late-Nov.–Mar. and Mon.–Tues. Labor Day–Apr. No lunch.*

$$–$$$ ✕ **Contrast at the Commons.** Sister to a similarly named restaurant in Dennis, Contrast is a warm, sophisticated place in which to eat excellent food and study the unique and carefully executed decor. The theme of contrast is highlighted by color-block walls, hand-painted tables, and modern sculpture that give a sense of sleek urban style. In addition to the fine dinner menu, you'll find innovative bistro fare and fancy sandwiches. Try the individual grilled pizzas served on a very thin, crisp Middle Eastern *lavash* crust; on the shrimp version you can actually see and taste good-size shrimp. Everything is available for takeout, too. ✉ *Market St., Mashpee Commons,* ☎ *508/477–1299. Reservations not accepted. AE, MC, V.*

$$–$$$ ✕ **Gone Tomatoes.** This bustling contemporary Italian grill is festive enough for a night out but still casual enough for a family dinner. The upstairs dining room, with its white tablecloths and candles, is best for a quieter evening; if you've brought the gang, sit in the lively room downstairs near the bar. The food takes its influences from several Italian regions, and the portions are hearty—the Tuscan sirloin almost hangs off the plate, while the pastas and grilled pizzas will sate those sun-and-surf-fueled appetites. The tasty Mediterranean shrimp pasta, with black olives, sun-dried tomatoes, and capers tossed over penne, is a fine choice for seafood lovers who've had enough of the fry-o-later. ✉ *11 Steeple St., Mashpee Commons,* ☎ *508/477–8100. MC, V.*

$$ ✕ **The Flume.** The Cape belonged to the Wampanoags for centuries
★ before the Pilgrims arrived, and the Flume, owned for more than 25 years by Wampanoag elder (and author) Earl Mills, pairs great food with reminders of that cultural tradition; Native American artifacts decorate the dining room. The food concentrates on a few New England

staples, and the chowder is considered to be among the best on the Cape. Traditional codfish cakes and beans, Yankee pot roast, soft-shell crabs in season, and Indian pudding are done to perfection. The Sunday roast turkey is a genuine treat, as are Aunt Jan's desserts. If you have any questions about Mashpee's remarkable Wampanoag history, Earl will happily provide the answers. ⊠ *Lake Ave. off Rte. 130,* ☎ *508/477–1456. MC, V. Closed Thanksgiving–Easter. No lunch.*

$-$$ ✕ **Marketplace Raw Bar.** At this funky little seafood joint tucked away in Popponesset Marketplace (☞ *below*), you can pull up a bar stool and chow down on littlenecks, cherrystones, oysters, steamers, and peel-your-own shrimp, all washed down with a local brew or a rum punch. Although there are a few picnic tables out back, the casual atmosphere here is more "bar" than "seafood shack." There's live music some nights, too. ⊠ *Popponesset Marketplace, New Seabury,* ☎ *508/539–4858. AE, MC, V. Closed late-Oct.–mid-May.*

$$$$ ✕🏨 **New Seabury Resort and Conference Center.** On a 2,000-acre point
★ surrounded by the waters of Nantucket Sound, this self-contained resort community rents apartments in some of its 13 "villages." For example, Maushop Village is a gray-shingle oceanfront complex of buildings set among narrow lanes of crushed seashells, with rugosa roses trailing over white picket fences and trellises; the interiors attractively mix Cape-style and modern furnishings. Town-house units in Sea Quarters have solariums with whirlpool baths and gas-log fireplaces. All units have full kitchens and washer-dryers. Among the amenities (many of them seasonal) are fine oceanfront dining, a lounge and restaurant overlooking the fairways, a vast tennis facility, a 3-mi private beach and an oceanfront pool, miles of jogging trails through the woods, and Popponesset Marketplace (☞ Shopping, *below*). Golf and other packages are available. ⊠ *Off Great Neck Rd. S, Box 549, New Seabury 02649,* ☎ *508/477–9400 or 800/999–9033,* 🖷 *508/477–9790. 140 1- or 2-bedroom units. 2 restaurants, 2 pools, 2 18-hole golf courses, 16 tennis courts, health club, jogging, beach, boating, bicycles, shops. AE, DC, MC, V.*

Nightlife and the Arts

Bobby Byrne's Pub (⊠ Mashpee Commons, Rtes. 28 and 151, ☎ 508/477–0600), now past the quarter-century mark, offers a comfortable pub atmosphere, an outdoor café, a jukebox, and good light and full menus.

The **Boch Center for the Performing Arts** (☎ 508/477–2580) presents top-name performers year-round and is home to the Annual New England Jazz Festival, held in late August. Plans are under way to construct a complex of buildings, including an amphitheater to accommodate 2,000 people, on an idyllic 10-acre tract of countryside in Mashpee. Until the complex is completed, performances are held at Mashpee Commons (☞ Shopping, *below*) or in the auditoriums of local high schools.

The 90-member **Cape Symphony Orchestra** (☎ 508/362–1111) comes to Mashpee in July for its annual Sounds of Summer Pops Concert (it also performs an August concert in Orleans). The performance takes place at the Mashpee Commons (☞ Shopping, *below*).

Outdoor Activities and Sports

BEACHES

Attaquin Park Beach (⊠ End of Lake Ave. off Rte. 130, near Great Neck Rd. N) is a pretty, sandy place, with a spectacular view of the interconnecting **Mashpee and Wakeby ponds**, the Cape's largest freshwater expanses. It's popular for swimming, fishing, and boating, but resident parking stickers are required in season.

South Cape Beach in Mashpee is a 2½-mi-long state and town beach on warm Nantucket and Vineyard sounds, accessible via Great Neck Road south from the Mashpee rotary. Wide, sandy, and pebbly in parts, with low dunes and marshland, it's a beach where you can walk to get a bit of privacy. Its only services are portable toilets, although there are lifeguards in season. A hiking trail loops through marsh areas and ponds, linking it to the Waquoit Bay National Estuarine Research Reserve (☞ East Falmouth and Waquoit, *above*). A $2 parking fee is charged in summer.

GOLF

New Seabury Country Club (⊠ Shore Dr., New Seabury, ☎ 508/477–9111) has a superior 18-hole, par-72 championship layout on the water as well as an 18-hole, par-70 course. Both are open to the public September–May, depending on availability; reservations four days in advance are recommended, and proper attire is required.

HIKING AND WALKING

The **Lowell Holly Reservation** (⊠ S. Sandwich Rd. off Rte. 130, ☎ 781/821–2977), administered by the Trustees of Reservations, has 4 mi of walking trails amid American beeches, hollies, white pines, and rhododendrons on a peninsula between Mashpee and Wakeby ponds. The reservation has picnic tables and a little swimming beach. There's a small free parking area open year-round and an additional parking lot open from Memorial Day to Labor Day ($6).

In summer, free **naturalist-led guided walks** of Mashpee's woods and conservation areas are frequently offered. Family nature walks, animal scavenger hunts, and "pond scoops" to explore aquatic life are among the choices for and their parents; sunrise walks on South Cape Beach and natural history tours of the Lowell Holly Reservation are also on the program. Call the **Mashpee Conservation Commission** (☎ 508/539–1400, ext. 540) for schedules.

Shopping

Mashpee Commons (⊠ Junction of Rtes. 28 and 151, ☎ 508/477–5400) has about 80 stores, including restaurants, art galleries, and a mix of local boutiques and national chains, in an attractive village square setting. There's also a multiscreen movie theater, and free outdoor entertainment in summer. Some of the more unique shops include: **M. Brann & Co.** (☎ 508/477–0299), a creative home-and-gift shop that carries everything from funky refrigerator magnets and unusual candlesticks to hand-crafted glassware, one-of-a-kind lamps, mirrors, and furniture, with many of the works by New England artists; **Signature Gallery** (☎ 508/539–0029), a high-end crafts gallery and store (with branches in Boston and in Westport, Connecticut) that stocks contemporary crafts, including textiles, ceramics, prints, and glass; and **Cape Cod Toys** (☎ 508/477–2221), crammed full of anything the children might possibly need (and then some!)—beach toys, board games, science projects, and more.

Popponesset Marketplace (⊠ Off Great Neck Rd. S, 2½ mi south of Rte. 28 from Mashpee rotary, New Seabury, ☎ 508/477–9111), open from late spring to early fall, has 20 shops (boutique clothing, antiques), eating places (a raw bar [☞ *above*], pizza, ribs, Ben & Jerry's), miniature golf, and weekend entertainment (bands, fashion or puppet shows, sing-alongs).

THE UPPER CAPE A TO Z

Arriving and Departing

By Bus

Bonanza Bus Lines (☎ 508/548–7588 or 800/556–3815) offers direct service to Bourne, Falmouth, and the Woods Hole steamship terminal from Boston's Logan Airport, downtown Boston, Providence, Rhode Island, Fall River, and New Bedford, as well as connecting service from New York, Connecticut, and Providence's T. F. Green Airport. Some of the buses from Boston also make stops in Wareham and Buzzards Bay.

Plymouth & Brockton Street Railway (☎ 508/746–0378) provides bus service to Provincetown from downtown Boston and Logan Airport, with stops en route. The Logan Direct airport express service bypasses downtown Boston and stops in Plymouth, Sagamore, Barnstable, and Hyannis.

By Ferry

Year-round ferries to Martha's Vineyard leave from Woods Hole. Seasonal Vineyard ferries leave from Falmouth. For details *see* Ferries *in* Smart Travel Tips.

By Car

If your destination is Sagamore, Sandwich, or points east along Cape Cod Bay, cross the Sagamore Bridge to reach U.S. 6 or Route 6A. If you're headed for Bourne, Falmouth, Woods Hole, or Mashpee, take the Bourne Bridge instead and pick up Route 28 south. To reach East Falmouth or Mashpee, get off Route 28 at either Route 151 or Brick Kiln Road to bypass Falmouth center—both rejoin Route 28 east of Falmouth.

By Plane

Barnstable Municipal Airport (✉ 480 Barnstable Rd., Rte. 28 rotary, Hyannis, ☎ 508/775–2020) is the main air gateway on the Cape.

Getting Around

By Bus

For general information on Cape buses, *see* Bus Travel *in* Smart Travel Tips.

Bonanza (☎ 508/548–7588 or 800/556–3815) runs between Bourne, Falmouth, and Woods Hole year-round.

By Car

If you're not in a hurry, get off the main highways and seek out the Upper Cape's more scenic byways. Route 6A heading east from Sandwich is a heavily traveled but still scenic route that parallels Cape Cod Bay all the way to Orleans. Watch for cars turning suddenly, though, as there are shops and side roads along many stretches of 6A. Heading from the Bourne Bridge toward Falmouth, County Road and Route 28A are prettier alternatives to Route 28, and Sippewisset Road meanders near Buzzards Bay between West Falmouth and Woods Hole. Just remember that some of these roads travel through residential areas, so keep your speed down.

By Taxi

Call **All Village Taxi** (✉ Falmouth, ☎ 508/540–7200).

By Trolley

The **Cape Cod Regional Transit Authority** (☏ 508/385–8326; 800/352–7155 in MA) runs seasonal trolleys in Falmouth, Mashpee, Hyannis, Yarmouth, and Dennis. Fares and times vary; call for more information.

Contacts and Resources

Children's Activities

Libraries usually offer regular children's story hours or other programs; check them out on a rainy day. Hours are listed in the newspapers each week.

The **Cape Cod Baseball League** (☏ 508/432–6909) offers summer day camps and clinics, run by the individual teams, for children ages 5–13; most teams run six weeks of camp, typically weekday mornings.

Emergencies

Ambulance, fire, police (☏ 911).

For rescues at sea call the **Coast Guard** (☏ 508/548–5151 in Woods Hole; ☏ 508/888–0335 in Sandwich and Cape Cod Canal). Boaters should use Channel 16 on their radios.

Massachusetts Poison Control Center (☏ 800/682–9211).

HOSPITALS

Falmouth Hospital (✉ 100 Ter Heun Dr., Falmouth, ☏ 508/548–5300) has a 24-hour emergency room.

LATE-NIGHT PHARMACIES

In summer **CVS** (✉ 105 Davis Straits, Falmouth, 508/540–4307) closes at midnight on weekdays, 10 PM on weekends.

WALK-IN CLINICS

Falmouth Walk-In Medical Center (✉ 309 Main St., Rte. 28, Teaticket, ☏ 508/540–6790).

Mashpee Family Medicine (✉ 800 Falmouth Rd., Mashpee, ☏ 508/477–4282).

Guided Tours

CRUISES

Patriot Boats offers two-hour day and sunset cruises from Falmouth Harbor on the 68-ft schooner *Liberté*. Another nightly sunset cruise passes six lighthouses in the Falmouth area. Also available is an afternoon excursion to Cuttyhunk Island, with a guided walk around the island; this trip runs weekdays in summer from noon to 5. Rates vary; call for details. ✉ *227 Clinton Ave., Falmouth,* ☏ *508/548–2626; 800/734–0088 in MA.*

House Rentals

Donahue Real Estate (✉ 850 Main St., Falmouth 02540, ☏ 508/548–5412, ℻ 508/548–5418, ✎) lists both apartments and houses in the Falmouth area.

Real Estate Associates (✉ Rtes. 151 and 28A, Box 738, North Falmouth 02556, ☏ 508/563–7173, ℻ 508/563–6943, ✎) lists properties ranging from beach cottages to waterfront estates, although the focus is on more expensive houses. It covers Falmouth, Bourne, and Mashpee, on the Upper Cape.

Outdoor Activities and Sports

BASEBALL

The **Cape Cod Baseball League** (☎ 508/432–6909, ✎), considered the country's best summer league, is scouted by all the major-league teams. Ten teams play a 44-game season from mid-June to mid-August; admission is free to games at all 10 fields, although donations are accepted.

BIKING

The Travel Center at the American Youth Hostels' Boston office (✉ 1105 Commonwealth Ave., Boston 02215, ☎ 617/779–0900) sells a "Cape Ann & North Shore/Cape Cod & Islands" bike map that includes information on the **Claire Saltonstall Bikeway** between Boston and Provincetown (135 mi) or between Boston and Woods Hole (85 mi). Brochures about the bikeway may also be available from the Cape Cod Chamber of Commerce.

CANOEING AND KAYAKING

Cape Cod Coastal Canoe & Kayak (✉ 36 Spectacle Pond Dr., East Falmouth 02536, ☎ 508/564–4051; 888/226–6393 in MA, ✎) runs daily paddling tours of tidal rivers, salt marshes, and coastal ponds as far north as Eastham from April through October. The company provides all equipment (including canoes and solo or tandem kayaks) and a naturalist guide for tours that average 3–3½ hours. Call for a schedule of trips, which depart from sites across the Cape. Tours are $30 per kayak (for solo boats), $50 per boat for canoes and tandem kayaks; children accompanying two adults in a canoe ride free. Trips are rated by difficulty, but you should be realistic about what you or your family can manage.

RUNNING

To run in the world-class **Falmouth Road Race** (✉ Box 732, Falmouth, 02541, ☎ 508/540–7000), in mid-August, send a stamped, self-addressed envelope to request an entry form; the race typically closes to entrants in early spring.

Visitor Information

The **Cape Cod Chamber of Commerce** (✉ Junction of U.S. 6 and 132, Hyannis, ☎ 508/862–0700 or 888/332–2732, ✎) is open year-round, Monday–Saturday 9–5 and Sunday 10–4. There's also a year-round visitor information center (☎ 508/759–3814) on Route 25, in a rest area about 3 mi west of the Bourne Bridge; it's open daily 9–5. From Memorial Day to Columbus Day there are extended hours: daily 8 AM–10 PM.

LOCAL CHAMBERS OF COMMERCE

Cape Cod Canal Region, for Sandwich and Bourne and Wareham (✉ 70 Main St., Buzzards Bay 02532, ☎ 508/759–6000, ✎); information centers at Sagamore rotary, at train depot in Buzzards Bay, and on Rte. 130 in Sandwich).

Falmouth (✉ 20 Academy La., Box 582, 02541, ☎ 508/548–8500 or 800/526–8532, ✎).

Mashpee (✉ N. Market St., Mashpee Commons [Rte. 151], 02649, ☎ 508/477–0792 or 800/423–6274, ✎).

4   THE MID CAPE

Band concerts on village greens, peaceful
beaches, and busy strips with saltwater
taffy shacks and T-shirt shops make the Mid
Cape a sort of New England Midwest.
Staid Barnstable Village, with its 300-year-
old homes, is just minutes from Hyannis,
the center of commerce for all Cape Cod.
Languid Yarmouth Port vies for attention with
motel-stacked South and West Yarmouth,
and the pristine ponds and beaches of
Dennis are colorfully adorned with umbrellas
from South Dennis minimalls.

Revised by
Karl Luntta

M ORE A COLLOQUIALISM than a proper name, the designation *Mid Cape* refers to central Cape Cod, the most heavily populated—and touristed—part of the peninsula. To the north lies calm Cape Cod Bay, lined with wide beaches, inlets, creeks, and marshes. The tides on the bay are dramatic; at dead low some beaches double in size as the tidal flats stretch out for hundreds, even thousands, of feet.

The main thoroughfare through the north side of the Mid Cape is Route 6A, a scenic section that dates from 1684, making it one of the first major roads constructed on Cape Cod. Alternately called Old King's Highway, Main Street, and Hallet Street, the road winds through the villages of West Barnstable, Barnstable, Cummaquid, Yarmouth Port, and Dennis, with short side trips to north-side harbors and beaches. More residential than commercial, Route 6A is lined with antique captains' mansions and farmhouses that now serve as year-round private homes, bed-and-breakfasts, art galleries, restaurants, and antiques shops.

On the south side of the Mid Cape, the crowd pleaser is Nantucket Sound and its miles of long beaches. The main thoroughfare here, from Centerville to Osterville, through Hyannis and on to West Yarmouth, South Yarmouth, and Dennisport, is the busy—in every sense of the word—Route 28. This stretch, particularly between West Yarmouth and Dennisport, is the original vacationland of Cape Cod, a honky-tonk paradise filled with strip motels, clam shacks, miniature golf courses, ice cream parlors, and tacky T-shirt outlets. It's sort of a Cape Cod Disneyland, the archetype seaside vacation area that saw its boom time in the 1960s and hasn't changed much since.

Between routes 6A and 28 is the "mid" of the Mid Cape, a mostly residential area with some historic sections and a few quiet, freshwater ponds. Included here are the commercial sections of Hyannis, as well as tony Osterville and Hyannis Port, a well-groomed enclave and site of the Kennedy compound.

Pleasures and Pastimes

Beaches
Beach lovers will find numerous Shangri-Las throughout the Mid Cape. Sandy Neck, a peninsular strip of land that stretches across the north side of Barnstable Harbor, is one of the top 10 of Cape Cod, perfect for those who like (mostly) gentle surf and long shoreline walks. Also on the north side of the Mid Cape, Dennis's Corporation Beach and Mayflower Beach are great places for children, with wide tidal flats, snack huts, and rest rooms. Barnstable's south-side beaches, on Nantucket Sound, include the busy Craigville Beach, popular with college students on break, and Kalmus Park Beach, in Hyannis, with a windy surf that attracts world-class wind-boarders. Yarmouth's best beaches lie along its Nantucket Sound side and include Seagull Beach and Smugglers Beach.

In and among Mid Cape towns are a number of freshwater kettle ponds, created by receding glaciers eons ago. Pond beaches are usually not as crowded as ocean beaches and have plenty of appeal for those who like cooling off in gentle water without the salt and sand. In Yarmouth Port, Dennis Pond attracts families to its shallow swimming area. Dennis's Scargo Lake has two public beaches, and Hathaway's Pond in Barnstable has a nice beach and rest rooms.

Biking

Bike enthusiasts are well placed on the Mid Cape: the scenic 25-mi Cape Cod Rail Trail begins in South Dennis, following the paved right-of-way of the old Penn Central Railroad, South Wellfleet (☞ Close-Up: Riding the Rail Trail, *below*).

Dining

The Mid Cape is chock-full of eateries, ranging from sedate, high-end haute cuisine houses such as Barnstable's Paddock, the Regatta of Cotuit, and Dennis's Red Pheasant to family places such as Barbyann's in Hyannis, or Jack's Outback in Yarmouth Port. Expect good fun and great eats at the area's dozens of clam shacks and other supercasual restaurants along Route 28 in Yarmouth and Dennis. If you simply want lots of choices, head to Barnstable and its villages, particularly Hyannis, where a stroll down Main Street will bring you to a dozen fine restaurants ranging from lunch joints to Thai, Italian, Cajun, and upscale American dining establishments.

For price ranges *see* Dining *in* Smart Travel Tips A to Z.

Lodging

On the northern (bay) side, Route 6A from Barnstable to Dennis has dozens of B&Bs, many in the elegant former homes of sea captains. In contrast, Route 28 on the south side has row after row of lodgings, from tacky roadside motels to medium-range family hotels, with larger seaside resorts along the side roads on Nantucket Sound. Main Street, Hyannis, is lined with motels, while several inns and B&Bs perch on side streets leading to Hyannis Harbor and Lewis Bay.

For price ranges *see* Lodging *in* Smart Travel Tips A to Z.

Nightlife and the Arts

Since you'll pass an art gallery almost every minute on the drive along Route 6A between Barnstable and Dennis, you should stop in at some of these places, such as Barnstable's Tao Water Art Gallery, which features art from China, and Cummaquid Fine Arts, for original contemporary art that's a decided improvement over the ubiquitous paintings of rowboats on beaches. Other gallery centers are on Main Street in Hyannis and on Main Street in Osterville.

As for summertime entertainment, the Mid Cape is ground zero. The Cape Cod Melody Tent, in Hyannis, features music, comedy, and even boxing matches, with internationally well-known performers ranging from Bill Cosby and George Carlin to singers Jimmy Cliff and Lyle Lovett. The Melody Tent—which really is a tent, albeit a large and comfortable one with a revolving stage—also produces children's matinee theater, with regular summer shows such as *Sleeping Beauty* and *The Frog Prince*. Your theater need can also be sated at the Cape Playhouse in Dennis, one of the country's oldest summer repertory theaters. Big stars who have come this way in the past include Henry Fonda and Jane Fonda; Jerry Stiller and Anne Meara are more recent attendees. The Cape Playhouse also offers children's theater during the season. The Barnstable Comedy Club on Route 6A in Barnstable Village presents drama, sketches, and, yes, comedic works throughout the summer.

Nightlife is abundant in the Mid Cape, from bistros and bars that offer regular entertainment—think Hyannis's Roadhouse Café for jazz or West Yarmouth's Molly's Restaurant and Pub for weekend bands—to such dance clubs as Pufferbellies in Hyannis, specializing in country line dancing. Special events such as the Boston Pops Esplanade Orchestra's Pops by the Sea concert, held on the Hyannis Village Green in August, are listed in local newspapers weekly.

Check out listings in the *Barnstable Patriot* and the Tuesday and Friday editions of the *Cape Codder,* as well as the pullout section "Cape Week" in the Friday edition of the *Cape Cod Times.* Visitors can pick up any of these publications at local supermarkets and convenience stores.

Outdoor Activities and Sports

Numerous fishing and tour boats depart Hyannis Harbor, Barnstable Harbor, and Dennis's Sesuit Harbor for trips ranging from deep-sea fishing excursions to harbor fishing, a favorite with the children. Barnstable Harbor is also the launch point for Hyannis Whale Watcher Cruises, which operates from spring through early fall. Canoeing and sea kayaking are excellent around the bay's marshy inlets, and windsurfing is popular at Hyannis's Kalmus Park Beach. Dennis's Swan River is great for kayaking and canoeing, and the Bass River, a border separating Yarmouth and Dennis, has river sightseeing excursions on a small boat, as well as fishing and, if you've got the permit, clamming.

Conservation-land walking trails are found in Yarmouth and Dennis, including a Dennis trail set up for hikers with impaired vision.

Many road races are held in season, and the Cape Codder Triathlon (✉ Box 307, West Barnstable 02668) takes place at Craigville Beach in Centerville in early summer.

Shopping

Throughout the villages and towns of the Mid Cape, and particularly along Route 6A and the main streets of Hyannis, Centerville, Osterville, and Dennisport, are numerous boutiques, crafts shops, bookstores, antiques centers, candy shops (saltwater taffy, yes, but also exquisite chocolates and homemade fudge), and galleries. In general, look to the smaller towns and villages for specialty craft items such as Nantucket baskets, wicker furniture, and bird-watching esoterica. The Cape Cod Mall, between Routes 132 and 28 in Hyannis, has recently expanded and now features a range of clothing boutiques such as Ann Taylor Loft, the Gap, and Abercrombie and Fitch, as well as jewelry stores; specialty shops; and the anchor stores Macy's, Filene's, and Sears. Everyone is wild about Christmas Tree Shops, a local chain with stores in Yarmouth Port, West Yarmouth, West Dennis, and Hyannis that sells all sorts of amusing things at discount prices, including lava lamps, lanai furniture, candles, and cookies.

Exploring the Mid Cape

The Mid Cape includes the towns of Barnstable, Yarmouth, and Dennis, each divided into smaller townships and villages. The town of Barnstable, for example, consists of Barnstable Village, West Barnstable, Cotuit, Marstons Mills, Osterville, Centerville, and Hyannis, with the smaller quasi-villages (distinguished by their separate zip codes), of Craigville, Cummaquid, Hyannis Port, West Hyannis Port, and Wianno. Yarmouth contains Yarmouth Port, along on the north shore, and the mid and south villages of West Yarmouth and South Yarmouth. The town of Dennis's villages are easy to remember: Dennis, West Dennis, South Dennis, East Dennis, and Dennisport. Route 6A winds along the north shore through tree-shaded scenic towns and village centers, while Route 28 dips south through some of the more overdeveloped parts of the Cape. Generally speaking, if you want to avoid malls, heavy traffic, and tacky motels, stay away from Route 28 from Falmouth to Chatham.

Great Itineraries

Numbers in the text correspond to numbers in the margin and on the Mid Cape map.

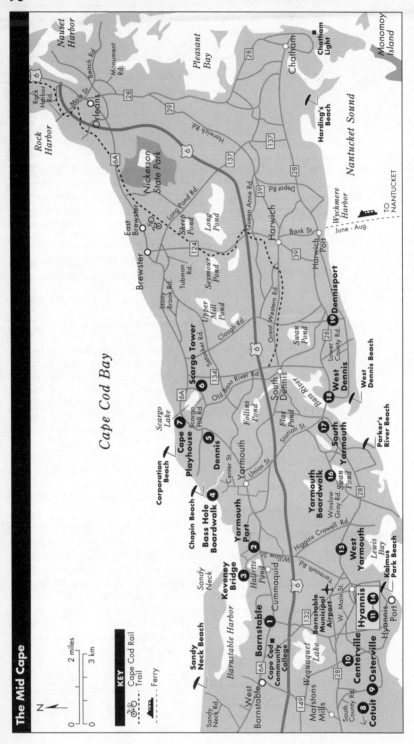

The Mid Cape

KEY

🚲🚲 Cape Cod Rail
- - - - Trail
⛴ Ferry

N

0 ——— 2 miles
0 ——— 3 km

Cape Cod Bay

Nantucket Sound

Monomoy Island

TO NANTUCKET
June - Aug.

Nauset Harbor

Pleasant Bay

Chatham Light

Chatham

Harding's Beach

Wychmere Harbor

Rock Harbor

Orleans

Nickerson State Park

Brewster

East Brewster

Harwich

Harwich Port

19 Dennisport

Scargo Tower **6**

Scargo Lake

7 Cape Playhouse

Dennis **5**

West Dennis **18**

West Dennis Beach

South Dennis

17 South Yarmouth

Parker's River Beach

Corporation Beach

Chapin Beach
Bass Hole
Boardwalk **4**

Yarmouth Port

2

Keveney Bridge

3

Yarmouth

Yarmouth Boardwalk **16**

West Yarmouth **15**

Kalmus Park Beach

Lewis Bay

Hyannis **11–14**

Hyannis Port

Barnstable **1**

Cape Cod Community College

Sandy Neck Beach

Sandy Neck

Barnstable Harbor

Cummaquid

Halletts Pond

Barnstable Municipal Airport

Centerville **10**

Osterville **9**

Cotuit **8**

West Barnstable

Marstons Mills

Wequaquet Lake

Long Pond

Sheep Pond

Seymour Pond

Upper Mill Pond

Swan Pond

Follins Pond

Flat Pond

Swan Pond

Nantucket Island

The crowded belly of the Cape is a center of activity unlike any other here, except perhaps Provincetown at the height of its summer crush. **Hyannis** ⑪–⑭ is the hub of Cape Cod, with plenty to do and see. Take a cruise around the harbor or go on a deep-sea fishing trip. There are shops and restaurants along Main Street and plenty of amusements for the youngsters. Kennedy fans will want to spend time at the JFK Museum. End the day with a concert at the Cape Cod Melody Tent. **Barnstable** ①, the county seat, has plenty of its own history and the wonderful Sandy Neck Beach to keep you occupied. Scenic Route 6A passes through **Yarmouth Port** ② and **Dennis** ⑤. There are beaches and salt marshes, museums, walking trails, and old graveyards all along this route if you feel like stopping. Yarmouth Port's **Bass Hole Boardwalk** ④ makes for a particularly beautiful stroll. In Dennis there are historic houses to tour, the Cape Museum of Fine Arts will introduce you to the work of Cape-associated artists, and the Cape Cod Rail Trail provides a premier path for bicyclists. Toward the end of the day, head for Scargo Hill and climb 30-ft **Scargo Tower** ⑥ to watch the sun set. At night you could catch a film at the Cape Cinema, on the grounds of the **Cape Playhouse** ⑦. The south shore has plenty of activities for children, from **Centerville** ⑩ to **Dennisport** ⑲.

When to Tour the Mid Cape

In the summer the Mid Cape bustles with tourists. But from Columbus Day weekend through April, the Mid Cape is a peaceful collection of towns and villages, with beaches (no fees) for strolling, trails for walking and biking, and a wealth of shopping and entertainment opportunities. Fall sees bursts of color in the easily accessed forests and marshes; winter brings a slower pace of life and a holiday spirit that locals love to celebrate with Christmas strolls featuring tours of shops, B&Bs, and old homes. Spring is also quiet, as the Mid Cape awakens to blooming trees, warmer days, reopened B&Bs, newly landscaped golf courses, and flower festivals. Boats come out of hibernation—the Hyannis Whale Watcher Cruises, for instance, starts its program in April.

Barnstable

❶ *11 mi east of Sandwich, 4 mi north of Hyannis.*

With more than 43,000 year-round residents, Barnstable is the largest town on the Cape. It's also the second oldest—it was founded in 1639, two years after Sandwich. You'll get a feeling for its age in Barnstable Village, on and near Main Street (Route 6A), a lovely area of large old homes dominated by the Barnstable County Superior Courthouse. Behind the courthouse are the county lockup and a complex of government buildings, all best avoided. The Village Hall is home to the Barnstable Comedy Club, one of the oldest community theater groups in the country. Just north of the village are the marshes and beaches of Cape Cod Bay, including beautiful Sandy Neck Beach, as well as busy Barnstable Harbor. The Cape Cod Conservatory of Music and Arts and Cape Cod Community College are also in the vicinity.

The **Olde Colonial Courthouse,** built in 1772 as the colony's second courthouse, is the home of the historical society **Tales of Cape Cod** (✉ 3018 Main St. [Rte. 6A], ☎ 508/362–8927), which is restoring the courthouse to serve as a museum. A series of slide-illustrated lectures given by guest speakers is held Tuesday night in July and August. From the courthouse take a peek across the street at the old-fashioned English gardens at **St. Mary's Episcopal Church.**

Set in a 1644 building listed on the National Register of Historic Places, the **Sturgis Library** was established in 1863. Its holdings date from the 17th century and include hundreds of maps and land charts, the definitive collection of Cape Cod genealogical material ($5 daily fee for nonresidents), and an extensive maritime history collection. ⊠ *3090 Main St. (Rte. 6A),* ☎ *508/362–6636.* ☉ *Mon. and Thurs. 10–2, Tues. 1–9, Wed., Fri., and Sun. 1–5, Sat. 10–4.*

Barnstable's maritime past is on display at the **Trayser Museum Complex.** On the National Register of Historic Places, the complex's red-painted brick main building houses a small collection of maritime exhibits—telescopes, captains' shaving boxes, items brought back from voyages, ship models, and paintings—as well as ivory, Sandwich glass, and arrowheads. The downstairs re-creates the building as it looked in 1856, when it served as a customs house; don't miss the ornate bronze Corinthian columns. A restored customs-keeper's office with an original safe and a view of the harbor are on the second floor. Also on the grounds are a jail, circa 1690, with two cells bearing former inmates' graffiti, and a carriage house with early tools, fishing implements, and a 19th-century horse-drawn hearse. ⊠ *3353 Main St. (Rte. 6A),* ☎ *508/362–2092.* ☜ *$2 suggested donation.* ☉ *Mid-June–Columbus Day, Tues.–Sun. 1:30–4:30.*

If you're interested in Cape history, the **Nickerson Memorial Room** at **Cape Cod Community College** has the largest collection of information on Cape Cod, including books, records, ships' logs, oral-history tapes, photographs, films, and more. It also has materials on the neighboring islands of Martha's Vineyard and Nantucket. ⊠ *2240 Iyanough Rd., off Rte. 132, West Barnstable,* ☎ *508/362–2131, ext. 4445.* ☉ *Mon., Wed., and Fri. 8:30–4, Tues. 8:30–3.*

Dining and Lodging

$$–$$$ ✕ **Barnstable Tavern & Grille.** This handsome old building right in the village center, across from the courthouse, holds both a serious restaurant and a more relaxed tavern. Partners Pat O'Mara and Jane Lebel took over in 2000 and refurbished it with new paint, new carpets, and a new menu. The pasta Livorno, with jumbo shrimp, scallops, and lobster over linguine, and the Tavern Keeper's Special, a medley of seafood in a casserole, are favorites of both patrons and chef Eddie Woelfle. Lunch fare is lighter, featuring burgers, salads, and sandwiches. Look for live music on the patio Friday night. ⊠ *3176 Main St. (Rte. 6A),* ☎ *508/362–2355. AE, MC, V.*

$$–$$$ ✕ **Dolphin Restaurant.** Want to know who's running for what local office, or what the next controversy is likely to be at the planning commission? Eavesdrop at the Dolphin. For decades this has been the place where opinions clash and deals are cut. There is a colonial feel inside, dark and inviting; the food clings to what might be called historically appropriate preparation. This is a place to go basic, ordering the baked stuffed haddock or the prime rib. The bar is small but inviting, and your political secrets are safe with Joseph, one of Cape Cod's famous bartenders. ⊠ *3250 Main St. (Rte. 6A),* ☎ *508/362–6610. AE, MC, V.*

$ ✕ **Mill Way Fish and Lobster.** This combination seafood market and
★   lunch place sits right on Barnstable Harbor, giving it access to the freshest seafood possible. It's tiny, with only six outside picnic tables and limited parking, but the fried clams and fish sandwiches are worth the inevitable wait. Arrive hungry and try the fat onion rings or the almost-too-big-for-lunch clambake, which comes with chowder, lobster, steamers, and an ear of corn. Mill Way is open until 7 for early dinners. ⊠ *275 Mill Way,* ☎ *508/362–2760. AE, D, MC, V. Closed Oct.–Mar.*

$ ✕ **Whistleberries.** Most people settle for takeout from this tiny sandwich shop, but the lucky few who get a seat (two tables and three counter spots) are in for a treat. Breakfast is fresh muffins; "scrambled" eggs (they're actually steamed by the cappuccino machine); bagels; or burrito sandwiches stuffed with cheese, bacon, veggies, rice, beans, and sour cream. For lunch, try a wrap—there are many tempting choices, from barbecued chicken, turkey, or roast beef to specialties such as the Mediterranean, with red pepper, hummus, tabbouleh, tomato, onion, and feta cheese folded up in a spinach tortilla. ☒ *3261 Main St. (Rte. 6A),* ☎ *508/362–6717. No credit cards. Closed Sun.; no dinner.*

$$–$$$ ⬚ **Ashley Manor.** Set back from the Old King's Highway by high private hedges and a wide lawn, this fine B&B is just a short walk from the village. The inn has preserved its antique wide-board floors and has open-hearth fireplaces, one with a beehive oven, in the living room, the dining room, and the keeping room. The rooms are toasty, too— all but one have a working fireplace or woodstove, and the four suites have whirlpool tubs. Antique and country furnishings, Oriental rugs, and glimmers of brass and crystal create an elegant atmosphere. Breakfast is served on the backyard terrace (overlooking fruit trees, a gazebo, and the tennis court) or in the formal dining room. Phones with data port and TVs can be put in the rooms on request. ☒ *3660 Main St. (Rte. 6A), Box 856, 02630,* ☎ *508/362–8044 or 888/535–2246,* ℻ *508/362–9927. 2 rooms, 4 suites. Air-conditioning, tennis court, bicycles. No smoking. D, MC, V. BP.* ❧

$$–$$$ ⬚ **Beechwood Inn.** Debbie and Ken Traugot's yellow and pale green
★ 1853 Queen Anne is trimmed with gingerbread, wrapped by a wide porch with wicker furniture and a glider swing, and shaded by old beech trees. Although the parlor is pure mahogany-and-red-velvet Victorian, guest rooms (all with queen- or king-size beds) are decorated with antiques in lighter Victorian styles, including Eastlake. Three have fireplaces (two additional rooms were scheduled to add fireplaces in 2000), and one has a water view. Bathrooms have pedestal sinks and antique lighting fixtures. Breakfast is served in the dining room, which has a pressed-tin ceiling, a fireplace, and lace-covered tables set with hurricane lamps and fresh flowers. Afternoon tea and homemade snacks are also available. ☒ *2839 Main St. (Rte. 6A), 02630,* ☎ *508/ 362–6618 or 800/609–6618,* ℻ *508/362–0298. 6 rooms. Air-conditioning, refrigerators, bicycles. No smoking. AE, D, MC, V. BP.* ❧

$$–$$$ ⬚ **Cobb's Cove.** Proprietors Henri-Jean and Evelyn Chester have created a rustic hideaway for guests who want both quiet and comfort. Lush, wild gardens filled with bird feeders and fountains surround the house. The interior has huge wood beams, rough burlap walls, and heavy wooden doors studded (just as they were in the olden days) with nail heads. Guest rooms are large; each has a dressing area and a private bath with whirlpool tub and robes. The two top-floor rooms have glass walls, and from the sitting areas you can enjoy the spectacular view of Cape Cod Bay—on a good day you can see all the way to Provincetown. Breakfast is served in the rustic dining room, dominated by a Count Rumford–designed fireplace. Historic Barnstable village, beaches, and even whale-watching boats in the marina are only a short stroll. ☒ *31 Powder Hill Rd., Box 208, 02630,* ☎ ℻ *508/362–9356. 6 rooms. No smoking. AE, D, MC, V. BP.* ❧

$$–$$$ ⬚ **Heaven on High.** There's no more appropriately named B&B on the
★ Cape. Deanna and Gib Katten's haven is indeed heaven, nestled high on a hill, on one of the Cape's oldest roads, overlooking dunes, Great Salt Marsh, and the Bay at Sandy Neck. The modern house's decor is a meld of California beach house and Cape Cod comfort—light, airy, and breezy. The great room is filled with overstuffed chairs and couches, a fireplace, TV, and natural oak floors. Sliding glass doors lead to the living room and also to the deck, which runs the full length of the house, offering panoramic views of sand and surf. Deanna is an avid collector of, well, you name it, and she has filled every nook with her trea-

sures. Each room is named for the expansive collection that it houses; the Silhouettes and Mirrors room, for instance, has both commodities in all shapes and sizes, as well as a queen-size bed, a fireplace, and a large private deck. Breakfast, served on fine china and Tiffany sterling, is heavenly. ⊠ *70 High St., Box 346, West Barnstable, 02668, ☎ 508/ 362–4441 or 800/362–4044, FAX 508/362–4465. 3 rooms. Air-conditioning, refrigerators, putting green. No smoking. D, MC, V. Closed Nov.–Dec. BP.* ✿

$$–$$$ 🛏 **Lamb and Lion Inn** The carved sign out front, a glimmering lion and lamb in white and gold, is your first hint this inn is something special. More than a typical B&B, Lamb and Lion occupies a 1740 farmhouse and barn, as well as several additions, with rooms and suites gathered around a courtyard and large swimming pool. On the pool deck is a year-round hot tub. Several rooms open directly onto the courtyard, while others have private decks and entrances. Inside, decor ranges from summery cottage rooms, bright with blue-and-white-stripe wallpaper and wicker chairs, to more staid rooms adorned with antiques and dark woods. The Innkeeper's Pride Suite has a fireplace and sunken tub that opens to a private deck, while the rustic but comfortable Barn-Stable, in the original barn, is outfitted with three sleeping lofts that can accommodate six. Personal service includes pickups and drop-offs from local ferries and the Barnstable Municipal Airport. The Lamb and Lion accepts children and pets (extra fee). ⊠ *2504 Main St. (Rte. 6A), Box 511, Barnstable 02630, ☎ 508/362–6823 or 800/909–6923, FAX 508/ 362–0227. 4 rooms, 6 suites. Pool, hot tub, shop. MC, V. CP.* ✿

$$ 🛏 **Acworth Inn.** Joan Tognacci, manager of an engineering lab in a former life, took over the Acworth in 2000. The historic 1860 house has four large rooms and a spacious two-room suite. The rooms are decorated with soft pastels, lacy designer linens, and tasteful hand-painted furniture. The suite, with modern furnishings, also has a fireplace, whirlpool tub, TV/VCR, and refrigerator. Breakfast is scrumptious, featuring homemade granola; fresh muffins and fruit; yogurt; and your choice of waffles, pancakes, or an omelet. The inn is 1 mi east of Barnstable Village. ⊠ *4352 Main St. (Rte. 6A), Box 256, Cummaquid 02637, ☎ 508/ 362–3330 or 800/362–6363, FAX 508/375–0304. 4 rooms, 1 suite. Air-conditioning, bicycles. No smoking. AE, D, MC, V. BP.* ✿

$$ 🛏 **Honeysuckle Hill.** Innkeepers Mary and Bill Kilburn ran an inn in Vermont before relocating to the Cape in 1998, and their experience and graciousness shine through in lots of little touches: a guest fridge stocked with sodas and water bottles, beach chairs with umbrellas (perfect for nearby Sandy Neck Beach), and an always-full cookie jar in the sunny dining room. The airy, country-style guest rooms in this expansive, gray-shingle 1810 Queen Anne–style cottage have lots of white wicker, featherbeds, checked curtains, and pastel-painted floors. The spacious second-floor Wisteria Room, overlooking the lush yard and flower gardens, is a particularly comfortable retreat, with its own entrance under a wisteria arbor. The screened-in porch is a peaceful place for early morning coffee. ⊠ *591 Rte. 6A, West Barnstable 02668, ☎ 508/362–8418 or 800/441–8418. 3 rooms, 1 suite. Air-conditioning. No smoking. AE, D, MC, V. BP.* ✿

Nightlife and the Arts

The **Barnstable Comedy Club** (⊠ Village Hall, Rte. 6A, ☎ 508/362– 6333), the Cape's oldest amateur theater group (it celebrated its 75th anniversary in 1997), gives much-praised musical and dramatic performances throughout the year. Some folks who appeared here before they made it big are Geena Davis; Frances McDormand; and Kurt Vonnegut, a past president of the BCC.

Outdoor Activities and Sports
BEACH
Hovering above Barnstable Harbor and the 4,000-acre **Great Salt Marsh, Sandy Neck Beach** stretches some 6 mi across a peninsula that ends at **Sandy Neck Light**. The beach is one of the Cape's most beautiful—dunes, sand, and sea spread endlessly east, west, and north. The marsh used to be harvested for salt hay; now it's a haven for birds, which are out and about in the greatest numbers morning and evening, at low tide, and during spring and fall migration. The lighthouse, standing just a few feet from eroding shoreline at the tip of the neck, has been out of commission since 1952. It was built in 1857 to replace an 1827 light, and it used to run on acetylene gas. It is now privately owned and no longer accessible from the beach. If you like to hike, ask at the ranger station for a trail brochure. The main beach at Sandy Neck has lifeguards, a snack bar, rest rooms, and showers. As you travel east along Route 6A from Sandwich, Sandy Neck Road is just *before* the Barnstable line, although the beach itself is in West Barnstable. ⊠ *Sandy Neck Rd., West Barnstable,* ☎ *508/362–8300.* 🚗 *Parking $10 Memorial Day–Labor Day.* ☉ *Daily 9–9, but staffed only until 5 PM.*

FISHING
The **Barnstable Harbor Charter Fleet** (⊠ 186 Millway, ☎ 508/362–3908) has fishing trips on 10 sportfishing vessels from spring through fall. Reservations are recommended but not required.

WHALE-WATCHING
On **Hyannis Whale Watcher Cruises** out of Barnstable Harbor, a naturalist narrates and comments on whale sightings and the natural history of Cape Cod Bay. Trips last about four hours, there are concessions on board, and in July and August you can cruise at sunset, too. Reservations are required; book a day or two in advance. ⊠ *Mill Way, Millway Marina, off Phinney's La.,* ☎ *508/362–6088 or 800/287–0374.* 🚗 *$26.* ☉ *Apr.–Oct.*

Shopping
Black's Handweaving Shop (⊠ 597 Rte. 6A, West Barnstable, ☎ 508/362–3955), in a barnlike shop with working looms, makes beautiful handwoven goods in traditional and jacquard weaves. If you don't see what you want on display, you can commission it.

The **Crystal Pineapple** (⊠ 1540 Rte. 6A, West Barnstable, ☎ 508/362–3128 or 800/462–4009) has cranberry glass and many collectibles lines, including Dept. 56, Snowbabies, Swarovski crystal, and Disney Classics.

Maps of Antiquity (⊠ 1022 Rte. 6A, West Barnstable, ☎ 508/362–7169) sells original and reproduction maps of Cape Cod, New England, and other parts of the world. Some date to the 1700s.

West Barnstable Tables (⊠ Rte. 149, West Barnstable, ☎ 508/362–2676) has handcrafted tables, chairs, chests, and a range of furniture made from the finest woods.

Whippletree (⊠ 660 Rte. 6A, West Barnstable, ☎ 508/362–3320) is a large barn, decorated for each season and filled with country gift items and a year-round Christmas section. Offerings include German nutcrackers, from Prussian soldiers to Casanovas.

Yarmouth Port

❷ *4 mi northeast of Hyannis, 21 mi east of the Sagamore Bridge, 4 mi east of Barnstable.*

Once known as Mattacheese, or "the planting lands," Yarmouth was settled in 1639 by farmers from the Plymouth Bay Colony. Yarmouth Port wasn't incorporated as a separate village until 1829. By then the Cape had begun a thriving maritime industry, and men turned to the sea to make their fortunes. Many impressive sea captains' houses—some now B&Bs and museums—still line the always-enchanting Route 6A, as well as side streets, and Yarmouth Port has some real old-time stores in town. Just a mile's drive north of Route 6A is the small but lovely Gray's Beach, where a boardwalk at the section called Bass Hole stretches hundreds of feet over the wide marsh and where the Callery-Darling conservation land trails loop through forest and marshland.

★ For a peek into the past, make a stop at **Hallet's,** a country drugstore preserved as it was in 1889, when the current owner's grandfather, Thacher Hallet, opened it. Hallet served not only as druggist but also as postmaster and justice of the peace. At the all-marble soda fountain with swivel stools, you can order the secret-recipe ice cream soda as well as an inexpensive lunch. Above Hallet's Store, the **Thacher Taylor Hallet Museum** displays photographs and memorabilia of Yarmouth Port and the Hallet family. ⊠ *139 Main St. (Rte. 6A),* ☎ *508/362–3362.* ☜ *Donations accepted for museum.* ⊘ *Apr.–mid-Nov.; call for hrs.*

The 1886 **Village Pump,** a black wrought-iron mechanism long used for drawing household water, is topped by a lantern and surrounded by ironwork with cutouts of birds and animals. In front is a stone trough that was used for watering horses. It's across from the Parnassus Book Service (⊠ 220 Main St.). The 1696 **Old Yarmouth Inn** (⊠ 223 Main St. (Rte. 6A), near Summer St. ☎ 508/362–9962), near the village pump, is the Cape's oldest inn and a onetime stagecoach stop.

The **Botanical Trails of the Historical Society of Old Yarmouth,** right behind the post office (⊠ 231 Main St.), provide a good look at the area's flora in 50 acres of oak and pine woods and a pond, accented by blueberries, lady's slippers, Indian pipes, rhododendrons, hollies, and more. Stone markers and arrows point out the 2 mi of trails; you'll find trail maps in the gatehouse mailbox. Just beyond the historical society's trails, the little **Kelley Chapel** was built in 1873 by a father for a daughter grieving over the death of a child. The simple interior is dominated by an iron woodstove and a pump organ. ⊠ *Off Main St. (Rte. 6A).* ☜ *$1 suggested donation.* ⊘ *Gatehouse July–Aug., daily 1–4. Trails during daylight hrs year-round.*

The 1780 **Winslow Crocker House** is an elegantly symmetrical two-story Georgian with 12-over-12 small-pane windows and rich paneling in every room. After Crocker's death, his two sons built a wall dividing the house in half. The house was moved here from West Barnstable in 1936 by Mary Thacher, who donated it—along with her collection of 17th- to 19th-century furniture, pewter, hooked rugs, and ceramics—to the Society for the Preservation of New England Antiquities, which operates it as a museum. Tours are given every hour on the hour. ⊠ *250 Main St. (Rte. 6A),* ☎ *508/362–4385.* ☜ *$4.* ⊘ *June–mid-Oct., weekends 11–4.*

Built in 1840 onto an existing 1740 house for a sea captain in the China trade, then bought by another, who swapped it with a third captain, the **Captain Bangs Hallet House** is a white Greek Revival building with a hitching post out front and a weeping beech in back. The house and its contents typify a 19th-century sea captain's home, with pieces of pewter, china, nautical equipment, antique toys and clothing, and more on display. The kitchen has the original 1740 brick beehive oven and butter churns. ⊠ *11 Strawberry La., off Rte. 6A,* ☎ *508/362–3021.* ⊡ *$3.* ⊙ *June–Oct., Sun. 1–3:30; tours at 1, 2, and 3.*

Purchased in 1640 and established as a prosperous farm in the late 1700s, the **Taylor-Bray Farm** (⊠ Bray Farm Rd., ☎ 508/385–6499) is still a working farm, listed on the National Register of Historic Places. The farm is open to the public by making an appointment with the tenants; it has picnic tables, walking trails, and a great view of the tidal marsh.

For a scenic loop with little traffic, turn north off Route 6A in town onto Church Street or Thacher Streets, then left onto Thacher Shore Road. In fall this route is especially beautiful, with its impressive stands of blazing-red burning bush. Wooded segments alternate with open views of marsh. Keep bearing right, and at the WATER STREET sign, the dirt road on the right will bring you to a wide-open view of marshland as it meets the bay. Don't drive in too far, or you may get stuck. As you ❸ come out, a right turn will take you to **Keveney Bridge,** a one-lane wooden bridge over marshy Hallet's Mill Pond, and back to Route 6A.

One of Yarmouth Port's most beautiful areas is Bass Hole, which ★ ⊚ ❹ stretches from Homer's Dock Road to the salt marsh. **Bass Hole Boardwalk** (⊠ Trail entrance on Center St. near Gray's Beach parking lot) extends over a marshy creek; amid the salt marshes, vegetated wetlands, and upland woods meander the 2½-mi **Callery-Darling nature trails.** Gray's Beach is a little crescent of sand with still water good for children—but don't go beyond the roped-in swimming area, the only section where the current isn't strong. At the end of the boardwalk, benches provide a place to relax and look out over abundant marsh life and, across the creek, the beautiful, sandy shores of Dennis's Chapin Beach. At low tide you can walk out on the flats for almost a mile. It's a far cry from the days when an 18th-century harbor here was the site of a schooner shipyard.

Dining and Lodging

$$$ ✕ **Abbicci.** Unassuming to a fault from the outside, Abbicci tells an entirely different story on the inside, with stunning modern decor, explosions of color, and a handsome black-slate bar. One of the first to bring northern Italian cooking to Cape Cod, chef-owner Marietta Hickey has remained true to the tradition and ahead of the crowd. She prepares rich and full-tasting yet heart-healthy fare, thanks to a light touch with olive oil and a watchful eye over the fat content of her dishes. One of the most pleasing is braised rabbit with fresh green beans and tiny onions over garlic mashed potatoes. In summer, fish and a dozen elegant pasta dishes take over. ⊠ *43 Main St. (Rte. 6A),* ☎ *508/362– 3501. AE, D, DC, MC, V.*

$$–$$$ ✕ **Howes Cottage.** The main dining area of this pretty 1849 Gothic Revival house contains knickknacks and antiques, and a striking maple bar dominates the lounge. You'll find wide-plank pine floors and antique hutches throughout, as well as a hearth in the back room. The menu concentrates on regional American cuisine and includes rack of lamb, seared beef tenderloin with red-chili chutney, and a variety of pastas and seafood. The restaurant is perhaps overly ambitious, serving breakfast, lunch, and dinner in season, plus an all-day tavern menu, and service doesn't always meet the standard of the food. ⊠ *134 Main St. (Rte. 6A),* ☎ *508/362–9866. Reservations essential. AE, D, MC, V. Closed Mon. in off-season; no breakfast.*

$$-$$$ ✕ **Inaho.** Yuji Watanabe, the chef-owner of the Cape's best Japanese
★ restaurant, makes early morning journeys to Boston's fish markets to
shop for the freshest local catch. His selection of sushi and sashimi is
vast and artful, and vegetable and seafood tempura come out of the
kitchen fluffy and light. If you're a teriyaki lover, you can't do any better than the chicken's beautiful blend of sweet and sour. One remarkable element of the restaurant is its artful lighting: small pinpoint
lights on the food accentuate the presentation in a dramatic way. The
serene and simple Japanese garden out back has a traditional goldfish
pond. ✉ 157 Main St. (Rte. 6A), ☎ 508/362–5522. MC, V. Closed
Mon.; no lunch.

$-$$ ✕ **Jack's Outback.** Tough to find, tough to forget, this eccentric little
★ serve-yourself-pretty-much-anything-you-want joint is right down the
driveway from Inaho (☞ above) and goes by the motto "Good food,
lousy service." The quintessential local hangout, it lives up to its motto
in every way. Solid breakfasts give way by midday to thick burgers,
freshly concocted sandwiches, pasta salads, homemade soups, and
then traditional home-cooked favorites such as Yankee pot roast and
fried chicken. One of the owners, Jack Braginton-Smith, is a local historian of note. (As far as locals are concerned, if he *doesn't* insult you
on the way in and out, you've been insulted.) Jack's has no liquor license, and you may not BYOB. ✉ 161 Main St. (Rte. 6A), ☎ 508/
362–6690. Reservations not accepted. No credit cards. No dinner.

$$-$$$ 🏨 **Blueberry Manor.** Owners Jerry Rosen and Victoria Schuh, who
moved from a Brooklyn loft to this quiet early 19th-century Greek Revival, have completely restored their new home to create a wonderfully
sophisticated yet homey B&B. The living room pairs Victorian furnishings
and a marble fireplace with modern amenities, including a TV/VCR, a
stereo, and a stash of puzzles, games, and books. Upstairs, the guest
rooms feel crisp and clean; although the furnishings are traditional, there
are no fussy lace treatments or curio shelves. The Lavender Room has
a queen-size four-poster bed with a handmade quilt, an antique armoire,
and a modern bath under the eaves with a skylight. Across the hall, the
Rose Room has an exquisitely painted queen-size bed and cheery pink
walls. The new Willow Garden Suite, with a loft, fireplace, and private
entrance, accommodates as many as four. The fruit from the blueberry
bushes in the lush backyard and garden turns up at breakfast in homemade coffee cakes and other baked goods. ✉ 438 Main St. (Rte. 6A),
02675, ☎ 508/362–7620, FAX 508/362–0053. 3 rooms, 1 suite. Air-conditioning. No smoking. AE, MC, V. BP. 🐾

$$-$$$ 🏨 **The Inn at Cape Cod.** A stately white Greek Revival building with
imposing columns, the inn sits back from Route 6A in a parklike lawn
adjacent to the Botanical Trails (☞ above). The interior is eclectic. On
the first floor, the large Joshua Sears Room, with a mahogany king four-
poster bed, Oriental rug, and antique furnishings, is a traditional Victorian chamber, while the Far East Room—iron-and-wicker bed, Chinese
curio chest, and wicker wing chairs—would feel at home in Beijing's
Forbidden City. Upstairs, the romantic Village Suite with its Italian armoire and cherry writing desk opens to the front porch, and the frilly
Victorian Room has its own fireplace. Some smaller rooms, particularly
the basic pine Guest Room, are pint-size. Innkeepers Doug and Mary
Heywood serve a hearty buffet breakfast and can accommodate children age 10 and older with a rollaway bed. ✉ 4 Summer St., 02675,
☎ 508/375–0590 or 800/850–7301, FAX 508/362–9520. 7 rooms, 2 suites.
Air-conditioning. No smoking. AE, D, DC, MC, V. BP. 🐾

$$-$$$ 🏨 **Wedgewood Inn.** This handsome Greek Revival building, white with
★ black shutters and a fanlight, is on the National Register of Historic
Places and dates from 1812. The interior is sophisticated but welcoming,
with a mix of fine colonial antiques, upholstered wing chairs, sport-

ing prints, and maritime paintings. In the guest rooms, antique quilts top handcrafted cherry pencil-post beds. Two spacious suites in the main building have canopy beds, fireplaces, and porches; one has a separate sitting room. Three additional suites are in the restored barn behind the house and have king-size beds, TVs, and large bathrooms. Innkeeper Gerrie Graham cooks elegant breakfasts such as Belgian waffles with whipped cream and strawberries or eggs with hollandaise sauce. Her husband, Milt, a former Boston Patriot (before the football team was renamed the New England Patriots) and FBI agent, serves breakfast and helps guests make plans for the day. ⊠ *83 Main St. (Rte. 6A), 02675,* ☎ *508/362–5157 or 508/362–9178,* FAX *508/362–5851. 4 rooms, 5 suites. Air-conditioning. No smoking. AE, MC, V. BP.*

$$ 🖫 **Lane's End Cottage.** Owner-innkeeper Valerie Butler's house indeed sits at the end of a dirt lane, moved here in 1860 by oxen to make room for the neighboring church. And what a magical setting it is: a white picket fence, an English cottage garden, an English antiques–filled common room–library with a fireplace. Each guest room has tasteful appointments and beds with firm mattresses, feather comforters, and white spreads. The sun-drenched first-floor Terrace Room has a fireplace and French doors that lead to a cobblestone patio overlooking a flower-rimmed garden. There's no air-conditioning, but the rooms have fans, and the cottage is shaded by trees. Pets are allowed with prior notice—but only in the off-season. ⊠ *268 Main St. (Rte. 6A), 02675,* ☎ *508/362–5298. 3 rooms. Library. No smoking. No credit cards. BP.*

$–$$ 🖫 **Village Inn.** Many guests who stay here will say it's just like staying at your grandmother's—provided, of course, your grandmother has the kind of clean, snug rooms found in Esther Hickey's 1795 sea captain's house. It's old-fashioned—some might say faded—but the rooms with their wide pine floorboards are lessons in history. The Provincetown Room, for instance, served as the house's schoolroom; the original (but no longer used) light fixtures are still in place. Room sizes and amenities fluctuate; the tiny Wellfleet Room, which has a half-size tub, may be too small for some, but it's a bargain. Families should note that the Brewster, Truro, and Hyannis rooms connect and that the first-floor Yarmouth Room is the most spacious, with its own library, bathroom with fireplace, and private entrance. The common rooms have as many books as some public libraries. Children of all ages are welcome. ⊠ *92 Main St. (Rte. 6A), Box 1, 02675,* ☎ *508/362–3182. 10 rooms, 8 with bath. No smoking. MC, V. BP.*

Nightlife and the Arts

Oliver's (⊠ 6 Bray Farm Rd., off Rte. 6A, ☎ 508/362–6062) has live acoustic music in its tavern on weekends year-round.

Shopping

Cummaquid Fine Arts (⊠ 4275 Rte. 6A, Cummaquid, ☎ 508/362–2593) has works by contemporary resident Cape Cod artists, beautifully displayed in an old home.

Parnassus Book Service (⊠ 220 Main St. [Rte. 6A], ☎ 508/362–6420), occupying a three-story 1840 former general store, has a huge selection of old and new books—Cape Cod, maritime, Americana, antiquarian, and others—and is a great place to browse. Its book stall, outside on the building's side, is open 24 hours a day and works on the honor system—tally up your purchases and leave the money in the mail slot.) Parnassus also carries Robert Bateman's nature prints.

Peach Tree Designs (⊠ 173 Main St. [Rte. 6A], ☎ 508/362–8317) carries home furnishings and decorative accessories, some from local craftspeople, all beautifully made.

Pewter Crafters of Cape Cod (✉ 933 Main St. [Rte. 6A], ☎ 508/362–3407) handcrafts traditional and contemporary pewter objects, from baby cups to tea services.

Dennis

❺ *4½ mi north of South Yarmouth, 4 mi east of Yarmouth Port, 5 mi north of Dennisport.*

The backstreets of Dennis still retain the colonial charm of seafaring days. The town was named for Reverend Josiah Dennis and incorporated in 1793. There were 379 sea captains living in Dennis when fishing, salt making, and shipbuilding were the main industries, and the elegant houses they constructed—now museums and B&Bs—still line the streets. In 1816 Dennis resident Henry Hall discovered that adding sand to his cranberry fields' soil improved the quality and quantity of the fruit. The decades after saw cranberry farming and tourism become the Cape's main commercial enterprises. The town has a number of conservation areas and nature trails and numerous freshwater ponds for swimming. The village center has antiques shops, general stores, a post office, and ice cream shops. There's also a village green with a bandstand, home to occasional summer concerts.

West Dennis and Dennisport, off Route 28 on the south shore of the Cape (the triceps, if you will), are covered separately below.

The **Josiah Dennis Manse,** a saltbox house with add-ons, was built in 1736 for Reverend Josiah Dennis. Inside, the rooms reflect life in Reverend Dennis's day. One room is set up as a child's room, with antique furniture and toys. The keeping room has a fireplace and cooking utensils, and the attic exhibits spinning and weaving equipment. Throughout you'll see china, pewter, and portraits of sea captains. The Maritime Wing has ship models, paintings, nautical artifacts, and more. On the grounds is a 1770 one-room schoolhouse, furnished with wood-and-wrought-iron desks and chairs. ✉ *77 Nobscussett Rd., at Whig St.,* ☎ *508/385–2232.* 🆓 *Donations accepted.* ☺ *July–Sept., Tues. 10–noon, Thurs. 2–4.*

❻ On a clear day, from the top of **Scargo Tower,** you'll have unbeatable panoramic views of Scargo Lake, the village's scattered houses below, Cape Cod Bay, and distant Provincetown. A wooden tower built on this site in 1874 was one of the Cape's first tourist attractions; visitors would pay 5¢ to climb to the top for the views. That tower burned down, and the present all-stone 30-ft tower was built in 1901 to replace it. Winding stairs bring you to the top; don't forget to read the unsightly, but amusing, graffiti on the way up. Expect crowds at sunrise and sunset. ✉ *Scargo Hill Rd., off Rte. 6A or Old Bass River Rd.* 🆓 *Free.* ☺ *Daily sunrise–sunset.*

NEED A BREAK?

Dip into homemade ice cream and frozen yogurt at the **Ice Cream Smuggler** (✉ 716 Main St. [Rte. 6A], across the street from the town green and cemetery, ☎ 508/385–5307).

★ ☙ **❼** For Broadway-style dramas, comedies, and musicals, as well as children's plays, you can attend a production at the **Cape Playhouse,** the oldest professional summer theater in the country. In 1927 Raymond Moore, who had been working with a theatrical troupe in Provincetown, bought an 1838 former Unitarian Meeting House and converted it into a theater. The original pews still serve as seats. The opening performance was *The Guardsman,* starring Basil Rathbone; other stars who performed here in the early days, some in their professional stage debuts, include

Bette Davis (who first worked here as an usher), Gregory Peck, Lana Turner, Ginger Rogers, Humphrey Bogart, Tallulah Bankhead, and Henry Fonda, who appeared with his then-unknown 20-year-old daughter, Jane. Cape resident Shirley Booth was such an admirer of the theater she donated her Oscar (for *Come Back Little Sheba*) and her Emmy (for *Hazel*) to the theater; both are on display in the lobby during the season. Behind-the-scene tours are also given in season; call for a schedule. The Playhouse offers children's theater on Friday morning during July and August. Also on the 26-acre property, now known as the Cape Playhouse Center for the Arts, are a restaurant, the **Cape Museum of Fine Arts** (☞ *below*), and the **Cape Cinema,** whose exterior was designed in the style of the Congregational church in Centerville. Inside, a 6,400-square-ft mural of heavenly skies—designed by Massachusetts artist Rockwell Kent, who also designed the gold-sunburst curtain—covers the ceiling. ⊠ *820 Main St. (Rte. 6A),* ☎ *508/385–3911 or 877/ 385–3911.* ⊙ *Call for tour schedule.* ⊜

The **Cape Museum of Fine Arts** exhibits a permanent collection of more than 850 works by Cape-associated artists. Important pieces include a portrait of a fisherman's wife by Charles Hawthorne, the father of the Provincetown art colony; a 1924 portrait of a Portuguese fisherman's daughter by William Paxton, one of the first artists to summer in Provincetown; a collection of wood-block prints by Varujan Boghosian, a member of Provincetown's Long Point Gallery cooperative; an oil sketch by Karl Knaths, who painted in Provincetown from 1919 until his death in 1971; and works by abstract expressionist Hans Hoffman and many of his students. The museum also hosts film festivals, lectures, art classes, and trips. ⊠ *60 Hope La. (on the grounds of the Cape Playhouse), off Rte. 6A,* ☎ *508/385–4477.* ⊠ *$5.* ⊙ *Late May–mid-Oct., Mon.–Sat. 10–5, Sun. 1–5; late Oct.–mid-May, Tues.– Sat. 10–5, Sun. 1–5.*

Dining and Lodging

$$$ ✕ **Red Pheasant.** This is one of the Cape's best cozy country inns, with a consistently good kitchen; the hearty American food is prepared with elaborate sauces and herb combinations. For instance, rack of lamb is served with an intense port-and-rosemary reduction, and exquisitely grilled veal chops come with a dense red wine and Portobello mushroom sauce. In fall look for the specialty game dishes, including venison and quail. Deep-fried goat cheese ravioli is another winner. Try to reserve a table in the more intimate Garden Room. The expansive wine list is excellent. Men may want to wear a jacket. ⊠ *905 Main St. (Rte. 6A),* ☎ *508/385–2133 or 800/480–2133. Reservations essential. D, MC, V. No lunch.*

$$ ✕ **Gina's by the Sea.** Some places are less than the sum of their parts; Gina's is more. The funky old building is tucked into a sand dune, so that the aroma of fine northern Italian cooking blends with a fresh breeze off the bay. The dining room is tasteful, cozy, and especially wonderful in the fall when the fireplace is blazing. Blackboard specials could include angel-hair pasta or linguine with clams. If you don't want a long wait, come early or late. ⊠ *134 Taunton Ave.,* ☎ *508/385–3213. Reservations not accepted. AE, MC, V. Closed Dec.–Mar. and Mon– Wed. Oct.–Nov.; no lunch Apr.–June and Sept.–Nov.*

$$ ✕ **Scargo Café.** Because the Cape Playhouse is right across the street, this café is a favorite before- and after-show haunt. Excellent early-bird specials for the show crowd include scallops cooked in Harpoon beer (a Boston brew) and fettuccine Alfredo. The menu focuses on lighter fare for summer, but there's still plenty of richness, as well as a rather good wine cellar to complement it. Mussels Ferdinand features farm-raised mussels with a buttery Pernod sauce over pasta. An added plus:

the kitchen stays open until midnight in summer. ⊠ *799 Main St. (Rte. 6A),* ☎ *508/385–8200. AE, D, MC, V.*

$ ✕ **Cap'n Frosty's.** This locally much-acclaimed though very modest fried seafood and ice cream joint has a regular menu, a small specials board, and a counter where you order and take a number written on a french fries box. The staff is young and hard working, pumping out fresh fried clams and fish-and-chips on paper plates. All frying is done in 100% canola oil, and rice pilaf is offered as a substitute for fries. There's seating inside as well as outside on a shady brick patio. ⊠ *219 Main St. (Rte. 6A),* ☎ *508/385–8548. Reservations not accepted. No credit cards. Closed Labor Day–Mar.*

$ ✕ **Red Cottage Restaurant.** Up Old Bass River Road just ½ mi north of the town hall, the Red Cottage is indeed a red cottage that serves breakfast and lunch year-round. This friendly place has a long counter with swivel stools, and the grill is in plain view. The breakfasts are actually better than the lunches, but both are no-nonsense and just plain reliably good. The menu has something of an emphasis on "health," meaning egg-white omelets are available alongside the usuals, and "lite" cheese is used. ⊠ *36 Old Bass River Rd.,* ☎ *508/394–2923. Reservations not accepted. No credit cards. No dinner.*

$$ ▦ **Scargo Manor.** Location, location, location: that's what this 1895 sea captain's home has, a prime one right on Scargo Lake. Inside, there's plenty of room to spread out on the big screened porch with green wicker chairs, in the sitting room (with TV and fireplace), in the more formal living room, or in a red wicker chair in the cozy third-floor reading room (also with a TV). If you want a lake view, choose the all-blue Hydrangea Room, with a pineapple-top, queen-size four-poster bed; you can watch the stars through the skylight overhead. If you need lots of space, the Captain Howe's Suite has a king-size canopy bed, plus a separate sitting room with a fireplace that's bigger than the guest rooms at many B&Bs. Take a walk down to the inn's private beach and dock, where you'll find a gazebo. Don't miss innkeeper Jane MacMillin's yummy cinnamon bread; it's enough to make you forget that the house's exterior, although a tasteful white, has been covered with nonwood siding. ⊠ *909 Main St. (Rte. 6A), 02638,* ☎ *508/385–5534 or 800/595–0034,* FAX *508/385–3992. 4 rooms, 2 suites. Breakfast room, beach. No smoking. AE, D, DC, MC, V. Jan.–Mar. CP.* ✑

$–$$ ▦ **Four Chimneys Inn.** This three-story, four-chimney 1881 Queen Anne Victorian gem, once home to the town doctor, is now a relaxing getaway. Rooms vary in size and decor, but all are tastefully furnished with cherry four-poster, wicker, or antique pine or oak beds; chenille comforters; and hand-stenciled trim. Three rooms have fireplaces, and all have views of either Scargo Lake (across the street) or of the surrounding woods and flowering gardens. You can enjoy breakfast in the high-ceiling dining room; the screened-in summer porch, with its lovely garden views, is an even more soothing place to start the day. Having afternoon tea under the wisteria-draped arbor is a wonderful way to wind down. ⊠ *946 Main St. (Rte. 6A), 02638,* ☎ *508/385–6317 or 800/874–5502,* FAX *508/385–6285. 7 rooms, 1 suite. No smoking. AE, MC, V. Closed Nov.–mid-Feb. CP.* ✑

$–$$ ▦ **Isaiah Hall B&B Inn.** Lilacs and pink roses trail along the white picket
★   fence outside this 1857 Greek Revival farmhouse on a residential road on the bay side of town. Inside, guest rooms are decorated with country antiques and floral-print wallpapers, have TVs, and are adorned with such homey touches as quilts and Priscilla curtains. In the attached carriage house, rooms have three walls stenciled white and one knotty pine, and some have small balconies overlooking a wooded lawn with gardens, grape arbors, and berry bushes. The carriage-house suite has a king-size bed, a separate sitting area with a pullout couch, and a re-

frigerator. Make-it-yourself popcorn, tea, coffee, and soft drinks are always available. ✉ *152 Whig St., Box 1007, 02638,* ☎ *508/385–9928 or 800/736–0160,* FAX *508/385–5879. 9 rooms, 1 suite. Picnic area, air-conditioning, badminton, croquet. No smoking. AE, MC, V. Closed mid-Oct.–mid-Apr. CP.* ✒

Nightlife and the Arts

The oldest professional summer theater in the country is the **Cape Playhouse** (✉ 820 Main St. [Rte. 6A], ☎ 508/385–3911 or 877/385–3911), an 1838 former Unitarian Meeting House, where top stars appear each summer (☞ *above*). The playhouse also mounts children's shows on Friday morning during July and August. On the grounds of the Cape Playhouse is the artsy **Cape Cinema** (☎ 508/362–2503), which shows foreign and first-run films throughout the summer (☞ *above*).

The **Nau-Sets** (✉ Dennis Senior Center, Rte. 134, ☎ 508/255–5079 or 508/385–9841) holds weekly square dances on Tuesday.

The **Reel Art Cinema** at the Cape Museum of Fine Arts (✉ 60 Hope La., ☎ 508/385–4477) shows avant-garde, classic, art, and independent films on weekends. Call for a schedule.

Outdoor Activities and Sports

BEACHES

Parking at all Dennis beaches is $10 a day in season for nonresidents.

Chapin Beach (✉ Chapin Beach Rd.) is a lovely dune-backed bay beach with long tidal flats so you can walk far out at low tide. It has no lifeguards or services.

Corporation Beach (✉ Corporation Rd.) has lifeguards, showers, rest rooms, and a food stand. At one time a packet landing owned by a corporation of the townsfolk, the beautiful crescent of white sand backed by low dunes now serves a decidedly noncorporate use as a public beach.

Mayflower Beach (✉ Dunes Rd. off Bayview Rd.) at low tide reveals hundreds of feet of tidal flats. The beach has rest rooms, showers, lifeguards, and a food stand.

For freshwater swimming, **Scargo Lake** (✉ Access off Rte. 6A or Scargo Hill Rd.) has two beaches that offer rest rooms and a picnic area. The sandy-bottom lake is shallow along the shore, which is good for youngsters. It's surrounded by woods and is stocked for fishing.

BIKING

A guidebook published by the Dennis Chamber of Commerce includes bike tours and maps. For background *see* Close-Up: Riding the Rail Trail, *below*. You can rent bikes at any number of places along the rail trail, including **Barbara's Bike Shop** (✉ Rte. 134, ☎ 508/760–4723) at the trail entrance, **Brewster Bike** (✉ Underpass Rd., Brewster, ☎ 508/896–8149), and **Idle Times** (✉ Rte. 6A, ☎ 508/896–9242) at the Brewster section of the trail.

You can pick up the Cape Cod Rail Trail at several points along its path. In fact, riding the entire trail in one day doesn't do justice to its sights and side trips (though it certainly can be done). Many bicyclists, especially those with small children, prefer the piecemeal method since they can relax and enjoy the sights—and not turn their legs into jelly.

The ride in Dennis starts as a flat, straight spin through a small pine forest, a good warming-up exercise. Your first road crossing is at busy Great Western Road, one of the town's major thoroughfares, after which you'll pass Sand Pond and Flax Pond in Harwich. The Dennis part of

RIDING THE RAIL TRAIL

IN THE LATE 1800S VISITORS to Cape Cod could take the train from Boston all the way to Provincetown. But with the construction of the Sagamore and Bourne bridges in the mid-1930s, the age of the automobile truly arrived on the Cape. Today, although passenger trains no longer serve Cape Cod, the former train paths provide another, more leisurely way to explore the Cape—by bicycle. For many people, riding the trail through the fragrant woods is as quintessential a Cape experience as leaping into the cold Atlantic on a dune-backed beach.

The Cape's premier bike path, the Cape Cod Rail Trail was constructed in 1978 and extended in the mid-1990s and now offers a scenic ride from South Dennis to South Wellfleet. Following the paved right-of-way of the old Penn Central Railroad, it is 25 mi long, passing salt marshes, cranberry bogs, ponds, and Nickerson State Park, which has its own path.

Some serious bikers whiz along at top speed, but that's not the only way to travel. Along the way there are plenty of tempting places to veer off to spend an hour or two on the beach, to stop for lunch or ice cream, or just to smell the pine trees and imagine what the Cape looked like years ago. So relax: the terrain is easy to moderate and is generally quite flat, making it great for youngsters.

The trail starts at the parking lot off busy Route 134 south of U.S. 6, near Theophilus Smith Road in South Dennis, a far-from-scenic place that will make you appreciate the trail even more. It ends at the post office in South Wellfleet. The Dennis Chamber of Commerce (☞ Visitor Information in The Mid Cape A to Z, *below*) will give you a free rail trail map, with distance markings to various points along the trail. It also notes the location of parking lots en route if you want to cover only a segment: in Harwich (across from Pleasant Lake Store on Pleasant Lake Avenue), in Brewster (at Nickerson State Park), and in Eastham (at the Salt Pond Visitor Center). Several bike

shops near the trail in Dennis, Brewster, and Eastham can also provide information as well as convenient rentals.

If you want to ride the entire length and back in one day, you're in for a long ride. Experienced rail-trailers suggest doing the trail in segments, perhaps starting in the middle near Nickerson State Park and looping to one end and back. If you want to return to your starting point by public transportation, the easiest way is to start in Dennis, ride to Orleans, and catch the bike-rack-equipped H20 line bus back to Dennis; contact the Cape Cod Regional Transit Authority (☞ Getting Around in The Mid Cape A to Z, *below*) for schedule and route information.

The Cape Cod Rail Trail is popular with in-line skaters and pedestrians as well as bicyclists. Remember that wheels yield to heels, so cyclists should give walkers the right of way. Pass slower traffic on the left, and call out a warning before you pass. Children under 13 must wear helmets. As you ride through Orleans, a stretch of the trail is on busy town streets rather than on a dedicated bike thoroughfare, so use extra caution. And at one point in Harwich, you will cross a major highway. The trail can get crowded at times, especially in summer; if you prefer solitude (or cooler temperatures), set out earlier in the morning or later in the afternoon.

Busy bike trails share the same fate as roads: maintenance projects and expansion. A 19-mi section of the rail trail is scheduled for resurfacing in 2001–2002. A new 3-mi spur leads from the rail trail through Harwich to the Chatham line; eventually this spur will go into Chatham center. Also in the works are plans to extend the trail westward into Yarmouth. Nickerson State Park (508/896–3491) maintains the rail trail; to view a map of the route before you leave home, go to www.magnet.state.ma.us/mhd/paths/webrt.htm. Other Web resources are listed under Web Sites in Smart Travel Tips A to Z.

— By Carolyn Heller

the trail is short, but it's worth starting here for the ample parking at the trail's entrance and for the several bike-rental places that set up shop on Route 134. For more information ☞ Close-up: Riding the Rail Trail.

FISHING

Sesuit Harbor, on the bay side of Dennis off Route 6A, is busy with fishing and pleasure boats. Several are available for fishing charters: the **Bluefish** (⊠ Sesuit Harbor, Box 113, Dennis 02638, ☎ 508/385–7265) makes four-, six-, and eight-hour trips; the **LAD-NAV** (⊠ Sesuit Harbor, Box 2002, East Dennis 02641, ☎ 508/385–8150) takes as many as six anglers per trip on a 36-ft fishing vessel.

Shopping

Armchair Bookstore (⊠ 619 Rte. 6A, ☎ 508/385–0900) carries a surprisingly large selection of current releases, plus numerous books about Cape lore, history, and sights. Also on hand are cards and knickknacks and a children's section with books, games, and toys.

Emily's Beach Barn (⊠ 708 Rte. 6A, ☎ 508/385–8328) has fashionable women's beachwear, from bathing suits and wraps to sun hats and summer dresses and tops.

Robert C. Eldred Co. (⊠ 1483 Main St. [Rte. 6A], East Dennis, ☎ 508/385–3116) holds more than two dozen auctions per year, dealing in Americana; estate jewelry; top-quality antiques; marine, Asian, American, and European art; tools; and dolls. Its "general antiques and accessories" auctions put less expensive wares on the block.

Scargo Pottery (⊠ 30 Dr. Lord's Rd. S, off Rte. 6A, ☎ 508/385–3894) is set in a pine forest, where potter Harry Holl's unusual wares—such as his signature castle birdhouses—sit on tree stumps and hang from branches. Inside are the workshop and kiln, plus work by Holl's four daughters. With luck you'll catch a potter at the wheel; viewing is, in fact, encouraged.

Cotuit

❽ *9 mi southwest of Barnstable, 2½ mi southeast of Mashpee.*

Once called Cotuit Port, this charming little town was formed around seven Crocker family homesteads. Much of the town lies along and just south of Route 28, west of Osterville and east of Mashpee, and its center is not much more than a crossroads with a post office, old-time coffee shop, local pizza parlor, and general store, which all seem unchanged since the 1940s. Large waterfront estates line sections of Main Street and Ocean View Drive, where small coves hide the uncrowded Loop Beach and Ropes Beach. It's best to get to the beaches by bike, since traffic is light and beach parking is for residents only.

The **Cahoon Museum of American Art** is in one of the old Crocker family buildings, a 1775 Georgian colonial farmhouse that was once a tavern and an overnight way station for travelers on the Hyannis–Sandwich stagecoach line. Its several rooms display selections from the permanent collection of American primitive paintings by Ralph and Martha Cahoon along with other 19th- and early 20th-century artists. Special exhibitions, classes, talks, and demonstrations are held throughout the summer. ⊠ *4676 Falmouth Rd. (Rte. 28), ☎ 508/428–7581. ▢ Free; donations accepted. ☉ Mar.–Jan., Tues.–Sat. 10–4.*

The first motor-driven fire-fighting apparatus on Cape Cod, a 1916 Model T chemical fire engine, is housed in the **Santuit-Cotuit Historical Society Museum,** behind the **Samuel Dottridge Homestead,** which itself dates from the early 1800s. ✉ *1148 Main St.,* ☎ *508/428–0461.* 🎦 *Free.* ☉ *Mid-June–mid-Oct., Thurs.–Sun. 2:30–5.*

Dining and Lodging

$$$$ ✕ **Regatta of Cotuit.** Like its sister restaurant in Falmouth (☞ Chapter 3), the Cotuit Regatta serves three nightly menus in a softly elegant setting. The menu reaches for a wider global cuisine, and a younger audience, but it's still much more haute than hot. The classic yet original fare includes pâtés of rabbit, veal, and venison and a signature seared loin of lamb with cabernet sauce, surrounded by chèvre, spinach, and pine nuts. The restored colonial stagecoach inn is plushly filled with wood, brass, and Oriental carpets, and the cozy taproom has its own bar menu. ✉ *4613 Falmouth Rd. (Rte. 28),* ☎ *508/428–5715. AE, MC, V. Reservations essential. No lunch.*

$ ✕ **The Mills.** With just 20 tables and a six-seat lunch counter, this busy breakfast and lunch spot has local and imported fans lining up to sample *linguica* (sausage) and cheese omelets, blueberry or cranberry pancakes, and thick cut (and intriguingly named) Texas French toast. The Mills also serves up fresh baked muffins, scones, and breads. Lunch is homemade soups and sandwiches, including burgers and veggie burgers. You can (and must) make reservations for the popular Friday-night fish dinners, the only dinner offered. ✉ *Rte. 149, just north of Cotuit, Marstons Mills,* ☎ *508/428–9814. No credit cards.*

$–$$ 🛏 **Josiah Sampson House.** This regal and imposing 1793 Federal-style house is a comfortable mix of colonial and casual. Owners Leonard and Carol Carter took over in 2000 and added new queen-size beds, updated decor, and air-conditioning to all the rooms. The spacious dining room has traditional colonial furnishings and an over-size fireplace. The guest rooms, some with fireplaces, have canopy beds, needlepoint rugs, and an attractive mix of antiques. Hannah's Room, formerly the kitchen, has a queen-size four-poster, built-in window seats, and a massive working fireplace. It's also the roomiest. Upstairs, Sampson Room has an extra-large bathroom and a view of the backyard. Guests have tennis privileges ($10 for 1½ hours) at the Kings Grant Racquet Club next door. ✉ *40 Old Kings Rd., off Main St., Box 226, 02635,* ☎ *508/428–8383 or 877/574–6873,* 🖷 *508/428–0116. 6 rooms. Outdoor hot tub, bicycles. AE, MC, V. CP.* ✐

Outdoor Activities and Sports

The **Cotuit Kettleers** (☎ 508/428–3358) of the collegiate Cape Cod Baseball League play home games at Lowell Park (✉ Lowell St., 2 mi south of Rte. 28) from mid-June to mid-August.

Shopping

The **Sow's Ear Antique Company** (✉ 4698 Rte. 28, ☎ 508/428–4931), next to the Cahoon Museum, specializes in folk art—dolls, ship's models, wood carvings, antique quilts, and paintings—in a house that dates from the late 1600s.

Osterville

⑨ *3 mi east of Cotuit, 7 mi southwest of Barnstable.*

A wealthy Barnstable enclave southwest of the town center, Osterville is lined with elegant waterfront houses, some of which are large "cottages" built in the 19th century, when the area became popular with a monied set. You'll find most beaches in the village, including the impressive **Dowses Beach,** are restricted to residents-only parking. If you want to swim locally, make sure your hotel or inn issues parking permits.

Despite its haute homes, the village of Osterville retains the small-town charm that permeates the Cape; its Main Street and Wianno Avenue area is a collection of trendy boutiques and jewelry shops mixed with a library, a post office, and country stores. The village's festivals of Daff O'ville Day (late April) and Christmas Stroll (mid-December) are heavily attended.

An 1824 sea captain's house is the setting for the **Osterville Historical Society Museum,** which displays antiques, dolls, and exhibits on Osterville's history. Two wooden boat museums, each showcasing various sailing vessels, as well as the Cammett House (dating from the early 18th century) are also on the property. ⊠ *155 W. Bay Rd.,* ☎ *508/428–5861.* ☞ *$3.* ☉ *Mid-June–Oct., Thurs.–Sun. 1:30–4:30.*

NEED A
BREAK?

Gone Chocolate (⊠ 858 Main St., ☎ 508/420–0202) will tempt you with old-fashioned chocolate-pecan turtles, saltwater taffy, ice cream, and other confections.

Dining

$$ ✕ **Wimpy's.** In spite of its name and namesake, this is not a fast-food hamburger joint but a Cape standby with an extensive menu that favors Italian food and fried fish, from chicken picatta to a seafood platter. The restaurant occupies an expanded space that began life as the 1821 Charles Boult House. Wimpy's has built a large and loyal clientele that fills a big family dining room, a sunny atrium, and a dark traditional tavern, the latter with cozy booths and a fine old bar. The frying batter and fish selections are on the bland side, so opt for the more inventive specials such as tortilla-crusted salmon topped in a caper sauce or a simple prime rib (when available). You can get takeout here, too. This is just about the only choice in town, so make the most of it. ⊠ *752 Main St.,* ☎ *580/428–6300; 508/428–3474 for takeout. AE, DC, MC, V.*

Outdoor Activities and Sports

Holly Hill Farm (⊠ 240 Flint St., Marstons Mills, ☎ 508/428–2621) offers horseback-riding instruction and day camp but no trail rides.

Shopping

Oak & Ivory (⊠ 1112 Main St., ☎ 508/428–9425) specializes in Nantucket lightship baskets made on the premises, as well as gold miniature baskets and scrimshaw. China, gold jewelry, and other gifts round out the selection.

Centerville

🔟 *2½ mi northeast of Osterville, 4 mi southwest of Barnstable.*

Centerville was once a busy seafaring town, a history evident in the 50 or so shipbuilders' and sea captains' houses along its quiet, tree-shaded streets. Offering the pleasures of both sheltered ocean beaches on Nantucket Sound, such as **Craigville Beach** (☞ *below*), and fresh-water swimming in Lake Wequaquet, it has been a popular vacation area since the mid-19th century. Shoot Flying Hill Road, named by Native Americans, is the highest point of land on the Cape, with panoramic views to Plymouth and Provincetown to the north and to Falmouth and Hyannis to the south.

Set in a 19th-century house, the **Centerville Historical Society Museum** exhibits furnished period rooms, Sandwich glass, miniature carvings of birds by Anthony Elmer Crowell, models of ships, marine artifacts, military uniforms and artifacts, antique tools, perfume bottles (dating from 1760 to 1920), 300 costumes (from 1650 to 1950), and quilts, and it has a research library. Each summer there are special costume exhibits or other shows. ⊠ *513 Main St.,* ☎ *508/775–0331.* ☞ *$3.* ☉ *June–Sept., Wed.–Sat. 12:30–4:30.*

The **1856 Country Store** (✉ 555 Main St., ☎ 508/775–1856) still sells penny candy, except that these days each candy costs at least 25 pennies. The store also carries newspapers, coffee, crafts, jams, and all kinds of gadgets and toys. You can sip your coffee—and take a political stance—by choosing a wooden bench out front, one marked DEMO-CRAT and the other REPUBLICAN.

NEED A BREAK? Sample the homemade offerings at **Four Seas Ice Cream** (✉ 360 S. Main St., ☎ 508/775–1394), a tradition for generations (67 years in 2001) of summer visitors. It's open Memorial Day–Labor Day until 10 PM.

Lodging

$$–$$$ 🛏 **Tradewinds Inn.** Cape Cod conjures up images of sand and surf, and since 1963 the motel-style Tradewinds Inn has offered both—and a lot more. The 6-acre property, overlooking the Atlantic Ocean, Lake Elizabeth, and the pretty village of Craigville, has large, family-friendly ocean-view rooms, each with a balcony or patio. There are also three efficiencies with fully equipped kitchenettes, but skip the less attractive non-water-view rooms in the detached buildings. The furnishings are simple but appealing: whitewashed furniture, floral quilts, and tasteful if somewhat unspectacular prints dotting the walls. All rooms have TV and phones. A small, sandy beach just for guests is down the path from the main lodge. The wicker-festooned, knotty-pine-paneled lobby has a fireplace and a cocktail bar. ✉ *780 Craigville Beach Rd., Box 477, 02632,* ☎ *508/775–0365 or 877/444–7966,* FAX *508/790–1404. 28 rooms, 4 suites, 3 efficiencies. Air-conditioning, lobby lounge, putting green, beach. AE, MC, V. Closed Nov.–Apr. CP.* 🐾

Outdoor Activities and Sports

Craigville Beach, on Craigville Beach Road, is a long, wide strand that is extremely popular with the collegiate crowd (it's also known by its nickname, Muscle Beach). The beach has lifeguards, showers, and rest rooms, and there is food nearby. A $10 parking fee is charged in summer.

Hyannis

⓫–⓮ *3½ mi east of Centerville, 23 mi east of the Bourne Bridge.*

Hyannis was named for the Native American Sachem Iyanno, who sold the area for £20 and two pairs of pants. He would have sold it for far more had there been any indication that Hyannis would become known as the "home port of Cape Cod" or that the Kennedys would have pitched so many tents here. Hyannis is effectively the transportation center of the Cape; it's near the airport, and ferries depart here for Nantucket and (in season) Martha's Vineyard. The busy roads feeding into the town are lined with big-box stores you'll find anywhere.

A bustling year-round hub of activity, Hyannis has the Cape's largest concentration of businesses, shops, malls, hotels and motels, restaurants, and entertainment venues. Main Street is lined with used-book and gift shops, jewelers, clothing stores, summer-wear and T-shirt shops, and ice cream and candy stores, but the street can have a somewhat forlorn, down-at-the-heels feeling, as the malls outside downtown have taken their toll on business. There are, however, plenty of eateries, both fun and fancy.

Perhaps best known for its association with the Kennedy clan, the Hyannis area was also a vacation site for President Ulysses S. Grant in 1874 and later for President Grover Cleveland. Hyannis is making an effort to preserve its historical connection with the sea. By 1840 more than

200 shipmasters had established homes in the Hyannis–Hyannis Port area. Aselton Park (at the intersection of South and Ocean streets) and the Village Green on Main Street are the sites of events celebrating this history, and Aselton Park marks the starting point of the scenic Walkway to the Sea, which extends to the dock area.

Three parallel streets run through the heart of town. Busy, shop-filled Main Street runs one-way from east to west; South Street runs from west to east; and North Street is open to two-way traffic. The airport rotary connects with heavily trafficked Routes 132 and 28, and with U.S. 6. Off Ocean Street and Sea Street lie several excellent beaches, including **Kalmus Park Beach,** renowned for its stiff winds and hordes of windsurfers, and the smaller **Veterans Park Beach,** next to the Kennedy Memorial.

⑪ In Main Street's Old Town Hall, the surprisingly sparse **John F. Kennedy Hyannis Museum** explores JFK's Cape years (1934–63) through enlarged and annotated photographs culled from the archives of the JFK Library near Boston, as well as a seven-minute video narrated by Walter Cronkite. The gift shop sells mugs, T-shirts, and presidential memorabilia. ⊠ *397 Main St.,* ☎ *508/790–3077.* ☞ *$3.* ☼ *Mid-Apr.–mid-Oct., Mon.–Sat. 10–4, Sun. 1–4; last admission at 3:30. Call for off-season hrs.*

⑫ The **St. Francis Xavier Church** (⊠ 347 South St., ☎ 508/775–0818) is where Rose Kennedy and her family worshiped during their summers on the Cape; the pew that John F. Kennedy used regularly is marked by a plaque.

Beyond the bustling docks where waterfront restaurants draw crowds, and ferries, harbor tour boats, and deep-sea fishing vessels come and
⑬ go, the quiet esplanade by the **John F. Kennedy Memorial** (⊠ Off

Ocean St. south of Channel Point) overlooks boat-filled Lewis Bay. JFK loved to sail these waters, and in 1966 the people of Barnstable erected a plaque and fountain pool here in his memory. Adjacent to the memorial is **Veterans Park,** with a beach, a tree-shaded picnic and barbecue area, and a playground.

⑭ Hyannis Port was a mecca for Americans during the Kennedy presidency, when the **Kennedy Compound** became the summer White House. The days of hordes of Secret Service men and swarms of tourists trampling down the bushes are gone, and the area is once again a community of quietly posh estates, though the Kennedy mystique is such that tourists still seek it out. The best way to get a glimpse of the compound is from the water on one of the many harbor tours or cruises.

Joseph P. and Rose Kennedy bought their house here—the largest one, closest to the water—in 1929 as a healthful place to summer with their soon-to-be-nine children. (Son Ted bought the house before his mother's death in 1995.) Sons Jack and Bobby bought neighboring houses in the 1950s. Jack's is the one at the corner of Scudder and Irving, with the 6-ft-high stockade fence on two sides. Bobby's is next to it, with the white fieldstone chimney. Ted bought a home on Squaw Island, a private island connected to the area by a causeway at the end of Scudder Avenue. It now belongs to his ex-wife, Joan. Eunice (Kennedy) and Sargent Shriver have a house near Squaw Island, on Atlantic Avenue.

The compound is relatively self-sufficient in terms of entertainment: Rose Kennedy's former abode (with 14 rooms and nine baths) has a movie theater, a private beach, a boat dock, a swimming pool, a tennis court, and a sports field that was the scene of the famous Kennedy touch-football matches. More recently, Maria Shriver, Caroline Kennedy Schlossberg, and other family members have had their wedding receptions here. In the summer of 1999 family members waited here for confirmation of John Kennedy Jr.'s death in a plane crash off Martha's Vineyard. He and his wife were flying her sister to the Vineyard before continuing on to a cousin's wedding in Hyannis; all three were killed.

☪ Perfect for a rainy day, **Smith Family Amusement** is replete with bowling lanes, video-game rooms, and that old seaside favorite, Skee-ball. ✉ *441 Main St.,* ☎ *508/775–3411.* ☉ *Daily; hrs vary.*

OFF THE   **CAPE COD POTATO CHIPS –** There's a standing invitation on the back of
BEATEN PATH   the bag: come for a free factory tour and get free samples of the
              crunchy all-natural chips hand-cooked in kettles in small batches. ✉ *Independence Dr. to Breeds Hill Rd., off Rte. 132,* ☎ *508/775–7253.* ☉ *July–Aug., weekdays 9–5, Sat. 10–4; Sept.–June, weekdays 9–5.*

Dining and Lodging

$$$ ✕ **Roadhouse Café.** For 20 years now, Dave and Melissa Colombo's
★   Roadhouse Café has been one of the smartest choices for a night out in Hyannis. Candlelight flickers off the white-linen tablecloths and dark-wood wainscoting. The roasted red pepper–and–goat cheese appetizer is a savory combination, and shrimp and basil pesto over linguine is full of sun-dried tomatoes and whole roasted garlic cloves. All desserts are made on the premises, so do indulge in the rich tiramisu. In the more casual bistro and the mahogany bar, you can order from a separate menu, which offers thin-crust pizza as well as burgers, sandwiches, and other lighter fare. On Monday night year-round in the bistro is the best straight-ahead jazz on Cape Cod, with such regulars as pianist Dave McKenna and Lou Colombo (the trumpet-playing father of Dave). There's a piano bar every other night of the week between July

4 and Labor Day; it continues on Friday and Saturday in the off-season. ⊠ *488 South St.,* ☎ *508/775–2386. Reservations essential. AE, D, MC, V. No lunch.*

$$–$$$ ✕ **The Paddock.** For more than 30 years the Paddock has been synonymous with excellent formal dining on the Cape—it's authentic Victorian style, with sumptuous upholstery in the main dining room and old-style wicker on the breezy summer porch. Its menu manages to be traditional yet deceptively innovative, combining fresh ingredients in novel ways. A salad of duck, apple, sharp Vermont cheddar, and walnuts on baby greens with cider-mustard vinaigrette is but one example. Steak au poivre, with the promise of five varieties of crushed peppercorns, is masterful; the superb Pacific Rim chicken is a grilled breast topped with oranges and mangoes, served on mixed greens and Asian noodles. Terrific brawny reds are on the award-winning wine list. An older crowd enjoys live music in the evening at the bar, where a Manhattan is still the drink of choice. ⊠ *W. Main St. rotary, next to Melody Tent,* ☎ *508/775–7677. AE, DC, MC, V. Closed mid-Nov.–Mar.*

$$–$$$ ✕ **Penguins Seagrill.** That a penguin is a bird that swims has symbolic import for this restaurant: although owner-chef Bobby Gold experiments carefully, he never loses sight of the fresh grilled seafood he prepares so well. Baked stuffed lobster (from 1 to 3 pounds) is outstanding, served with crabmeat stuffing topped with fresh sea scallops. There are a number of excellent pasta dishes, again with seafood, such as pasta Fiore: shrimp, scallops, and lobster with mushrooms, scallions, sherry, and cream sauce on angel-hair pasta. All the breads and desserts are homemade. The dining room is on two levels, with wood and brick and carvings of sea life galore. ⊠ *331 Main St.,* ☎ *508/775–2023. AE, DC, MC, V. No lunch weekends.*

$$–$$$ ✕ **RooBar.** A bit of Manhattan on Main Street, RooBar has a dark, sophisticated feel, aided by good music, low light, and a crowded, hip bar scene at night. It's all crowned by a flickering wood-fired oven in the back wall. From this oven come "hand-spun to order" pizzas such as scallop and prosciutto with asparagus and goat cheese. The scene gleams at night, but the lunch menu is fresh and inventive and not to be overlooked. Try the Big-Ass Grilled Shrimp appetizer, three enormous grilled shrimp in a red curry and coconut sauce, and the fire-roasted half chicken entrée, rubbed with toasted fennel and cumin seeds. The owner is a member of actor Christopher Reeve's family, and a portion of all profits goes to the Christopher Reeve Foundation for Spinal Cord Research. ⊠ *586 Main St.,* ☎ *508/778–6515. Reservations essential. AE, MC, V.*

$$ ✕ **Fazio's.** Set in an old Italian bakery building, Fazio's looks like the trattoria it is, with wood floors, high ceilings, and a deli case full of fresh pasta, breads, and cheeses (not for sale). There's also an espresso and cappuccino bar. Chef Tom Fazio's menu leans on simple, fresh ingredients and herbed pastas, such as thick, rough-cut black pepper tagliatelle with sausage and eggplant chunks in a garlicky tomato sauce. All ravioli, pastas, and breads are homemade. Take home some fresh cannoli for dessert. ⊠ *294 Main St.,* ☎ *508/775–9400. Reservations not accepted. AE, MC, V. No lunch.*

$$ ✕ **Harry's.** Homesick for a little bit of the French Quarter on Cape Cod? Harry's feels as though it's transplanted from New Orleans and serves accordingly—both Cajun and creole—with great spices and sizable portions. The menu features a number of meal-size sandwiches and blackened local fish that's done to perfection, with a jambalaya that makes you wonder if there isn't a bayou nearby. It's also a prime location for music: you can hear blues, zydeco, and folk music Tuesday through Sunday in summer, weekends in the slower months. ⊠ *700 Main St.,* ☎ *508/778–4188. Reservations not accepted. AE, DC, MC, V.*

$$ ✕ **Starbuck's.** No, it's not another branch of the Seattle-based coffee company but something more like a T. G. I. Friday's with an edge. Walls and rafters are hung with doodads and hoo-has of every description, but there's no theme: a tuba here, a couple of mannequins there, a miniature World War I fighter plane from out of nowhere. The menu matches the decor, with selections yanked from all over the planet: ostensibly Asian shrimp deep-fried in a coconut-tempura batter, Buck's beef burrito from the Tex-Mex column, and Italian standards such as spaghetti and meatballs. There's also an assortment of burgers and Buckwiches. This might not be for everyone, but it's good if you're in the mood for something raucous. Reservations are essential on weekends. ⊠ *624 Iyannough Rd. (Rte. 132),* ☎ *508/778–6767. AE, D, DC, MC, V.*

$$ ✕ **Ying's.** The huge menu at this little pan-Asian place combines the best of Thai, Korean, and Japanese cuisines. Ying's sushi and sashimi combos are artful, and its wealth of different curried Thai seafood, noodles, and fried rice dishes range from spicy to, well, really spicy. For something different try the Korean *bibimbap* (vegetables, beef, and egg on rice with hot sauce). Tables are set up by the windows, and there's a sushi bar as well as a small lounge area with a selection of Asian beers. Avoiding alcohol? Try the sweet and thick Thai iced tea—you won't need dessert. But if you do, the fried ice cream is a treat. ⊠ *59 Center St.,* ☎ *508/790–2432. AE, MC, V. No lunch weekends.*

$–$$ ✕ **Barbyann's.** Sooner or later your children are likely to reach their limit of seafood, even fish-and-chips. When that happens, pack everyone off to Barbyann's for an inexpensive family meal—steak and seafood, pizza and burgers, a couple of hardly authentic but child-pleasing Mexican dishes, and loads of appetizers. Best of all are the Buffalo chicken wings, hot and spicy and filling. There's an outdoor patio with umbrella tables, and "night bird" specials are offered all evening Monday–Thursday. ⊠ *120 Airport Rd.,* ☎ *508/775–9795. Reservations not accepted. AE, D, DC, MC, V.*

$–$$ ✕ **Baxter's Fish N' Chips.** Fried seafood being the Cape staple that it is, you may want to plan ahead for a trip to pay homage to one of the best fry-o-lators around. Fried clams are delicious and generous, cooked up hot to order with french fries and homemade tartar sauce. Outside, a number of picnic tables, some set up on an old floating ferry outside the main restaurant, allow you to lose no time in the sun while eating, with lobster, burgers, or something from the excellent raw bar. Indoors, Baxter's Boat House Club, slightly more upscale, serves the same menu but with a number of very good specials as well; no one under 21 is allowed here, however. The restaurant is right on Hyannis Harbor, and since 1955 it's been a favorite of boaters and bathers alike. ⊠ *Pleasant St.,* ☎ *508/775–4490. Reservations not accepted. AE, MC, V. Closed Columbus Day–Apr. and weekdays Labor Day–Columbus Day.*

$–$$ ✕ **Sam Diego's.** The bar is busy with people seeing and being seen, and the menu has satisfyingly authentic Mexican tortillas, burritos, and delicious *mole poblano* (chicken with a spicy, bittersweet cocoa sauce). The prop-shop decor may be a little cheesy—sombreros, Aztec birds, and the like—but the atmosphere is fun and friendly. Especially in the early evening, this recently expanded place is popular with families, thanks in part to the all-you-can-eat chili and taco bar—a good option when the children need a little change of culinary pace. An interesting dessert, crusty deep-fried ice cream, is served in a giant goblet. Later on, the bar scene picks up steam; dinner is served until midnight. ⊠ *950 Iyanough Rd. (Rte. 132),* ☎ *508/771–8816. AE, D, MC, V.*

$$$–$$$$ 🏨 **Sheraton Hyannis Resort.** For its beautifully landscaped setting, extensive services and pampering, and superior resort facilities, it's hard to beat the Sheraton. The lobby area is elegant, but the rooms, each with a private balcony, are admittedly a bit dull—standard contemporary hotel style. All, however, come with amenities such as hair dryers, ironing boards, and coffeemakers. ⊠ *Scudder La., West End rotary, 02601,* ☎ *508/775–7775 or 800/325–3535 (reservations center off Cape Cod),* ℻ *508/778–6423. 230 rooms. Restaurant, pub, room service, air-conditioning, 1 indoor and 1 outdoor pool, beauty salon, 18-hole golf course, putting green, 2 tennis courts, health club, business services. AE, D, DC, MC, V.* ☜

$$$ ⌂ **Simmons Homestead Inn.** This 1820 former sea captain's country estate is a delightful, inviting escape from the world, even though it's only two minutes from congested downtown Hyannis. Gregarious innkeeper Bill Putman doesn't hesitate to share his opinions, and he encourages guests to return around 6 each evening for a wine-and-socializing hour. If you can't stand smoke, though, beware: although the bedrooms are no-smoking, Putnam—a smoker himself—allows smoking in some public spaces. Each room in the main house or the detached barn is named for an animal. They have antique, wicker, or canopied four-poster beds topped with brightly colored quilts; some have fireplaces and private decks. The Bird Room, the largest and cheeriest, has an old-fashioned cast-iron tub and a private deck. You can borrow the 10-speed mountain bikes to explore the town, or simply enjoy the expansive backyard from the wraparound porch. Simmons Pond is a short jaunt on the property's trail. Check out Putnam's collection of vintage sports cars. Children are welcome; dogs are permitted with advance notice for an additional $25. ⊠ *288 Scudder Ave., Box 578, Hyannis Port 02647,* ☎ *508/778–4999 or 800/637–1649,* ℻ *508/790–1342. 12 rooms, 1 suite. No-smoking rooms, hot tub, bicycles, billiards. AE, D, MC, V. BP.* ☜

$$ ⌂ **Anchor-In.** All rooms have harbor views at this inviting hotel on the
★ north end of Lewis Bay and Hyannis Harbor. The hotel's simple streetside appearance belies its spacious accommodations and fairly extensive grounds—and the rates are hard to beat. Most rooms have small balconies overlooking the water and standard amenities such as air-conditioning, cable TV, and phones. The deluxe and executive rooms' wraparound porches make them worth the extra money. The Arnett family owns this hotel, delivering the warm, personal service of a small B&B. Main Street restaurants are minutes away, and ferries for Nantucket and Martha's Vineyard are just around the corner. ⊠ *1 South St. 02601,* ☎ *508/775–0357,* ℻ *508/775–1313. 43 rooms. Air-conditioning, pool. AE, D, MC, V.* ☜

$$ ⌂ **Breakwaters.** If you were any closer to the water, you'd be in it—
★ that's how close these weathered gray-shingle cottages are to Nantucket Sound. Privately owned condos rented as cottages by the week (or day if vacancies occur), the one-, two-, and three-bedroom units offer all the comforts of home, including linens and towels. There's an inground heated pool less than 200 ft from the lifeguarded town beach. Each unit has one or two full baths; kitchens with microwave, coffeemaker, refrigerator, toaster, and stove; TV and phone (local calls are free); and a deck or patio with grill and picnic table. Most have water views. Another plus is the daily (except Sunday) maid service. The laundromat at the end of the street (at the corner of North Street) will wash and fold your dirty duds for a nominal fee. From June through August you must rent by the week. ⊠ *432 Sea St., Box 118, 02601,* ☎ ℻ *508/775–6831. 18 cottages. Refrigerators, pool, beach, baby-sitting. No credit cards. No smoking. Closed mid-Oct.–Apr.* ☜

$$ ⌂ **Comfort Inn Cape Cod.** All the rooms at this business- and family-oriented cinder-block motel just off the highway have white-oak-veneer furnishings and include one king-size or two double beds, a table and chairs or a desk and chair, and a wardrobe. Some king rooms have sofa beds. The quietest rooms are those on the top floor that face the pond and woods; all have free HBO movies and Nintendo, and pets are allowed. Guests have free use of the nearby Barnstable Athletic Club, and children under 18 stay free. Although the location is convenient to the highway, keep in mind that Route 132 is painfully busy during the summer months. ✉ *1470 Iyanough Rd. (Rte. 132), 02601, ☎ 508/771–4804 or 800/228–5150, ℻ 508/790–2336. 103 rooms, 1 suite. Indoor pool, sauna, hot tub, exercise room. AE, D, DC, MC, V. CP.* ✎

$–$$ 🖭 **HoJo Express Inn.** This centrally located inn—squarely placed on downtown Main Street—is in walking distance to all of Hyannis's major sights. The no-surprises rooms have large double beds and typical motel-chain furniture; most, unfortunately, have views of the drab parking lot. A value-conscious package plan includes discount shopping coupons and a meal allowance at four nearby restaurants. ✉ *447 Main St., 02601, ☎ 508/775–3000, ℻ 508/771–1457. 39 rooms, 1 suite. Restaurant, bar, indoor pool. AE, D, DC, MC, V. CP.*

$–$$ 🖭 **Hyannis Inn Motel.** The second-oldest motel in Hyannis, this modest two-story motel has been family-owned and -run for the past 45 years. It also has a link to the Kennedys: during JFK's presidential campaign, the main building served as press headquarters. The main building's immaculate rooms, nicely decorated in shades of dark blue and rose, have double, queen-size, or king-size beds, cable TV, and direct-dial phones; some have whirlpool tubs. The newer deluxe rooms—built in 1981 in a separate wing out back—are larger, sunnier, and quieter (they don't face Main Street) and offer queen- or king-size beds, sleeper sofas, walk-in closets, and refrigerators. The restaurant serves breakfast only. Children under 12 stay free. ✉ *473 Main St., 02601, ☎ 508/775–0255 or 800/922–8993, ℻ 508/771–0456. 77 rooms. Restaurant, pub, air-conditioning, indoor pool, sauna. AE, D, MC, V. Closed Dec.–Jan.* ✎

$–$$ 🖭 **Inn on Sea Street.** Charming and relaxed, this B&B is just a short walk from the beach and downtown Hyannis. Guest rooms, in the 1849 main house or the mansard-roof Victorian across the street, have canopy beds, antique furnishings, and claw-foot tubs. The across-the-street rooms are generally larger; all have queen-size beds, one has a private porch, and there's also a common living room and shared kitchen. Innkeepers Sylvia and Fred LaSelva, who took over the inn in 1999, are gracious and welcoming hosts. Breakfasts are served on china, silver, and crystal in the antiques-and-lace dining room of the main house or in the glassed-in sunporch. Out back, the small one-bedroom Honeymoon Cottage, all in white, has its own kitchen. Guests have privileges at the nearby 18-hole golf course at the Sheraton Hyannis Resort. ✉ *358 Sea St., 02601, ☎ 508/775–8030, ℻ 508/771–0878. 9 rooms, 7 with bath; 1 cottage. Air-conditioning. No smoking. AE, D, MC, V. Closed Nov.–late-Apr. BP.* ✎

$–$$ 🖭 **Sea Breeze Inn.** The Irish accent of owner-innkeeper Patricia Gib-
★ ney helps make this cedar-shingle B&B two blocks from the beach even more welcoming. Each room has antique or canopied beds and is simply decorated with well-chosen antiques. Larger families may want to stay in one of the three detached cottages; the nicest is the Rose Garden, with three bedrooms (two on the second level), two baths, a TV room, a fireplace, even a washer and dryer. If that's booked, try the Honeymoon Cottage, which has a canopy bed and inviting double Jacuzzi (the cottage is fenced in for total privacy). Patricia's breakfasts are worth getting up early for; you can eat in the dining room or in the outdoor gazebo, surrounded by winsome gardens. ✉ *270 Ocean Ave., at Sea St., 02601, ☎ 508/771–7213, ℻ 508/862–0663. 14 rooms, 3 cottages. Air-conditioning. No smoking. AE, D, MC, V. CP.* ✎

$ 🖭 **Capt. Gosnold Village.** An easy walk to the beach and town, this colony of motel rooms and pink-shutter cottages is ideal for families. Children can ride their bikes around the quiet street, and the pool is fenced in and watched by a lifeguard. In some rooms walls are attractively paneled with painted pine; floors are carpeted, and furnishings are colonial or modern, simple, and pleasant. All cottages have decks and gas grills and receive maid service (except Sunday). The cottages are divided into rooms, efficiencies, and 1- to 3-bedroom cottages. ⊠ *230 Gosnold St., 02601,* ☎ *508/775–9111. 18 cottages. Picnic area, pool, basketball. MC, V. Closed Nov.–mid-Apr.* ✎

Nightlife and the Arts

THE ARTS

The **Boston Pops Esplanade Orchestra** (☎ 508/362–0066) wows a crowd with its annual Pops by the Sea concert, held in August at the Hyannis Village Green. Each year a celebrity guest conductor strikes up the band for a few selected numbers; recent baton bouncers have included Olympia Dukakis, Joan Kennedy, Mike Wallace, and Art Buchwald.

In 1950 the actress Gertrude Lawrence and her husband, producer-manager Richard Aldrich, opened the **Cape Cod Melody Tent** (⊠ 21 W. Main St., at West End rotary, ☎ 508/775–9100) to showcase Broadway musicals and concerts. Today it's the Cape's top venue for pop concerts and comedy shows; performers who have played here, in the round, include Aretha Franklin, Willie Nelson, Tom Jones, Ziggy Marley, KC and the Sunshine Band, Anne Murray, and Tony Bennett. The Tent also hosts a Wednesday-morning children's theater series in July and August.

The 90-member **Cape Symphony Orchestra** (☎ 508/362–1111), under former D'Oyly Carte Opera conductor Royston Nash, gives regular classical and children's concerts with guest artists October through May. Performances are held at the Barnstable Performing Arts Center at Barnstable High School (⊠ 744 W. Main St., Hyannis).

Opera New England of Cape Cod (☎ 508/771–3600 for schedules and locations and reservations) has two or three performances a year, in spring and fall, by the National Lyric Opera Company.

In July and August **town-band concerts** (☎ 508/362–5230 or 800/449–6647) are held on Wednesday evening starting at 7:30 on the Town Green on Main Street.

NIGHTLIFE

Bobby Byrne's Pub (⊠ Rte. 28 at Bearses Way, ☎ 508/775–1425) is a branch of this local chain; it's comfortable and unpretentious.

Bud's Country Lounge (⊠ Bearses Way and Rte. 132, ☎ 508/771–2505) has pool tables and provides live country music, dancing, and line-dancing lessons year-round.

Club 477 (⊠ 477 Yarmouth Rd., ☎ 508/771–7511), in the old Hyannis train station, is the Upper and Mid Cape's only gay club. There's a piano bar on the lower level and a dance bar on the upper floor with music almost as hot as the crowd.

The **Prodigal Son** (⊠ 10 Ocean St., ☎ 508/771–1337) is home to some of the best up-and-coming bands and musicians in New England. The lineup includes acoustic, blues, jazz, and rock, and even spoken-word performers. Their high-octane java keeps the joint jumpin'. Call for schedule.

Pufferbellies (⊠ 183 Iyanough Rd. (Rte. 28), ☎ 508/790–4300 or 800/233–4301), in an old railroad roundhouse by the Hyannis tracks, is the Mid Cape's largest dance club, with four dance floors of swing, country line dancing, and DJ tunes, as well as eats, Internet terminals, and, yes, volleyball courts.

The **Roadhouse Café** (⊠ 488 South St., ☎ 508/775–2386; ☞ Dining, *above*) has great jazz year-round.

Starbuck's (⊠ 645 Iyanough Rd., ☎ 508/778–6767; ☞ Dining, *above*) presents live acoustic entertainment in its bar many nights year-round.

Outdoor Activities and Sports

BASEBALL

The **Hyannis Mets** (☎ 508/420–0962), of the collegiate Cape Cod Baseball League, play home games at McKeon Field (⊠ High School Rd.) from mid-June to mid-August.

BEACHES

Kalmus Park Beach, at the south end of Ocean Street, is a fine, wide sandy beach with an area set aside for windsurfers and a sheltered area that's good for children. It has a snack bar, rest rooms, showers, and lifeguards. Parking fee is $10 in season.

Veterans Park, next to the John F. Kennedy Memorial on Ocean Street, has a small beach that's especially good for children; it's sheltered from waves and fairly shallow. There are picnic tables, barbecue facilities, showers, rest rooms, and a playground. The parking fee is $10 in season.

BIKING

Cascade Motor Lodge (⊠ 201 Main St., ☎ 508/775–9717), by the bus and train station, rents three-speed and mountain bikes by the half day, full day, and week.

BOATING

Eastern Mountain Sports (⊠ 1513 Iyanough Rd. (Rte. 132), ☎ 508/362–8690) rents kayaks and camping gear.

Sailing tours aboard the catboat **Eventide** (⊠ Ocean St. Dock, ☎ 508/775–0222) offer a variety of 1½-hour cruises through Hyannis Harbor and out into Nantucket Sound, including a nature tour and a sunset cruise.

Hy-Line (⊠ Ocean St. Dock, ☎ 508/778–2600) offers cruises on replicas of old-time Maine coastal steamers. The one-hour tours of Hyannis Harbor and Lewis Bay include a view of the Kennedy compound and other points of interest.

FISHING

Hy-Line (⊠ Ocean St. Dock, ☎ 508/790–0696) leads fishing trips on a walk-on basis in spring and fall, but reservations are mandatory in summer.

GOLF

Sheraton Hyannis Resort (⊠ West End rotary, ☎ 508/775–7775) has a beautifully landscaped, challenging 18-hole, par-3 course open to nonguests. You may bump into some famous faces: many performers from the Cape Cod Melody Tent tee off here while in town.

HEALTH AND FITNESS CLUBS

Barnstable Athletic Club (⊠ 55 Attucks La., Independence Park, off Rte. 132, ☎ 508/771–7734) has four racquetball-wallyball courts (wallyball is volleyball played on a racquetball court), a squash court, basketball, an aerobics room, whirlpools, sauna and steam rooms, and cardiovascular and free-weight equipment. Day care and day and short-term memberships are available.

Hyannis Athletic Club (⊠ Sheraton Hyannis Resort, West End rotary, ☎ 508/862–2535) has two outdoor tennis courts, a fitness club, and indoor and outdoor pools. Day and short-term memberships are available.

The **Joseph P. Kennedy Jr. Memorial Skating Rink** (✉ 141 Bassett La., ☎ 508/790–6345), named after the late Kennedy scion and war hero, offers skating October through March, with special times reserved for teenagers, youngsters, and families; you can rent skates there.

Cape Cod Storyland Golf is a 2-acre miniature golf course set up as a mini–Cape Cod, with each of the 18 holes a Cape town. The course winds around small ponds and waterfalls, a full-size working gristmill, and reproductions of historic Cape buildings. The picture possibilities are great. There's an additional charge of $5 for the bumper boats. ✉ *70 Center St., by railroad depot,* ☎ *508/778–4339.* ⌨ *$6.50.* ⊙ *Mid-Apr.–Oct., daily 8 AM–midnight.*

Shopping

Cape Cod Mall (✉ Between Rtes. 132 and 28, ☎ 508/771–0200), already the Cape's largest, completed a major expansion in 1999–2000. It now has 120 shops, including department stores from Macy's to Marshall's, and a 12-screen movie complex.

A mix of Disney-esque fantasy and Victorian excess, the Hyannis branch of the **Christmas Tree Shops** (✉ 655 Iyanough Rd. [Rte. 132], ☎ 508/778–5521) is the largest on the Cape. Many people come just to gawk at the glass-enclosed clock out front, made in the 1920s in Cincinnati.

Colonial Candle of Cape Cod (✉ 388 Main St., ☎ 508/771–2790 or 508/771–3916) is touristy, but the candles are top-notch.

Hyannis Antique Co-op (✉ 500 Main St., ☎ 508/778–0512) has a large selection of jewelry, glassware, porcelain, furniture, dolls, prints, and collectibles at good prices.

Nantucket Trading Company (✉ 354 Main St., ☎ 508/790–3933), sort of a local version of Pier 1, sells an incredible array of neat necessities for your home, including edibles, table linens, cooking gadgets, and kitchen accessories.

The handsome flagship **Puritan** (✉ 408 Main St., ☎ 508/775–2400) store carries upscale clothing brands from North Face to Eileen Fisher and Ralph Lauren and also sells outdoor gear. Service is great here; there are five other stores around the Cape.

If you're tired of wearing T-shirts and beach cover-ups, duck into **12 West** (✉ 558 Main St., ☎ 508/771–7000) for upscale-casual women's clothing and accessories.

West Yarmouth

🔟 *4 mi south of Yarmouth Port, 3 mi east of Hyannis.*

There's no getting around it: the part of the Cape people love to hate is Route 28. Passing through the area, it's one motel, strip mall, nightclub, and miniature golf course after another. In 1989, as *Cape Cod Life* magazine put it, "the town [began] to plant 350 trees in hopes that eventually the trees' leaves, like the fig leaf of Biblical lore, cover the shame of unkempt overdevelopment." Regardless of the glut of tacky tourist traps, there are some interesting sights in the little villages along the way. So take Route 28 if you want to intersperse amusements with your sightseeing, because you really can amuse yourself to no end on this section of 28. A sensible option if you want to avoid this road entirely: take speedy U.S. 6 to the exit nearest what you want to visit and then cut south across the interior. If you must travel the Route 28 area, take Buck Island Road, which runs north of and parallel to much of the busy route in West and South Yarmouth.

The village of West Yarmouth was settled in 1643 by Yelverton Crowe, who acquired his land from a Native American sachem. The deal they struck was that Crowe could have as much land as he could traverse in an hour in exchange for an "ox-chain, a copper kettle. . . and a few trinkets." The first settlers were farmers; in the 1830s, when Central Wharf near Mill Creek was built, the town turned to more commercial ventures as it became headquarters for the growing packet service that ferried passengers from the Cape to Boston.

Listed on the National Register of Historic Places, the 1710 **Baxter Grist Mill,** by the shore of Mill Pond, is the only mill on Cape Cod powered by an inside water turbine; the others use either wind or paddle wheels. The mill was converted to the indoor metal turbine in 1860 because of the pond's low water level and the damage done to the wooden paddle wheel by winter freezes. The original metal turbine is displayed on the grounds, and a replica powers the restored mill. A videotape tells the mill's history. ⊠ *Rte. 28,* ☎ *508/398–2231, ext. 292.* ☞ *Free.* ☉ *Early June–Labor Day, weekends 1–5; also open Mon. or Fri. 1–5 on some holiday weekends.*

16 A unique and lovely walking trail, the **Yarmouth Boardwalk** (⊠ Off Meadowbrook La.) stretches through swamp and marsh and leads to the edge of Swan Pond, a pretty pond ringed with woods. To get here, take Winslow Gray Road northeast from Route 28, turn right on Meadowbrook Lane, and take it to the end.

An entertaining, educational, and occasionally hokey stop for children, **ZooQuarium** has sea-lion shows, a petting zoo with native wildlife, wandering peacocks, pony rides in summer, aquariums, and educational programs. The Children's Discovery Center presents changing exhibits such as *Bone Up on Bones* (all about skeletons), *Zoo Nutrition* (in which children prepare meals), and the self-explanatory *Scoop on Poop.* ⊠ *674 Main St. (Rte. 28),* ☎ *508/775–8883.* ☞ *$8.* ☉ *Mid-Feb.–June and Sept.–late Nov., daily 9:30–5; July–Aug., daily 9:30–6.*

NEED A **Jerry's Seafood and Dairy Freeze** (⊠ 654 Main St. , ☎ 508/775–
BREAK? 9752) offers fried clams and onion rings, along with thick frappes (milk shakes), frozen yogurt, and soft ice cream at good prices.

Dining and Lodging

$ ✕ **Red Rose Inn.** The breakfast and lunch menus are solid and the ocean views are hard to beat at this small inn and restaurant next to Englewood Beach. Red Rosbrough, with his wife, Rose—get it?—opened the inn, and it's now in the hands of grandson Rick Wilkey, the third-generation chef and innkeeper. Rose was fond of the classic women's dress hats of the flapper days and collected them, apparently with a passion—they hang, delicate but by the hundreds on hooks and shelves throughout the small, sunlighted dining room. Rick's breakfast menu is simple and hearty, with a few gems—eggs Oscar combines the classic Benedict recipe with crabmeat and asparagus, while Titanic French toast, a house favorite, flies off the griddle. Big eaters will gravitate to the hearty Innkeeper's Special of two eggs, two pancakes, and ham or sausage. ⊠ *6 New Hampshire Ave.,* ☎ *508/775–2944. No credit cards. Closed Mon.–Wed., off-season. No dinner.*

$–$$ 🛏 **Inn at Lewis Bay.** This 1920s Dutch Colonial overlooks Lewis Bay and is steps from the beach. Enjoy—but be back by 4, when innkeeper Liz Latshaw serves tea and home-baked cookies. Each room is furnished

ONE LAST TRAVEL TIP:

Pack an easy way to reach the world.

Wherever you travel, the MCI WorldCom Card[SM] is the easiest way to stay in touch. You can use it to call to and from more than 125 countries worldwide. And you can earn bonus miles every time you use your card. So go ahead, travel the world. MCI WorldCom[SM] makes it even more rewarding. For additional access codes, visit **www.wcom.com/worldphone**.

EASY TO CALL WORLDWIDE

1. Just dial the WorldPhone® access number of the country you're calling from.

2. Dial or give the operator your MCI WorldCom Card number.

3. Dial or give the number you're calling.

Aruba (A) ⊹	800-888-8
Australia ◆	1-800-881-100
Bahamas ⊹	1-800-888-8000
Barbados (A) ⊹	1-800-888-8000
Bermuda ⊹	1-800-888-8000
British Virgin Islands (A) ⊹	1-800-888-8000
Canada	1-800-888-8000
Costa Rica (A) ◆	0800-012-2222
New Zealand	000-912
Puerto Rico	1-800-888-8000
United States	1-800-888-8000
U.S. Virgin Islands	1-800-888-8000

(A) Calls back to U.S. only.   ⊹ Limited availability.   ◆ Public phones may require deposit of coin or phone card for dial tone.

EARN FREQUENT FLIER MILES

When it Comes to Getting Cash at an ATM, Same Thing.

Whether you're in Yosemite or Yemen, using your Visa® card or ATM card with the PLUS symbol is the easiest and most convenient way to get cash. Even if your bank is in Minneapolis and you're in Miami, Visa/PLUS ATMs make getting cash so easy, you'll feel right at home. After all, Visa/PLUS ATMs are open 24 hours a day, 7 days a week, rain or shine. And if you need help finding one of Visa's 627,000 ATMs in 127 countries worldwide, visit **visa.com/pd/atm**. We'll make finding an ATM as easy as finding the Eiffel Tower, the Pyramids or even the Grand Canyon.

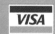

It's Everywhere You Want To Be.®

in country-antiques style, with Laura Ashley linens, fresh flowers, claw-foot tubs, and antique or canopy beds. The rooms also have a name and a theme, such as Secret Garden (ivy-print linens and wallpaper) and Sea Grass. Whalewatch, with its distinctive navys and maroons, is the one decidedly masculine room and one of two with water views. Bountiful breakfasts are served in the dining room, where the hand-stenciled strawberries on the ceiling match the wallpaper. ⊠ *57 Maine Ave., 02673,* ☎ *508/771–3433 or 800/962–6679,* FAX *508/394–1400. 6 rooms. Air-conditioning, beach. No smoking. AE, MC, V. BP.*

$ 🏨 **Americana Holiday Motel.** If you want the convenience of staying
★ on Route 28, this family-owned and -operated strip motel is a good choice. All rooms have cable TV and a phone; those in the rear Pine Grove section overlook serene sea pines and one of the motel's three pools rather than traffic snarls. In the off-season the rates simply can't be beat. ⊠ *99 Main St. (Rte. 28), 02673,* ☎ *508/775–5511 or 800/445–4497,* FAX *508/790–0597. 149 rooms, 4 suites. Coffee shop, air-conditioning, refrigerators, 1 indoor and 2 outdoor pools, hot tub, sauna, putting green, shuffleboard, video games, playground. AE, D, DC, MC, V. Closed Nov.–Mar. CP.*

$ 🏨 **Mariner Motor Lodge.** Say what you will about Route 28—it's crowded and cheesy, but there's no shortage of action, and there are several value-packed hotels. The Mariner, near the Hyannis-West Yarmouth line, is a good family lodging and a bargain, to boot. Although the rooms are standard-issue motel—think basic furnishings like floral bedcovers, carpets that can take a direct hit from a spilled soft drink, and long balcony windows (but no step-out balconies)—they all come with a small refrigerator, TV, and phone. The outdoor pool is heated and large, and a heated indoor pool, with an oversize whirlpool hot tub, is great for rainy days. Also on site is a miniature golf course and vending machines for snacks. Children stay free, and rates on weekdays are reduced. ⊠ *573 Rte. 28, 02673,* ☎ *508/771–7887 or 800/445–4050,* FAX *508/771–2811. 100 rooms. Coffee shop, air-conditioning, in-room safes, no-smoking rooms. AE, D, MC, V.*

Nightlife and the Arts

Cape Cod Irish Village (⊠ 512 Main St. [Rte. 28], ☎ 508/771–0100) has dancing to two- or three-piece bands performing traditional and popular Irish music year-round. The crowd is mostly couples and people over 35.

Clancy's (⊠ 175 Main St. [Rte. 28], ☎ 508/775–3332) offers live entertainment, typically a mix of Irish, folk, and soft rock performed by acoustic guitarist and vocalist Terry Brennan, on weekends year-round.

Mill Hill Club (⊠ 164 Rte. 28, ☎ 508/775–2580) provides something for everyone, from more than 20 TVs to live music, hypnotist's acts, and the occasional men's and women's bikini contests—it's a young, and loud, crowd.

West Yarmouth's summertime **town-band concerts** are held on Monday in July and August at 7 PM at Mattacheese Middle School (⊠ Off Higgins Crowell Rd., ☎ 508/778–1008).

Outdoor Activities and Sports

BIKE RENTAL

All Right Bike & Mower (⊠ 627 Main St. [Rte. 28], ☎ 508/790–3191) rents bikes and mopeds and does on-site repairs.

FISHING

Truman's (⊠ 608 Main St. [Rte. 28], ☎ 508/771–3470) can supply you with a required freshwater license and rental gear.

Shopping

The **Cranberry Bog Outlet Stores** (✉ Rte. 28, ☎ no phone) are on the edge of a working cranberry bog. Bass, Van Heusen, and Izod are a few of the shops here.

South Yarmouth

⓱ *3 mi east of West Yarmouth, 6 mi east of Hyannis.*

The Bass River divides the southern portions of the towns of Yarmouth and Dennis. People also generally refer to the area of South Yarmouth as Bass River. Here you'll find charter boats and boat rentals, as well as a river cruise, plus seafood restaurants and markets. Like West Yarmouth, the town has its stretch of blight and overdevelopment on Route 28, but it also has some nice beaches that are good for families. For a good indication of what the town looked like 100 years ago, take a drive down Pleasant Street and the Main Street section south of Route 28 to view old homes in the Federal and Greek Revival style. This section, along Bass River, was home to the elite businessmen, bankers, and sea merchants.

South Yarmouth was once called Quaker Village for the large numbers of Quakers who settled the area in the 1770s after a smallpox epidemic wiped out the local Native American population.

The 1809 **Quaker Meeting House** is still open for meetings. Two separate entrance doors and the partition down the center were meant to divide the sexes. The adjacent cemetery has simple markers with no epitaphs, an expression of the Friends' belief that all are equal in God's eyes. Behind the cemetery is a circa-1830 one-room Quaker schoolhouse. ✉ *58 N. Main St.,* ☎ *508/398–3773.* ☉ *Services Sun. at 10.*

☙ **Pirate's Cove** is the most elaborate of the Cape's many miniature golf setups, with a hill, a waterfall, a stream, and the 18-hole Blackbeard's Challenge course. ✉ *728 Main St. (Rte. 28),* ☎ *508/394–6200.* ☒ *$6.50.* ☉ *July–Aug., daily 9 AM–11 PM; Apr.–June and Sept.–Oct., most days 10–8, but call.*

☙ For rainy-day fun, the **Ryan Family Amusement Center** offers video-game rooms, Skee-Ball, and bowling. ✉ *1067 Main St. (Rte. 28),* ☎ *508/394–5644.* ☉ *Daily; hrs vary.*

Dining and Lodging

$$–$$$ ✕ **The Skipper.** The new owners of the Skipper had a bang-up second season in 2000, and with good reason. With expanded seating, an expanded menu, and terrific ocean views, this classic Cape restaurant has been getting better and better since its inception in 1936. Sit downstairs in the nautically themed main room or upstairs on the new outside deck featuring views of Nantucket Sound. Skipper's menu is an odd but compelling mix of classic New England seafood, Italian favorites, and international dishes, from Thai pasta to Jamaican jerk chicken. The Skipper is open in season for breakfast, lunch, and dinner. ✉ *152 South Shore Dr.,* ☎ *508/394–7406. Reservations not accepted. AE, D, MC, V. Closed Nov.–March.*

$$$ ▥ **Ocean Mist.** This three-story, upscale motel-style resort sits on its own private (but tiny) beach on Nantucket Sound. The rooms are designed to cover the bases: all have modern furnishings, cable TV, and either wet bars or fully stocked kitchenettes. The duplex loft suites are a step above, with cathedral ceilings, a sitting area with pullout sofa, skylights, and one or two private balconies. ✉ *97 S. Shore Dr., 02664,* ☎ *508/398–2633 or 800/248–6478,* ℻ *508/760–3151. 32 rooms, 31 suites. Coffee shop, air-conditioning, indoor pool, hot tub, beach, coin*

*laundry. AE, D, MC, V. Closed Dec. (except for Christmas holidays)–
mid-Feb.* ✍

$$–$$$ 🏨 **Capt. Farris House.** Steps from the Bass River Bridge dividing South
Yarmouth and West Dennis and a short spin away from congested Route
28 sits this imposing 1845 Greek Revival home, built by the sea captain for whom it's named. The rooms and suites—large and comfortable—have either antique or canopied queen- or king-size beds, extra
pillows, plush comforters, fancy drapes, TVs, and tile baths (all but
one with a whirlpool tub). Some have fireplaces and sundecks, and the
Honeymoon Suite has a private sundeck and a two-person whirlpool
tub. Breakfast is served in the formal dining room or in the interior
glassed-in, brick courtyard, and might feature quiche with pumpkin-
pecan scones or thick French toast. Fresh baked goods and sherry are
available for later-in-the-day nourishment. ⊠ *308 Old Main St., 02664,*
☎ *508/760–2818 or 800/350–9477,* 🖷 *508/398–1262. 6 rooms, 4
suites. Air-conditioning. No smoking. AE, D, MC, V. BP.* ✍

$$ 🏨 **Belvedere B&B.** Elisha Baker, a local sea captain, built this quaint
Federal home around 1820. The Hamilton Room is the most spacious,
with some frilly touches: lace curtains, a lacy bedspread, green floral
wallpaper, and old pink-velvet chairs. Romantics may prefer the first-
floor Boston Room, with green wicker chairs, a two-person whirlpool
tub, and a queen-size bed topped with a rose quilt. The Virginia An-
thony Room (with pink-and-white quilts on the twin four-poster beds)
and the Florilla Room (with a queen-size bed, white wicker furnishings,
and a pink wide-board floor) are both small but cozy and sunny; they
share a bath across the hall. All rooms are air-conditioned. Those who
want privacy might consider the Carriage House, an efficiency unit be-
hind the main house. Breakfast, which may include sour cream cran-
berry bread or chocolate-covered bananas and fresh muffins, is served
in the formal dining room or on the screened-in porch. ⊠ *167 Old Main
St., 02664,* ☎ *508/398–6674 or 800/288–4080,* 🖷 *508/398–8297. 4
rooms, 2 with bath; 1 efficiency. No smoking. AE, D, MC, V. BP.* ✍

$$ 🏨 **Seaside.** Right on a warm Nantucket Sound beach, this 5-acre village of Cape-style cottages (studios and one- or two-bedroom units)
has a view of scalloped beaches in both directions. Seaside was built
in the 1940s, and the decor varies from cottage to cottage, as each is
individually owned. All have kitchens or kitchenettes, and many have
wood-burning fireplaces. The oceanfront cottages, right off a strip of
grass set with lounge and Adirondack chairs, have the best view and
decor. Cottages in the adjacent pine grove are generally very pleasant,
and most have been updated within the past two years. Shoulder-sea-
son rates are very attractive. ⊠ *135 S. Shore Dr., 02664,* ☎ *508/398–
2533,* 🖷 *508/398–2523. 43 cottages. Kitchenettes, picnic area, beach.
MC, V. Closed mid-Oct.–Apr.*

Nightlife and the Arts

Feel like it's been too long since you last fox-trotted? **Betsy's Ballroom**
(⊠ 528 Forest Rd., ☎ 508/362–9538) has Saturday-night ballroom
dancing year-round to live bands on the Cape's largest dance floor. The
bands deliver swing, waltzes, and fox-trot 8 PM–11 PM; it's BYO for
drinks and snacks, and Betsy will provide the ice and cups. Admission
is $7.50.

Outdoor Activities and Sports

BASEBALL

The **Yarmouth-Dennis Red Sox** (☎ 508/394–9466) of the collegiate Cape
Cod Baseball League play home games at Red Wilson Field (⊠ Station Ave.) from mid-June to mid-August.

SOCCER

The **Cape Cod Crusaders** (☎ 508/790–4782) of the D-3 League, play action-packed home matches at the Alan Carlsen Field at Dennis-Yarmouth Regional High School (✉ Station Ave.) from April to mid-August.

BEACHES

The **Flax Pond** (✉ N. Main St. between High Bank and Great Western Rds.) recreation area offers freshwater swimming, a lifeguard, and ducks, but no sand beach, just pine-needle-covered ground. There's a pine-shaded picnic area with grills, as well as tennis and basketball courts and plenty of parking.

Parker's River Beach (✉ S. Shore Dr.), a flat stretch of sand on warm Nantucket Sound, is perfect for families. It has a lifeguard, a concession stand, a gazebo and picnic area, a playground, outdoor showers, and rest rooms. There's a $10 parking fee in season.

BIKE RENTAL

Outdoor Shop (✉ 50 Long Pond Dr., ☎ 508/394–3819) rents bikes and mopeds and does repairs.

GOLF

Blue Rock Golf Course (✉ Off Great Western Rd., ☎ 508/398–9295) is a highly regarded, easy-to-walk 18-hole, par-3, 3,000-yard public course crossed by a pond. The pro shop rents clubs; reservations are mandatory in season.

HEALTH AND FITNESS CLUBS

Mid Cape Racquet Club (✉ 193 White's Path, ☎ 508/394–3511) has one racquetball, one squash, and nine indoor tennis courts; indoor basketball; a sauna, steam room, and whirlpools; massage services; and a free-weight and cardiovascular room—plus day care. It also offers spinning, kick boxing, and body pump classes. Daily rates are available.

West Dennis

⑱   *6 mi south of Dennis, 1 mi east of South Yarmouth.*

In another one of those tricks of Cape geography, the village of West Dennis is actually south of South Dennis on the east side of the Bass River. Dennisport is farther east, near the Harwich town line. If you're driving between West Dennis and Harwich, Lower County Road, with occasional glimpses of the sea between the cottages and beach-front hotels, is a more scenic alternative to overdeveloped Route 28.

Dining and Lodging

$$–$$$ ✕ **Christine's.** This family-run restaurant is sprawling, spacious, and a little generic—the type that attracts bus tours—with a big bar in its own room, a private function room, and a separate show club with a glittering stage offering cabaret acts, comedians, impersonators, and bands from all over the country. The menu here is mostly typical American restaurant fare, with basic Italian dishes and some seafood and steak. A nice touch is Lebanese specials such as a pine-nut- and almond-crusted haddock with tahini sauce, and *kafta*, fresh ground lamb and beef blended with onions, mint, and Lebanese spices, grilled and served with almond rice and hummus. To help work off dinner, there's dancing year-round (☞ Nightlife and the Arts, *below*). Christine's has a 30-ft cruise ship–style buffet every Sunday from 10 to 2. ✉ *581 Main St. (Rte. 28),* ☎ *508/394–7333. AE, D, MC, V.*

$$$$ 🏨 **Lighthouse Inn.** On a small private beach adjacent to West Dennis Beach, this traditional Cape resort has been in family hands since 1938. The main inn was built around a still-operational 1855 lighthouse and has five guest rooms. Scattered along a landscaped lawn are 23 individual weathered, shingle Cape cottages (one room to three bedrooms, no kitchens) and five multiroom buildings. Cottages have decks, knotty-pine and some painted walls, and generally nice, cabiny bedrooms. The oceanfront Guest House has a common room with a fireplace. In the main inn are a living room, a library, and a restaurant in three waterfront rooms that serves New England cuisine and seafood. In summer supervised activities and dinners for children give parents some private time. ⊠ *1 Lighthouse Rd., Box 128, 02670, ☎ 508/398–2244, ℻ 508/398–5658. 40 rooms, 23 cottages. Restaurant, bar, room service, pool, miniature golf, tennis court, shuffleboard, beach, fishing, billiards, nightclub, recreation room, library, children's programs (ages 3–12), playground. MC, V. Closed mid-Oct.–mid-May. BP; MAP available.* ◈

$ ☷ **Beach House Inn.** This is the kind of house you'd expect when Nantucket Sound is your backyard: shingles weathered gray from the salt air; white wicker and natural oak furniture that's practical yet comfortable; walls of glass that frame the beauty—and sometimes ferocity—of Mother Nature. Some rooms have brass or four-poster beds, and all have TVs, ceiling fans, and decks, some of which overlook the front yard. The best room is undoubtedly Room 2, with its second-story waterfront deck and a private staircase leading to the inn's beach. The common room has a TV and wide assortment of hit movies on video. For cooking meals you can use the barbecue grills or the fully equipped kitchen, which has a microwave. In the off-season the inn must be rented as a whole, and is not run as a B&B. ⊠ *61 Uncle Stephen's Rd., Box 494, 02670, ☎ 508/398–4575, 617/489–4144 Columbus Day–Memorial Day. 7 rooms. Beach, playground. No smoking. No credit cards. CP.* ◈

Nightlife and the Arts

Christine's (⊠ 581 Main St. [Rte. 28], ☎ 508/394–7333; ☞ Dining, *above*) stages nightly entertainment in season in its 300-seat showroom. Concerts, sometimes with dancing, feature name bands from the 1950s to 1970s, Top 40 bands, or jazz. There are also stand-up comedy nights. Off-season the schedule includes live entertainment and dancing to a DJ on weekends, as well as special events.

The **Sand Bar** (⊠ Lighthouse Rd., ☎ 508/398–7586) presents the boogie-woogie piano playing of local legend Rock King, who's been tickling the ivories—and people's funny bones—here every summer for more than 40 years. The club is closed from mid-October to mid-May.

Sundancer's (⊠ 116 Main St. [Rte. 28], ☎ 508/394–1600) has dancing to a DJ and live bands in season. It's closed December and January.

Outdoor Activities and Sports

BEACHES

The **West Dennis Beach** (⊠ Lighthouse Rd. off Lower County Rd.) is one of the best on the south shore. A breakwater was started here in 1837 in an effort to protect the mouth of Bass River but was abandoned when a sandbar formed on the shore side. It is a long, wide, and popular sandy beach, stretching for 1½ mi, with marshland and the Bass River across from it. Popular with windsurfers, the beach also has bathhouses, lifeguards, a playground, concessions, and parking for 1,000 cars. Nonresidents pay a $10 parking fee per day in season.

ICE-SKATING

Fall through spring, plus summer Saturdays and some evenings (call for schedule), ice-skating is available at the **Tony Kent Arena** (⊠ 8 Gages Way, South Dennis, ☎ 508/760–2400). Keep your eyes peeled: this is where Nancy Kerrigan and Paul Wylie train. Rental skates are available.

JOGGING

Lifecourse (✉ Bob Crowell Rd. and Old Bass River Rd., South Dennis) is a 1½-mi jogging trail through woods, with 20 exercise stations along the way. It's part of a recreation area that includes basketball and handball courts, ball fields, a playground, and a picnic area.

Dennisport

⑲ *1 mi east of West Dennis, 10 mi west of Chatham.*

The Mid Cape's last southern village is Dennisport, a prime summer-resort area, with gray-shingle cottages, summer houses and condominiums, and lots of white picket fences covered with rambling roses. The Union Wharf Packing Company was here in the 1850s, and the shore was lined with sail makers and ship chandlers. The beach where sea clams were once packed in the sands is now packed with sunbathers.

♻ The **Cape Cod Discovery Museum** is a small but lively indoor play space for children from preschool age through about second grade. Legos, musical instruments, play dinosaurs, magnetic word games, and puzzles, plus visits from iguanas, snakes, or the resident parrot, will amuse the little ones. Also on hand are a shadow room and a puppet theater. ✉ *444 Main St. (Rte. 28),* ☎ *508/398–1600.* 💲 *$4.50.* ☉ *Daily 9:30–4:30.*

NEED A
BREAK?

Set in a rustic mid-19th-century barn decorated with such memorabilia as a working nickelodeon, the **Sundae School Ice Cream Parlor** (✉ 387 Lower County Rd., ☎ 508/394–9122), open mid-April–mid-October, serves great homemade ice cream and frozen yogurt with lots of toppings, sugar-free ice cream, real whipped cream, and old-fashioned sarsaparilla and cream soda from an antique marble soda fountain.

Dining and Lodging

$$–$$$ ✕ **Clancy's.** A local landmark set on the bucolic Swan River, Clancy's is popular, with a parking lot that's often jammed by 5 PM. Calling itself a county (not country) tavern, this is an enormous operation, with long family tables, round tables, bar tables, booths, a deck overlooking the river, two bars, and many, many servers. On the seemingly endless menu are several variations of nachos, salads, and chili. Clancy's likes to put cute names on things, so you'll find items such as steak Lucifer (sirloin topped with lobster, asparagus, and béarnaise sauce) and a Sunday-brunch menu with the like of crab, steak, or eggs Benny. ✉ *8 Upper County Rd.,* ☎ *508/394–6661. Reservations not accepted. AE, DC, MC, V.*

$$ ✕ **Swan River Seafood Restaurant.** From the right table you can have a beautiful view of the Swan River marsh and Nantucket Sound beyond at this informal little eatery, which turns out great fresh fish, both traditional and creative. Besides the usual fried and broiled choices, try mako shark au poivre or scrod San Sebastian, simmered in garlic broth with littleneck clams. ✉ *5 Lower County Rd.,* ☎ *508/394–4466. AE, MC, V. Closed mid-Sept.–late May. No lunch late May–mid-June.*

$–$$ ✕ **Bob Briggs' Wee Packet.** Cute as can be—maybe a little too cute—this tiny dinette is decorated in classic Cape kitsch, with screaming-yellow tables, seascapes on the walls, and driftwood, seashells, and little bits of moss everywhere. The food is very good, very traditional, and very plain: plenty of local seafood (broiled swordfish and fish-and-chips are very reliable) as well as sandwiches and salads. Try bread pudding with lemon sauce for dessert. You can pick up homemade freshly baked goods of all kinds at the adjoining bakery and doughnut shop. Bob Briggs himself will greet you at the door, no doubt wearing his signature suspenders, just as he has been greeting customers for more than 30 years. ⊠ *79 Depot St., at Lower County Rd.,* ☎ *508/398–2181. Reservations not accepted. MC, V. Closed Oct.–Apr.*

$ ✕ **Bob's Best Sandwiches.** Bob Theobald is a hands-on owner in the best sense; he makes his own bread, roasts his own turkey, opens every day at 7 AM, and doesn't close until around dinnertime. The result is one of the better breakfast and lunch spots around, as well as a busy catering business. The French toast for breakfast is a true treat, even better than the excellent omelets. For lunch get a big roast beef sandwich, and you're ready for anything. ⊠ *613 Main St. (Rte. 28),* ☎ *508/394–8450. Reservations not accepted. No credit cards. No dinner.*

$ ✕ **Kream 'N Kone.** This is how it's been since 1953: order up some fried clams and a shake or a soda, get a number, wait five minutes, and sit down to some of the best fast food anywhere. For some reason the onion rings in particular are a knockout. The fried food will overflow your paper plate onto a plastic tray, but it's so good that what you thought you'd never be able to finish somehow vanishes. At times the prices seem surprisingly high, but not for what you get. A sister restaurant of the same name, owned and operated by the same family, serves up the same great stuff down Route 28 a few miles into Chatham. ⊠ *Main St. (Rte. 28),* ☎ *508/394–0808. No credit cards. Closed Nov.–Apr.*

$$$ ⊞ **Pelham House.** The ocean-side Pelham House, south of Route 28, underwent major refurbishments in 1999–2000, adding new bathroom tiles, fresh paint, and rugs. The result is a modern, if not particularly exciting, collection of clean and spacious rooms, strategically angled to maximize ocean views. All are equipped with phone, cable TV, a small refrigerator, and a fan (no air-conditioning). Atop the property's ocean-facing section are several "penthouse" rooms with spacious sitting areas, excellent views of Nantucket Sound, and more upscale furniture. But really it's Pelham's location that generates a buzz—with about 400 ft of private beachfront, it's a great place to spend all day in the sun and sand. A complimentary full breakfast is served in season, a Continental breakfast in the cooler months. ⊠ *14 Sea St., Box 38 02639,* ☎ *508/398–6076 or 800/497–3542,* 𝔽𝔸𝕏 *508/760–3999. 39 rooms. Breakfast room, pool, tennis, beach. AE, D, MC, V. Closed Nov.–Mar. BP.* ✍

$$ ⊞ **The Garlands.** There are innumerable strip motels and cottage colonies lining Old Wharf Road in Dennisport, but few places offer comfort and views to match this bilevel motel-style complex. There are 20 units in all—18 are two-bedroom suites. Each unit has a fully equipped kitchen, cable TV, private sundeck or patio, and daily maid service. The oceanfront VIP suites, simply named A and B (two bedrooms) and C and D (one bedroom), are the best picks here—the nearly floor-to-ceiling windows offer unobstructed water views; at high tide you're almost in the surf. ⊠ *117 Old Wharf Rd., Box 506, 02639,* ☎ *508/398–6987. 20 suites. Beach. No credit cards. Closed mid-Oct.–mid-Apr.*

Nightlife and the Arts

Clancy's (⊠ 8 Upper County Rd., ☎ 508/394–6661; ☞ Dining, *above*) has contemporary piano year-round.

Improper Bostonian (⊠ Rte. 28, ☎ 508/394–7416), open only in summer, has a mix of live music and DJ-spun dance tunes Wednesday–Saturday and attracts a youngish crowd.

Outdoor Activities and Sports

Cape Cod Waterways (⊠ 16 Main St. [Rte. 28], ☎ 508/398–0080) rents canoes, kayaks, and electric paddleboats for leisurely travel on the Swan River.

Shopping

Factory Shoe Mart (⊠ 271 Main St. [Rte. 28], ☎ 508/398–6000) has such brand names as Capezio, Dexter, Clark, Esprit, Nike, Reebok, L. A. Gear, and Rockport.

THE MID CAPE A TO Z

Arriving and Departing

By Car

U.S. 6 and Routes 6A and 28 are heavily congested eastbound Friday evening, westbound Sunday afternoon, and in both directions on Saturday in summer.

By Plane

Barnstable Municipal Airport (⊠ 480 Barnstable Rd., Rte. 28 rotary, ☎ 508/775–2020) is in Hyannis, minutes from Barnstable village.

CARRIERS

Airline service is extremely unpredictable because of the seasonal nature of Cape travel—carriers come and go, while others juggle their routes.

Cape Air/Nantucket Airlines (☎ 508/771–6944 or 800/352–0714, ✈) flies direct from Boston to Hyannis and Provincetown year-round and from New Bedford to Martha's Vineyard and Nantucket. Cape Air has joint fares with Continental, Delta, Midwest Express, and US Airways and ticketing and baggage agreements with eight major U.S. airlines and with KLM.

US Airways Express (☎ 800/428–4322) flies nonstop from Boston and New York to Hyannis year-round. Connect in Boston with the airline's other routes.

For charters contact **Cape Air** (☞ *above*). **Westchester Air** (☎ 800/759–2929) offers charter service from White Plains, New York, to Hyannis, Martha's Vineyard, and Nantucket.

Getting Around

By Bus

The **Cape Cod Regional Transit Authority** (☎ 508/385–8326; 800/352–7155 in MA; ✈) operates several bus services that link Cape towns. All buses are wheelchair-accessible and equipped with bike racks. The SeaLine operates along Route 28 Monday–Saturday between Hyannis and Woods Hole (average fare is $3.50 one-way from Hyannis to Woods Hole). Its many stops include Mashpee Commons, Falmouth, and the Woods Hole Steamship Authority docks. The SeaLine connects in Hyannis with the Plymouth & Brockton line, as well as the Villager, another bus line that runs along Route 132 between Hyannis and Barnstable Harbor. The driver will stop when signaled along the route.

The b-Bus is a fleet of minivans that will transport passengers door to door between any towns on the Cape. Service runs seven days a week, year-round, though reservations must be made in advance. The cost is $2 per ride, plus 10¢ per mi, half that for seniors.

The H2O Line offers daily regularly scheduled service year-round between Hyannis and Orleans along Route 28. The Hyannis–Orleans fare is $3.50; shorter trips cost less. Buses connect in Hyannis with the SeaLine, Villager, and Plymouth & Brockton lines.

Plymouth & Brockton Street Railway (☎ 508/746–0378) has service between Boston and Provincetown, with stops at many towns in between.

By Limousine

John's Taxi & Limousine (☎ 508/394–3209) picks up in Dennis and Harwich only but will take passengers all over the Cape.

By Taxi

There are taxi stands at the Hyannis airport, the Hyannis bus station, and the Cape Cod Mall. In Hyannis call **Checker Taxi** (☎ 508/771–8294), **Hyannis Taxi** (☎ 508/775–0400 or 800/773–0600), or **Town Taxi** (☎ 508/771–5555 or 888/771–8696).

By Trolley

The **Cape Cod Regional Transit Authority** (☎ 508/385–8326, 800/352–7155 in MA) runs seasonal trolleys in Falmouth, Mashpee, Hyannis, Yarmouth, and Dennis. Fares and times vary; call for more information.

Contacts and Resources

Camping

Eastern Mountain Sports (✉ 1513 Rte. 132, Hyannis, ☎ 508/362–8690) rents tents and sleeping bags.

Nickerson State Park (✉ 3488 Rte. 6A, Brewster, ☎ 508/896–3491 or 877/422–6762) is huge (almost 2,000 acres with 420 campsites) and hugely popular. It has plenty of facilities and guest programs.

Sandy Terraces (✉ Box 98, Marstons Mills 02648, ☎ 508/428–9209), a surprise in this very traditional area, is a seasonal family nudist campground.

Car Rentals

You can rent wheels at Barnstable Municipal Airport. **Avis** (☎ 508/775–2888 or 800/831–2847). **Budget** (☎ 508/771–2744 or 800/527–0700). **Hertz** (☎ 508/775–5825 or 800/654–3131). **National** (☎ 508/771–4353 or 800/227–7368).

Children's Activities

The **Cape Cod Community College** (✉ Rte. 132, West Barnstable 02668, ☎ 508/362–2131, ext. 4365) offers summer sports programs.

Children's concerts, plays, and programs are offered by the **Cape Cod Melody Tent** (☎ 508/775–9100), the **Cape Cod Symphony Orchestra** (☎ 508/362–1111), the **Cape Rep Theatre** (☎ 508/896–1888), and the **Cape Playhouse** (☎ 508/385–3911).

The **Cape Cod YMCA** (✉ Box 188, Rte. 132, West Barnstable 02668, ☎ 508/362–6500) offers one-week Fun Clubs (sports, crafts, nature) during school vacation weeks, as well as children's evenings, summer day camps, swimming classes, and more.

Hyannis Public Library (✉ 401 Main St., Hyannis, ☎ 508/775–2280) has a children's multicultural center, created in collaboration with the Barnstable public schools, with books, tapes, and videos (some in foreign languages), programs, a play area with puzzles and games, and a children's reading club in summer.

Emergencies

Ambulance, fire, police (☎ 911).

For rescues at sea, call the **Coast Guard** (☎ 508/888–0335 in Sandwich and Cape Cod Canal, ☎ 508/945–0164 in Chatham). Boaters should use Channel 16 on their radios.

Massachusetts Poison Control Center (☎ 800/682–9211).

DENTISTS

Dental Associates of Cape Cod (⊠ 262 Barnstable Rd., Hyannis, ☎ 508/778–1200) accepts emergency walk-ins.

HOSPITALS

Cape Cod Hospital (⊠ 27 Park St., Hyannis, ☎ 508/771–1800) has a 24-hour emergency room.

LATE-NIGHT PHARMACIES

CVS (⊠ 176–182 North St., Hyannis, ☎ 508/775–8346) is open 24 hours.

WALK-IN CLINICS

Health Stop (⊠ Cape Town Plaza, Rte. 132, Hyannis, ☎ 508/771–7520) takes walk-in patients weekdays 8–8, Saturday 9–5, and Sunday 11–5.

Mid Cape Medical Center (⊠ 489 Bearses Way, at Rte. 28, Unit A-4, Hyannis, ☎ 508/771–4092) is open every day 8–7:30 in summer, 8–6:30 after Labor Day.

Guided Tours

CRUISES

Cape Cod Duck Mobile takes you on a land-and-sea tour of downtown Hyannis and the harbor in a restored U.S. military amphibious vehicle. These 45-minute narrated tours depart on the hour, roll through downtown, then splash into Lewis Bay to cruise past the Kennedy compound and other sights. Tickets go on sale daily at 9:30 and in summer often sell out by noon. Tours run on the hour 10–4. Call for details about where to purchase tickets. ⊠ *447 Main St., Hyannis,* ☎ *508/ 362–1117.* ☞ *$12.*

Hy-Line runs one-hour narrated tours of Hyannis Harbor, including a view of the Kennedy compound. Sunset and evening cocktail cruises are available. ⊠ *Ocean St. dock, Pier 1,* ☎ *508/778–2600.* ☞ *$10–$14.*

Starfish River Cruise offers 1½-hour water safari tours of the Bass River, past windmills, marshlands, and old captains' houses, all seen from a 32-ft aluminum boat with an awning. Trips run at 11, 1, 4, and 6, and there's a snack bar on board. ⊠ *Rte. 28, West Dennis, just east of Bass River Bridge,* ☎ *508/362–5555.* ☞ *$12.*

FLIGHTSEEING

Sightsee from above with the **Cape Cod Flying Service** (⊠ Cape Cod Airport, 1000 Race La., Marstons Mills, ☎ 508/428–8732), or **Cape Flight LTD** (Barnstable Municipal Airport, ⊠ 480 Barnstable Rd., Rte. 28 rotary, Hyannis, ☎ 508/775–8171). **Cape Cod Soaring Adventures** (☎ 508/420–4305) offers glider flights and lessons out of Marstons Mills.

TRAIN TOURS

The **Cape Cod Central Railroad** offers two-hour, 42-mi narrated rail tours from Hyannis to the Cape Cod Canal, as well as a three-hour dinner train where you can settle back and watch the scenery as you nosh. The dinner train runs Wednesday through Sunday, and the cost is $50 per person. Another dinner train, created for families, with a children's menu and activities, runs on Tuesday evening. ⊠ *Hyannis Train Depot, 252 Main St., Hyannis,* ☎ *508/771–3800 or 888/797–7245.* ☞ *2-hr tours $13.* ☉ *Memorial Day–Oct., Tues.–Sun.; off-season, call for schedule.*

House Rentals

Mid Cape rentals are handled by **Century 21, Sam Ingram Real Estate** (⊠ 938 Rte. 6A, Yarmouth 02675, ☎ 508/362–8844 or 800/697–3340, FAX 508/362–7889).

Commonwealth Associates (⊠ 551 Main St., Harwich Port 02646, ☎ 508/432–2618, FAX 508/432–1771) can assist in finding vacation rentals in the Harwiches, including waterfront properties.

Great Vacations Inc. (⊠ 2660 Rte. 6A, Brewster 02631, ☎ 508/896–2090) specializes in locating vacation rentals in Brewster, Dennis, and Orleans.

Peter McDowell Associates (⊠ 585 Main St. [Rte. 6A], Dennis 02638, ☎ 508/385–9114 or 888/385–9114; ⊠ 11 Main St. [Rte. 28], Dennisport 02639, ☎ 508/394–5400 or 800/870–5401, ✎) offers a wide selection of properties for rent by the week, month, or season; the company also rents larger homes for family reunions and other gatherings. Most places are in Dennis.

Waterfront Rentals (⊠ 20 Pilgrim Rd., West Yarmouth 02673, ☎ 508/778–1818, FAX 508/771–3563, ✎) covers Bourne to Truro, listing everything from one-bedroom condos to a seven-bedroom, seven-bath beachfront estate.

Libraries

Several area libraries have special collections. The **Centerville Library** (⊠ 585 Main St., ☎ 508/790–6220) has a 42-volume noncirculating set of transcripts of the Nuremberg Trials. **Cotuit Library** (⊠ 871 Main St., ☎ 508/428–8141) holds a noncirculating set of luxurious leather-bound classics. **Hyannis Public Library** (⊠ 401 Main St., ☎ 508/775–2280) has a case full of books on JFK. Barnstable's **Sturgis Library** (⊠ 3090 Rte. 6A, ☎ 508/362–6636) has extensive Cape genealogical and maritime materials.

Visitor Information

The **Cape Cod Chamber of Commerce** (⊠ Junction of U.S. 6 and 132, Box 790, Hyannis 02601, ☎ 508/862–0700 or 888/332–2732, ✎) is open year-round, Monday–Saturday 9–5 and Sunday 10–4.

LOCAL CHAMBERS OF COMMERCE

Dennis (⊠ Junction of Rtes. 28 and 134, West Dennis; ⊠ Box 275, South Dennis 02660, ☎ 508/398–3568 or 800/243–9920, ✎).

Hyannis (⊠ 1481 Rte. 132, 02601, ☎ 508/362–5230 or 877/492–6647, ✎).

Yarmouth (⊠ 657 Rte. 28, West Yarmouth 02673; ⊠ Box 479, South Yarmouth 02664, ☎ 508/778–1008 or 800/732–1008, www.yarmouth-capecod.com; information center on U.S. 6 heading east between Exits 6 and 7, ☎ 508/362–9796).

5 THE LOWER CAPE

This quieter, gentler part of the Cape holds some of the peninsula's most breathtaking natural scenery and gives a glimpse of the region's rich history. Brewster holds on to the past with aged oak trees and 19th-century sea captains' homes. Harwich and Harwich Port combine rural beauty with the bustle of boats and beachgoers. Elegant Chatham has a lively downtown, and Eastham is all about the sea, with splendid Atlantic and bay beaches.

Revised by
Laura V. Scheel

S PECKLED with still-active cranberry bogs, sturdy trees, and pasture, the Lower Cape exudes a peaceful, residential aura. You won't find roadways cluttered with mini-golf complexes, trampolines, or bumper boats here. Although the current building boom has filled many once-vacant expanses with sparkling new homes, the region is still marked by a quiet sense of history and simple purpose.

Rich in history and Cape flavor, Brewster and Harwich stand opposite one another in the area just shy of the elbow. Harwich, inland, has antique homes; rambling old burial grounds; and a modest town center with shops, restaurants, museums, churches, and public parks. Brewster is similarly historic; examples of Victorian, Greek Revival, and colonial architecture abound, most of it meticulously preserved. Many homes have been converted to welcoming guest houses and bed-and-breakfasts, while others are privately owned.

The traditional, elegant town of Chatham perches dramatically at the end of the peninsular elbow. It's here the Atlantic begins to wet the shores of the Cape, sometimes with frightening strength. Chatham has shown vulnerability to the forces of nature over the years, as little by little its shores have succumbed to the insatiable sea.

North of Chatham is Orleans, supply center of the Lower and Outer Capes, replete with large grocery chains and shopping plazas. The famed Nauset Beach is here, its dune-backed shores crammed with sunseeking revelers in summer. Orleans does have a rich history; you just have to leave the maze of industry to find it. Continuing north, you'll reach Eastham, a town often overlooked because of its position on busy Route 6 but perfectly charming if you know where to look.

The Lower Cape is blessed with large tracts of open space, set aside for conservation. South of Chatham, the Monomoy National Wildlife Refuge is a twin-island bird sanctuary. Here dozens of species of birds are free to feed, nest, and expand their numbers without human meddling. Recreation seekers should head straight to Nickerson State Park in Brewster to frolic in freshwater ponds or enjoy a serene bike ride under the shade of trees. In Eastham, where the Cape Cod National Seashore officially begins, the Salt Pond Visitor Center has a wealth of area information, educational programs, and guided tours.

Pleasures and Pastimes

Beaches

The Cape is straddled by water—which means beach lovers have plenty of choices. Visitors to the Lower Cape can pick from four major bodies of water: the bracing and grand Atlantic Ocean or three more mild-mannered bays—Nantucket Sound, Pleasant Bay, and Cape Cod Bay. For those who prefer freshwater swimming, there are many ponds—some left over from the ancient glacial carving of the peninsula—sprinkled throughout the entire area.

On the south side, Harwich Port, Harwich, and Chatham dip into the shallower and warmer Nantucket Sound. The beaches here, which tend to be divided into smallish partitions designated according to public or private ownership, are popular with families, ice cream trucks, jet skiers, and windsurfers. Harwich and Chatham swimmers can also find a spot along Pleasant Bay. The waters here are very shallow, which makes it ideal for kayaks, canoes, and peace-seeking swimmers.

Brewster's glory is Cape Cod Bay, and there are dozens of beaches (public and private) extending for acres at low tide. Although swimmers won't have much luck at this time, treasure hunters can stroll the sands, keeping an eye out for shells and creatures left behind by the retreating waters. There's plenty of room to wander on the bayside, and you won't find a better spot to catch the nightly sunset.

The Lower Cape's ocean beaches are unbroken by dictates of ownership or man-made barriers from Chatham onward, so you're free to roam. Note that Chatham's ocean beaches are easily accessible by bike or foot, but there's no parking for cars. Orleans has Nauset Beach, a Cape Cod favorite. In Eastham the National Seashore and the town maintain several beaches that provide exhilarating ocean swimming.

Biking

The Cape's top bike route, the 25-mi Cape Cod Rail Trail, follows the paved right-of-way of the old Penn Central Railroad, from South Dennis to South Wellfleet (☞ Close-Up: Riding the Rail Trail *in* Chapter 4). You can pick up the trail in Harwich, Brewster, Orleans, and Eastham. Nickerson State Park, in Brewster, has 8 mi of its own forested trails, some with access to the rail trail. From the Salt Pond Visitor Center in Eastham, take a jaunt off the rail trail for meandering paths leading to Nauset Beach, Coast Guard Beach, and beautiful Nauset Marsh. Cyclists in Chatham can follow the little green signs that denote the Chatham Bike Route; but use caution, as the roadway is shared with folks in cars who are just as eagerly taking in the view as you are. The trail runs beside the ocean and all the stunningly majestic homes that dominate the waterfront.

Dining

In a highly controversial policy change, many Cape towns have banished smoking from restaurants and bars. The towns of Chatham and Orleans were quick and eager to pass the new law, and recently Eastham, Brewster, and Harwich have followed suit. Despite the law, which has enraged many a business owner, dining out still remains one of the region's most popular pastimes, and seekers of fine food will not be disappointed. Cape Cod is a casual place, in that even most top restaurants do not require a dress code.

Each town has its own batch of treasured and traditional restaurants, though all will be crowded in the summer. A significant number of restaurants close their doors once the crowds thin in October— including the beloved fried-seafood shacks—but plenty remain open throughout the year. Seafood is, not surprisingly, a major staple in these parts.

If you're in the mood for fine dining, a couple of good choices are Brewster's Chillingsworth for French cuisine in a European country-inspired setting, and Chatham Bars Inn for an elegant waterfront meal. Not sure what you want? In Chatham you can just stroll down Main Street and see what tickles your palate; diners in Orleans, Brewster, Harwich, and Eastham will have to do some driving if unsure of their eating desire, as restaurants are more spread out.

For price ranges *see* Dining *in* Smart Travel Tips A to Z.

Lodging

Money made in early maritime fortunes helped build exquisite historic homes, many of which are now unique and lovely inns. Chatham is blessed with dozens of these aged beauties, most with all the modern conveniences—so you can sleep in a home built in the 18th century, then get up and surf the Internet. B&Bs and intimate guest houses are the primary lodging choices, but there are several larger hotels such as Chatham Bars Inn, Chatham Wayside Inn, and the Bradford. Even these giants specialize in carefully designed decor and comfort. Outside town are roadside or waterfront hotel complexes, usually a bit softer on the budget and welcoming to families with small children.

Brewster is essentially a B&B kind of town, offering lodging in former sea captains' homes. Harwich and Orleans have a pleasant mixture of both family-friendly hotel complexes and lovingly restored inns. Eastham has quite a few large-scale hotels along Route 6, including Sheraton. Don't expect to find bargains in the summertime.

Other options include camping or weekly cottage rentals; all towns have the ubiquitous cottage colonies. Note that in summer these must be secured well in advance, usually through a local real estate agent.

For price ranges *see* Lodging *in* Smart Travel Tips A to Z.

Nightlife and the Arts

Chatham's Main Street is lined with galleries and studios showcasing local and national artists. In Orleans weekly outdoor art shows sell the works of local painters and craftspeople, and offer free demonstrations. Eastham and Harwich also host outdoor arts and crafts forays. Harwich's biggie is the Professional Arts and Crafts Festival, held in July and August.

The theater tradition remains strong throughout the Lower Cape. In Harwich the Harwich Junior Theatre stages a variety of performances year-round and offers children's classes in the summer. Community theater dominates the scene in Orleans and Chatham. Off-season, Eastham shines with the First Encounter Coffee House, a lively place for local music and poetry readings in an alcohol-free setting. Brewster is home to the professional Cape Cod Repertory Theatre, where performances are staged both indoors and out under the stars.

Popular and free town-band concerts are held all over the Cape, and other concerts are presented by various church groups and community organizations. There's a continuous, lively schedule of events throughout the summer in each town; pick up a free guide at information centers and stores.

Nightlife on the Lower Cape is never wild, but it's certainly not dull. Many bars in Orleans, Chatham, and Harwich feature live local bands, including the Chatham Squire, the Land Ho! in Orleans, Brewster's rustic Woodshed, and the spirited Irish Pub in West Harwich. More peaceful nighttime diversions include solitary beach walking by moonlight, and stargazing (watch for the extraordinary Perseid meteor shower display in August). The National Seashore schedules storytelling nights around a beach bonfire.

Outdoor Activities and Sports

Cape Cod, especially the Lower and Outer regions, is an outdoor playground. From Eastham to Provincetown, the Cape Cod National Seashore offers miles of hiking and biking trails, several historic sites, and many beautiful, natural places to explore.

The Cape's rivers, ponds, inlets, and harbors are great for canoeing or kayaking. Whether on your own or as part of a guided tour (the Cape Cod Museum of Natural History, in Brewster, offers a full schedule of such trips), these peaceful ventures provide a break from the crowds and an up-close look at the local flora and fauna. Several rental shops provide equipment and instruction in Eastham, Orleans, and elsewhere. Ambitious anglers in search of striped bass, bluefish, flounder, or cod will find plenty of charter boats for hire. In general, fishing is a tremendous industry on Cape Cod, both commercial and recreational.

In Eastham, the National Seashore's Salt Pond Visitor Center maintains walking and biking trails in the woods and around Nauset Marsh. In Brewster, the Punkhorn Parklands include nearly 2,000 acres open to walkers, horseback riders, and mountain bikers. Chatham visitors can hike over to Morris Island (mindful of the tides), which affords spectacular views of the ocean and the dunes.

Shopping

Shoppers in Cape Cod can find everything from a sweatshirt to a hand-crafted reproduction of an early American brass lantern. Absent on the Lower Cape are the national chain stores so popular on the mainland and on the upper Cape. Out in these parts, stores are individually owned and feature a selection of unique merchandise. Certainly, the area has its fill of kitsch-laden gift shops, selling all manner of magnets, T-shirts, mugs, and beach towels—all emblazoned with local themes such as lobsters and lighthouses. But don't let this hinder your shopping hunger.

Cape Cod has long been a center for artists and craftspeople, who have been inspired by the natural environment. The massive tourist trade helps sustain them, as most artisans spend the winter busily creating and replacing stock wiped out with visitors' dollars the season before. The high number of resident artisans on the Cape gives you an immense body of one-of-a-kind work to peruse. Choose from ceramics, jewelry, works in fabric, sculpture, paintings, photography, or glass.

Exploring the Lower Cape

U.S. 6 is the fastest way to get from the mainland to Harwich, Chatham, Orleans, and Eastham. Route 6A to Brewster winds along the north shore through scenic towns.

Numbers in the text correspond to numbers in the margin and on the Lower Cape and Chatham maps.

Great Itineraries

Brewster ① has something for everyone—antiques shops, museums, an old gristmill open to the public, Bassett's Wild Animal Farm for children, freshwater ponds for swimming or fishing, the beach and tidal flats to explore when the water is low, and miles of biking and hiking trails through **Nickerson State Park** ④. Don't miss the **Cape Cod Museum of Natural History** ③, which will take a couple of hours to explore. Main Street in the handsome town of **Chatham** ⑥–⑪ is perfect for strolling, shopping, and dining. A trip to the Monomoy Islands is a must for bird-watchers. Back in town, you can watch glassblowing in process at the Chatham Glass Company, visit the Old Atwood House and Railroad Museums, and drive over to take in the view from Chatham Light.

On the way north from Chatham, take the less commercial end of Route 28 to **Orleans** ⑫, driving alongside sailboat-speckled views of Pleasant Bay. You might want to allow time for a good long bike ride on the Cape Cod Rail Trail or for an afternoon relaxing at Nauset Beach. **Eastham** ⑬ is the next stop on the way up the arm, where the **Fort Hill Area** ⑭ has the historic Penniman House Museum and some wonderful walks along the adjacent trails. Stop at the National Seashore's **Salt Pond Visitor Center** ⑮ for some interesting information about the area; then take the bike trails to Coast Guard Beach and Nauset Light, with a view of the Three Sisters Lighthouses, now settled in a small park area.

When to Tour the Lower Cape

Although the crowds of summer are testament to the appeal of the lower Cape—its spectacular beaches, outdoor pursuits, crafts and art shows,

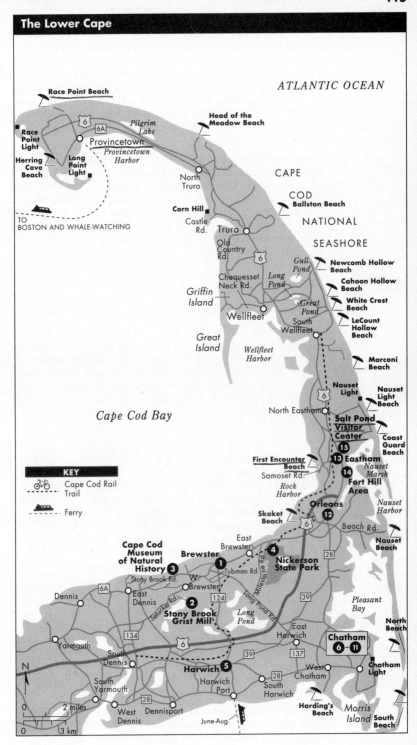

The Lower Cape

ATLANTIC OCEAN

Race Point Beach

Race Point Light

Herring Cove Beach

Long Point Light

Pilgrim Lake

Head of the Meadow Beach

Provincetown

Provincetown Harbor

North Truro

Corn Hill

Castle Rd.

Truro

Old Country Rd.

Gull Pond

Chequesset Neck Rd.

Griffin Island

Long Pond

Wellfleet

Great Pond

South Wellfleet

Great Island

Wellfleet Harbor

CAPE

COD

Ballston Beach

NATIONAL

SEASHORE

Newcomb Hollow Beach

Cahoon Hollow Beach

White Crest Beach

LeCount Hollow Beach

Marconi Beach

Nauset Light

Nauset Light Beach

North Eastham

Salt Pond Visitor Center

Coast Guard Beach

15 Eastham

13

Nauset Marsh

14 Fort Hill Area

First Encounter Beach

Samoset Rd.

Rock Harbor

Skaket Beach

Orleans **12**

Cape Cod Bay

KEY

🚲 Cape Cod Rail Trail

⛴ Ferry

Cape Cod Museum of Natural History **3**

Brewster **1**

East Brewster

Tubman Rd.

Nickerson State Park **4**

Nauset Harbor

Beach Rd.

Nauset Beach

28

Dennis

6A

East Dennis

Stony Brook Rd.

W. Brewster

Saucier Rd.

2

Stony Brook Grist Mill

124

Long Pond

Millstone Rd.

Long Pond Rd.

Pleasant Bay

North Beach

Yarmouth

134

South Dennis

6

39

East Harwich

Chatham

6 **11**

Chatham Light

N

South Yarmouth

Harwich **5**

Harwich Port

39

137

West Chatham

Morris Island

South Beach

0   2 miles

0   3 km

West Dennis

28

Dennisport

28

South Harwich

Harding's Beach

June-Aug.

concerts, and special events—more and more visitors are beginning to appreciate the surrounding seasons. Because of the ocean-side climate, spring and fall are simply lesser shades of full-blown summer. In late May and early June businesses closed in the winter months open their doors, lodging rates are lower, and the agonies of summertime traffic, long waits at restaurants and parking restrictions at area beaches can all be avoided. September, October and even November are the same. The waters usually remain warm enough to swim well into October, and seasonal businesses do their best to rid their stocks of merchandise by having generous sales.

You won't get the expected splendors of New England foliage on the Lower Cape, because the landscape changes more subtly. Swaying salt-marsh grasses turn golden, cranberry bogs explode in a vividness of ruby harvest, and the ocean relaxes into a deep, deep blue. The light becomes softer and its patterns more dramatic on both land and sea. In the towns of Harwich, Brewster, and Orleans, where the soil is substantial enough to support mighty oaks and maples, the colors of autumn do come through. A drive along Route 6A under the canopy of changing leaves is just as breathtaking as a summer jaunt past blooming gardens.

Brewster

❶ *6 mi north of Chatham, 5 mi west of Orleans, 20 mieast of Sandwich.*

Calling itself "the Sea Captains' Town," Brewster retains a firm and appreciative grip on its past. The town flourished under the boon of maritime-related profit, giving it an essence of old-world elegance that still lingers. Historic Route 6A, the Old King's Highway, winds through the center of town. This road, the old stagecoach route, was once nearly the only one at this end of the Cape, and both residents and legislators are determined to keep it well preserved. Homes and businesses must adhere to historic detail—there are no neon signs, no strip malls—only the gentle accoutrements of a more graceful era.

Named for Plymouth leader William Brewster, the area was settled in 1659 but was not incorporated as a separate town until 1803. In the early 1800s Brewster was the terminus of a packet cargo service from Boston. In 1849 Thoreau wrote that "this town has more mates and masters of vessels than any other town in the country." A large number of mansions built for sea captains remain today, and quite a few have been turned into handsome B&Bs. In the 18th and 19th centuries the bay side of Brewster was the site of a major salt-making industry. Of the 450 salt-works operating on the Cape in the 1830s, more than 60 were here.

Brewster's location on Cape Cod Bay makes it a perfect place to learn about the natural history of the Cape. The Cape Cod Museum of Natural History is here, and the area is rich in conservation lands, state parks, forests, freshwater ponds, and brackish marshes. When the tide is low in Cape Cod Bay, you can stroll the beaches and explore tidal pools up to 2 mi from the shore on the Brewster flats. When it's high tide, the water is relatively warm and very calm for swimming. Both Nickerson State Park and the Punkhorn Parklands offer up thousands of acres through which to wander.

Windmills used to be prominent in Cape Cod towns; the Brewster area once had four. The 1795 **Higgins Farm Windmill** (⊠ Off Rte. 6A, just west of the Cape Cod Museum of Natural History; ☞ *below*)—an octagonal type mill shingled in weathered pine with a roof like an upturned boat—was moved here in 1974 and has been restored. The millstones are original. At night the mill is often spotlighted and makes quite a sight.

On the grounds of the Higgins Farm Windmill (☞ *above*) is a one-room house from 1795, the **Harris-Black House.** Once, amazingly enough, home to a family of 13, the restored building is today partially furnished and dominated by a brick hearth and original woodwork. ✉ *Off Rte. 6A, just west of Cape Cod Museum of Natural History (☞ below),* ☎ *508/896–9521.* ⌑ *Free.* ☉ *July–Aug., Tues.–Fri. 1–4.*

❷ A short drive outside Brewster is the **Stony Brook Grist Mill,** a restored, operating, 19th-century fulling mill (a mill that shrinks and thickens cloth), now also a museum. The scene is a pleasing eyeful, with the old mill's waterwheel slowly turning in a small, tree-lined brook. Inside, exhibits include old mill equipment and looms; you can watch cornmeal being stone-ground and get a lesson in weaving on a 100-year-old loom. Out back, across wooden bridges, a bench has a pleasant view of the pond and of the sluices leading into the mill area.

Early each spring, in April and early May, Stony Brook's **Herring Run** boils with alewives (herring) making their way to spawning waters; it is an amazing sight. The fish swim in from Cape Cod Bay up Paine's Creek to Stony Brook and the ponds beyond it. The rushing stream is across the street from the mill. The herring run consists of ladders that help the fish climb the rocky waters. Farther down the path to the stream, there is an ivy-covered stone wishing well and a wooden bridge with a bench. ✉ *Setucket Rd. off Rte. 6A,* ☎ *no phone.* ⌑ *Donations accepted.* ☉ *May–Aug., Thurs.–Sat. 2–5.*

👆 **❸** For nature enthusiasts, a visit to the **Cape Cod Museum of Natural History** is a must; it's just a short drive west from the heart of Brewster along Route 6A. The museum and grounds include guided field walks; a shop; a natural history library; lectures; classes; nature and marine exhibits such as a working beehive and a pond- and sea-life room with live specimens; and self-guided trails (one goes out to the bay) through 80 acres of forest, marshland, and ponds, all rich in birds and other wildlife. The exhibit hall upstairs has a wall display of aerial photographs documenting the process by which the famous Chatham sandbar was split in two.

Combining art and nature, the monthly exhibitions in the Personal Response to the Earth gallery display artists' interpretations of the environment; most of the multimedia works are for sale. The museum also offers guided canoe and kayak trips from May through September and several cruises that explore different Cape waterways: Nantucket Sound, Pleasant Bay, and Nauset Marsh. Onboard naturalists point out the wildlife and relay historical information unique to each habitat. Call for tour times and fees, and sign up as early as you can. The museum has wildlife movies and slide lectures on Wednesday at 7:30, early July through August, in the auditorium. There's a full program of children's and family activities in summer, including one-day workshops and one- and two-week day camps of art and nature classes for preschoolers through grade 9. ✉ *869 Main St. (Rte. 6A),* ☎ *508/896–3867; 800/479–3867 in MA.* ⌑ *$5.* ☉ *Mon.–Sat. 9:30–4:30, Sun. 11–4:30.*

👆 Set on a re-created 19th-century common with a picnic area, the **New England Fire & History Museum** exhibits 35 antique vehicles, including the only surviving 1929 Mercedes-Benz fire engine, the late Boston Pops conductor Arthur Fiedler's private collection of fire-fighting memorabilia, 14 mannequins in historical uniforms depicting firefighters through the centuries, a Victorian apothecary shop, an animated diorama of the Chicago Fire of 1871 complete with smoke and fire, a historic working forge, and medicinal herb gardens. Guided tours are given. ✉ *1439 Main St. (Rte. 6A),* ☎ *508/896–5711.* ⌑ *$5.* ☉ *Mid-May–Labor Day, weekdays 10–4; Labor Day–Columbus Day, weekends noon–4.*

At the junction of Route 124, the **Brewster Store** (⊠ 1935 Main St. [Rte. 6A], ☎ 508/896–3744) is a local landmark. Built in 1852 as a church, it is a typical New England general store—God love 'em!—providing such essentials as the daily papers, penny candy, and benches out front for conversation. There's even a selection of Cape books to add to your collection. It's a good stop for quick grocery-type refreshments, as the bicycles piled up out front in summer attest. The Brewster Scoop out back serves ice cream mid-June through Labor Day. Upstairs, the old front of the store has been re-created, and memorabilia from antique toys to World War II bond posters are displayed. Downstairs is an antique nickelodeon that you can play.

Known as the Church of the Sea Captains, the handsome **First Parish Church** (⊠ 1969 Main St. [Rte. 6A], ☎ 508/896–5577), with Gothic windows and a capped bell tower, is full of pews marked with the names of famous Brewster seamen. Out back is an old graveyard where militiamen, clergy, farmers, and sea captains rest side by side.

🐾 For a look at some nonnative species, visit the 20-acre **Bassett Wild Animal Farm,** home to domestic and exotic birds, a lion, a tiger, monkeys, llamas, and the animals at a petting zoo. Hayrides, pony rides, a snack bar, and a picnic area are available. ⊠ *Tubman Rd. between Rtes. 124 and 137,* ☎ *508/896–3224.* 🎫 *$6.75.* ⊙ *Mid-May–mid-Sept., daily 10–5.*

The **Brewster Historical Society Museum,** in an 1830s house, is made up of a sea captain's room with paintings and artifacts, an 1890 barbershop, a child's room with antique toys and clothing, a room of women's period gowns and accessories, and other exhibits on local history and architecture. Out back, a ¼-mi nature trail over dunes leads to the bay. ⊠ *3371 Main St. [Rte. 6A],* ☎ *508/896–7593.* 🎫 *Free.* ⊙ *June and Sept., weekends 1–4; July–Aug., Tues.–Sun. 1–4.*

For a lovely hike or run through the local wilds, try the **Punkhorn Parklands,** studded with freshwater kettle-hole ponds, which has 45 mi of scenic trails meandering through 800 acres of meadows, marshes, and pine forests. ⊠ *End of Run Hill Rd., off Stony Brook Rd.*

Although today they are open to the public for recreation, the 1,961 ❹ acres encompassed by **Nickerson State Park** were once part of a vast estate belonging to Roland C. Nickerson, son of Samuel Nickerson, a Chatham native who became a multimillionaire and founder of the First National Bank of Chicago. At their long, private beach or their hunting lodge, Roland and his wife, Addie, lavishly entertained such visitors as President Grover Cleveland in English country-house style, with coachmen dressed in tails and top hats and a bugler announcing carriages entering the front gates.

The estate was like a village unto itself. Its gardens provided much of the household's food, supplemented by game from its woods and fish from its ponds. It also had its own electric plant and a nine-hole golf course by the water. The enormous mansion Samuel built for his son in 1886 burned to the ground 20 years later, and Roland died two weeks after the event. The even grander stone mansion built to replace it in 1908 is now part of the Ocean Edge resort (☞ Dining and Lodging, *below*). In 1934 Addie donated the land for the state park in memory of Roland and their son, who died during the 1918 flu epidemic.

The park itself consists of acres of oak, pitch pine, hemlock, and spruce forest dotted with seven freshwater kettle ponds formed by glacial action. Some ponds are stocked with trout for fishing. Other recreational opportunities include swimming in the ponds, canoeing, sailing, motorboating, biking along 8 mi of paved trails that have access to the Cape Cod Rail Trail, picnicking, and cross-country skiing in winter. Bird-watchers seek out the thrushes, wrens, warblers, woodpeckers, finches, larks, Canada geese, cormorants, great blue herons, hawks, owls, ospreys, and other species that frequent the park. Occasionally, red foxes and white-tailed deer are spotted in the woods. Tent and RV camping (☞ Dining and Lodging, *below*) is extremely popular here, and visitor programs are offered in season. A map of the park is available on-site. ⊠ *3488 Rte. 6A,* ☎ *508/896–3491.* ⊡ *Free.* ☉ *Daily dawn–dusk.*

Dining and Lodging

$$$$ ✕ **Chillingsworth.** Although generally regarded as the crown jewel of Cape
★ restaurants for many years, Chillingsworth's extremely formal and somewhat stiff presentation seems a less essential experience as other dining has become more sophisticated here. Even so, the excellent, terribly pricey classic French menu and wine cellar continue to win award after award. Every night the seven-course table d'hôte menu rotates through an assortment of appetizers, entrées, and "amusements." Recent favorites have been a superrich risotto, roast lobster, and grilled venison. At dinner a more modest bistro menu is served in the Garden Room, a sort of patio in the front of the restaurant. The whole experience is as close as you get on the Cape to formal extravagance. If you want to linger, there are some guest rooms here, too. ⊠ *2449 Main St. (Rte. 6A),* ☎ *508/896–3640. AE, DC, MC, V. Closed Thanksgiving–Memorial Day; closed Mon. mid-June–Thanksgiving; closed some weekdays Memorial Day–mid-June and mid-Oct.–Thanksgiving.*

$$$$ ✕ **High Brewster.** High Brewster is the real thing: a working country
★ inn that serves up some of the finest food on the Cape. The restored colonial farmhouse has low ceilings and exposed overhead beams, and it overlooks a perfect New England landscape. The five-course prix-fixe menu ($35–$55) changes frequently as it explores classic interpretations of American regional cooking. Longtime favorites include squash soup, grilled duck breast with black-currant reduction, and apple-rum ice cream. Rack of lamb is always on the menu and always perfectly prepared. Summertime sees the arrival of swordfish and striped bass. A six-course tasting dinner ($40–$42) is offered once a week in the summer (call ahead for the schedule). Accommodations at the inn are also available. ⊠ *964 Setucket Rd.,* ☎ *508/896–3636 or 800/203–2634. Reservations essential. AE, MC, V. Closed 1st 2 wks in Jan.; call for weekday hrs off-season. No lunch.*

$$–$$$ ✕ **Brewster Fish House.** Long overshadowed by its pricier neighbors, the Fish House finally has carved a niche for itself: Old Cape standards are starting to take a backseat to new ideas, and there's an expanded menu. Management doesn't seem entirely convinced that a wholesale shift to an upscale menu will carry the day, so classic scrod and boiled dinners still play backup to evolving experimentations with duck, rack of lamb, Cornish game hen, and tenderloin of beef in the classic style. The wine list offers a half-dozen whites and a half-dozen reds that you don't often see by the glass. ⊠ *2208 Rte. 6A,* ☎ *508/896–7867. Reservations not accepted. MC, V. Call for information about off-season closing.*

$$–$$$ ✕ **Spark Fish.** The "spark" in the name explains this new establishment's commonly used meal-preparation method, which involves the use of a wood-fire grill. New owner Steven Parrott, formerly on the management team of Boston's Legal Seafoods, began wowing Brewster diners with his expertise in July 2000. The menu focuses on simple ingredients—fresh herbs, garlic, and fruit salsas—and lets the flavors of local seafood, quality meats, and good vegetables shine through without complicated sauces. In the off-season, fireside dining adds to the comfortable aura of the place. The inside decor is as unfussy as the menu and, like the meals offered, is more about elegant understatement than elaborate decoration. A full wine list is available. ⊠ *2671 Rte. 6A,* ☎ *508/896–1067. MC, V.*

$$ ✕ **Brewster Inn and Chowder House.** A real institution in these parts, this local-flavor-infused restaurant has been around for a long, long time. Home cooking in the traditional New England style is the rule; you'll find no fancy or fussy fusion recipes here—just comfort food in a casual setting. Look for simple but tasty meat and seafood standards, and don't miss the rich and full-bodied New England clam chowder. The inn is somewhat small and dark—it's not unlike eating with some old Yankee salt's relatives in the old homestead. The service is friendly, the prices are kind, and you won't leave hungry. The restaurant serves lunch and dinner daily year-round. ⊠ *1993 Rte. 6A,* ☎ *508/896–7771. MC, V.*

$$ ✕ **Laurino's Cape Cod Tavern.** With warm wood paneling, generous booth-style seating, and red-and-white-check tablecloths, there's something timeless about Laurino's in a basic American-Italian way. It's an easy place to feed the whole family lunch and dinner but not a place for Cape Cod fish, so steer yourself instead to the burgers or the specialty pizzas that come in two sizes. Try a Buffalo Chicken Pizza or the Kitchen Sink, which, as you might expect, has plenty of toppings. At the long, friendly bar you can sit with a buddy over a beer and a big plate of Macho Nachos. In summer live music serenades the late-night crowd of revelers. Look for the staggered flock of plastic pink flamingos out front. ⊠ *3668 Main St. (Rte. 6A),* ☎ *508/896–6135. Reservations not accepted. AE, MC, V.*

$$$$ 🏨 **Ocean Edge.** This huge, self-contained resort is almost like a town. Sports facilities are superior, and activities such as concerts, tournaments, and clambakes are scheduled throughout the summer. Accommodations range from oversize hotel rooms in the conference center, with sitting areas and direct access to the health club and tennis courts, to luxurious one- to three-bedroom condominiums in the woods. Two- to three-bedroom beachfront villas offer immediate access to the resort's private beach. All are decorated with pastel fabrics and fresh wood furnishings in modern style. Each condominium has a washer-dryer; some units have fireplaces, and many have ocean views. The resort is so spread out you may need a car to get from your condo to the pool. MAP plans are subject to availability. ⊠ *2907 Main St. (Rte. 6A), 02631,* ☎ *508/896–9000 or 800/343–6074,* 🆐 *508/896–9123. 197 condominium units, 90 rooms. 4 restaurants, pub, room service, 2 indoor and 4 outdoor pools, ponds, saunas, driving range, golf privileges, putting greens, 11 tennis courts, basketball, exercise room, beach, bicycles, children's programs (ages 4–17), concierge. AE, D, DC, MC, V.* ✍

$$–$$$$ 🏨 **Captain Freeman Inn.** A splendid 1866 Victorian built for a packet-
★   schooner-fleet owner continues to show off its original opulence with a marble fireplace, herringbone-inlay flooring, ornate Italian plaster ceiling medallions, tall windows, and 12-ft ceilings.Guest rooms have hardwood floors, antiques and Victorian reproductions, and beds with eyelet spreads and fishnet or lace canopies. The eight "luxury rooms" are truly indulgent, with queen-size canopy beds, sofas, fireplaces, TVs with VCRs, mini-refrigerators, and French doors leading to small enclosed porches with private whirlpool spas. Winter weekend cooking schools allow participants to learn from the innkeeper's skills, as can diners (on request for an extra charge) in the off-season. ⊠ *15 Breakwater Rd., 02631,* ☎ *508/896–7481 or 800/843–4664,* 🆐 *508/896–5618. 12 rooms. Pool, badminton, croquet, bicycles. No smoking. AE, MC, V. BP.* ✍

$$–$$$ 🏨 **Brewster Farmhouse.** This restored 1846 farmhouse on historic Route 6A has several comforting touches, from the goose-down pillows in the guest rooms to the turndown service with bedside sherry and chocolates. One room has a fireplace, another a king-size canopy bed and sliders out to a private deck. In 1999 an ambitious expansion produced an additional structure that added three luxury-size rooms with antiques and reproduction pieces, including a white wrought-iron canopy bed. These new rooms all have fireplaces and whirlpool baths. In good weather a breakfast prepared by the inn's owners, Carol and Gary Concors, is served on a patio looking onto the 2-acre backyard, which has apple trees and gardens on its edges and a heated pool and whirlpool in its center. ✉ *716 Main St. (Rte. 6A), 02631,* ☎ *508/896–3910 or 800/892–3910,* FAX *508/896–4232. 8 rooms, 1 suite. Pool, bicycles. No smoking. AE, D, DC, MC, V. BP.* ✎

\$\$–\$\$\$ ⊞ **Isaiah Clark House.** A former sea captain's residence just west of the town proper, this inn provides modern amenities without sacrificing its 18th-century heritage and character. The original inhabitants are not forgotten here, from the scrawled signature of 13-year-old son Jeremiah in a closet and framed historic documents and photographs to the namesake of each of the rooms (all Clark family women). Having been lovingly preserved and updated, the inn retains all its old touches of wide-plank flooring and low, sloping ceilings and is further enhanced by a varied selection of antiques. Most rooms have queen-size four-poster or canopy beds, braided rugs, and fireplaces. The extensive gardens yield some of the fruit used in the homemade pies, muffins, and breads. ✉ *1187 Main St. (Rte. 6A), 02631,* ☎ *508/896–2223 or 800/822–4001. 7 rooms. AE, D, DC, MC, V. BP.* ✎

\$\$–\$\$\$ ⊞ **The Ruddy Turnstone.** Built in the early 1800s, this beautifully preserved Cape homestead is set on 3 acres that gently slope to a marsh at the edge of the property. Modern amenities make life easy while antiques, quilts, and pine-board floors with braided rugs (in the main house) or original barn-board walls (in the Carriage House) take you back in time, while modern amenities pamper you. Rooms have queen-size beds and large baths, most with shower-tub combos. An upstairs common sitting room offers an incredible vista of the marsh and the bay beyond; another common room has a fireplace and small library. One spectacular upstairs room has fine bay views through generous windows (no need to lift your head from the pillow). A delicious country breakfast is served at little tables on the porch or in the dining room. ✉ *463 Main St. (Rte. 6A), 02631,* ☎ *508/385–9871 or 800/654–1995,* FAX *508/385–5696. 5 rooms. Air-conditioning. No smoking. MC, V. Closed Nov.–Apr. BP.* ✎

\$–\$\$\$ ⊞ **Old Sea Pines Inn.** Fronted by a white-column portico and
★ wraparound veranda overlooking a broad lawn, the Old Sea Pines evokes the atmosphere of a summer estate from an earlier time. A sweeping staircase leads to guest rooms decorated with reproduction wallpaper, antiques, and framed old photographs. Many rooms are very large; some have fireplaces, including the inn's best room, which also has a sitting area in an enclosed sunporch. Rooms in a newer building are sparsely but well decorated, with bright white modern baths, and have cast-iron queen-size beds. The shared-bath rooms are *very* small but sweetly done, and a steal in summer. There's a Sunday dinner theater, also open to the public, in season. ✉ *2553 Main St. (Rte. 6A), Box 1070, 02631,* ☎ *508/896–6114,* FAX *508/896–7387. 24 rooms, 19 with bath; 3 suites and 2 family-size rooms. Restaurant. No smoking. AE, D, DC, MC, V. Closed Jan.–Mar. BP.* ✎

\$\$ ⊞ **Greylin House.** Set slightly back off Route 6A and surrounded with prettily manicured gardens is this 1837 B&B, where good things actually do come in smaller packages. The five guest rooms are individually decorated with reproduction antiques, canopy beds, and painted wide-pine flooring. The baths (one bath is a quick hop across the hall) are on the small side but comfortable and well equipped; you'll probably be spending more time on the outdoor brick patio overlooking the gardens and greenhouse. ✉ *2511 Main St. (Rte. 6A), 02631,* ☎

508/896–0004 or 800/233–6662. 5 rooms. AE, D, DC, MC, V. Closed Nov.–mid-Apr. BP. ✍

$ ⚠ **Nickerson State Park.** The Cape's largest and most popular camping site is on almost 2,000 acres teeming with wildlife, white pine, hemlock, and spruce forest. The area is jammed with opportunities for trout fishing, walking, or biking along 8 mi of paved trails and for canoeing, sailing, motorboating, and bird-watching. New state park regulations have increased both rates and services; basic sites cost $15 from June to October and $5 from October to December 31; the park is closed to campers the rest of the year. Yurts are also available for rental ($25 for a small one and $30 for a large; both sizes include electricity and water). RVs must be self-contained. Facilities include showers, bathrooms, picnic tables, barbecue areas, and a store. Maps and schedules of park programs are available at the park entrance. ✉ *3488 Main St. (Rte. 6A), 02631,* ☎ *508/896–3491; 877/422–6762 for reservations;* FAX *508/896–3103. 418 sites. No credit cards.*

Nightlife and the Arts

The **Cape Cod Repertory Theatre Co.** (✉ 3379 Main St. [Rte. 6A], ☎ 508/896–1888) performs several impressive productions each summer, from original works to classics, in its new indoor Arts and Crafts–style theater way back in the woods. Mesmerizing entertainment for children, in the form of lively outdoor (and often interactive) theater, is provided here, too. Performances of fairy tales, music, and folktales are given on Tuesday and Friday mornings at 10 in July and August. The theater is just west of Nickerson State Park.

Sunday evenings by the bay are filled with the sounds of the **town-band concerts,** held in the gazebo on the grounds of Drummer Boy Park (✉ Rte. 6A). The park is about ½ mi west of the Cape Cod Museum of Natural History, on the western side of Brewster. Families with little ones will delight in the park's new playground with ornate wood facilities.

The **Woodshed** (✉ 1993 Main St. [Rte. 6A], ☎ 508/896–7771), the rustic bar at the Brewster Inn, is a good place to soak up local color and listen to pop duos or bands that perform nightly. It's open May through October.

Outdoor Activities and Sports

BASEBALL

The **Brewster Whitecaps** (☎ 508/896–9284 in summer; 781/784–7409 in winter) of the collegiate Cape Cod Baseball League play home games at Cape Cod Regional Tech High School (✉ Rte. 124, Harwich) from mid-June to mid-August.

BEACHES

Flax Pond in Nickerson State Park (3488 MainSt. [Rte. 6A], ☎ 508/896–3491), surrounded by pines, offers picnic areas, a bathhouse, and water-sports rentals.

Breakwater Landing, Linnell Landing, Paine's Creek, Point of Rocks, and **Robin's Hill** bay beaches all have access to the flats that at low tide make for very interesting tidal-pool exploration. Eponymous roads to each beach branch off Route 6A; there's limited parking. Some beaches have a daily $8 parking fee; ask at the town hall (☎ 508/896–3701) about various seasonal parking passes, which may require a proof-of-stay form.

BIKING

The **Cape Cod Rail Trail** (☞ Dennis, *above*) has many access points in Brewster, among them Long Pond Road, Underpass Road, and Millstone Road.

Open during summer only but located right alongside the Cape Cod Rail Trail is the tiny **Idle Times Bike Shop** (✉ Rte. 6A, just west of Nickerson State Park, ☎ 508/896–9242), with bikes both big and small for rent. You can't beat the proximity to the trail and the easy parking.

The **Rail Trail Bike Shop** (✉ 302 Underpass Rd., ☎ 508/896–8200) rents bikes, including children's bikes, and in-line skates. Parking is free, and there's a picnic area with easy access to the Rail Trail.

FISHING

Many of Brewster's freshwater ponds offer good fishing for perch, pickerel, and more; five ponds are well stocked with trout. Especially good for fishing is Cliff Pond in Nickerson State Park. You'll need a **fishing license,** available from the town hall (✉ 3918 Main St. [Rte. 6A], ☎ 508/896–3701).

When fishing guidance is in order, you can sign up with **Brewster Flats Fishing & Outfitters** (✉ 2655 Main St. [Rte. 6A], ☎ 508/896–2460) for custom sport-fishing trips that include bait, tackle, and all-weather gear.

GOLF

The par-72, 18-hole **Captain's Golf Course** (✉ 1000 Freeman's Way, ☎ 508/896–5100) is an excellent public course.

Ocean Edge Golf Course (✉ Villages Dr., off Rte. 6A, ☎ 508/896–5911), an 18-hole, par-72 course winding around five ponds, features Scottish-style pot bunkers and challenging terrain. Three-day residential and commuter golf schools are offered in spring and early summer.

HORSEBACK RIDING

Moby Dick Farm (✉ 179 Great Fields Rd., ☎ 508/896–3544) offers instruction and trail rides to riders of all levels.

Woodsong Farm (✉ 121 Lund Farm Way, ☎ 508/896–5555) has instruction and day programs but no trail rides; it also has a horsemanship program for children 5–18.

NEED A BREAK?

Box Lunch (✉ Underpass Rd. near Cape Cod Rail Trail crossing, Brewster, ☎ 508/896–1234), famous for its unique "rollwiches," is quickly spreading around the Cape. This new location, opened in the summer of 2000, has the same tasty selection of breakfast and lunch roll-ups, perfect for a break and a bite while on the Cape Cod Rail Trail or just touring around. In summer the Box Lunch stays open until 9 PM; it closes at 4 PM when the weather turns cooler.

TENNIS

The **Ocean Edge** resort (✉ 2907 Main St. [Rte. 6A], ☎ 508/896–9000) has five clay and six Plexipave courts. It offers lessons and round-robins and hosts a tennis school, with weekend packages and video analysis.

Run by the town and open to the public at no charge are four **public tennis courts,** all just behind the fire and police stations on Route 6A. Two basketball courts are also for public use.

WATER SPORTS

Cape Cod Sea Camps (✉ Box 1880, Brewster 02631, ☎ 508/896–3451) teaches sailing and water sports to children ages 7–17.

Jack's Boat Rentals (✉ Flax Pond, Nickerson State Park, Rte. 6A, ☎ 508/896–8556) rents canoes, kayaks, Seacycles, Sunfish, pedal boats, and sailboards; guide-led kayak tours are also offered.

Shopping

B. D. Hutchinson (⊠ 1274 Long Pond Rd., ☎ 508/896–6395), a watch-and clock maker, sells antique and collectible watches, clocks, and music boxes.

Brewster Book Store (⊠ 2648 Main St. [Rte. 6A], ☎ 508/896–6543) prides itself on being a special Cape bookstore. It's filled to the rafters with all manner of books by local and international authors and has an extensive children's section. A full schedule of author signings and children's story times continues year-round.

Kemp Pottery (⊠ 258 Main St. [Rte. 6A], ☎ 508/385–5782) has functional and decorative stoneware and porcelain, fountains, garden sculpture, pottery sinks, and stained glass.

Kingsland Manor (⊠ 440 Main St. [Rte. 6A], ☎ 508/385–9741) has ivy covering the facade, fountains in the courtyard, and everything "from tin to Tiffany"—including English hunting horns, full-size antique street lamps, garden and house furniture, weather vanes, jewelry, and chandeliers.

Kings Way Books and Antiques (⊠ 774 Main St. [Rte. 6A], ☎ 508/896–3639) sells out-of-print and rare books, including a large medieval section, plus small antiques, china, glass, silver, coins, and linens.

Lemon Tree Village (⊠ Main St. [Rte. 6A, about 1 mi west of town center]) is a cheery shopping complex filled with many unusual stores. You'll find garden statuary, top-of-the-line cooking implements, locally made arts and crafts, pottery, birding supplies, clothing, gifts, jewelry and toys. There's even a nice café next door if all that shopping makes you hungry.

Punkhorn Bookshop (⊠ 672 Main St. [Rte. 6A], ☎ 508/896–2114), an antiquarian and out-of-print bookseller, specializes in natural history, information on the Cape and the region, fine arts, and biography, and also sells antique prints and maps.

Open from April through October, the **Satucket Farm Stand** (⊠ 76 Harwich Rd. [Rte. 124], just off Rte. 6A, ☎ 508/896–5540) is reminiscent of the well-stocked and freshly fragrant side-of-the-road farm stands that make us all nostalgic. Most produce is grown on the premises, and you can fill your basket with the finest of the harvest, from home-baked scones and breads to fruit pies, produce, herbs, and flowers.

The **Spectrum** (⊠ 369 Main St. [Rte. 6A], ☎ 508/385–3322) has a great selection of imaginative American arts and crafts, including pottery, stained glass, art glass, and more.

Sydenstricker Galleries (⊠ 490 Main St. [Rte. 6A], ☎ 508/385–3272) stocks glassware handcrafted by a unique process, which you can watch in progress.

Harwich

❺ *3 mi east of Dennisport, 6 mi south of Brewster.*

Originally known as Setucket, Harwich separated from Brewster in 1694 and was renamed for the famous seaport in England. Like other townships on the Cape, Harwich is actually a cluster of seven small villages, including Harwich Port. Historically, the villages of Harwich were marked by their generous number of churches and the styles of worship they practiced—small villages often sprang up around these centers of faith.

Harwich and Harwich Port are the commercial centers, and although the two have very different natures, both are blessed with graceful old architecture and a rich history. Harwich Port is the more bustling of the two: Brimming with shops, calm-water beaches, restaurants, and hotel complexes, it packs all manner of entertainment and frivolity along its roadways. Harwich is more relaxed, its commerce more centered, and its outlying areas graced with expanses of greenery, large shade trees, and historic homesteads. The Harwich Historical Society has a strong presence here, maintaining exhibits and artifacts significant to the town's past.

The Cape's famous cranberry industry took off in Harwich in 1844, and Alvin Cahoon was its principal grower at the time. Each September Harwich holds a great **Cranberry Festival** to celebrate the importance of this indigenous berry; the festival is usually scheduled during the week after Labor Day. There are cranberry bogs throughout Harwich.

Three naturally sheltered harbors on Nantucket Sound make the town, like its English namesake, popular with boaters. You'll find dozens of elegant sailboats and elaborate yachts in Harwich's harbors, plus plenty of charter fishing boats. Each year in August the town pays celebratory homage to its large boating population with a grand regatta, Sails Around the Cape.

Beaches are plentiful in Harwich, and nearly all rest on the warm and mild waters of Nantucket Sound. Freshwater ponds also speckle the area, ideal for swimming as well as small-scale canoeing and kayaking. Several conservation areas offer miles of secluded walking trails, many alongside the vivid cranberry bogs that have made the town famous.

Once the home of a private school offering the first courses in navigation, the pillared 1844 Greek Revival building of the **Brooks Academy Museum** now houses the museum of the **Harwich Historical Society**. In addition to a large photo-history collection and exhibits on artist Charles Cahoon (grandson of cranberry grower Alvin), the sociotechnological history of the cranberry culture, and shoemaking, the museum displays antique clothing and textiles, china and glass, fans, toys, and much more. There is also an extensive genealogical collection for researchers. On the grounds is a powder house used to store gunpowder during the Revolutionary War, as well as a restored 1872 outhouse that could spur your appreciation for indoor plumbing. ⊠ *80 Parallel St.,* ☎ *508/432–8089.* 🎟 *Donations accepted.* ☉ *June–mid-Oct., Wed.–Sat. 1–4.*

☺ **Brooks Park** on Main Street (Rte. 28) is a good place to stretch your legs, with a playground, picnic tables, a ball field, tennis courts, and a bandstand that's the site of summer concerts.

☺ **Grand Slam Entertainment** has softball and baseball batting cages and pitching machines, including one with fastballs up to 80 mph, a Wiffle-ball machine for younger children, a bumper-boat pool, and a video-arcade room. ⊠ *322 Main St. [Rte. 28], Harwich Port,* ☎ *508/430–1155.* 🎟 *$1.50 for 10 pitches, $5 for 40 pitches, or $10 for 100 pitches; $5 per bumper-pool ride.* ☉ *Apr.–May and Sept.–mid-Oct., Mon.–Sat. 11–7, Sun. 11–9; June–Aug., daily 9 am–11 pm.*

For children who have spent too much time in the car watching you drive, a spin behind the wheel of one of 20 top-of-the-line go-carts at
☺ **Bud's Go-Karts** may be just the thing. ⊠ *9 Sisson Rd., off Rte. 28, Harwich Port,* ☎ *508/432–4964.* 🎟 *$5 for 6 mins.* ☉ *June–Labor Day, Mon.–Sat. 9 am–11 pm, Sun. 1–11.*

☺ The **Trampoline Center** has 12 trampolines—a perfect activity to release some of that boundless, bouncing energy. They are set up at ground level over pits for safety. ⊠ *296 Main St. [Rte. 28], West Harwich,* ☎ *508/432–8717.* 🎟 *$4 for 10 mins.* ☉ *Apr.–mid-June, weekends (hrs vary widely, call ahead); mid-June–Labor Day, daily 9 am–11 pm.*

Dining and Lodging

\$\$–\$\$\$ ✕ **Cape Sea Grille.** Because it's settled primly on a side street off hectic Route 28, this culinary gem stays free of thundering hordes. Elegant in both decor and cuisine, it's a favorite of both locals and visitors. Fresh flowers, beautiful wood tables, colorful linens, and vibrant wall murals delight the eye while dinner teases the palate—specialties always include local fish, dressed in such fineries as applewood-smoked bacon or an orange-and-ginger marinade. The menu changes frequently in order to feature the freshest ingredients. Save room for dessert—the bananas Foster Napoléon is heavenly. Dinner is served nightly from 5 in the height of summer; call for hours in the slower season. ⊠ *31 Sea St., Harwich Port,* ☎ *508/432–4745. AE, DC, MC, V. Closed Nov.–mid-Apr.*

\$\$–\$\$\$ ✕ **L'alouette.** Lovers of authentic French cuisine will feel happily at home here, where the full-bodied essence of country cooking is the house specialty. Owners Danielle and Jean-Louis hail from France, so their knowledge is true. Look for traditional and rich offerings such as duckling and rack of lamb; veal chops with Portabello mushrooms; and the favorite, chateaubriand. The setting is casual and comfortable. ⊠ *787 Rte. 28, Harwich Port,* ☎ *508/430–0405. AE, DC, MC, V. Closed late-Feb.–mid-Mar.*

\$\$ ✕ **Brax Landing.** In this local stalwart perched alongside busy Saquatucket Harbor, you'll get a menu tip-off as you pass by tanks full of steamers and lobsters in the corridor leading to the dining room. The restaurant sprawls around a big bar that serves drinks such as the Moxie (pink lemonade and vodka, "calm seas guaranteed"). The swordfish and the Chatham scrod are favorites, both served simply and well. There's a notable children's menu, and Sunday brunch, served from 10 to 2, is an institution. ⊠ *Rte. 28 at Saquatucket Harbor, Harwich Port,* ☎ *508/ 432–5515. Reservations not accepted. AE, DC, MC, V.*

\$\$ ✕ **Country Inn Restaurant and Tavern.** This year-round beauty has more than withstood the test of time, offering up traditional New England cuisine in a gentle pastoral setting. The main dining room rests upon wide-plank floors and looks out onto the inn's 6 acres of greenery. Fresh flowers, candlelight, and—in the off-season—firelight set a romantic mood. The tavern room is darker and smaller, but still comfortable. Menu specials include the Country Inn Platter for Two—filet mignon, lobster, scallops, and shrimp scampi—and the local favorite, Lazy-Man's Lobster; it's pre-dismantled, so you get all the meat without the mess. Friday and Saturday evenings meals are accompanied by live piano serenades; lots of folks push back their napkins and hit the dance floor on Saturday night, when music is liveliest. ⊠ *86 Sisson Ave. (Rte. 39), Harwich Port,* ☎ *508/432–2769. AE, MC, V.*

\$\$ ✕ **400 East.** This big, dark restaurant buzzing with conversation is in a nondescript shopping plaza. The menu includes teriyaki tuna and chicken, prime rib, and baked scrod but lists excellent pizza offerings as well, with toppings such as wild mushrooms, blue cheese, and Cajun chicken and corn. Eating at the busy, U-shape bar can be a great alternative to waiting for a table, provided you don't mind a television set in the picture. The 400 has a cousin restaurant (also called the 400) on Main Street that is not as much fun. ⊠ *1421 Rte. 39,* ☎ *508/432– 1800. AE, D, MC, V.*

\$ ✕ **Ay! Caramba Cafe.** Brand new and thriving so completely that plans are already in the works for a second location, this tiny but vibrant café is a welcome dining alternative in the Harwich area. Here you can fill up on authentic Mexican fare without cleaning out your wallet. Choose from tasty quesadillas, burritos, tostadas, and tacos, or go for one of the large combination plates, complete with rice and either refried beans or vegetables. The fish tacos and seafood quesadillas are especially good. Once you have your food, sidle up to the salsa bar, where three varieties are made throughout the day—but be sure to have your water handy for the hottest stuff. ☒ *703 Main St., Harwich,* ☎ *508/432–9800. AE, DC, MC, V.*

$$$–$$$$ 🏠 **Winstead Inn and Beach Resort.** Two equally inviting properties, one in the heart of historic Harwich, the other on a private Nantucket Sound beach, combine to make an enticing getaway. Since they're under the same management, the facilities of both are open to all guests; an old "woodie" shuttles between the two. The inn is a grand colonial building, with fireplaces and a baby grand piano in the common room. The antiques-filled guest rooms are in two separate wings; many have balconies or decks that overlook the pool and garden. The beach resort is reminiscent of an earlier era, with a turret and a wraparound porch. Its elegant guest rooms are also dotted with antiques, and some baths have whirlpool tubs. From umbrella tables on the deck you can watch the sweep of coast and surrounding grasslands while enjoying a generous Continental breakfast. Off-season, there's a fire burning in the common room. ☒ *328 Bank St., 02645;* ☒ *4 Braddock La., Harwich Port 02646,* ☎ *508/432–4444 or 800/870–4405. 44 rooms. Restaurant, pool. MC, V. CP.* 🐾

$$–$$$$ 🏠 **Dunscroft by the Sea.** With romance as its main motto, this gambrel-roof, cedar-shingle inn provides such lush amenities as antique sleigh, laced canopy, and four-poster beds; two-person whirlpool tubs; and terry robes for its guests. Rooms are generously sized and individually and colorfully decorated, with floral curtains and reproduction pieces; some have working fireplaces. The calming waters of Nantucket Sound are just a few paces away. ☒ *24 Pilgrim Rd., Harwich Port 02646,* ☎ *508/432–0810 or 800/432–4345. 8 rooms, 1 cottage. Beach. AE, D, MC, V. BP.* 🐾

$$$ 🏠 **Augustus Snow House.** This grand old Victorian is the epitome of
★ elegance. Common areas include the oak-paneled front room, with tall windows and a fireplace, and a wicker-filled screened porch. The stately dining room is the setting for the three-course breakfast, with dishes such as baked pears in raspberry and cream sauce. Guest rooms are individually decorated with Victorian-print wallpapers, luxurious carpets, and fine antique and reproduction furnishings. All have quilts, TVs, fireplaces, and antique brass bathroom and lighting fixtures; three also have whirlpool tubs. Downstairs, a lovely gardenlike tearoom is open to the public on Thursday, Friday, and Saturday for afternoon tea. Planned to be completed by this year is the new Carriage House Suite with fireplace, dining area, kitchenette, and living room. ☒ *528 Main St. (Rte. 28), Harwich Port 02646,* ☎ *508/430–0528 or 800/320–0528,* 🆁🆇 *508/432–6638 ext. 15. 5 rooms. Air-conditioning. AE, D, MC, V. BP.* 🐾

$$ 🏠 **Sea Heather Inn.** Resting majestically amid sculptured lawns with views of Nantucket Sound, this is one of the grand dames of the area. The main house, a stately and rambling Cape-style building built in the 1840s, is in the perpetual process of renewing itself; currently the owners are adding painted wainscoting and wide-plank flooring. The eight rooms in the main house are filled with antiques and reproductions and several offer water views. A larger, hotel-style complex on the property provides rooms with more modern furnishings in a decidedly hotel-style area, complete with game room for those in need of entertainment. The inn is a short walk from several beaches. ☒ *28 Sea St., Harwich Port 02646,* ☎ *508/432–1275 or 800/789–7809. 20 rooms. Air-conditioning. AE, D, MC, V. BP.* 🐾

$–$$ 🏠 **Seadar Inn.** Although it won't win any awards for elegant decor, the
★ friendly Seadar brings comfort and cleanliness with a great draw—location. The only obstacle between you and the beach on Nantucket Sound is the small parking lot and possibly the ice cream truck. The homey,

motel-style rooms are unfussy and practical in a colonial style, with knotty-pine walls, frilly curtains, and the kind of furniture you might see in your grandmother's house; some have water views. Outdoor grills are available. To keep up with visitor comforts, all rooms have recently been furnished with air-conditioning. ⊠ *Braddock La. at Bank St. Beach, Harwich Port 02646,* ☎ *508/432–0264 or 800/888–5250. 23 rooms. Air-conditioning. AE, D, MC, V. Closed mid-Oct.–May. BP.* ✎

$ ⌧ **Handkerchief Shoals Motel.** This single-story property about 2 mi from Harwich Port and 3 mi from downtown Chatham is set back from the highway on a deep skirt of lawn. The large rooms are sparkling clean, with sitting and desk areas, tile baths, cable TV, and a refrigerator and microwave. All in all, it's a very good value for the area. ⊠ *888 Rte. 28, at Deep Hole Rd., Box 306, South Harwich 02661,* ☎ *508/432–2200. 26 rooms. Pool, Ping-Pong, shuffleboard. D, MC, V. Closed mid-Oct.–mid-Apr.* ✎

Nightlife and the Arts

THE ARTS
The **First Congregational Church** (⊠ Main St. at corner of Rtes. 39 and 124, Harwich, ☎ 508/432–1053) closes its day of worship with Sunday-evening Candlelight Concerts at 7:30 from July through September.

Harwich Junior Theatre (⊠ 105 Division St., West Harwich, ☎ 508/432–2002) gives theater classes for children year-round and presents four family-oriented summer productions.

Town band concerts in Harwich take place in summer on Tuesday at 7:30 in Brooks Park (☎ 508/432–1600).

NIGHTLIFE
Country Inn (⊠ 86 Sisson Rd. [Rte. 39], West Harwich Port, ☎ 508/432–2769) complements its dinner menu with dancing every Friday and Saturday evening. You can dance between courses to music of the 1940s with a piano player on Friday night and a pianist and bass player on Saturday evening after 7.

Irish Pub (⊠ 126 Main St. [Rte. 28], West Harwich, ☎ 508/432–8808) has dancing to bands—playing Irish, American, and dance music—as well as sing-alongs, pool, darts, sports TV, and pub food in the bar.

Jake Rooney's Pub (⊠ 119 Brooks Rd., off Rte. 28, Harwich Port, ☎ 508/430–1100) has a comfortable pub atmosphere, keno, and live entertainment five nights a week.

Outdoor Activities and Sports

BASEBALL
The **Harwich Mariners** (☎ 508/432–0662) of the collegiate Cape Cod Baseball League play home games at Whitehouse Field (⊠ Harwich High School, Oak St.) from mid-June to mid-August.

BEACHES
Harwich has 22 beaches, more than any other Cape town. Most of the ocean beaches are on Nantucket Sound, where the water is a bit calmer and warmer. Freshwater pond beaches are also abundant.

BOATING
Whether you're in the mood to sail under the moonlight, hire a private charter or learn to navigate yourself, **Cape Sail** (⊠ 337 Saquatucket Harbor, off Rte. 28, Harwich Port, ☎ 508/896–2730) can accommodate any whim.

Cape Water Sports (⊠ 337 Main St. [Rte. 28], Harwich Port, ☎ 508/432–7079) rents Sunfish, Hobie Cats, Lasers, powerboats, surf bikes, day sailers, and canoes and gives instructions.

The year 2000 marked the 10th annual **Sails Around Cape Cod** regatta (☎ 508/430–1165). The late-August race circumnavigates the Cape, a distance of 140 nautical mi, beginning at the east end of the Cape Cod Canal and ending at the west end.

FISHING

Fishing trips are operated on a walk-on basis from spring through fall on the *Golden Eagle* (⊠ Wychmere Harbor, Harwich Port, ☎ 508/432–5611).

The *Yankee* (⊠ Saquatucket Harbor, Harwich Port, ☎ 508/432–2520) invites passengers aboard its 65-ft party boat in search of fluke, scup, sea bass, and tautog. Two trips depart daily Monday through Saturday, and there's one on Sunday. Reservations are recommended.

GOLF

Cranberry Valley Golf Course (⊠ 183 Oak St., ☎ 508/430–7560) has a championship layout of 18 well-groomed holes surrounded by cranberry bogs.

Harwich Port Golf Club (⊠ South and Forest Sts., Harwich Port, ☎ 508/432–0250) has a nine-hole course that's great for beginners.

Shopping

Cape Cod Braided Rug Co. (⊠ 537 Main St. [Rte. 28], Harwich Port, ☎ 508/432–3133) specializes in braided rugs made on the premises in a variety of colors, styles, and sizes.

Carriage House Designs (⊠ 100 Main St. [Rte. 28], West Harwich, ☎ 508/432–7800) has a fine selection of dried and silk flower arrangements, folk art, and antiques.

820 Main Gallery (⊠ 820 Main St. [Rte. 28], Harwich Port, ☎ 508/430–7622) sells original works in oil, acrylics, watercolors and photography, as well as limited-edition prints by established local artists. The gallery specializes in regional land- and seascapes.

The **Mews at Harwich Port** (⊠ 517 Main St. [Rte. 28], Harwich Port, ☎ 508/432–6397) has a varied and changing selection of antiques, from baskets to early American glassworks.

The **Potted Geranium** (⊠ 188 Main St. [Rte. 28], West Harwich, ☎ 508/432–1114) has a wide selection of country-inspired gifts and home-related items, including colorful wind flags, handcrafted items, and wind chimes.

Pottery Plus (⊠ 551 Main St. [Rte. 28], Harwich Port, ☎ 508/430–5240) offers the pottery of artist Scott Sullivan, as well as other works by local artists.

Treasure Tyme (⊠ 815 Main St. [Rte. 28], Harwich Port, ☎ 508/430–5475) features an array of locally made arts and crafts. Six rooms of goodies display pottery, glassworks, photography, and dolls, among other items. The shop is open year-round.

Wychmere Book & Coffee (⊠ 587 Main St. [Rte. 28], Harwich Port, ☎ 508/432–7868) is a place to savor the comforts of browsing, reading, and sipping good coffee. Special events with authors and a children's summer reading hour further enhance the scene.

Chatham

❻–⓫ *5 mi east of Harwich, 8 mi south of Orleans.*

Originally populated by Native Americans, Chatham came into the hands of white settlers from Plymouth when, in 1656, William Nickerson traded a boat for the 17 square mi of land that make up the town. In 1712 the area separated from Eastham and was incorporated as a town; the surnames of the Pilgrims who first settled here still dominate the census list. Although Chatham was originally a farming community, the sea finally lured townspeople to turn to fishing for their livelihood, an industry that has held strong to this day.

At the bent elbow of the Cape, with water nearly surrounding it, Chatham has all the charm of a quietly posh seaside resort, with relatively little commercialism. And it is charming: gray-shingle houses with tidy awnings and cheerful flower gardens, an attractive Main Street with crafts and antiques stores alongside homey coffee shops, and a five-and-dime. It's a traditional town, where elegant summer cottages share the view with stately houses of purebred Yankee architecture, including some of the finest bow-roof houses in the country. There's none of Provincetown's flash, yet it's not overly quaint—just well-to-do without being ostentatious, casual and fun but refined, and never tacky (unless you feel that a few large new "trophy houses" qualify as tacky).

Because of its location at the elbow, Chatham is not a town you just pass through—it's a destination in itself. And this position gives the town an exclusive aura. The atmosphere is casual and quaint in the New England way, yet there's also that quiet essence of privilege and class here. Summer is truly beautiful in Chatham, when the streets are lined with exquisite hydrangea bushes in varying shades, from cobalt blue to indigo and deep violet.

Its position on the confluence of Nantucket Sound and the Atlantic Ocean makes Chatham especially vulnerable to the destructive wrath of stormy seas. Many a home and beachfront have been lost to the tumultuous waters. But like any stalwart, New England character, Chatham will continue to hold on to its fortunes, its past, and its future.

❻ Authentic all the way, the **Railroad Museum** is set in a restored 1887 depot. Exhibits include a walk-through 1910 New York Central caboose, old photographs, equipment, thousands of train models, and a diorama of the 1915 Chatham rail yards. ⊠ *153 Depot Rd., ☎ no phone.* 🖾 *Donations accepted.* ☉ *Mid-June–mid-Sept., Tues.–Sat. 10–4.*

☽ A unique playground, the **Play-a-round,** a multilevel wooden playground of turrets, twisting tubular slides, jungle gyms, and more, was designed with the input of local children and built by volunteers. There's a section for people with disabilities and a fenced-in area for small children. ⊠ *Depot Rd., across from Railroad Museum.*

On **Queen Anne Road** around Oyster Pond, half-Cape houses, open fields, and rolling pastures reveal the area's colonial and agricultural history.

Built by sea captain Joseph C. Atwood in 1752 and occupied by his descendants until it was sold to the Chatham Historical Society in 1926, **❼** the **Atwood House Museum** has a gambrel roof, variable-width floor planks, fireplaces, an old kitchen with a wide hearth and a beehive oven, and some antique dolls and toys. The New Gallery displays portraits of local sea captains. The Joseph C. Lincoln Room has the manuscripts, first editions, and mementos of the Chatham writer, and in the basement is an antique tool room. The 1974 Durand Wing houses collections of seashells from around the world and threaded Sandwich glass, as well as Parian ware figures, unglazed porcelain vases, figurines, and busts. In a remodeled freight shed are murals (1932–45) by Alice Stallknecht Wight portraying religious scenes in Chatham settings. On the grounds are an herb garden, the old turret and lens from the Chatham Light, and a simple camp house rescued from eroding North Beach. ⊠ *347 Stage Harbor Rd., ☎ 508/945-2493.* 🖾 *$3.* ☉ *Mid-June–Sept., Tues.–Fri. 1–4.*

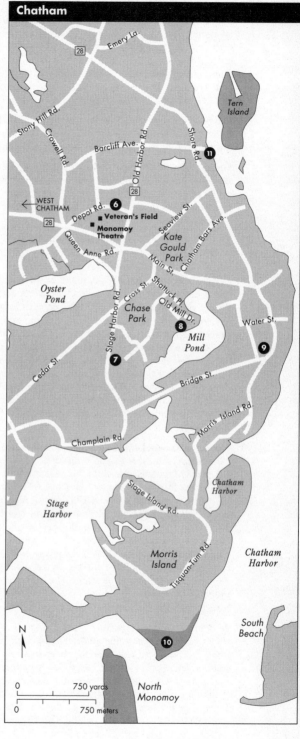

Chatham

❽ The **Old Grist Mill,** one of a number of windmills still on the Cape, was built in 1797 by Colonel Benjamin Godfrey for the purpose of grinding corn. How practical the mill actually was is a matter of debate: for it to work properly, a wind speed of at least 20 mph was necessary, but winds more than 25 mph required the miller to reef the sails or to quit grinding altogether. Moved to its present location from Miller Hill in 1956, the mill was extensively renovated and opened to the public in 1957. ⊠ *Old Mill Dr.* ☼ *July–Aug., weekdays 10–3.*

Mill Pond is a lovely place to stop for a picnic. There's fishing from the bridge, and often the bullrakers can be seen at work, plying the pond's muddy bottom with 20-ft rakes in search of shellfish.

Stage Harbor, sheltered by Morris Island, is where Samuel de Champlain anchored in 1606. The street on its north side is, not surprisingly, called Champlain Road. A skirmish here between Europeans and Native Americans marked the first bloodshed in New England between Native people and the new arrivals.

★ ❾ The famous view from **Chatham Light** (⊠ Main St., near Bridge St., ☎ 508/945–5199)—of the harbor, the offshore sandbars, and the ocean beyond—justifies the crowds that gather to share it. The lighthouse is especially dramatic on a foggy night, as the beacon's light pierces the mist. Coin-operated telescopes allow a close look at the famous "Chatham Break," the result of a fierce 1987 nor'easter that blasted a channel through a barrier beach just off the coast; it is now known as North and South beaches. The Cape Cod Museum of Natural History in Brewster (☞ *above*) has a display of photos documenting the process of erosion leading up to and following the break. The U.S. Coast Guard auxiliary, which supervises the lighthouse, offers tours on the first and third Wednesdays, April–September. The lighthouse is also open by appointment, and on three special occasions during the year: Seafest, an annual tribute to the maritime industry held in mid-October; mid-May's Cape Cod Maritime Week; and June's Cape Heritage Week.

★ Monomoy National Wildlife Refuge is a 2,500-acre preserve including the Monomoy Islands, a fragile 9-mi-long barrier-beach area south of Chatham. Monomoy's North and South islands were created when a storm divided the former Monomoy Island in 1978. Monomoy was itself separated from the mainland in a 1958 storm. A paradise for bird-watchers, the island is an important stop along the North Atlantic Flyway for migratory waterfowl and shore birds—peak migration times are May and late July. It also provides nesting and resting grounds for 285 species, including gulls—great black-backed, herring, and laughing—and several tern species. White-tail deer also live on the islands, and harbor and gray seals frequent the shores in winter. The only structure on the islands is the **South Monomoy Lighthouse.** Built in 1849, the shiny red-orange structure, along with the keeper's house, was refurbished in 1988.

Monomoy is a quiet, peaceful place of sand and beach grass, of tidal flats, dunes, marshes, freshwater ponds, thickets of bayberry and beach plum, and a few pines. Because the refuge harbors several endangered species, visitors' activities are limited. Certain areas are fenced off to protect nesting areas of terns and the threatened piping plover. The Massachusetts Audubon Society in South Wellfleet, the Cape Cod Museum of Natural History in Brewster, and other groups conduct tours of the islands, many with a focus on bird-watching. The *Rip Ryder* (☎ 508/945–5450) will take you over from Chatham in season for some lone bird-watching. Rates vary greatly: if you catch a ride out with the seal-watching cruise, it's $14 per person; if you charter a private ride, rates are $45 per person round-trip or $10 per person for three or more passengers.

⑩ The **Monomoy National Wildlife Refuge headquarters,** on the misleadingly named Morris Island (it is connected to the mainland), has a visitor center and bookstore (⊠ Off Morris Island Rd., ☎ 508/945–0594), open daily 8–5, with gaps, where you can pick up pamphlets on Monomoy and the birds, wildlife, and flora and fauna found there. A ¾-mi interpretive walking trail, closed at high tide, around Morris Island gives a good view of the refuge and the surrounding waters.

⑪ The **Fish Pier** (⊠ Shore Rd. and Barcliff Ave.) bustles with activity when Chatham's fishing fleet returns, sometime between noon and 2 PM daily, depending on the tide. The unloading of the boats is a big local event, drawing crowds who watch it all from an observation deck. From their fishing grounds 3–100 mi offshore, fishermen bring in haddock, cod, flounder, lobster, halibut, and pollack, which are packed in ice and shipped to New York and Boston or sold at the fish market here. You might also see sand sharks being unloaded. Typically they are sent, either fresh or frozen, to French and German markets. Also here is *The Provider,* a monument to the town's fishing industry, showing a hand pulling a fish-filled net from the sea.

Known for their artful contemporary treatment of blown glass, Jim Holmes and Deborah Doane of the **Chatham Glass Company** (☞ Shopping, *below*) create everything from candleholders to unique vases in a vast spectrum of colors. You can watch the fascinating process of glassblowing here. ⊠ *758 Main St.,* ☎ *508/945–5547.* ☉ *Memorial Day–Labor Day, Mon.–Sat. 10–5; Labor Day–Memorial Day, daily 10–5.*

Dining and Lodging

$$$ ✕ **Christian's.** The influences at this landmark town establishment stem from two continents. Downstairs, the dining room mixes Old Cape and country French decor: Pilgrim blue with lace. Lunch and dinner are also both French and New England: boneless roast duck with raspberry sauce and flaky sautéed sole with lobster and lemon-butter sauce. The mahogany-paneled bar and deck upstairs serve a lighter menu that remains strong on seafood but adds some Mexican influences, such as tacos and quesadillas, that are well suited to the summer. In some ways this is one of those situations where less is more; as nice as the formal downstairs remains, the upstairs is more of a happening scene. ⊠ *443 Main St.,* ☎ *508/945–3362. AE, D, DC, MC, V. Closed weekdays Jan.–Mar.*

$$–$$$ ✕ **Vining's Bistro.** Chatham's restaurants have tended to the conserva-
★ tive end of the culinary spectrum, but this bistro is convincing everyone that it deserves mention not only for its exceptionally inventive menu but for its determination not to rest on its laurels. The wood grill is the center of attention here, where the chef employs zesty rubs and spices from all over the globe. The wonderful, exotic Bangkok fisherman's stew has almost too much seafood crammed in; spit-roasted Jamaican chicken competes with a Portobello mushroom sandwich as the restaurant's signature dish. Go for the Mahogany Fire Noodles, an awe-inspiring shrimp and chicken dish. The restaurant is upstairs at the Gallery Building, and many windows look out on the art below. ⊠ *595 Main St.,* ☎ *508/945–5033. Reservations not accepted. AE, D, MC, V. Closed mid-Jan.–Apr.*

$$ ✕ **Chatham Squire.** What had been a bar and not much more has now
★ evolved into an excellent dining experience. This is the kind of place where if you order anything local, you can't go wrong. The fish is as fresh and good as you get on Cape Cod, and the kitchen continues to innovate while not forgetting its Cape roots. The calamari is always tender, the oysters a lovely mouthful. The Squire is not as inexpensive as it was (or as its exterior implies), but it is much finer. Expect a long wait in season, in which case a visit to the bar side is not the worst fate. ⊠ *487 Main St.,* ☎ *508/945–0945. Reservations not accepted. AE, D, MC, V.*

$$ ✕ **High Tide Restaurant.** A long-established (and typically crowded) favorite, this high-spirited place has an ample and varied menu. Local seafood is generously represented, as are several creative meat dishes, daily specials, and Italian entrées. A classic is the Neptune High Tide: shrimp, scallops, and lobster bathed in a creamy garlic sauce and heaped over pasta. There's also a children's menu. Live entertainment is offered on the weekends. ✉ *1629 Main St.,* ☎ *508/945–2582. AE, MC, V.*

$$ ✕ **Marley's.** Shaking up traditional New England fare with international flavors, this restaurant is not afraid to be a little creative. Try the scallops Barbados, prepared with pineapple, rum, and brown sugar and topped with a coconut-macaroon crust. More traditional entrées include steaks, chicken potpie, lobster, and steamers; there are also several vegetarian options. Filled with flowers and greenery, it's also a comfortable and good bet for weekend breakfast; try to get a seat out on the garden patio when the weather cooperates. It seems the owners are as inventive with their hours of operation as they are with the menu—after late October, visitors need to call to see if the restaurant is open. It all depends on fate, say the owners. ✉ *1077 Main St.,* ☎ *508/945–1700. AE, MC, V.*

$$ ✕ **Pate's.** This popular spot has been grilling up meats and local seafood since 1957. You can expect such items as succulent lamb chops, filet mignon, sirloin, and swordfish to arrive marked with the telltale stripes of the open flame. Seafood is taken seriously here; that baked lobster on your plate weighs in at more than 2 pounds. The setting is comfortable and casual, and dinner is consistently tasty. ✉ *1260 Main St.,* ☎ *508/ 945–9777. AE, MC, V. Closed mid-Jan.–Apr.*

$$ ✕ **The Sou'wester.** You're more likely to see someone in a yellow slicker and rubber boots than a sports jacket and loafers in this small spot, the most unpretentious bar-restaurant in Chatham, if not the Lower Cape. The decor, such as it is, can barely be called that: eight booths, low light, and what look like fake Oriental rugs for wall hangings. The handwritten menu is heavy on steak tips, sirloin, and pork chops, with fish cakes and beans for the fishermen patrons who haven't had their fill of fish for the day. A long-neck Bud seems the appropriate accompaniment. On weekends there's good, loud, get-down live music in the bar, known as the Lincoln Lodge. ✉ *1563 Main St.,* ☎ *508/945–4424. AE, MC, V.*

$$$$ ✕🏨 **Chatham Bars Inn.** This 1914 landmark inn is an oceanfront resort in the old, extravagant style. High above the beach on a windswept bluff, the inn claims a stunning view of the ocean through floor-to-ceiling windows. The formal dining-room menu leans on current American hits such as rich, seared foie gras and steamed swordfish with clams. Grand Sunday dinner buffets include a raw bar with caviar and half lobsters. The Tavern is open for a more casual lunch and dinner, and the Beach House Bar opens in season for breakfast and lunch down by the water. The inn consists of a main building flanked by wings—on the ground floor the grand lobby gives way to the formal restaurant on one side and a porch-fronted lounge on the other—with 26 one- to eight-bedroom cottages on 22 landscaped acres overlooking the ocean. Under seemingly perpetual renovation, the once-bland rooms are now filled with hand-painted furnishings by local artists and colorful fabrics depicting sunny seaside scenes. Although the ocean views from some rooms may be spectacular, when push comes to shove, the value for the money is not exceptional. ✉ *Shore Rd., 02633,* ☎ *508/945–0096 or 800/527–4884,* 🅵🅰🆇 *508/945–5491. 205 rooms. 3 restaurants, bar, lobby lounge, pool, putting green, 4 tennis courts, exercise room, volleyball, beach, baby-sitting, children's programs. AE, DC, MC, V.*☙

$$$$ 🏨 **Wequassett Inn Resort & Golf Club.** This exquisite traditional resort
★ offers first-rate accommodations in 20 Cape-style cottages and an attractive hotel complex. Partly surrounded by the mild waters of Pleasant Bay and shaded by oaks and pines on its 22 acres, the Wequassett provides lux-

ury in an informal setting. Along with attentive service and evening entertainment, you'll find plenty of sunning and sporting opportunities, including the brand-new, very exclusive Cape Cod National Golf Club (guests have golf privileges). Thoughtfully decorated with fresh pine furniture, floral bedcovers, or handmade quilts and such homey touches as overflowing window boxes and duck decoys, rooms are spacious and welcoming. ⊠ *173 Orleans Rd. (Rte. 28), Pleasant Bay, 02633,* ☎ *508/432–5400 or 800/225–7125,* FAX *508/432–5032. 102 rooms, 2 suites. Restaurant, grill, piano bar, room service, pool, 4 tennis courts, exercise room, windsurfing, boating. AE, D, DC, MC, V. Closed Nov.–Apr. FAP.* ⊗

$$$–$$$$ 🏠 **Chatham Wayside Inn.** Once a stop on a turn-of-the-20th-century stagecoach route, the inn may still be an oasis for weary travelers, but its decor does not hark back to those earlier times. Everything is crisp and colorful here, from the floral comforters and wallpapers to freshly painted walls and bright wall-to-wall carpeting. Some rooms include private balconies, fireplaces, and whirlpool tubs. You'll find modern, tasteful comfort here, with the added benefit of a location smack in the center of town: you may not have to leave your room to hear the sounds of the weekly town band concerts. ⊠ *512 Main St., 02633,* ☎ *508/945–5550 or 800/391–5734,* FAX *508/945–3407. 56 rooms. Restaurant, pool. AE, D, MC, V. BP.* ⊗

$$$–$$$$ 🏠 **Cranberry Inn.** Within close range of the heart of town, the inn has the added benefit of a protected marsh area in its backyard—a fine spot from which to spy great blue herons and the occasional deer or fox. Billed as the oldest continuously operating lodging establishment in Chatham, the inn reinforces that tradition with decor reflecting a country-inspired theme, such as antique and reproduction furniture and an array of handmade quilts. Rooms have telephones and televisions; some offer fireplaces or private balconies. ⊠ *359 Main St., 02633,* ☎ *508/945–9232 or 800/332–4667,* FAX *508/945–3769. 18 rooms. Restaurant. AE, D, MC, V. BP.* ⊗

$$$–$$$$ 🏠 **Queen Anne Inn.** Built in 1840 as a wedding present for the daugh-
★   ter of a famous clipper-ship captain, the building first opened as an inn in 1874, at which time a north wing was added; a south wing was added much later, in the 1950s. The quite-grand resulting structure has large guest rooms furnished in a casual yet elegant style. Some have working fireplaces, private balconies, and hot tubs. Lingering and lounging are encouraged—around the large heated outdoor pool, at the tables on the veranda, in front of the fireplace in the cozy sitting room, and in the plush parlor. The tastefully designed restaurant, which serves a delicious breakfast, is also open to the public for dinner. ⊠ *70 Queen Anne Rd., 02633,* ☎ *508/945–0394 or 800/545–4667,* FAX *508/945–4884. 31 rooms. Restaurant, bar, air-conditioning, pool, 3 tennis courts. AE, D, MC, V.* ⊗

$$–$$$$ 🏠 **Captain's House Inn.** Finely preserved architectural details, superb
★   interiors, and an overall feeling of warmth and quiet comfort are just part of what makes Jan and Dave McMaster's inn one of the Cape's finest. Each room in the four inn buildings has its own personality. Some are quite large, and most have fireplaces; some are lacy and feminine, others refined and elegant. Authentic details of another era abound, from a Victorian tile ceiling to wide-board floors and elaborate moldings and wainscoting. The gorgeous Hiram Harding Room, in the bow-roof Captain's Cottage, has 200-year-old hand-hewn ceiling beams; a wall of raised walnut paneling; and a large, central working fireplace. The luxury suites in the former stables are particularly spacious and have every amenity imaginable, including whirlpool baths, fireplaces, TV/VCR, mini-refrigerators, and private patios or balconies. ⊠ *371 Old Harbor Rd., 02633,* ☎ *508/945–0127,* FAX *508/945–0866. 16 rooms, 3 suites. Croquet, bicycles. No smoking. AE, D, MC, V. BP.* ⊗

$$–$$$ 🏠 **Moses Nickerson House.** Each room in this 1839 house has an individual look: one with dark woods, leathers, Ralph Lauren fabrics, and English hunting antiques; another with a high canopy bed and a hand-hooked rug. Still others are bedecked with handmade quilts, floral wall-coverings, and canopy or four-poster beds. Some rooms have gas-log fireplaces. The constants are the queen-size beds, televisions, telephones, and complete modem and computer hookups. Breakfast is served in a pretty glassed-in sunroom with views of the garden and fishpond. ⊠ *364 Old Harbor Rd., 02633,* ☎ *508/945–5859 or 800/ 628–6972,* 𝖥𝖠𝖷 *508/945–7087. 7 rooms. Air-conditioning, in-room data ports. No smoking. AE, D, MC, V. BP.* 🐾

$$ 🏠 **Chatham Highlander.** A great bargain considering its location near the center of Chatham, this clean motel offers generously sized rooms on prettily manicured grounds. The rooms have modern decor, with floral bedspreads and curtains. Most rooms have double beds, though there is a room with a king-size bed, as well as a suite and two efficiencies for larger families. All the standard amenities are offered, from cable TV to small refrigerators, and there are two outdoor pools on the grounds. ⊠ *946 Main St., 02633,* ☎ *508/945–9038. 28 rooms. Air-conditioning, 2 pools. No smoking. AE, D, MC, V. Closed Thanksgiving.–Apr.* 🐾

$$ 🏠 **Hawthorne Motel.** Known not just for its immediate proximity to the water, this popular motel overlooking Pleasant Bay, the Atlantic, and Chatham Harbor is also cherished for its reasonable prices. Nearly all the rooms, whether they are the spotless no-nonsense, simply decorated motel rooms or the fully equipped efficiency units, have the advantage of stunning water views. The center of town is just a short walk. ⊠ *196 Shore Rd., 02633,* ☎ *508/945–0372. 16 rooms, 10 efficiencies. AE, D, MC, V. Closed mid-Oct.–mid-May.* 🐾

$$ 🏠 **Ridgevale Beach Inn Resort Motel.** This complex, just a few miles from Chatham's town center, is nestled on 6 acres of wooded green land. The warm waters of Nantucket Sound are not far, nor are all the in-town activities. Standard rooms have two double beds while the condolike suites are equipped with kitchens, dining areas, fireplaces, and private decks. Decor is simple, comfortable, and most important, very clean. For larger groups, there are also two-bedroom suites, and cottages are available on the grounds for weekly rentals. ⊠ *2045 Main Street, West Chatham, 02633,* ☎ *508/432–1169,* 𝖥𝖠𝖷 *508/432–1877. 8 condos, 23 rooms. AE, D, MC, V. Closed late-Oct.–Apr.* 🐾

Nightlife and the Arts

THE ARTS

Chatham Drama Guild (⊠ 134 Crowell Rd., ☎ 508/945–0510) stages several productions in the summer season, including musicals, comedies, and dramas.

The **Creative Arts Center** (⊠ 154 Crowell Rd., ☎ 508/945–3583) is a thriving year-round arts center with classes, changing gallery exhibitions, demonstrations, lectures, and other activities.

In July and August the **Guild of Chatham Painters** presents an outdoor art gallery on Thursday and Friday from 9:30 to 5 on the lawn of the Main Street School (⊠ Main St.).

The **Monomoy Theatre** (⊠ 776 Main St., ☎ 508/945–1589) presents summer productions—thrillers, musicals, classics, modern drama—by the Ohio University Players.

Chatham's summer **town-band concerts** (⊠ Kate Gould Park, Main St., ☎ 508/945–5199) begin at 8 on Friday and draw up to 6,000 people. As many as 500 fox-trot on the roped-off dance floor, and there are special dances for children and sing-alongs for all.

Chatham Squire (⊠ 487 Main St., ☎ 508/945–0945; ☞ Dining and Lodging, *above*), with four separate bars including a raw bar, is a rollicking year-round local hangout, drawing a young crowd to the bar side and a mixed crowd of locals to the restaurant.

Wequassett Inn Resort & Golf Club (⊠ 173 Orleans Rd. (Rte. 28), Pleasant Bay, ☎ 508/432–5400; ☞ Dining and Lodging, *above*) has a jazz duo or piano music nightly in its lounge in July and August (jacket requested).

Sou'wester (⊠ 1563 Main St., ☎ 508/945–4424; ☞ Dining and Lodging, *above*) maintains an active schedule of live music—rock and roll, the blues, oldies, and swing—in a raucous and locally flavored setting.

Outdoor Activities and Sports

BASEBALL

The **Cape Cod Baseball League,** begun in 1885, is an invitational league of college players that counts Carlton Fisk, Ron Darling, and the late Thurman Munson as alumni. Considered the country's best summer league, it is scouted by all the major-league teams. Players have included Mo Vaughn and Nomar Garciaparra. Ten teams play a 44-game season from mid-June to mid-August; games held at all 10 fields are free (☞ Close-Up: The Cape Cod Baseball League, *below*). The **Chatham A's** games (⊠ Veterans' Field, Main and Depot Sts. by rotary, ☎ 508/996–5004 for schedule) are great entertainment.

Baseball clinics (⊠ Veterans' Field, Main and Depot Sts. by rotary, ☎ 508/432–6909) for children 6–8, 9–12, and 13–17 are offered in one-week sessions by the Chatham A's in summer. The other nine town teams in the Cape league also conduct clinics (☎ 508/996–5004 for information).

BEACHES

If you're looking for a crowd-free sandy beach, boats at Chatham Harbor—such as the ***Rip Ryder*** (☎ 508/945–5450)—will ferry you across to North Beach ($10–$12 per person), which is a sand spit adjoining Orleans's Nauset Beach, to South Beach ($10), or to Monomoy ($45, or $10 per person for three or more passengers).

Outermost Harbor Marine (⊠ Morris Island Rd., ☎ 508/945–2030) runs shuttles to South Beach; rides cost $10 round-trip for adults. The cost includes parking.

Harding's Beach (⊠ Harding's Beach Rd., off Barn Hill Rd.), west of Chatham center, is open to the public and charges daily parking fees to nonresidents in season. Lifeguards are stationed in summer. This beach can get crowded, so plan to arrive early or late.

BIKING

Bert & Carol's Lawnmower & Bicycle Shop (⊠ 347 Orleans Rd. [Rte. 28], North Chatham, ☎ 508/945–0137) rents a variety of bikes.

Bikes & Blades (⊠ 195 Crowell Rd., ☎ 508/945–7600) rents all manner of bikes as well as in-line skates.

BOATING

Monomoy Sail & Cycle (⊠ 275 Orleans Rd., North Chatham, ☎ 508/945–0811) rents sailboards and Sunfish.

GOLF

Chatham Seaside Links (⊠ Seaview St., ☎ 508/945–4774), a nine-hole course, is good for beginners.

138

THE CAPE COD BASEBALL LEAGUE

AT THE BASEBALL HALL OF FAME in Cooperstown, New York, you'll find a poster announcing a showdown between arch rivals Sandwich and Barnstable. The date? July 4, 1885. In the 100-plus years since that day, the Cape's ball-playing tradition has continued unabated, and if you're a sports fan, a visit to a Cape Cod Baseball League summer game is a must. Seeing a game on the Cape is to come into contact with baseball's roots. You'll remember why you love the sport, and you'll have a newfound sense of why it became the national pastime.

As they have since the 1950s, top-ranked college baseball players from around the country descend on the Cape when school lets out, in time to begin the season in mid-June. This is no sandlot, catch-as-catch-can scene. Each player joins one of the league's 10 teams, which are based in Bourne, Wareham, Falmouth, Cotuit, Hyannis, Dennis-Yarmouth, Harwich, Brewster, Chatham, and Orleans. The teams are the Bourne Braves, Wareham Gatemen, Falmouth Commodores, Cotuit Kettleers, Hyannis Mets, Dennis-Yarmouth Red Sox, Harwich Mariners, Brewster Whitecaps, Chatham Athletics (A's), and the Orleans Cardinals.

Players lodge with local families and work day jobs cutting lawns, painting houses, or giving baseball clinics in town parks. In the evening, though, their lives are given over to baseball, as they don uniforms and head for the field.

To judge by the past, Cape League veterans are tomorrow's major-league stars. By latest count, one of every eight active major-league ballplayers spent a summer in the Cape League on the way up. The Boston Red Sox's recent starting infield—Mo Vaughn, John Valentin, Tim Naehring, and Nomar Garciaparra—all played in the Cape League in different years, for different teams. Add names such

as Frank Thomas, Jeff Bagwell, Albert Belle (before he lost his manners), Will Clark, and Walt Weiss, and you could build an all-star roster.

To enshrine these heroes past, the Cape League recently announced the opening of its own Hall of Fame, which will be housed in a special building at the Heritage Plantation in Sandwich. The first-ever induction ceremony, scheduled for January 20, 2001, will honor 12 players including Thurman Munson, Mike Flanagan, Jeff Reardon, Mo Vaughn, and Frank Thomas.

Yet as good as the baseball is—and you'll often see bunches of major-league scouts at a game—another great reason to come out to the ballpark is. . . the ballpark. **Chatham**'s Veterans Field is the Cape's 3Com Park at Candlestick Point because, much like the San Francisco version, fog tends to engulf the games. **Orleans's** Eldredge Park is a local favorite—immaculate, cozy, and comfortable. Some parks have bleachers, while in others it's up to you to bring your own chair or blanket and stretch out behind a dugout or baseline. Children are free to roam and can even try for foul balls—which they are, however, asked to return because, after all, balls don't grow on trees. When hunger hits, the ice cream truck and hot-dog stand are never far away.

Games start at either 5 or 7, depending on whether the field has lights (there are occasionally afternoon games). Each team plays 44 games in a season, so finding one is rarely a problem. And, best of all, they're always free. The Cape's baseball scene is so American, the ambience so relaxed and refreshing, it's tempting to invoke the old *Field of Dreams* analogy. But the league needs no Hollywood comparison. This is the real thing. It was built a long time ago, and they are still coming.

—Seth Rolbein

SURFING

The Lower and Outer Cape beaches, including North Beach in Chatham, are the best for surfing, which is tops when there's a storm offshore. Chatham does not have any surf shops, but you'll find them in nearby Orleans (☞ Outdoor Activities and Sports *in* Orleans, *below*).

TENNIS

Chatham Bars Inn (⊠ Shore Rd., ☎ 508/945–0096 ext. 1155) offers three waterfront all-weather tennis courts, open to the public by reservation for $30 an hour. You can also take lessons and visit the pro shop.

The town maintains two public tennis parks, one on Depot Road next to the Railroad Museum at No. 153 and the other at the middle school on Crowell Road.

NEED A BREAK?

If you're looking for a fat and fancy sandwich, a morning bagel, or an afternoon cappuccino pick-me-up, stop in at the **Chatham Village Café** (⊠ 400 Main St., ☎ 508/945–2525) and choose from an impressive selection of eats. Eat inside at one of the few tables for some good street-side people-watching or head over to the Village Green for an impromptu picnic.

Shopping

Main Street is a busy shopping area, with upscale and conservative merchandise. Here you'll find galleries, crafts, clothing stores, bookstores, and a few good antiques shops.

Aquitaine Antiques (⊠ 35 Cross St., ☎ 508/945–5787 or 945–9746) has a good selection of marine and Americana antiques.

Cabbages and Kings Bookstore(⊠ 628 Main St., ☎ 508/945–1603) is a good independent bookstore. In addition to a full stock of literary and regional books, look for a host of unusual games, cards, and toys and a regular schedule of author appearances.

Cape Cod Cooperage (⊠ 1150 Queen Anne Rd., at Rte. 137, ☎ 508/432–0788), set in an old barn, sells woodenware made in a century-old tradition by an on-site cooper (barrel maker), as well as hand-decorated furniture, crafts supplies, and more. Daily classes are also scheduled in everything from stenciling to basket making, from decorative painting to birdhouse building.

Chatham Glass Company (⊠ 758 Main St., ☎ 508/945–5547) is a glassworks where you can watch glass being blown and buy it, too—objects including marbles, Christmas ornaments, jewelry, and art glass.

Chatham Jam and Jelly Shop (⊠ 10 Vineyard Ave., at Rte. 28, West Chatham, ☎ 508/945–3052) sells preserves such as cranberry with strawberries and Maine wild blueberry, nutty conserves, and ice cream toppings, all made on-site in small batches.

Clambake Celebrations (⊠ 1223C Main St., ☎ 508/945–7771 or 800/423–4038) prepares full clambakes, including lobsters, clams, mussels, corn, potatoes, onions, and sausage, for you to take out; it'll even loan a charcoal grill. The company also delivers, even via air, year-round. The food is layered in seaweed in a pot and ready to steam.

The **East Wind Silver Co.** (⊠ 878 Main St., ☎ 508/945–8935) specializes in artful silver jewelry but also sells watercolor paintings, pottery, fountains, and Tiffany-style lighting.

Fancy's Farm of Chatham (⊠ 1291 Main St. [Rte. 28]), West Chatham, ☎ 508/945–1949) sells local and exotic produce, fresh-baked breads, pies, and pastries, dried flowers, baskets, frozen prepared gourmet foods, spices, and potpourri. A delicatessen provides take-out meats and sandwiches.

Journey on a Small Planet (⊠ 746 Main St., ☎ 508/945–1771) has a good selection of antique prints, books, and unique gifts.

Marion's Pie Shop (⊠ 2022 Main St. [Rte. 28], West Chatham, ☎ 508/432–9439) sells homemade and home-style fruit breads; pastries; prepared foods such as lasagna; Boston baked beans; chowder base; and, of course, pies, both savory and sweet.

The **Spyglass** (⊠ 618 Main St., ☎ 508/945–9686) carries telescopes, barometers, writing boxes, maps, and other nautical antiques.

S. Wilder & Co. (⊠ 304 Rte. 28, North Chatham, ☎ 877/794–5337) sells old-style colonial crafts. Handcrafted brass and copper lanterns are made here.

Yankee Ingenuity (⊠ 525 Main St., ☎ 508/945–1288) stocks a varied selection of unique jewelry and lamps and a wide assortment of unusual, beautiful trinkets at reasonable (especially for Chatham) prices.

Yellow Umbrella Books (⊠ 501 Main St., ☎ 508/945–0144) has an excellent selection of new books, many about Cape Cod, as well as used books.

En Route   North of Chatham, Route 28 winds through wooded upland toward **Pleasant Bay,** from which a number of country roads will take you to a nice view of Nauset spit and the islands in the bay.

Orleans

⑫ *8 mi north of Chatham, 4 mi southwest of Eastham, 35 mi east of Sagamore Bridge.*

Named for Louis-Philippe de Bourbon, *duc d'Orléans* (duke of Orléans), who reputedly visited the area during his exile from France in the 1790s, Orleans was incorporated as a town in 1797. Historically, it has the distinction of being the only place in the continental United States to have received enemy fire during either world war. In July 1918 a German submarine fired on commercial barges off the coast. Four were sunk, and one shell is reported to have fallen on American soil.

Today Orleans is part quiet seaside village and part bustling center with strip malls. The commercial hub of the Lower Cape, Orleans is one of the more steadily populated areas, year-round, of the Lower Cape. Yet the town retains a fervent commitment to preserving its past, and residents maintain an active refusal policy of many big-time corporations. A few years back a local woman tried to prohibit a Dunkin' Donuts from opening, fearful that the megachain would drive the local mom-and-pop doughnut shops out of business. Although she was ultimately unsuccessful, her fight is testament to the spirit of Orleans.

Orleans has a long heritage in fishing and seafaring, and many beautifully preserved homes remain from the colonial era. Much of this beauty is found in the small village of East Orleans, home of the town's Historical Society and Museum. In other areas of town, such as down by Rock Harbor, more modestly grand homes stand near the water's edge. Recently completed, the dramatic cathedral of the Community of Jesus stands watch over the bustle of fishing fleets at Rock Harbor; this religious community owns a large portion of the prime real estate in the area.

As you head north, this is the first Cape town to touch both Cape Cod Bay and the Atlantic Ocean. Nauset Beach, on the Atlantic, is enormously popular. Backed by towering dunes dotted with sea grass and colorful *rosa Rugosa,* this beach begins what could be a long but beautiful trek clear to the very tip of the Cape. Skaket Beach, just south of Rock Harbor, is the main bayside beach and affords both scenic views and calm, warm waters for swimming.

A walk along Rock Harbor Road, a pleasant winding street lined with gray-shingle Cape houses, white picket fences, and neat gardens, leads to the bay-side **Rock Harbor,** a former packet landing and site of a War of 1812 skirmish in which the Orleans militia kept a British warship from docking. In the 19th century Orleans had an active saltworks and a flourishing packet service between Rock Harbor and Boston developed. Today the former packet landing is the base of charter-fishing and party boats in season, as well as of a small commercial fishing fleet whose catch hits the counters at the fish market and small restaurant here. Sunsets over the harbor are spectacular.

The 1890 **French Cable Station Museum** was the stateside landing point for the 3,000-mi-long transatlantic cable that originated in Brittany. Another cable laid between Orleans and New York City completed the France–New York link, and many important messages were communicated through the station. In World War I it was an essential connection between army headquarters in Washington and the American Expeditionary Force in France, and the station was under guard by the marines. By 1959 telephone service had rendered the station obsolete, and it closed. The equipment is still in place. ⊠ *41 S. Orleans Rd.,* ☎ *508/240–1735.* 🎟 *Donations accepted.* ☉ *June–Labor Day, Mon.–Sat. 1–4.*

The **Jonathan Young Windmill,** a pretty if somewhat incongruous sight on the busy highway, is a landmark from the days of salt making in Orleans, when it would pump saltwater into shallow vaults for evaporation. A program explaining the history and operation of the mill demonstrates the old millstone and grinding process. ⊠ *Rte. 6A and Town Cove.* ☉ *July–Aug., daily 11–4; June and Sept., weekends 11–4.*

☾ The **Academy of Performing Arts** (⊠ 5 Giddiah Hill Rd., ☎ 508/255–5510) offers two-week sessions of theater, music, and dance classes to children ages 8–12, with a show at the end of each session. It also schedules year-round classes for ages four to adult in dance, music, and drama. The academy's theater is at 120 Main Street.

Dining and Lodging

$$–$$$ ✕ **Kadee's Lobster & Clam Bar.** A summer landmark that harks back to an era when drive-ins were the norm and not the exception, Kadee's serves good clams and fish-and-chips that you can grab on the way to the beach from the take-out window. Or sit down in the smoke-free indoor dining room for steamers and mussels, pasta and seafood stews, or the famous Portuguese kale soup. Even the service staff seems plucked from a few decades ago—clean-cut college students working their way through the summer. There's also a gift shop as well as a miniature golf course out back. Unfortunately, the prices seem to have gone through the roof, especially for what is being served—the only serious drawback here. ⊠ *212 Main St.,* ☎ *508/255–6184. Reservations not accepted. MC, V. Closed day after Labor Day–week before Memorial Day and weekdays in early June.*

$$–$$$ ✕ **Nauset Beach Club.** What once was the unsung local hero has now
★ become widely known for its fine dining. You might feel as if you're eating in someone's former living room (you are), but the sophisticated food, rooted in contemporary Italian cuisine, is beyond that of even the finest home cooks. *Zuppa di pesce* (seafood stew) features shrimp, scallops, calamari, and lobster in a sauce Provençale served on pasta. The penne *puttanesca* (with olives, garlic, peppers, and anchovies) de-

livers a medley of tastes. Unfortunately, the bar is too small and uncomfortable for the long waits (reservations are accepted only for parties of six or more), so stop in early or late for what will prove to be a superb meal. ⊠ *222 Main St., East Orleans,* ☎ *508/255–8547. Reservations not accepted. AE, D, DC, MC, V. No lunch; no dinner Sun. and Mon., mid-Oct.–Memorial Day.*

$$–$$$ ✕ **Rosina's Cafe.** Originally a classic mom-and-pop Italian restaurant off Main Street, Rosina's has expanded into a full-blown full-service place. Some feel that the food, which was some of the best home-style Italian cooking on Cape Cod, has not survived the move all that well, but with a little care in your choice, you can still find that fresh, natural style. The pasta primavera makes the grade, as does Angela's stuffed halibut (often on special), a good chunk of fish stuffed with scallops, cheeses, pine nuts, bread crumbs, and garlic. The spaghetti puttanesca remains a rewarding signature dish. The wine list mimics the food, veering toward the conventional. ⊠ *15 Cove Rd.,* ☎ *508/240–5513. AE, D, MC, V.*

$$ ✕ **The Beacon Room.** Adorned with crisp linens, frilly curtains, and handsome wood furnishings, this little bistro serves a nice mix of seafood and meats enhanced with sophisticated and inventive flavors. The Gorgonzola, pear, and walnut salad is especially nice and makes for a rich beginning to such delights as potato-crusted salmon or the house favorite, chicken saltimbocca. There's a bit of everything here, from quesadillas to calamari, and each dish is treated with the same care and attention to quality. In the warmer months dinner out on the lantern-lighted garden patio is particularly gracious. An ambitious wine list complements the fine selection. ⊠ *23 West Rd.,* ☎ *508/255–2211. Reservations not accepted. D, MC, V.*

$$ ✕ **The Jailhouse.** The symbol next to the entrance of this rambling restaurant, added on to what was an old stone lockup, is a big set of golden jailer's keys. The theme continues, with a light touch, throughout the decor and menu. On the long, varied menu are headings such as "A Light Sentence," for salads and appetizers, and "The Lineup," for the sandwich list. Foods for sharing include a whole wheel of baked Brie with homemade Boursin cheese, crackers, and fruit; and deep-fried fresh vegetables with ranch dip. Entrées lean toward basic seafood, steak, veal, and chicken dishes. The restaurant has a flower-hung atrium, a long oak bar, and the new Courthouse addition for group events. ⊠ *28 West Rd.,* ☎ *508/255–5245. Reservations not accepted. D, MC, V.*

$$ ✕ **Lobster Claw.** If you're over 6 ft tall, keep an eye out for the fishnets hanging from the ceiling in this goofy little seafood spot. Tables are lacquered turquoise, portions are huge, and the lobster roll is one of the best. You can get all the Cape basics here: fish and seafood poached, broiled, baked, or fried, along with an assortment of steaks for variety. The children's choices include some good seafood picks as well as the usual chicken tenders. ⊠ *Rte. 6A,* ☎ *508/255–1800. Reservations not accepted. AE, D, DC, MC, V.*

$$ ✕ **Mahoney's Atlantic Bar and Grill.** A recent arrival, Mahoney's has overcome some bad vibes at an excellent location and now seems ready to make a good go of it. The chef, indeed a Mahoney who cooked for years at one of Provincetown's busiest restaurants, really knows his stuff. The lunch and dinner menu are extending appetizers to new heights, emphasizing grilled vegetables and polenta; drunken littlenecks steamed in ale; and a New Orleans classic, oyster po'boys (why this hasn't come to Cape Cod sooner is a mystery). The bar is long and comfortable, although the California wine list is a little overpriced and the beer selection should improve. ⊠ *28 Main St.,* ☎ *508/255–5505. AE, D, DC, MC, V.*

$–$$ ✕ **Abba Cafe.** This brand-new place has given a much-needed boost of flavor to the Orleans's restaurant scene. Specializing in Mediterranean cuisine, the café serves robust sandwiches and pizzas unlike anything else you can get around here. Try the Gran Huevon—a sandwich of eggs, saffron-basil mayonnaise, onions, and capers—or La Bruja pizza, topped with walnut-and-spinach ricotta, marinated wild mushrooms, and Gorgonzola. An impressive range of salads is also available, including such treats as tabbouleh and baba ghanouj. Other good choices are falafel, *shawarma*, and anything from the extensive bakery selection. All items are made on the premises. ⊠ *West Rd. and Old Colony Way,* ☎ *508/255–8405. No credit cards.*

$–$$ ✕ **Land Ho!** The scene at Orleans's flagship local restaurant is definitely fun and boisterous even if the typical tavern fare on the blackboard menu doesn't always live up to the atmosphere. Hanging from the rafters are dozens of homemade wooden signs; anybody who's anybody in town has one made up. The burgers and the sea-clam pie are both excellent—much better than the fish-and-chips. The conversation is generally tastier (and saltier) than the chowder. At one table near the back a group of local thinkers often chews over the world's problems. It's a good place for a rainy-day lunch. The place has expanded not only into the store next door but also down to Costa Rica, where owner John Murphy has set up another Land Ho! ⊠ *Rte. 6A and Cove Rd.,* ☎ *508/255–5165. Reservations not accepted. AE, MC, V.*

$–$$ ✕ **Sir Cricket's Fish and Chips.** If you have a sudden craving for a beautifully turned-out fish sandwich, you can pull off the highway into this tiny local favorite, a hole-in-the-wall attached to the Nauset Lobster Pool. Built mainly for takeout, this clean, no-frills fried-food joint does have three or four tiny tables and a soda machine. Try the fresh oyster roll or go for a full fisherman's platter. Be sure to check out the chair seats as you gobble those fries. Each is an exquisitely rendered minimual of Orleans history or a personality painted by legendary local artist Dan Joy. ⊠ *Rte. 6A, near Stop & Shop,* ☎ *508/255–4453. Reservations not accepted. No credit cards.*

$–$$ ✕ **The Yardarm.** Orleans's version of a roadhouse, the Yardarm feels smoky even though smoking is not allowed anymore. The tube over the bar is likely to be tuned to a sports game, and the only pool table in town is always busy (though not in use when dinner is being served). The hearty, well-cooked food is a great value, especially the baked sole, barbecued ribs or chicken, and the pot roast; thanks to the big portions, you can expect to take some of your dinner home. It's also a great place to stop in for a burger-and-beer lunch. If you're lucky, Lenny will be holding court behind the bar, and Patience will take your order into the kitchen. ⊠ *48 Rte. 28,* ☎ *508/255–4840. Reservations not accepted. AE, DC, MC, V.*

$$ ✕🏠 **Barley Neck Inn.** The hotel-like lodge, adjacent to the restaurant building, has spacious rooms outfitted in pretty florals and colored wicker or wood furnishings. Modern conveniences such as televisions and small refrigerators are standard. It took a little time, but the inn's restaurant, in a restored 1850s sea captain's house, has shucked off its staidness and become a popular new destination. The fairly formal main dining area and a buzzing, relaxed bar called Joe's have equally satisfying menus (the bar is cheaper); the chef updates classic Cape fish dishes with a French influence. The kitchen hums with innovation, particularly in its new array of salsas and sauces. Off-season, there is often live jazz on Sunday afternoon and a good fire burning in the huge stone fireplace. ⊠ *5 Beach Rd., East Orleans 02643,* ☎ *508/255–8484, 508/255–0212 for restaurant,* 🖷 *508/255–3626. 18 rooms. 2 restaurants, refrigerators, pool. AE, MC, V.* ✍

$$ 🏠 **Kadee's Gray Elephant.** A mile from Nauset Beach, next to shops,
★ a grocery store, a farm stand, a post office, and Kadee's Lobster & Clam Bar (☞ *above*), this 200-year-old house offers small vacation studio and one-bedroom apartments. They're a cheerful riot of color, from

wicker painted lavender or green to bright pink bows and flowers painted on furniture to beds layered in quilts and comforters mixing plaids and florals. Kitchens are fully equipped with microwaves, attractive glassware, irons and boards—even lobster crackers. ⊠ *216 Main St., Box 86, East Orleans 02643,* ☎ *508/255–7608,* FAX *508/240–2976. 6–8 apartments. Restaurant, miniature golf, shop. MC, V.*

$–$$ ⊞ **Nauset House Inn.** You could easily spend a day trying out all the places to relax here. There's a parlor with comfortable chairs and a large fireplace, an orchard set with picnic tables, and a lush conservatory with a weeping cherry tree in its center. Rooms in both the main building and the adjacent Carriage House have stenciled walls, quilts, and unusual antique pieces, as well as hand-painted furniture, stained glass, and prints done by one of the owners. The beach is only ½-mi distant (they'll set you up with beach chairs and towels), and the attractions of town are close but not too close. ⊠ *143 Beach Rd., Box 774, East Orleans 02643,* ☎ *508/255–2195. 14 rooms. Breakfast room. D, MC, V. Closed Nov.–Mar. BP.* ✎

$–$$ ⊞ **Orleans Holiday Motel.** This complex has been around for a while and has recently been redone so rooms once musty and outdated are now cleaner and far more freshly adorned. Smack in the middle of a commercial area, this is not a totally peaceful place, but its position does put you in the midst of restaurants and other services; it's also an easy walk to the center of town. Motel rooms are set around the giant outdoor pool and are furnished with either two double, one queen-size, or two queen-size beds. A bonus for beachgoers: There's a complimentary boat shuttle to Nauset Beach. ⊠ *Rtes. 6A and 28, 02643,* ☎ *508/255–1514 or 800/451–1833,* FAX *508/255–7284. 45 rooms. Picnic area, air-conditioning, refrigerators, pool. AE, MC, V. CP.* ✎

$–$$ ⊞ **Sea Breeze Motel.** In the historic area of East Orleans and about a
★ mile from famed Nauset Beach, this little motel complex offers reasonably priced, clean standard rooms. They're nothing fancy, but each room has either a queen-size or two twin-size beds, wall-to-wall carpeting, televisions with cable TV, radios, and decent-size tile bathrooms. You can walk to town restaurants, shops, and a post office. A Continental breakfast is offered for weekend visitors. ⊠ *Nauset Beach Road, 02643,* ☎ *508/240–5500 or 877/648–6732. 16 rooms. Picnic area, air-conditioning, refrigerators. MC, V. Closed late Sept.–Memorial Day.* ✎

$–$$ ⊞ **Skaket Beach Motel.** This convenient-to-everything motel prides it-
★ self on its commitment to absolute cleanliness. Rooms are traditional motel style but are sparkling and well sized, available in standard, deluxe, or poolside variety. Outdoors are a number of distractions—from horseshoes to the heated pool; you can even use one of the outdoor grills. The location on the busy roadside is less appealing, though the motel is convenient to local amenities from shops to beaches and still retains a semblance of privacy. ⊠ *203 Rte. 6A, 02643,* ☎ *508/255–1020 or 800/835–0298,* FAX *508/255–6487. 46 rooms. Pool, croquet, horseshoes. MC, V. Closed late Nov.–Mar. CP.* ✎

Nightlife and the Arts

The **Academy Playhouse** (⊠ 120 Main St., ☎ 508/255–1963), one of the oldest community theaters on the Cape, presents 12 or 13 productions year-round, including original works.

The **Cape & Islands Chamber Music Festival** (⊠ Box 2721, 02653, ☎ 508/255–9509) presents three weeks of top-caliber performances, including a jazz night, at various locations in August.

The 90-member **Cape Symphony Orchestra** (☎ 508/362–1111) sails into Orleans in late August for one of two Sounds of Summer Pops concerts (the other is in Mashpee in July). The performance takes place at the Eldredge Park, adjacent to the Nauset Middle School. (✉ Rte. 28 and Eldredge Pkwy.). Call for a year-round schedule of events.

Joe's Beach Road Bar & Grille (✉ Main St. at Beach Rd., ☎ 508/255–0212) features live piano on Thursday through Sunday nights in summer; check for off-season entertainment schedules.

Land Ho! (✉ Rte. 6A and Cove Rd., ☎ 508/255–5165) has live local bands frequently and throughout the year.

Mahoney's Atlantic Bar and Grill (✉ 28 Main St., ☎ 508/255–5505) schedules live jazz and blues in the bar area on a regular basis; call for times.

Free ocean-side concerts are held in the gazebo at **Nauset Beach** each Monday evening from 7 to 9 in July and August. The resident fried-clam shack stays open until 10.

Outdoor Activities and Sports

BASEBALL

The **Orleans Cardinals** (☎ 508/240–2867) of the collegiate Cape Cod Baseball League play home games at Eldredge Park (✉ Rte. 28) from mid-June to mid-August.

BEACHES

The town-owned **Nauset Beach** (✉ Beach Rd.)—not to be confused with Nauset Light Beach, up a ways at the National Seashore—is a wide 10-mi-long sweep of sandy ocean beach with low dunes and large waves good for bodysurfing or board surfing. The beach has life-guards, rest rooms, showers, and a food concession (something the National Seashore beaches lack). Despite its size, the massive parking lot often fills up when the sun is strong; it's best to arrive quite early or in the late afternoon if you want to claim a spot. The beach is open to off-road vehicles with a special permit. Daily parking fees of $8 are charged, or you can buy a one-week pass for $25, a two-week pass for $45, or a season pass for $65. Entrance is free with a resident sticker. For more information call the parks department (☎ 508/240–3775).

Freshwater seekers can access **Pilgrim Lake** (✉ Pilgrim Lake Rd. off Monument Rd. and Rte. 28) with the same parking and sticker fees as Nauset Beach (☞ *above*).

Skaket Beach (✉ Skaket Beach Rd.) on Cape Cod Bay is a sandy stretch with calm warm water good for children. It's a good place to watch motorboats, fishing charters, and sailboats as they leave the channel at Rock Harbor, not to mention the spectacular evening sunsets. There are rest rooms, lifeguards, and a snack bar. Daily parking fees are the same as at Nauset Beach (☞ *above*). For more information call the parks department (☎ 508/240–3775).

BOATING

Arey's Pond Boat Yard (✉ 43 Arey's La., off Rte. 28, South Orleans, ☎ 508/255–0994) has a sailing school with individual and group lessons.

FISHING

Many of Orleans's freshwater ponds offer good fishing for perch, pickerel, trout, and more. The required fishing license, along with rental gear, is available at the **Goose Hummock Shop** (✉ 15 Rte. 6A, ☎ 508/255–0455).

Bait, equipment rentals, and tide charts can be found at **MacSquids** (✉ 85 Lowell Sq., ☎ 508/240–0778).

The **Osprey** (☎ 508/255–1266) leaves Rock Harbor for both half-and full-day sportfishing trips. All tackle, bait, and cleaning services are provided.

Rock Harbor Charter Boat Fleet (✉ Rock Harbor, ☎ 508/255–9757; 800/287–1771 in MA) goes for bass and blues in the bay from spring through fall. Walk-ons and charters are both available.

ICE-SKATING
Ice-skating, lessons, hockey, clinics, and camps are available at the **Charles Moore Arena** (✉ O'Connor Way, ☎ 508/255–5902). Children ages 9–14 ice-skate to DJ-spun rock and flashing lights at Rock Night, which takes place Friday from 8 to 10.

SPORTING GOODS—RENTALS
Nauset Sports (✉ Jeremiah Sq., Rte. 6A at rotary, ☎ 508/255–4742) rents surf, body, skim, and wake boards; kayaks; wet suits; in-line skates; and tennis racquets.

For bike rentals just across the way from the Cape Cod Rail Trail, head to **Orleans Cycle** (✉ 26 Main St., ☎ 508/255–9115).

SURFING
The Lower and Outer Cape beaches, including Nauset Beach in Orleans, are the best spots for surfing, especially when there's a storm offshore. For a surf report—water temperature, weather, surf, tanning factor—call 508/240–2229.

Pump House Surf Co. (✉ 9 Rte. 6A, ☎ 508/240–2226) rents wet suits and sells other surf gear.

NEED A
BREAK?   **Sunset Grill** (✉ 84 Rte. 6A, ☎ 508/240–3282) is great for takeout or a quick sit-down bite. This smoky (from the barbecue grill, that is) little place has a large menu that includes big burgers, tacos, and barbecued chicken and beef. Cold salads and sandwiches are also available, as are beer and wine.

Shopping
Baseball Shop (✉ 26 Main St., ☎ 508/240–1063) sells licensed products relating to baseball and other sports—new and collectible cards (and nonsports cards) as well as hats, clothing, and videos.

Bird Watcher's General Store (✉ 36 Rte. 6A, ☎ 508/255–6974 or 800/562–1512) sells nearly everything avian but the birds themselves: feeders, paintings, houses, books, binoculars, calls, bird-theme apparel—ad infinitum.

Compass Rose Bookshop (✉ 43 Main St., ☎ 508/255–1545) is just what an independent bookstore should be: friendly, comfortable, and full of books on all kinds of subjects, including works by local authors and those of regional interest. You'll also find a generous collection of unique greeting cards and specialty items. Changing art exhibits showcase the talents of local artists, and Internet access is available on a sign-up fee basis.

Countryside Antiques (✉ 6 Lewis Rd., East Orleans, ☎ 508/240–0525) specializes in European and Asian antique furniture, home-accent pieces, china, and silver.

Fancy's Farm Stand (✉ 199 Main St., East Orleans, ☎ 508/255–1949) sells local produce, fresh sandwiches and roll-ups, salads (salad bar or prepared varieties), homemade soup, ice cream, fresh-baked breads, and other supplies for a great picnic. A wide assortment of flowers, both dried and fresh, are sold, adding great color to the beautiful, beamed old-style barn.

Hannah (⊠ 47 Main St., ☎ 508/255–8234) has women's casual dresses, scarves, and hats with flair by such labels as Hannah, No Saint, and Angel Heart. •

Heaven Scent You (⊠ 13 Cove Rd., ☎ 508/240–2508) offers massage, spa services, and beauty treatments—everything you need for some relaxation and rejuvenation.

Karol Richardson (⊠ 47 Main St., ☎ 508/255–3944) sells fine contemporary clothing. There's also a selection of silk wraps and scarves, hats, shoes, handbags, and handcrafted jewelry. You'll pay well for the quality, but if you're fortunate enough to be around for one of the off-season warehouse sales, you'll hit the jackpot.

Kemp Pottery (⊠ 9 Rte. 6A, ☎ 508/255–5853) has functional and decorative stoneware and porcelain, fountains, garden sculpture, sinks, and stained glass.

Oceana (⊠ 1 Main St. Sq., ☎ 508/240–1414) has a beautiful selection of nautical-theme home accents, gifts, and jewelry, as well as colorful hooked rugs made by Cape artist Claire Murray.

The **Orleans Farmers' Market** (⊠ Cape Cod Five Operations Center, 19 West Rd.), held Saturday morning throughout the summer, features local delicacies such as fresh shellfish, produce, flowers, and homemade goodies. It opens at 8, and early birds get the best selection—things tend to disappear quickly.

XO Clothing (⊠ 50 Main St., ☎ 508/255–4407) carries a full stock of designer warehouse excess at unbeatable prices. The inventory changes frequently, but expect scores of casual linen dresses, pants sets, shirts, and colorful cotton pieces.

ART AND CRAFTS GALLERIES

The **Addison Holmes Gallery** (⊠ 43 Rte. 28, ☎ 508/255–6200), in four rooms of a brick-red Cape house, represents more than two dozen regional artists and sells a broad range of contemporary works, many of which are inspired by life on Cape Cod. The sculpture garden in the side yard is a perfect complement to the tasteful gallery. Receptions, where you can often meet the week's featured artist, are held from 5 to 7 Saturday night.

The **Hogan Art Gallery** (⊠ 39 Main St., ☎ 508/240–3655) features the colorful white-line woodblock, paintings, and pastels by artist Ruth Hogan, as well as 20th-century American regional paintings by her husband, Frank. There's also a nice selection of painted furniture.

Left Bank Gallery (⊠ 8 Cove Rd., ☎ 508/247–9172) carries an eclectic mix of handcrafted jewelry, fine art by both local and national artists, hand-painted furniture, pottery, and handmade clothing.

In July and August, **Nauset Painters** presents outdoor juried art shows every Tuesday (⊠ Depot Sq. at Old Colony Way) from 10 to 5 and Sunday (⊠ Sandwich Cooperative Bank, 51 Main St.) from 10 to 5.

The **Orleans Art Association** holds outdoor art shows from 10 to 5 each Thursday and Friday in July and August on the grounds of the American Legion Hall (⊠ 137 Main St.).

At various times in June, July and August, the **Orleans Professional Arts and Crafts Association** holds a giant outdoor show featuring the works of more than 100 artists and craftsmen on the grounds of the

Nauset Middle School (⊠ Rte. 28). For specific dates and times check the free town chamber of commerce guide.

The **Star Gallery** (⊠ 76 Rte. 6A, ☎ 508/240–7827) specializes in contemporary and less traditional art by artists both local and beyond; watch for Saturday-evening artist receptions in July and August.

Tree's Place (⊠ Rte. 6A, at Rte. 28, ☎ 508/255–1330), one of the Cape's best and most original shops, has a collection of handcrafted kaleidoscopes, as well as art glass, hand-painted porcelain and pottery, hand-blown stemware, jewelry, imported ceramic tiles, and fine art. Tree's displays the work of New England artists including Robert Vickery, Don Stone, and Elizabeth Mumford (whose popular folk art is bordered in mottoes and poetic phrases). Champagne openings are held on Saturday night in summer.

Eastham

❸ *3 mi north of Orleans, 6 mi south of Wellfleet.*

Often overlooked on the speedy drive up toward Provincetown on Route 6, Eastham is a town full of hidden treasures. Unlike the other towns, it has no official town center or Main Street; the highway bisects Eastham, and the town is spread out on both Cape Cod Bay and the Atlantic. Stocked with gas stations, convenience stores, restaurants, and large motel complexes, it takes a little exploring to find Eastham's wealth of natural beauty.

One such gem is the National Seashore, which officially begins here. Beyond the commercial buildup are thousands of acres of wooded areas, salt marshes and wild, open ocean beaches. The Salt Pond Visitor Center rests just off Route 6 and is one of Cape Cod National Seashore's main centers. This is a fine place to stop for information on the area; the center also hosts numerous nature and history programs and lectures and maintains a paved bike path. Nearby is the much-beloved Nauset Light, the red-and-white-stripe lighthouse moved from its perilous place on the cliffs of the Atlantic back in 1996. The Fort Hill area is another pretty spot, with lots of walking trails and the stately old mansion called the Penniman House.

It was here in 1620 that an exploring band of *Mayflower* passengers met the Nauset tribe on a bayside beach, which was then named First Encounter Beach. The meeting was peaceful, but the Pilgrims moved on to Plymouth anyway. Nearly a quarter century later, they returned to settle the area, which they originally called by its Native American name, Nawsett. Eastham was incorporated as a town on June 7, 1651.

Like many of the towns on the Cape, Eastham started as a farming community and later turned to the sea and to salt making for its livelihood; at one time there were more than 50 saltworks in town. A more atypical industry here was asparagus growing; from the late 1800s through the 1920s, Eastham was known as the asparagus capital of the United States. The runner-up crop, Eastham turnips, are still the pride of many a harvest table.

❹ The road to the Cape Cod National Seashore's **Fort Hill Area** (⊠ Fort Hill Rd., off U.S. 6) winds past the **Captain Edward Penniman House** (☞ *below*), ending at a parking area with a lovely view of old farmland traced with stone fences that rolls gently down to **Nauset Marsh** (☞ *below*) and a red-maple swamp. Appreciated by bird-watchers and nature photographers, the 1-mi **Red Maple Swamp Trail** begins outside the Penniman House and winds through the area, branching into two separate paths, one of which eventually turns into a boardwalk that meanders through wetlands. The other path leads directly to Skiff Hill, an overlook with benches and informative plaques that quote Samuel de Champlain's account of the area from when he moored off Nauset Marsh in 1605. Also on Skiff Hill is Indian Rock, a large boulder moved to the hill from the marsh below. Once used by the local Native American tribe as a sharpening stone, the rock is cut with deep grooves and smoothed in circles where ax heads were whetted.

The French Second Empire–style **Captain Edward Penniman House** was built in 1868 for a whaling captain. The impressive exterior is notable for its mansard roof; its cupola, which once commanded a dramatic view of bay and sea; and the whale-jawbone entrance gate. Though still in the process of renovation, the interior is open for guided tours or for browsing through changing exhibits. Call ahead to find out when tours are available. ⊠ *Fort Hill Rd., Fort Hill Area,* ☎ *508/255–3421.* ▭ *Free.* ⊙ *Weekdays 1–4.*

The park at Samoset Road has as its centerpiece the **Eastham Windmill,** the oldest windmill on Cape Cod. A smock mill built in Plymouth in the early 1680s, it was moved to this site in 1793 and is the only Cape windmill still on the site where it was used commercially. The mill was restored by local shipwreck historian William Quinn and friends. The park often comes alive with town festivals and concerts, and occasionally demonstrations are given on the inner workings of the mill. Each September, just after Labor Day, Eastham celebrates its history and the change of the season with the annual Windmill Weekend, an event with a full roster of activities for all ages. ⊠ *U.S. 6 at Samoset Rd.* ▭ *Free.* ⊙ *Late June–Labor Day, Mon.–Sat. 10–5, Sun. 1–5.*

Frozen in time, the 1741 **Swift-Daley House** was once the home of Gustavus Swift, founder of the Swift meatpacking company. Inside the full Cape with bow roof you'll find beautiful pumpkin-pine woodwork and wide-board floors; a ship's-cabin staircase that, like the bow roof, was built by ships' carpenters; and fireplaces in every downstairs room. The colonial-era furnishings include an old cannonball rope bed, tools, a melodeon, and a ceremonial quilt decorated with beads and coins. Among the antique clothing is a stunning 1850 wedding dress. Out back is a tool museum. ⊠ *U.S. 6, next to Eastham post office,* ☎ *no phone.* ▭ *Free.* ⊙ *July–Aug., weekdays 1–4; Sept., Sat. 1–4.*

A great spot for watching sunsets over the bay, **First Encounter Beach** (⊠ End of Samoset Rd. off U.S. 6) is rich in history. Near the parking lot, a bronze marker commemorates the first encounter between local Native Americans and passengers from the *Mayflower,* led by Captain Myles Standish, who explored the entire area for five weeks in November and December 1620 before moving on to Plymouth. The remains of a navy target ship retired after 25 years of battering now rest on a sandbar about 1 mi out.

★ The Cape's most expansive national treasure, the **Cape Cod National Seashore** was established in 1961 under the administration of President John F. Kennedy, for whom Cape Cod was home and haven. The 27,000-acre seashore, extending from Chatham to Provincetown, encompasses and protects 30 mi of superb ocean beaches, great rolling dunes, swamps, marshes, and wetlands, pitch pine and scrub oak forest, all kinds of wildlife, and a number of historic structures. Self-guided nature trails, as well as biking and horse trails, lace through these landscapes. Hiking trails lead to a red-maple swamp, **Nauset Marsh,** and to **Salt Pond,** in which breeding shellfish are suspended from floating "nurseries"—their offspring will later be used to seed the flats. Also in the seashore, the Buttonbush Trail is a nature path for people with vision impairments. A hike or bike ride to Coast Guard Beach leads to a turnout looking out over marsh and sea. A section of the cliff here was washed away in 1990, revealing remains of a prehistoric dwelling.

⓯ Salt Pond Visitor Center is the first visitor center of the Cape Cod National Seashore; the other, the **Province Lands Visitor Center,** is in Provincetown (☞ Provincetown, *below*). The Salt Pond center, overlooking pretty Salt Pond, offers guided walks, tours, boat trips, demonstrations, and lectures from mid-April through Thanksgiving, as well as evening beach walks, campfire talks, and other programs in summer.

The center includes a museum with several displays: on whaling and the old saltworks, early Cape Cod artifacts including scrimshaw, the journal that Mrs. Penniman kept while on a whaling voyage with her husband, and some of the Pennimans' possessions, such as their tea service and the captain's top hat. A good bookstore and an air-conditioned auditorium showing films on geology, sea rescues, whaling, Henry David Thoreau, and Marconi are also here. Something's up most summer evenings at the outdoor amphitheater, from slide-show talks to military-band concerts. ⊠ *Doane Rd. off U.S. 6,* ☎ *508/255–3421.* 🎟 *Free.* ⊙ *Mar.–June and Sept.–Dec., daily 9–4:30; July–Aug., daily 9–5; Jan.–Feb., weekends 9–4:30.*

Roads and bicycle trails lead to **Coast Guard and Nauset Light beaches** (⊠ Off Ocean View Dr.), which begin an unbroken 30-mi stretch of barrier beach extending to Provincetown—the "Cape Cod Beach" of Thoreau's 1865 classic, *Cape Cod.* You can still walk its length, as Thoreau did, though the Atlantic continues to claim more of the Cape's eastern shore every year. The site of the famous beach cottage of Henry Beston's 1928 book, *The Outermost House,* is to the south, near the end of Nauset spit. Designated as a literary landmark in 1964, the cottage was, alas, completely destroyed in the Great Blizzard of February 1978.

Moved 350 ft back from its perch at cliff's edge in 1996, the much-photographed red-and-white **Nauset Light** (⊠ Ocean View Dr. and Cable Rd.) still tops the bluff where the Three Sisters Lighthouses once stood; the Sisters themselves can be seen in a little landlocked park surrounded by trees, reached by paved walkways off Nauset Light Beach's parking lot. How the lighthouses got there is a long story. In 1838 three brick lighthouses were built 150 ft apart on the bluffs in Eastham overlooking a particularly dangerous area of shoals (shifting underwater sandbars). In 1892, after the eroding cliff dropped the towers into the ocean, they were replaced with three wooden towers. In 1918 two were moved away, as was the third in 1923. Eventually the National Park Service acquired the Three Sisters and brought them together here, where they would be safe, rather than returning them to the eroding coast. The Fresnel lens from the last working lighthouse is on display at the **Salt Pond Visitor Center** (☞ *above*). Lectures on, and guided walks to, the lighthouses are conducted throughout the season. In 2000 tours of Nauset Light were given on Sunday between 4:30 and 7:30 in July and August, on Sunday from 1 to 4 after Labor Day, and by appointment; the plan was to repeat this schedule in 2001, but call in advance (☎ 508/240–2612) to confirm.

Dining and Lodging

$–$$ ✕ **Arturo's.** Now in its new location within the Sheraton (☞ *below*), there's finally room for this great little Italian kitchen to spread out a bit. Come for a huge selection of pasta, including such favorites as fettuccine Alfredo, linguini and clam sauce, and eggplant and chicken Parmesan. Everything is made on the premises, from the rich red sauce to the flaky and spiced focaccia bread. Freshly baked bread comes with each dish, and the portions are generous while the prices remain very reasonable. You won't leave hungry. ✉ *At Four Points Sheraton, Rte. 6,* ☎ *508/240–7828. AE, D, DC, MC, V.*

$–$$ ✕ **Beach Break Grill and Lounge.** After changing ownership, this place has found it's niche. The dining room serves a full breakfast, then clears the way for dinner. The menu is basic and varied, with seafood (even a raw bar), lots of burgers, fajitas, pasta, and steak. The decor is all Hawaiian surfer, complete with old photos, long boards on the ceiling, and grassy adornments on the bar. Pub food and late-night bites can be had in the lively bar, which also has a pool table. All in all, it's an affordable and fun place to eat—and as a bonus, children under age 10 eat free at dinner. In fair weather there's also an outdoor deck for dining. ✉ *Main St. Mercantile off Rte. 6,* ☎ *508/240–3100. AE, D, DC, MC, V.*

$–$$ ✕ **Fairway Restaurant and Pizzeria.** The newly renovated family-run Fairway is not as cozy as it used to be but still serves up Italian comfort food in a casual, friendly setting. Attached to the Hole in One Donut Shop (very popular among locals), the Fairway puts a jar of crayons on every paper-covered table and sells its own brand of root beer. Entrées come with salad and homemade rolls. Try the orange tequila shrimp and scallops with a little Cajun heat, eggplant Parmesan, or a well-stuffed calzone. You can order from the extensive breakfast menu from 6:30 to 11:30. ✉ *4295 U.S. 6,* ☎ *508/255–3893. Reservations not accepted. AE, D, DC, MC, V.*

$–$$ ✕ **The Friendly Fisherman.** Not just another roadside lobster shack with buoys and nets for decoration, this is a place serious about its fresh seafood. It's both a great place to pick up ingredients to cook at home—there's a fish and produce market on hand—and a good bet for dining out on such favorites as fish-and-chips, fried scallops, and lobster. The market also sells homemade pies, breads, soups, stews, and pasta. ✉ *Rte. 6, North Eastham,* ☎ *508/255–6770 or 508/255–3009. AE, MC, V.*

$$$$ 🏠 **Four Points Sheraton.** At the entrance to the National Seashore, this Sheraton offers standard modern-decor rooms with two double beds or one king-size bed and tile baths. Rooms have views of the tropical indoor pool (complete with lush plants, pirate-theme bar, and resident live parrot), the parking lot, or the woods. Outside rooms are a little bigger and brighter and have mini-refrigerators. Children under 17 stay free. ✉ *3800 U.S. 6, 02642,* ☎ *508/255–5000 or 800/533–3986,* ℻ *508/240–1870. 107 rooms, 2 suites. Restaurant, lobby lounge, no-smoking rooms, room service, 2 pools, saunas, 2 tennis courts, exercise room, video games. AE, D, DC, MC, V. BP.* ✎

$$$–$$$$ 🏠 **Whalewalk Inn.** Named for the widow's walk atop the building, this 1830 whaling master's home is on 3 acres of rolling lawns, gardens, and meadows. Lots of windows give the place an open, airy feeling, while wide-board pine floors, fireplaces, and 19th-century country antiques provide historical appeal. Guest rooms are spacious, with four-poster twin, double, or queen-size beds; floral fabrics; and antique or reproduction furniture. Besides the rooms in the main inn, there are suites with fully equipped kitchens in the converted barn and guest house. A secluded saltbox cottage has a fireplace, kitchen, and private patio. Deluxe rooms in the carriage house have fireplaces, whirlpool tubs, and air-conditioning. Breakfast is served each morning in the cheerful sunroom or on the garden patio. ✉ *220 Bridge Rd., 02642,* ☎ *508/255–0617. 11 rooms, 5 suites. Bicycles. No smoking. MC, V. BP.* ✎

$$$ 🏠 **Overlook Inn.** If it weren't for the vivid yellow paint job on this three-story inn, it would be lost among the trees, even though it's right along U.S. 6. Both the Cape Cod Rail Trail and the Salt Pond Visitor Center are just across the road from this 19th-century oasis. Victorian touches abound, from the graceful high ceilings to the intricate interior wood molding. Each room has antiques, brass beds, and soft down comforters; some have genuine claw-foot tubs, which are great to slide into after a day at the beach. The innkeeper's Scottish hospitality promises some unusual and traditional breakfast fare each morning. ✉ *3085 U.S. 6, 02642,* ☎ *508/255–1886,* 𝖥𝖠𝖷 *508/240–0345. 14 rooms. AE, D, MC, V. BP.* 🐾

$$–$$$ 🏨 **Penny House Inn.** Tucked behind a wave of privet hedge, this rambling gray-shingle inn offers mostly spacious rooms, furnished with a combination of antiques, collectibles, and wicker. Captain's Quarters, the grandest room, has a sitting area with a wood-burning fireplace, a king-size brass bed, a miniature library, and a lovely view of the garden. Common areas include the Great Room, with a fireplace and lots of windows, a combination sunroom-library, and a garden patio set with umbrella tables. A full homemade breakfast starts the day, and afternoon tea is available. ✉ *4885 County Rd., U.S. 6, 02642,* ☎ *508/ 255–6632 or 800/554–1751,* 𝖥𝖠𝖷 *508/255–4893. 11 rooms. Air-conditioning, library. No smoking. AE, D, MC, V. BP.* 🐾

$–$$ 🏨 **Cove Bluffs Motel.** Nestled among the trees and very near the waters of Town Cove and several nature trails is this old-fashioned haven for families. The entire complex is reminiscent of a cottage colony, with several structures dotted beneath the pines, divided among standard motel rooms and several fully equipped one- to two-bedroom housekeeping units. Decor is simple, consisting of painted knotty-pine interiors and plain but practical bedcoverings. Outdoors holds plenty for busy children—basketball courts, shuffleboard, swing sets, a playhouse, and a sandbox—as well as a selection of swinging hammocks in the shade. You're welcome to use the outdoor grills, too. ✉ *U.S. 6 and Shore Rd., 02642,* ☎ *508/240–1616. 5 rooms, 8 housekeeping units. No-smoking rooms, pool, basketball, shuffleboard, coin laundry. MC, V. Closed Nov.–Mar.* 🐾

$–$$ 🏨 **Ocean Park Inn.** Recently purchased by the owners of the Four Points Sheraton, this large hotel complex shares some amenities with its sibling next door—but is much softer on the budget. Rooms are clean, simple, and straightforward. There are larger family units available—one with a fireplace—but most rooms are for double occupancy, with full or queen-size beds. Take advantage of the Sheraton's indoor pool and tennis courts. ✉ *Next to Four Points Sheraton, U.S. 6, 02642,* ☎ *508/ 255–1132 or 800/862–5550,* 𝖥𝖠𝖷 *508/255–5250. 55 rooms. Picnic area, no-smoking rooms, 2 pools, sauna, 2 tennis courts, exercise room, video games, coin laundry. AE, D, DC, MC, V. Closed Nov.–Mar.*

$ 🏨 **Hostelling International–Mid Cape.** On 3 wooded acres near the Cape Cod Rail Trail and a 15-minute walk to the bay, this hostel has eight cabins that sleep six–eight each; two can be used as family cabins. It has a common area and a kitchen, and a number of programs are available for guests. ✉ *75 Goody Hallet Dr., 02642,* ☎ *508/255–2785. 8 cabins. Ping-Pong, volleyball. MC, V. Closed mid-Sept.–mid-May.*

$ 🏕 **Atlantic Oaks Campground.** This campground is conveniently located less than a mile north of the Salt Pond Visitor Center. Primarily an RV camp, it offers limited tenting as well. The setting is a pine and oak forest, and you're minutes from Cape Cod National Seashore. There are bikes for rent and direct access to the Cape Cod Rail Trail. Movies for children are shown at night. RV hookups, including cable TV, cost $40 for two people; RV hookups cost $40 for two people, including cable TV; tent sites are $28 for two people. Showers are free. ✉ *3700 U.S. 6, 02642,* ☎ *508/255–1437 or 800/332–2267. 100 RV sites, 30 tent sites. Bicycles, playground, coin laundry. D, MC, V. Closed Nov.–Apr.*

Nightlife and the Arts

The **Cape Cod National Seashore** (☎ 508/255–3421 for information) offers summer-evening programs, such as slide shows, sunset beach walks, concerts by local groups or military bands, and campfire sing-alongs.

The **Eastham Painters Guild** holds outdoor art shows every Thursday, Friday, and holiday weekend from 9 to 5, July through October, at the Schoolhouse Museum (⊠ Next to Salt Pond Visitor Center, off U.S. 6).

First Encounter Coffee House (⊠ Chapel in the Pines, Samoset Rd., ☎ 508/255–5438) presents a mixture of professional and local folk and blues in a no-smoking, no-alcohol environment, with refreshments available during intermission. National acts are booked for the second and fourth Saturdays. It's closed May and December.

Outdoor Activities and Sports

BEACHES

On the bay side of the Outer Cape, **First Encounter Beach** (⊠ End of Samoset Rd. off U.S. 6) is open to the public and charges daily parking fees of $5 (weekly and season passes are also available; call the town hall at ☎ 508/240–5972) to nonresidents in season. Parking fees or passes also apply to several other bay beaches and ponds, both saltwater and freshwater.

Coast Guard Beach (⊠ Off Ocean View Dr.), part of the National Seashore, is a long beach backed by low grass and heathland. A handsome former Coast Guard station is also here, though it is not open to the public. The beach has no parking lot of its own, so park at the Salt Pond Visitor Center (☞ *above*) or at the lot up Doane Road from the center and take the free shuttle to the beach. At high tide the size of the beach shrinks considerably, so watch your blanket. There are showers, and lifeguards are posted between June and August. A daily charge of $7 for cars or a season pass (by far the best bargain) for $20 grants admission to all seven National Seashore beaches.

Nauset Light Beach (⊠ Off Ocean View Dr.), adjacent to Coast Guard Beach, continues the National Seashore landscape of long, sandy beach backed by tall dunes, grass, and heathland, with the lighthouse for a little extra Cape atmosphere. It has showers and lifeguards in summer, but as with other National Seashore beaches, there is no food concession. For fees *see* Coast Guard Beach, *above*.

BIKING

The **Idle Times Bike Shop** (⊠ U.S. 6 and Brackett Rd., ☎ 508/255–8281) provides bikes of all sizes and kinds and is right near the Cape Cod Rail Trail.

The **Little Capistrano Bike Shop** (⊠ Salt Pond Rd. across from Salt Pond Visitor Center, ☎ 508/255–6515) rents a variety of bikes and trailers and is conveniently located between the Cape Cod Rail Trail and the National Seashore Bike Trail.

Nauset Trail is maintained by the Cape Cod National Seashore and stretches 1⅗ mi from Salt Pond Visitor Center through groves of apple and locust trees to Coast Guard Beach.

HEALTH AND FITNESS CLUBS

The **Norseman Athletic Club** (⊠ 4730 U.S. 6, North Eastham, ☎ 508/255–6370 or 508/255–6371) has four racquetball courts, two squash courts, and six indoor tennis courts; one NBA indoor basketball court; an Olympic-size, heated indoor pool; swimming lessons; aerobics and children's self-defense classes; plus Nautilus, free weights, and cardiovascular machines. You can relax in the whirlpool, steam room, or sauna; you'll also find a pro shop and a restaurant. There are daily and weekly guest membership passes.

THE LOWER CAPE A TO Z

Arriving and Departing

By Ferry

HARWICH PORT–NANTUCKET

The **Freedom Cruise Line** runs express 90-minute ferries to Nantucket between May 15 and October 15, allowing you to explore the rose-covered isle without having to brave the crowds of Hyannis. Parking is free for the first 24 hours, then it's $10 per day. ⊠ *Saquatucket Harbor, Harwich Port,* ☎ *508/432–8999.* ⊞ *$39 round-trip, $10 extra with bicycle; $25 one-way, $5 extra with bicycle.*

Getting Around

By Bus

The **Cape Cod Regional Transit Authority** (☎ 508/385–8326; 800/352–7155 in MA, 🖎) operates several buses between Cape towns. The lower Cape route begins in Hyannis and follows Route 28 all the way to Orleans, stopping in Harwich Port and Chatham; buses will stop according to passenger discretion. Rates vary. This service operates year-round.

By Car

On the north shore, the Old King's Highway, Route 6A, parallels U.S. 6 but is a scenic country road passing through equally eye-pleasing towns. When you're in no hurry, use back roads—they're less frustrating and much more rewarding. Route 28, which begins at the upper Cape in Woods Hole and continues all the way to Orleans on the south side of the Cape, is notorious for its heavy traffic and slow going. Once past Harwich Port, the route is not as frustrating, and it even becomes scenic from Chatham to Orleans, winding past the shores of Pleasant Bay. In Orleans, when heading east, the large rotary can create problems. Remember, when approaching a rotary, you must yield to drivers already in the circle, and once within the rotary, you should not stop your vehicle.

By Limousine

John's Taxi & Limousine (☎ 508/394–3209) picks up only in Dennis and Harwich but will take you anywhere on the Cape.

By Taxi

Always Available Transport (⊠ Orleans, ☎ 508/255–7557 or 800/339–9732). **Eldredge Taxi** (⊠ Chatham, ☎ 508/945–0068).

Contacts and Resources

Camping

Nickerson State Park (⊠ 3488 Rte. 6A, Brewster, ☎ 508/896–3491 or 877/422–6762 for reservations) is huge—almost 2,000 acres—and hugely popular. It has plenty of facilities and guest programs. Because of its immense popularity, significant advance registration is necessary if you want a site.

Emergencies

For rescues at sea, call the **United States Coast Guard** in Chatham (☎ 508/945–0164).

Long Pond Medical Center (⊠ 525 Long Pond Dr., Harwich, ☎ 508/432–4100).

Outer Cape Health Services (⊠ 81 Old Colony Way, Orleans, ☎ 508/255–9700).

Guided Tours

CRUISES

Guided natural history tours of Chatham's Monomoy Islands are offered by the **Cape Cod Museum of Natural History** (☎ 508/896–3867) and **Wellfleet Bay Wildlife Sanctuary** (☎ 508/349–2615) on a year-round basis.

The **Cape Cod Museum of Natural History** (☎ 508/896–3867) also offers a two-hour cruise from Orleans through Nauset Marsh. Early morning cruises include breakfast in a nearby restaurant; evening tours feature cocktails and appetizers on board. Tours run daily, Tuesday through Friday until Labor Day, and then weekends until Columbus Day.

FLIGHTSEEING

To sightsee from above, contact **Chatham Municipal Airport** (⊠ George Ryder Rd., West Chatham, ☎ 508/945–9000).

House Rentals

Commonwealth Associates (⊠ 551 Main St., Harwich Port 02646, ☎ 508/432–2618, FAX 508/432–1771) can assist in finding vacation rentals in the Harwiches, including waterfront properties.

Compass Vacation Rentals (⊠ Main St. Mercantile Unit 19, U.S. 6, Eastham 02642, ☎ 508/240–7600 or 800/724–1307, FAX 508/240–6943, ✍) is one of many realtors with a listing of available apartments and houses on the Lower Cape.

Great Vacations Inc. (⊠ 2660 Rte. 6A, Brewster 02631, ☎ 508/896–2090) specializes in locating vacation rentals in Brewster, Dennis, and Orleans.

Libraries

The **Brewster Ladies' Library** (⊠ 1822 Main St. [Rte. 6A], ☎ 508/896–3913) occupies a restored Victorian building and a 1997 addition.

In Chatham, the **Eldredge Public Library** (⊠ 564 Main Street, ☎ 508/945–5170) has a special genealogy department.

Snow Library (⊠ Main Street and Rte. 28, ☎ 508/240–3760), in Orleans, has been in operation since around 1876; today there are children's story hours and numerous lecture programs.

Outdoor Activities and Sports

BASEBALL

The **Cape Cod Baseball League** (☎ 508/996–5004), considered the country's best summer league, is scouted by all the major-league teams. Ten teams play a 44-game season from mid-June to mid-August; admission is free to games at all 10 fields (☞ Close-Up: The Cape Cod Baseball League, *below*).

BIKING

There are a few parking lots along the Cape Cod Rail Trail (☞ Close-Up: Riding the Rail Trail *in* Chapter 4) for those who'd rather ride a segment of the trail than tackle all 25 mi. In Harwich there's a lot on Route 124, just off Exit 10 from U.S. 6 and directly across from the Pleasant Lake Store. In Orleans, park on West Road across from Old Colony Way. There is also a small parking area on Rock Harbor Road, between Bridge Road and the Route 6 traffic rotary.

Each town has its share of road races throughout the summer season.
In August, Brewster has its annual **Brew Run** (☎ 508/896–7771), a 5.25-
miler sponsored by the Brewster Inn and Chowder House. The **Irish
Pub Road Race** (☎ 508/432–8808) takes place in West Harwich every
August.

Visitor Information

Some local chambers of commerce are open only in season.

Brewster (✉ 2198 Main St. [Rte. 6A], Box 1241, 02631, ☎ 508/896–
3500), in the Brewster town offices building. The office includes a visitor center and the offices of the Brewster Chamber of Commerce and
Board of Trade United.

Chatham (✉ Box 793, 02633, ☎ 508/945–5199 or 800/715–5567;
visitor center: ✉ 2377 Main St., South Chatham; information booth:
✉ 533 Main St., Chatham).

Eastham (✉ U.S. 6 at Fort Hill Rd., Box 1329, 02642, ☎ 508/240–
7211).

Harwich (✉ Rte. 28, Box 34, Harwich Port 02646, ☎ 508/432–1600
or 800/441–3199).

Orleans (✉ Box 153, 02653, ☎ 508/255–1386; information booth:
✉ Eldredge Pkwy. off Rte. 6A, ☎ 508/240–2484).

6 THE OUTER CAPE

As the large trees and greenery fade to twisted pitch pine and sandy terrain, so too does the essence of the Outer Cape seem to grow a little wilder, a little less traditional than its neighbors. Though still proud of their histories, the towns of Wellfleet, Truro, and Provincetown are flavored by a more spirited attitude, one that seems more focused on the raw beauty of this area and the creativity it so often inspires.

Revised by
Laura V. Scheel

Technically part of the Lower Cape, the Outer Cape is nonetheless its own entity, forming the wrist and fist of Cape Cod. There's a sense of abandon here, in the hedonistic summertime frenzy of Provincetown and out on the windswept landscape of dunes and marshes. As you drive down here, the land flattens out, vegetation gets sparser and more coniferous, and the sea feels closer as the land narrows. Much of the region is undeveloped, protected by the Cape Cod National Seashore. Long, straight, dune-backed beaches appear to go on forever; inland, trails wind through wind-stunted forests of scrub pine, beech, and oak. Wellfleet is a quiet town, with art galleries, upscale shops, and a calmly active harbor. With an expanse of high dunes, estuaries, salt marshes, pine forests, rivers, and winding back roads, Truro is the least-populated, least-developed town on the entire Cape.

The promise of solitude has long drawn artists and writers out here. Provincetown has two faces—a quiet little fishing village in winter and a magnet for throngs of pleasure seekers in summer, who come for the rugged beaches, photogenic streets lined with historic homes, zany nightlife, shops selling everything from antiques to zoot suits, and the galleries, readings, and art classes that carry on Provincetown's rich history as an art colony.

Pleasures and Pastimes

Beaches

Ocean beaches on the Cape Cod National Seashore have cold water and serious surf and are backed by dunes. They're also contiguous: you can walk from Eastham to Provincetown if you've got the stamina.

On the Cape Cod Bay side, swimmers are greeted with warmer and more gentle waters. The tides are pivotal here: at low tide the flats expose vast sandy expanses, and to get thoroughly wet, you'll have to trek out a ways. Bay-side beachgoers also get more time in the sun—the majestic dunes on the ocean side block the descending late-afternoon sun—and sunsets on the Bay are spectacular.

Biking

The Cape Cod National Seashore maintains three bicycle trails. Head of the Meadow Trail is 2 mi of easy cycling between dunes and salt marshes from High Head Road, off Route 6A in North Truro, to the Head of the Meadow Beach parking lot. Province Lands Trail is a 5¼-mi loop off the Beech Forest parking lot on Race Point Road in Provincetown, with spurs to Herring Cove and Race Point beaches and to Bennett Pond. The paths wind up and down hills amid dunes, marshes, woods, and ponds and offer spectacular views—on an exceptionally clear day, you can see the Boston skyline. There's a picnic grove at Pilgrim Spring.

South Wellfleet is the beginning (or the end, depending on how you look at it) of the Cape Cod Rail Trail (☞ Close-Up: Riding the Rail Trail *in* Chapter 4, a 25-mi flat, paved route to Dennis that winds past cranberry bogs and ponds and through wooded areas. A good-size parking lot is open to cyclists just behind the South Wellfleet General Store, off LeCount Hollow Road.

Dining

Dining on the Outer Cape means everything from humble fried-clam shacks to candlelight elegance. Most restaurants have withstood the test of time and fashion and have developed a loyal following that keeps their doors open year after year. Menus frequently feature local seafood as a staple. In Wellfleet restaurants are known more for their creative cuisine than reasonable prices—going out with the whole family won't come cheap. Truro lacks a concentration of restaurants (the town itself has no real center); its offerings are spread out along the byways. Provincetown opens a world of great variation to the eager diner. There are a number of fine dining restaurants in town, all aglow with candles, crystal, and fine linens, but there are an equal number of lively and boisterous café spots. Many offer outdoor seating, providing for a good view of the town's constant the action.

In the height of the summer season, expect a long wait for a table, sometimes despite a reservation—the sheer volume of visitors is to blame. To make matters worse, in the last few years Cape Cod has been experiencing a labor shortage, so good help is at a premium, leading more than a few restaurants to close their doors. Others have been forced to shorten their season.

For price ranges *see* Dining *in* Smart Travel Tips A to Z.

Lodging

The Outer Cape's lodging options can be summed up in one word: diverse. Wellfleet has several cozy inns and bed-and-breakfasts in the center of town, with a few larger motels on busy Route 6. Despite the strict building codes, there are a surprising number of large (though not so imposing) hotel complexes and cottage colonies spread out along Cape Cod Bay in North Truro. It's crowded, but it's also right on the sand, with commanding views of sunsets and the Provincetown skyline.

Provincetown lodging varies from bare-bones lodging in a tiny room in an old house to the utmost luxury in one of the many meticulously restored and grand homes. Prices vary just as greatly as the offerings. Although it seems that every other building is an inn or guest house, a place to spend the night is not so easy to come by. Provincetown fills up fast and has a longer season than its neighbors. Minimum stays of at least three nights are often the norm during the peak season and holiday times.

For price ranges *see* Lodging *in* Smart Travel Tips A to Z.

Nightlife and the Arts

Many credit the unusual light and extraordinary beauty of the Outer Cape with creating such a strong and vibrant artistic tradition. In Wellfleet's town center are nearly two-dozen art galleries, all representing local and national artists. The works aren't limited to sea and landscapes either; you'll also find abstract works and fine crafts.

Truro has fewer art galleries, but its history is rich. Painter Edward Hopper spent many years here in his modest home overlooking Cape Cod Bay; numerous recognizable scenes of Truro exist among his work. The Center for the Arts at Castle Hill is a longtime organization that for more than 30 years has been holding summer classes in art, writing and crafts.

As Provincetown enters its second century, the town remains a center for the arts. Its history is great; many world-famous artists made their homes here—some started art schools still in operation. Provincetown may have more galleries per block than any other New England town. Friday night is gallery night; stroll the streets and pop in on one of many champagne artist receptions.

Provincetown also has an active nightlife, from pulsating dance clubs to pool halls, with lots of live entertainment. Drag shows, theater, comedy routines, and music happen on a continual basis throughout the summer season. Wellfleet has a few more peaceful options such as restaurant taverns that occasionally feature live music. Truro seems to prefer the silence, leaving the revelry to its bordering towns.

Outdoor Activities and Sports

The waters off Provincetown are one of the finest whale-watching areas in the world. The Cape Cod National Seashore has nine walking trails through varied terrain. In winter, ponds and shallow flooded cranberry bogs sometimes freeze hard enough for skating—but you should check conditions with the local fire department before venturing into unfamiliar territory.

Shopping

Shoppers on the Outer Cape never have to worry about the uniqueness of their purchases—all stores are individually owned and are one of a kind.

Wellfleet shoppers will find a wealth of fine art and crafts to choose from which to choose as well as a healthy dose of small designer-clothing stores. The word here is chic. On one street, you could walk away with a funky Indonesian sarong for the beach and a handcrafted, multi-thousand-dollar gold and gem-studded ring. Out on Route 6, far from the sophistication of town, are a few shops specializing in the $2 T-shirt, plastic lawn ornaments, and saltwater taffy. The Wellfleet Flea Market—great for bargain hunting—is held four days a week in summer.

Like the vast array of characters who make up the town, the Provincetown shopping experience is richly diverse. From the most civilized and expensive art gallery to the sunglasses hut, there's a little bit of everything. Commercial Street, aptly named, is a tightly packed thoroughfare dominated by pedestrians ambling in and out of the shops and galleries. Off-season visitors can benefit from some fine sales, when shops are eager to clean out their inventories before winter sets in.

Exploring the Outer Cape

Numbers in the text correspond to numbers in the margin and on the Lower and Outer Cape, Wellfleet, and Provincetown maps.

The Outer Cape refers to the wrist and fist of Cape Cod, the towns that rooted and grew amid dunes and marshland—Wellfleet, Truro, and Provincetown. **Wellfleet** ①, with pleasant shops and galleries along Main Street, is also rich in dune-backed ocean beaches and marshes great for canoeing and kayaking. Historic **Marconi Station** ② was the landing point for the transatlantic telegraph early in the 20th century, and its White Cedar Swamp Trail is quite beautiful. In Wellfleet visit art galleries, browse through great bookstores, take a dip in the bay or the ocean, rent a canoe or kayak and tour the marshes, and have dinner at one of the fine area restaurants. Don't leave without visiting the **Massachusetts Audubon Wellfleet Bay Wildlife Sanctuary** ③, especially if you're a bird-watcher. It's a fantastic place to catch a sunset over the bay. **Truro** ④ solidly represents the quietude of this end of the Cape, at least until you reach the seasonally bustling **Provincetown** ⑦–⑱, out at the tip. Catch a whale-watch boat from P-town (as Provincetown is almost universally known)—the Cape ranks fourth in the world for sighting whales. Take a trolley tour in town or bike through the National Seashore on its miles of trails. Climb the Pilgrim Monument for a spectacular view of the area—on an exceptionally clear day you can see the Boston skyline. Visit the museums and shops and art galleries, or spend the afternoon swimming and sunning on one of the beaches. To escape the crowds, walk across the breakwater to Long Point. Rent a sailboat or

relax in the sand, taking in the splendid views of the bay. Then choose from an abundance of restaurants and the Cape's wildest nightlife.

When to Tour the Outer Cape

Prime time on the Outer Cape—when everything is open—is from Memorial Day to around Columbus Day. July and August are by far the most crowded times; it's a wonder that the entire peninsula doesn't sink under the weight of the the the bulk of tourists. The shoulder seasons of late May–June, and after Labor Day, have become more and more popular with visitors who aren't locked into a school schedule. Rates are lower during these times, and restaurants and shops are open. If the weather has been generous, swimming is still a pleasant possibility.

Wellfleet pretty much seals itself up after Columbus Day; most galleries and restaurants close, leaving just a handful of year-round business. But there's the entire outside world to explore, now free of thousands of others trying to do the same thing. Ocean climates keep winters milder than on the mainland. It's quiet—beautifully so—and distractions and pleasures take on a more basic flavor.

Provincetown clears out as well, but not as fully as Wellfleet. Various theme weekends throughout the year have boosted tourism in the off-season, and there are always readings, films, and places to eat. The off-season is truly a time to discover the essence of the place, see its changing natural beauty, and experience a more restful and relaxed pace.

Wellfleet and South Wellfleet

➊ *6 mi north of Eastham, 13 mi southeast of Provincetown.*

Still famous for its world-renowned and succulent namesake oysters and, with Truro, a colonial whaling and cod-fishing port, Wellfleet is also a center for artists and writers. Less than 2 mi wide, it's one of the more tastefully developed Cape resort towns, with a number of fine restaurants, historic houses, art galleries, and a good old Main Street in the village proper. South Wellfleet borders North Eastham and is home to a wonderful Audubon sanctuary and a drive-in theater that doubles on weekends as a flea market.

The downtown center of Wellfleet is quite compact, so it's actually best to leave your car in one of the public parking areas and take off on foot. Historic buildings that once housed oyster and fish drying shacks or stately residences are now home to upscale art galleries, clothing designers' stores, and restaurants. Wellfleet's small-town nature still somehow accommodates the demands of a major tourist industry; the year-round population of around 3,000 residents explodes to more than 18,000 people in July and August.

Tourism isn't the only industry, though. Fishing boats still head out from the harbor daily in search of scallops, cod, and other fish. Shell-fishing accounts for a major portion of the town's economy and many of its residents' livelihoods. Whaling played a role in the 18th and 19th centuries; out on the now-sunken Billingsgate Island, a raucous whaling tavern once thrived. The wealth of world-traveling sea captains found its way to Wellfleet as well, its impact evident in many of the grand old houses that line the narrow streets of town. The Wellfleet Historical Society is a fine stop for those who wish to see the town as it was in its early days.

Visitors today are attracted to Wellfleet's alluring combination of history, sophisticated artistic culture, and natural splendor. The beaches of Wellfleet are spectacular, with their towering sand dunes, bracing surf, and miles of unfettered expanse. Seemingly endless wooded trails in the domain of the National Seashore provide terrific walking and hiking opportunities, and the sheltered waters of the tidal Herring River and Wellfleet Harbor are a favorite destination for canoeists, kayakers, windsurfers, and sailors. There's a vast outdoor playground for those who seek it.

② **Marconi Station,** on the Atlantic side of the Cape's forearm, is the site of the first transatlantic wireless station erected on the U.S. mainland. From here Italian radio and wireless-telegraphy pioneer Guglielmo Marconi sent the first American wireless message to Europe—"most cordial greetings and good wishes" from President Theodore Roosevelt to King Edward VII of England—on January 18, 1903. The station broadcast news for 15 years. An outdoor shelter contains a model of the original station, of which only fragments remain as a result of cliff erosion; parts of the tower bases are sometimes visible on the beach below, where they fell. The Cape Cod National Seashore's administrative headquarters is here, and though it is not an official visitor center, it can provide information at times when the centers are closed. Inside there is a mock-up of the spark-gap transmitter used by Marconi. Off the parking lot a 1¼-mi trail and boardwalk lead through the **Atlantic White Cedar Swamp;** it's one of the most beautiful trails on the seashore. Free maps and guides are available at the trailhead. **Marconi Beach,** south of the station on Marconi Beach Road, is another of the National Seashore's ocean beaches (☞ Beaches, *below*). ⊠ *Marconi Site Rd., South Wellfleet,* ☎ *508/349–3785.* 🎟 *Free.* ☉ *Daily 8–4:30.*

For a **scenic loop** through a classic Cape landscape near Wellfleet's Atlantic beaches—with scrub and pines on the left, heathland meeting cliffs and ocean below on the right—take LeCount Hollow Road just north of the Marconi Station turnoff. All the beaches on this strip rest at the bottom of a tall grass-covered dune, which lends dramatic character to this outermost shore. The first of the four, **LeCount Hollow,** is restricted to residents or temporary residents in season, as is the last, **Newcomb Hollow,** with a scalloped shoreline of golden sand. In between, **White Crest** and **Cahoon Hollow** are town-managed public beaches. On breezy days hang gliders fly from the cliffs. Cahoon has a hot restaurant and dancing spot, the Beachcomber (☞ Nightlife and the Arts, *below*). Backtrack to Cahoon Hollow Road and turn west for the southernmost entrance to the town of Wellfleet proper, across U.S. 6.

Wellfleet's **First Congregational Church** (⊠ 200 Main St., ☎ 508/349–6877), a handsome 1850 Greek Revival building, is said to have the only town clock in the world to strike on ship's bells. The church's interior is lovely, with pale blue walls, a brass chandelier hanging from an enormous gilt ceiling rosette, subtly colored stained-glass windows, and pews curved to form an amphitheater facing the altar and the 1873 738-pipe Hook and Hastings tracker-action organ. To the right is a Tiffany-style window depicting a clipper ship, with a dedication to the memory of a sea captain. Concerts are given in July and August on Sunday at 8 PM.

For a glimpse into Wellfleet's past, the **Wellfleet Historical Society Museum** exhibits furniture, paintings, shipwreck salvage, needlework, navigation equipment, early photographs, Native American artifacts, clothing, and more. The society's Samuel Rider House is no longer open to the public. In July and August short guided walks around the center of town are given Tuesday and Friday mornings at 10:15 for $3. ⊠ *266 Main St.,* ☎ *508/349–9157.* 🎟 *$1.* ☉ *Late June–mid-Sept., Tues.–Sat. 1–4.*

The comfortable **Wellfleet Public Library** (✉ 55 W. Main St., ☎ 508/349–0310) is a great place to spend a rainy afternoon. The library is a reflection of the literary life of Wellfleet. Among the writers who have spent time here are Mary McCarthy, Edmund Wilson, Annie Dillard, and Marge Piercy.

Main Street is a good place to start if you're in the mood for shopping (☞ Shopping, *below*). **Commercial Street** has all the flavor of the fishing town that Wellfleet remains. Galleries and shops occupy small weathered-shingle houses, some of which look like fishing shacks. A good stroll around town would take in Commercial and Main streets, ending perhaps at **Uncle Tim's Bridge** (✉ Off E. Commercial St.). The short walk across this arching landmark—with its beautiful, much-photographed view over marshland and a tidal creek—leads to a small wooded island.

Follow Commercial Street to the **Wellfleet Pier,** busy with fishing boats, sailboats, yachts, charters, and party boats. At the twice-daily low tides you can fish on the tidal flats for oysters, clams, and quahogs (☎ 508/349–9818 for a permit).

Chequessett Neck Road makes for a pretty 2½-mi drive from the harbor to the bay past Sunset Hill—a great place to catch one. At the end, on the left, is a parking lot and wooded picnic area from which nature trails lead off to **Great Island** (✉ Off Chequessett Neck Rd.), perfect for the beachcomber and solitude seeker. The "island" is actually a peninsula connected by a sand spit built by tidal action. More than 7 mi of trails wind along the inner marshes and the water; these are the most difficult on the seashore because they're mostly in soft sand. In the 17th century lookout towers for shore whaling as well as a tavern stood here. The residents pastured animals and engaged in oystering and cranberry harvesting. By 1800 the hardwood forest that had covered the island had been cut down for use in ship- and home building. The pitch pines and other growth you see here (and all over the Cape) today were introduced in the 1830s to keep the soil from washing into the sea. Cape Cod National Seashore offers occasional guided hikes on Great Island and, from February through April, seal walks. To the right of the Great Island lot, a road leads to **Griffin Island,** with its own walking trail.

★ ❸ A trip to the Outer Cape isn't complete without a visit to the informative **Massachusetts Audubon Wellfleet Bay Wildlife Sanctuary,** a 1,000-acre haven for more than 250 species of birds attracted by the varied habitats found here. The jewel of the Massachusetts Audubon Society, the sanctuary is a superb place for walking, birding, and looking west over the salt marsh and bay at wondrous sunsets.

The Audubon Society hosts a great variety of naturalist-led wildlife tours around different parts of the Cape, including the Monomoy Islands (☞ Chatham, *in* Chapter 5), year-round. There are bay cruises; bird, wildlife, and insect walks; hikes; snorkeling; winter seal cruises; and birding, canoe, and kayak trips. The sanctuary also has camps for children in July and August and weeklong field schools for adults. Phone reservations are required ahead of time, as some programs are very popular. ✉ Off U.S. 6, Box 236, South Wellfleet 02663, ☎ 508/349–2615. ⊞ $3. ☉ Daily 8 AM–dusk.

Dining and Lodging

$$$ ✕ **Aesop's Tables.** A worthy choice for a special dinner, Aesop's spe-
★   cializes in seafood entrées and appetizers that often take the local Wellfleet oyster to new heights. Inside this 1805 captain's house are five dining rooms; aim for a table on the porch overlooking the center of town. The signature dish is an exotic bouillabaisse, with mounds

of fresh-off-the-boat seafood in a hot saffron broth; the homemade sour-dough bread is the perfect accompaniment. The marinated duck breast is another favorite. When it's time for dessert, you're likely to see lots of diners tempting fate with Death by Chocolate, a heavy mousse cake. Some nights in summer there's live jazz in the tavern, where the mood and the menu are more casual; the chairs are so comfortable, you may have trouble getting up. ⊠ *316 Main St.,* ☎ *508/349–6450. AE, DC, MC, V. Closed Columbus Day–Mother's Day. No lunch.*

$$–$$$ ✕ **Painter's.** Named for chef-owner Kate Painter (not for all the local artists), this fresh restaurant has survived its start-up years but still seems to be in flux. A redesign has now closed the upstairs to the public; harder to understand is the elimination of a lovely old bar for a new one that is just as cramped but not as atmospheric. One moment the food seems fresh and excellent; the next, uncertain and unsophisticated. The 10–15 seafood dishes run from traditional Portuguese fare such as clam *cataplana* (hearty clam stew with a spicy red wine sauce) to a new American version of pan-seared tuna, encrusted with sesame and mustard seeds. All the desserts are homemade as well; the flourless chocolate Armagnac fig cake begs to be devoured. Be careful ordering wine; even the house chardonnay is seriously overpriced. ⊠ *50 Main St.,* ☎ *508/ 349–3003. AE, MC, V. Closed Dec.–Apr.*

$$ ✕ **Captain Higgins.** Fish is the obvious specialty at this popular spot at the turn of the road across from Wellfleet's town pier. Besides being close to the fishing fleet and town beach, Captain Higgins has a broad outdoor deck overlooking a beautiful green and gold marsh. You can watch the slender reeds sway in the breeze as you sip an icy Seabreeze and finish a plate of fresh Wellfleet oysters or a marinated calamari appetizer. This is a good place to get a big boiled lobster dinner or fresh bluefish with a sweet mustard glaze. A more surprising option is a de-licious 100% ostrich burger, similar to beef but lower in fat and calo-ries. Reservations are accepted if you call before 6. ⊠ *Across from Wellfleet Town Pier,* ☎ *508/349–6027. MC, V. Closed Nov.–Apr.*

$$ ✕ **Finely JP's.** This unassuming little roadside spot right on U.S. 6 gives
★ no hint that chef John Pontius consistently turns out wonderful food full of the best Italian influences and ingredients. The dining room is small and noisy, but the fish and pasta dishes (which emphasize good olive oil and plenty of lemon) silence all. Appetizers are especially good, among them a warm spinach-and-scallop salad or blackened beef with charred pepper relish. The Wellfleet paella draws raves and a steady hand-ful of locals, but the chef is not afraid to cook a Delmonico steak, ei-ther. Be sure not to confuse this place with PJ's (☞ *below*). ⊠ *U.S. 6, South Wellfleet,* ☎ *508/349–7500. Reservations not accepted. D, MC, V. Closed Mon.–Wed. Thanksgiving–Memorial Day; Mon.–Tues. Memo-rial Day–mid-June and Oct.–Thanksgiving; Tues. Labor Day–Oct.*

$$ ✕ **Serena's.** The name is Italian for "mermaid," and images of the sirens crop up everywhere. A family place that caters to children, Serena's offers an assortment of blackboard specials every night. The Italian menu is short on the contemporary northern cuisine you'll find at many other places; red sauces still prevail here. Try the seafood *fra diavolo,* a bouillabaisselike stew that can be ordered hot or extremely hot. ⊠ *U.S. 6, South Wellfleet,* ☎ *508/349–9370. Reservations not accepted. AE, D, DC, MC, V. No lunch.*

$–$$ ✕ **Bayside Lobster Hutt.** The sides of this lovably scruffy wooden building are draped with fishing nets, dangling from a rooftop effigy of a lobsterman and his boat. Inside, you share long tables with strangers and, often as not, wind up neighbors on the beach the next day. The menu is all about lobster—you just choose the size, don a nap-kin, and set to work with a nutcracker and some melted butter. A few other dishes satisfy the lobster-averse; try the sea-clam pie (in fact, a clam potpie). You're encouraged to bring your own beer or wine. Sadly, this Wellfleet institution suffered greatly from the Cape's lack of help—in 2000 the restaurant was unable to open its doors. It is hoped that the restaurant will find enough workers to reopen this year. ⊠ *91 Commercial St.,* ☎ *508/349–6333. Reservations not accepted. No credit cards. BYOB. Closed mid-Sept.–Memorial Day.*

$–$$ ✕ **PJ's Family Restaurant.** There's always a good-size but fast-moving line in front of this entrenched Wellfleet tradition, waiting for a heap of steamers or a creamy soft-serve cone. The inside is clean, airy, and unpretentious, with slanting knotty-pine paneling, swirling overhead fans, the ubiquitous starfish-studded fishnet—and the requisite view of the vast parking lot. The open kitchen gleams and the staff hustles. At PJ's you place your order and take a number. Food is served in utilitarian style: Styrofoam soup bowls, paper plates, plastic forks. The lobster-and-corn chowder doesn't have much lobster in it, so stick to the traditional clam chowder. Fried calamari and clam or oyster plates are generous and fresh. Try the dense, spicy stuffed clams and a pile of crispy homemade onion rings, but stay far, far away from the veggie burger. ⊠ *U.S. 6 at 1st turn into town,* ☎ *508/349–2126. Reservations not accepted. No credit cards. Closed mid-Oct.–mid-Apr.*

$ ✕ **Lighthouse Restaurant.** There are no fireworks, but there's still a line out the door on summer mornings for a classic bacon-and-egg breakfast—this place is authentic all the way down the line. A plate of steamers and a beer for lunch? Chowder, burger, and another beer for dinner? You got it. ⊠ *Main St.,* ☎ *508/349–3681. Reservations not accepted. D, MC, V.*

$ ✕ **Mac's Seafood.** Right at Wellfleet Harbor, this newly renovated and ambitious little spot has some of the freshest seafood around. There's not a whole lot of seating here—some inside and some out on picnic tables—but when you've got a succulent mouthful of raw oyster in your mouth, who cares? The lunch and dinner menu includes all types of seafood, plus a sushi bar and a raw bar for your perusal. For takeout there are deli items, a selection of smoked fish, pâtés, fish, and lobster. You can even order a full traditional lobster clambake to go. ⊠ *Wellfleet Town Pier,* ☎ *508/349–0404. MC, V. Closed Columbus Day–Memorial Day.*

$ ✕ **Moby Dick's.** A meal at this good-natured, rough-hewn fish shack named for you-know-who is an absolute Cape Cod tradition for some people. Many, many clams have given their lives to make the sparkling white driveway. Moby Dick's has a giant blackboard menu (order up front, and food is brought to you); a big, breezy screened-in porch in which to eat; and red-check tablecloths. The owners claim to serve the freshest seafood and to buy from local fishermen whenever possible, and what they serve supports the claim. The frying oil is filtered twice daily—essential for light and crisp clams, fish, and scallops. Go for the Nantucket Bucket: one pound of Monomoy steamers, one pound of native mussels, and corn on the cob served in a bucket. Don't miss the unique Outer Cape Onion, a whole onion cut in such a way that it opens like a flower when dipped in batter and deep-fried. ⊠ *U.S. 6 on Truro side of town center,* ☎ *508/349–9795* FAX *. Reservations not accepted. Closed Oct.–Apr.*

$$–$$$ ☷ **Holbrook House.** This fairly new inn, set in an immaculate and crisply elegant 1818 home, is surrounded by gardens and brick patios. A mixture of antiques, sea-grass floor coverings, and artwork adorns the interior (keep an eye out for the beautifully painted furnishings created by one of the owners). Because there are only two rooms and a studio apartment, privacy is guaranteed and cherished. The room on the first floor has a private entrance and twin beds that can be converted to a king. Upstairs, the second room has a sitting area and a large bedroom with a queen-size bed. Awake to the aromas of a full homemade breakfast—no boxed muffins here. Leave your car in the lot while in Wellfleet—the inn is close to town and to the harbor. ⊠ *223 Main St., Wellfleet 02667,* ☏ *508/349–6706. 2 rooms, studio apartment. MC, V. BP.* ✍

$$–$$$ 🏨 **Surf Side Colony Cottages.** There's very little in the way of accom-
★ modations on the Atlantic shore of the Outer Cape, so these one- to three-bedroom cottages are an especially good find. Scattered on either side of Ocean View Drive, they range from units in a piney grove to well-equipped ocean-side cottages; the two closest to the water have the best views. The cottages are a one-minute walk from Maguire's Landing town beach (Le Count Hollow), a beautiful, wide strand of sand, dunes, and surf. Though the exteriors are retro Florida, with pastel shingles and flat roofs, cottage interiors are tastefully decorated in Cape style, including knotty-pine paneling. All units have phones, wood-burning fireplaces, screened porches, kitchens, (mostly) tile baths, rattan furniture, carpeting, and grills. Some have roof decks with an ocean view and outdoor showers. Ocean-side cottages have dishwashers. ⊠ *Ocean View Dr., Box 937, South Wellfleet 02663,* ☏ *508/349–3959,* 𝔽𝔸𝕏 *508/349–3959. 18 cottages. Picnic area, coin laundry. 1- to 2-wk minimum in summer. MC, V. Closed Nov.–Mar.* ✍

$$–$$$ 🏨 **Wellfleet Motel & Lodge.** A mile from Marconi Beach, opposite the Audubon sanctuary, is this well-maintained and tasteful highway-side complex, which sits on 12 wooded acres. In the single-story motel, the rooms, renovated each winter, are decorated in rich green and burgundy, with standard oak furniture. Rooms in the two-story lodge are bright and spacious, with king- or queen-size beds, TV with HBO, and balconies or patios. The property offers direct access to the Cape Cod Rail Trail. ⊠ *146 U.S. 6, Box 606, South Wellfleet 02663,* ☏ *508/349–3535 or 800/852–2900,* 𝔽𝔸𝕏 *508/349–1192. 57 rooms, 8 suites. Bar, coffee shop, air-conditioning, 2 pools, hot tub, basketball, meeting room. AE, DC, MC, V. Closed Dec.–Mar.* ✍

$–$$$ 🏨 **The Moorings.** If you want simple accommodations in a perfect setting, this beauty is ideal. The main house, an 1850s Queen Anne–style Victorian sea captain's home, has just one suite for overnight guests, a two-bedroom space with a separate and pleasant sitting room. Outside, for the unfussy, several housekeeping cottages (meaning no maid service) sit on what may be the most splendid backyard in Wellfleet: Spacious, shaded by large trees, and dotted with inviting chairs, the lawn practically sits on Duck Creek. Two one-bedroom cottages are tiny but sufficient—just large enough for a bed, a dresser, and a small bathroom—and share the adjacent shower room. The two- and three-bedroom cottages, with full kitchens and private baths, are rented by the week. Walk to town and the harbor, and leave your car in the drive. At press time this inn had just been put up for sale, so call before visiting. ⊠ *149 Commercial St., Wellfleet 02667,* ☏ *508/349–3379. 1 suite, 2 1-room cottages, 1 2-bedroom cottage, 1 3-bedroom cottage. MC, V. Closed Columbus Day–Memorial Day.*

$–$$ 🏨 **Even'tide.** Long a summer favorite, this motel is set back off the main road, surrounded by trees and sitting close to the Cape Cod Rail Trail. A central attraction is the 60-ft indoor pool (although Wellfleet's beaches are not far), but guests return year after year for the hospitality and the motel's reputation for cleanliness. Rooms are furnished in simple motel style and include some with queen-size or double beds, two-room family suites, and efficiencies with kitchens. Speckled about the property are cottages, available for stays of a week or longer. ⊠ *650 U.S. 6, South Wellfleet 02663,* ☏ *508/349–3410,* 𝔽𝔸𝕏 *508/349–7804. 31 units, 10 cottages. Air-conditioning, refrigerators, indoor pool, playground. 1- or 2-wk minimum for cottages in summer. MC, V. Closed Nov.–Apr.* ✍

$-$$ ☎ **Holden Inn.** If you're watching your budget and can deal with modest basics, try this old-timey place just outside the town center. Rooms have hardwood floors and are simply decorated with grandma's house–type wallpapers, ruffled sheer or country-style curtains, and antiques such as brass-and-white-iron or spindle beds or a marble-top table. Private baths with old porcelain sinks are available in adjacent 1840 and 1890 buildings. A suite has a queen-size bed and two twins, suitable for a small family. The lodge has shared baths, an outdoor shower, and a large screened-in porch with a lovely view of the bay and Great Island, far below. The main house has a common room and a screened front porch with rockers and a bay view through trees. There are picnic tables and gardens in the backyard. ⊠ *140 Commercial St., Box 816, Wellfleet 02667,* ☎ *508/349–3450. 25 rooms, 10 with bath. No credit cards. Closed mid-Oct.–mid-Apr.*

$ ☎ **Inn at Duck Creek.** Set on 5 wooded acres by a duck pond, creek, and salt marsh, this old inn consists of the circa-1815 main building and two other old houses. Rooms in the main inn (except rustic third-floor rooms) and in the Saltworks house have a simple charm. Typical furnishings include claw-foot tubs, country antiques, lace curtains, chenille spreads, and rag rugs on hardwood floors. The two-room Carriage House is cabinlike, with rough barn-board and plaster walls. There's fine dining at Sweet Seasons or pub dining with entertainment at the Tavern Room (☞ Nightlife and the Arts, *below*). ⊠ *70 Main St., Box 364, Wellfleet 02667,* ☎ *508/349–9333,* ⅁ₓ *508/349–0234. 25 rooms, 17 with bath. 2 restaurants. 2-night minimum weekends July–Aug. AE, MC, V. Closed mid-Oct.–mid-Apr. CP.* 🍽

Nightlife and the Arts

THE ARTS

Jim Wolf, Master Storyteller (☎ 508/349–0103 for information) beguiles folks of all ages with his dramatic tales of both past and present Cape Cod lore and legend. July and August show times are Wednesday through Friday at 7:30 PM at the Wellfleet United Methodist Church (⊠ Main St.).

During July and August the First Congregational Church (⊠ 200 Main St., ☎ 508/349–6877) trades the serenity of worship for **Sunday evening concerts.** The music begins at 8 PM and has included opera, blues, jazz, and chamber music.

The drive-in movie is alive and well on Cape Cod at the **Wellfleet Drive-In Theater** (⊠ 51 U.S. 6, South Wellfleet, ☎ 508/349–7176 or 508/255–9619). Films start at dusk nightly in season, and there's a miniature golf course.

On Saturday evening in July and August during the **Wellfleet Gallery Crawl,** Wellfleet's art galleries are open for cocktail receptions to celebrate show openings. You can walk from gallery to gallery meeting the featured artists and checking out their works.

The well-regarded **Wellfleet Harbor Actors Theater** (⊠ Kendrick St. past E. Commercial St., ☎ 508/349–6835) presents world premieres of American plays, satires, farces, and black comedies in its mid-May–mid-October season. This is the place for provocative experimental theater.

NIGHTLIFE

Beachcomber (⊠ Ocean View Dr., Cahoon Hollow Beach, off U.S. 6, ☎ 508/349–6055) is big with the college crowd. It's right on the beach, with national touring acts most nights, weekend happy hours with live reggae, and dancing nightly in summer. Indoors or at tables by the beachfront bar, you can order from a menu of fun appetizers, salads, burgers, seafood, barbecue, and frozen drinks. There's also a raw bar.

A number of organizations sponsor outdoor activities at night, including the **Massachusetts Audubon Wellfleet Bay Wildlife Sanctuary**'s (☞ *above*) night hikes and lecture series.

The **Tavern Room** (✉ 70 Main St., ☎ 508/349–7369), set in an 1800s building with a beam ceiling, a fireplace, and a bar covered in nautical charts, has live entertainment from jazz to pop to country to Latin ensembles. Munchies are served alongside the menu of traditional and Latin/Caribbean-inspired dishes.

Kick up your heels and grab a twirling partner for a long-standing Wellfleet tradition, the **Wednesday Night Square Dance.** Down at the town pier in July and August, the music and live calling by master caller Toots begins at 7 and lasts as long as *you* can.

Outdoor Activities and Sports

Brand new in 2000 and already bustling is the state-of-the-art Skateboard Park down at **Baker's Field** (✉ Kendrick Ave. just past Wellfleet Town Pier). Professionally designed for tricks and safety, the park is manned by local teens. For the little ones, the town has built a good-size play area with all kinds of slides, tunnels, and places to climb.

BEACHES

Public Beaches. The spectacular dune-backed Atlantic beaches **White Crest** and **Cahoon Hollow** charge daily parking fees of $10 to nonresidents in season only. Extensive storm-induced erosion has made the cliffs to most of Wellfleet's ocean beaches quite steep—so be prepared for an exerting trek up and down the dune slope. White Crest is a prime surfer hangout where the dudes often spend more time waiting for waves than actually riding them. Cahoon Hollow has lifeguards, rest rooms, and a restaurant and music club on the sand (☞ Nightlife and the Arts, *above*). Both beaches tend to attract younger and slightly rowdier crowds; Cahoon Hollow in particular is known as a big Sunday afternoon party place. **Marconi Beach,** part of Cape Cod National Seashore, charges $7 for daily parking or $20 for a season pass that provides access to all seven National Seashore beaches. **Mayo Beach** just west of Wellfleet Harbor is free. But swimming here is only pleasant around high tide—once the water recedes, it's all mud and sharp shells. You can park free at the small lot by **Great Island** on the bay.

Restricted Beaches. Resident or temporary resident parking stickers are required for access to Wellfleet beaches in season only, from the last week of June through Labor Day (some hotels and rental agencies give parking stickers to their guests or to people renting houses). To get a weekly ($25) or season ($75) pass, visit the Beach Sticker Booth on the town pier with your car registration in hand and a proof-of-stay form, available from rental agencies and hotels. For the rest of the year anyone can visit the beaches for free. Note that people arriving on foot or by bicycle can visit the beaches at any time; the sticker is for parking only. **LeCount Hollow** and **Newcomb Hollow** are the restricted ocean beaches; the **Indian Neck** harbor beach and the **Duck Harbor** bay beach past Great Island are also restricted. For more information call the Wellfleet Chamber of Commerce (☎ 508/349–2510).

The **Wellfleet Ponds,** nestled in the woods between U.S. 6 and the ocean, were formed by glaciers and are fed by underground springs. Mild temperatures and clear, clean water make swimming pleasant for the whole family, a refreshing change from the bracing salty surf of the Atlantic. They are also perfect for canoeing, sailing, or kayaking (boats are available from Jack's Boat Rentals; ☞ *below*). These fragile ecosystems have called for restricted use, and a Wellfleet beach sticker (☞ *above*) is required in season. The sticker is only for cars, however; so anyone can walk over or ride a bike to the ponds and dive in. Motorized boats are not allowed.

BIKING

The Cape Cod Rail Trail (☞ Close-Up: Riding the Rail Trail *in* Chapter 4) ends at the South Wellfleet post office. Other scenic routes for bicyclists include the winding, tree-lined Old County Road, just outside Wellfleet center at the end of West Main Street. Ambitious riders can bike all the way to Truro on this often bumpy road, but do watch for vehicular traffic around the tight curves. Ocean View Drive, on the ocean side, provides for many miles of cycling in wooded areas. If you get too hot, there are several ponds along the route perfect for a quick dip.

The Wellfleet Chamber of Commerce publishes a pamphlet, "Bicycling in Wellfleet," with an annotated map.

Black Duck Sports Shop (⊠ U.S. 6 at LeCount Hollow Rd., South Wellfleet, ☎ 508/349–9801, 508/349–2335 off season) rents a variety of bikes.

Idle Times Bike Shop, Inc. (⊠ U.S. 6, just west of Cahoon Hollow Rd., ☎ 508/349–9161) opens Memorial Day and rents bikes, trail-a-bikes (a tandem bike with a backseat for children who are big enough to pedal), and trailer attachments for the littler passengers. The shop also offers repairs and sells parts and assorted accessories. Depending on the crowds and weather, it usually remains open until Columbus Day.

Wellfleet Cycles Ltd. (⊠ 54 E. Commercial St., ☎ 508/349–9322) rents bicycles in a convenient, in-town location. Sailing lessons are also available.

BOATING

Fun Seekers (☎ 508/349–1429) offers windsurfing instruction and guided mountain-bike and kayak tours by appointment. Children's programs are available; the company closes in the off-season.

Jack's Boat Rentals (⊠ Gull Pond, ☎ 508/349–7553; ⊠ U.S. 6, ☎ 508/349–9808 for long-term rentals) provides canoes, kayaks, sailboards, Sunfish, pedal boats, surfboards, boogie boards, and sailboards. Guided tours are also available.

Wellfleet Marine Corp. (⊠ Wellfleet Town Pier, ☎ 508/349–2233) rents motorboats in various sizes and sailboats by the hour or the day.

FISHING

You can climb aboard the charter boat *Jac's Mate* (⊠ Wellfleet Town Pier, ☎ 508/255–2978) for fishing expeditions in search of bass and blues.

Fishing trips are operated on a walk-on basis from spring through fall on the *Navigator* (⊠ Wellfleet Town Pier, ☎ 508/349–6003). Rods, reels, and bait are included.

Fishing licenses are not required for saltwater fishing, and many anglers hit the outer beaches to surf-cast for bluefish and striped bass. Rods, bait, and some advice are available at the **Black Duck Sports Shop** (☞ *above*).

GOLF AND TENNIS

Wellfleet maintains several tennis courts down at **Baker's Field** near the Town Pier. Court time, from late June until the end of August, is $10 per hour for singles and $12 per hour for doubles; call the Recreation Department to reserve (☎ 508/349–0330).

Chequessett Yacht Country Club (⊠ Chequessett Neck Rd., ☎ 508/349–3704) is a semiprivate club (public use on space-available basis) with a nine-hole golf course and five hard-surface tennis courts by the bay. Lessons are available.

Oliver's (⊠ U.S. 6, ☏ 508/349–3330) has one Truflex and seven clay courts, offers lessons, and arranges matches.

SURFING

The Atlantic-coast **Marconi** and **White Crest** beaches are the best for surfing. Surfboard rentals can be arranged at Jack's Boat Rentals (☞ *above*).

NEED A BREAK?

Chances are, you've seen this place before. The popular franchise **Box Lunch** (⊠ 50 Briar La., ☏ 508/349–2178) serves up hot and cold roll-up sandwiches, a style they claim to have invented and perfected. For breakfast, lunch, or dinner, the fillings vary, but they're always tasty. This tiny place gets ferociously busy in the summer season—call your order in ahead of time if you can.

Shopping

Blue Heron Gallery (⊠ 20 Bank St., ☏ 508/349–6724) is one of the Cape's best galleries, with contemporary works—including Cape scenes, jewelry, sculpture, and pottery—by regional and nationally recognized artists, among them Steve Allrich and Del Filardi.

Cape Impressions Gallery (⊠ 313 Main St., ☏ 508/349–6479) is one of the few shops open year-round in Wellfleet and has a nice selection of fine art, gifts, and the beautiful stained-glass works of Thomas Brophy.

Cove Gallery (⊠ 15 Commercial St., ☏ 508/349–2530) features the works of John Grillo, Tomi dePaola, and Leonard Baskin, among others, with Saturday night artist receptions in July and August.

Davis Gallery (⊠ 2766 U.S. 6, ☏ 508/349–0549) makes its home in what was once a hideously ugly building on the highway. New owners have turned the place into a very respectable and attractive gallery featuring contemporary art and fine crafts.

Eccentricity (⊠ 361 Main St., ☏ 508/349–7554) keeps the corner of Main and Briar offbeat. One of the most interesting stores on the Cape, it sells gorgeous kimonos, ethnic-inspired cotton clothing, African carved-wood sculptures, barbershop paintings, odd Mexican items, and trinkets.

Herridge Books (⊠ 11 E. Main St., between U.S. 6 and town center, ☏ 508/349–1323) is a perfect store for a town that has hosted so many writers. Its dignified literary fiction, art and architecture, literary biography and letters, mystery, Americana, sports, and other sections are full of used books in very nice condition. Herridge also carries new books on the Cape and its history.

I Used to Be a Tree (⊠ 326 Main St.,, ☏ 508/349–1234) is an odd name considering conservation and preservation are the themes here. At any rate, the little barn is full of all manner of curious games, toys, frames, puzzles, jewelry, gadgets, clocks, and carved figures all made from— you guessed it—wood.

Jacob Fanning Gallery (⊠ 25 Bank St., ☏ 508/349–9546) represents the work of several established local artists, including Joyce Zavorskas, Jane Lincoln, and Lynn Shaler.

Jules Besch Stationers (⊠ 15 Bank St., ☏ 508/349–1231) brings back the art of elegance and extreme good taste with an extraordinary collection of cards, fine stationery, journals, papers, and pens. Proprietor

Michael Tuck's warm and welcoming nature is as beautiful as his products. He also offers full calligraphy services.

Karol Richardson (⊠ 11 W. Main St., ☎ 508/349–6378) fashions women's wear in luxurious fabrics and sells interesting shoes, hats, and jewelry. The store may look and sound a little New York for Wellfleet, but the clothing is original.

Kendall Art Gallery (⊠ 40 E. Main St., ☎ 508/349–2482) carries contemporary art, including Harry Marinsky's bronzes in the sculpture garden, John French's brightly colored ceramic renderings of real and whimsical building facades, and watercolors by Walter Dorrell.

Left Bank Gallery (⊠ 25 Commercial St., ☎ 508/349–9451; ⊠ 3 West Main St., ☎ 508/349–7939) has two branches. The larger one, on Commercial Street, features a display of the larger works of local and national artists and sells fine crafts in the back room facing Duck Creek. The other gallery has fine handcrafted jewelry, silk and chenille scarves, hats, and small works of original art and photography.

Nicholas Harrison Gallery (⊠ 275 Main St., ☎ 508/349–7799) is quite new but is already making a name for itself in the area of lovely and unusual American crafts. Owners Mark and Laura Evangelista are also accomplished potters, so you'll see their vibrant ceramic works.

Off Center (⊠ Off Main St., diagonally across from Eccentricity, ☎ 508/349–3634), another of the Eccentricity (☞ *above*) owners' enterprises, sells mainstream yet stylish women's clothing.

Pickle and Puppy (⊠ 355 Main St., ☎ 508/349–0606) opened in spring 2000 and seems to have found a niche. There's a bit of everything in this shop: housewares, T-shirts, gourmet foodstuffs, ceramics, luxury bath and beauty-parlor items, and a selection of unusual children's toys, games, and puzzles.

Puritan of Cape Cod (⊠ Main St.) represents a family-owned chain of sportswear stores that sells brands such as Tommy Bahama, Sperry Top-Sider, C.C. Collection, and Woolrich from Memorial Day to Labor Day. Watch for some good sales.

Secret Garden (⊠ Main St., ☎ 508/349–1444) doesn't waste any precious space—from floor to ceiling are whimsical folk art pieces, handbags, clothing, decorative accessories, and good buys on sterling silver jewelry. In the back room are the gallery pieces, prints, and paintings from the old Wellfleet Collection, now closed.

The giant **Wellfleet Flea Market** (⊠ 51 U.S. 6, South Wellfleet, ☎ 508/349–2520) sets up shop in the parking lot of the Wellfleet Drive-In Theater mid-April–June and September–October, weekends and Monday holidays 8–4; July and August, Monday holidays, Wednesday–Thursday, and weekends 8–4. You'll find antiques, sweat socks, old advertising posters, books, Beanie Babies, Guatemalan sweaters, plants, trinkets, and plenty more. On Monday and Tuesday in July and August the vendors make way for large arts and crafts shows. A snack bar and playground keep fatigue at bay.

En Route If you're in the mood for a quiet, lovely ride winding through what the Cape might have looked like before Europeans arrived, follow **Old County Road** from Wellfleet to Truro on the bay side. It's bumpy and beautiful—let's hope it stays that way—with a stream or two to pass. So cycle on it, or drive slowly, or just stop and walk to take in the nature around you.

Truro

❹ *2 mi north of Wellfleet, 7 mi southeast of Provincetown.*

Settled in 1697, Truro has had several names. It was originally called Pamet after the local Indians, but in 1705 the name was changed to Dangerfield in response to all the sailing mishaps off its shores. "Truroe" was the final choice, and Truro became the namesake of a Cornish town that homesick settlers thought it resembled. The town relied on the sea for its income—whaling, shipbuilding, and cod fishing were the main industries.

Today a town of high dunes, estuaries, and rivers fringed by grasses, rolling moors, and houses sheltered in tiny valleys, Truro is a popular retreat of artists, writers, politicos, and numerous vacationing psychoanalysts. Edward Hopper summered here from 1930 to 1967, finding the Cape light ideal for his austere brand of realism.

One of the largest towns in terms of area—almost 43 square mi—it is the smallest in population, with about 1,400 year-round residents. If you thought neighboring Wellfleet's downtown was small, wait until you see—or don't see—Truro's. It's a post office, a town hall, a shop or two. You'll know it by the sign that says DOWNTOWN TRURO at a little plaza entrance. Truro also has a library, a firehouse, and a police station, but that's about all. It's the Cape's narrowest town, and from a high perch you can see the Atlantic Ocean on one side and Cape Cod Bay on the other.

NEED A BREAK?

Jams (⊠ 14 Truro Center Rd., off U.S. 6 in Truro Center, ☎ 508/349–1616) has the answer for whoever is looking for a great picnic lunch, sandwiches, fresh produce, a bottle of wine or Evian, or a sweet treat. You won't be able to stay for lunch unless you're content getting your knees knocked on the bench outside, but with the best part of the Cape just outside the door, who would want to?

☉ For a few hours of exploring, take the children to **Pamet Harbor** (⊠ Depot Rd.). At low tide you can walk out on the flats and discover the creatures of the salt marsh. A nearby plaque identifies the plants and animals and tells of the ecological importance of the area.

On **Corn Hill** (⊠ Off Corn Hill Rd.), near the beach area of the same name, a tablet commemorates the finding of a buried cache of corn by Miles Standish and the *Mayflower* crew. They took it to Plymouth and used it as seed, returning later to pay the Native Americans for the corn they'd taken.

The **Truro Center for the Arts at Castle Hill,** housed in a converted 19th-century barn, offers summer arts-and-crafts workshops for children, as well as courses and single classes in art, crafts, photography, and writing for adults. Teachers have included notable New York– and Provincetown-based artists. ⊠ *10 Meeting House Rd.; or write to Box 756, Truro 02666,* ☎ *508/349–7511,* ℻ *508/349–7513.*

Built at the turn-of-the-20th-century as a summer hotel, the **Truro Historical Museum** is a great little gem, a repository of 17th-century firearms, mementos of shipwrecks, early fishing and whaling gear, ship models, a pirate's chest, scrimshaw, and more. One room exhibits wood carvings, paintings, blown glass, and ship models by Courtney Allen, artist and founder of Truro's historical society. The museum also hosts some ambitious local art and artifact shows each year. ⊠ *6 Lighthouse Rd., off S. Highland Rd., North Truro,* ☎ *508/487–3397.* ⊠ *$3.* ☉ *Memorial Day–Sept., daily 10–4:30.*

⑤ Truly a breathtaking sight, **Highland Light,** also called Cape Cod Light, is the Cape's oldest lighthouse. It was the last to have become automated, in 1986. The first light on this site, powered by 24 whale-oil lamps, began warning ships of Truro's treacherous sandbars in 1798—the dreaded Peaked Hills Bars alone, to the north, have claimed hundreds of ships. The current light, a white-painted 66-ft tower built in 1857, is powered by two 1,000-watt bulbs reflected by a huge Fresnel lens. Its beacon is visible for 20 mi.

One of four active lighthouses on the Outer Cape, Highland Light has the distinction of being listed in the National Register of Historic Places. Thoreau used it as a stopover in his travels across the Cape's backside, as the Atlantic side of the Outer Cape is called. Erosion threatened to cut this lighthouse from the 117-ft cliff on which it stood and drop it into the sea. Thanks to a concerted effort by local citizens and lighthouse lovers, the necessary funds were raised, and the lighthouse was moved back 450 ft to safety in 1996; it is still surrounded by the Highland Links golf course, however. Twenty-five-minute tours of the lighthouse are given daily in the summer. For those with children, all must be 51" tall to climb the tower. ⊠ *Off S. Highland Rd.,* ☎ *508/ 487–1121.* ☞ *$3.* ☉ *Mid-June–Sept., daily 10–sunset.*

The gardens of **A Touch of Heaven** are a beautiful place and, unlike most other gardens, are meant to be picked. The lawns are set with benches and birdbaths. The flowers are so abundant you don't feel guilty gathering a bunch to take home. ⊠ *Pond Village Heights, North Truro,* ☎ *no phone.* ☞ *Free.* ☉ *Daily, dawn–dusk.*

⑥ At the **Pilgrim Heights Area** of the Cape Cod National Seashore (⊠ Off U.S. 6), a short trail leads to the spring where members of a Pilgrim exploring party stopped to refill their casks, tasting their first New England water in the process. Walking through this still-wild area of oak, pitch pine, bayberry, blueberry, beach plum, and azalea gives you a taste of what it was like for these voyagers in search of a new home. "Being thus passed the vast ocean . . ." William Bradford wrote in *Of Plimoth Plantation.* "They had no friends to welcome them, no inns to entertain them or refresh their weather-beaten bodies; no houses, or much less towns to repair to, to seek for succour."

From an overlook you can see the bluffs of High Head, where glaciers pushed a mass of earth before melting and receding. Another path leads to a swamp, and a bike trail leads to Head of the Meadow Beach (☞ Outdoor Activities and Sports, *below*), often a less crowded alternative to others in the area.

Dining and Lodging

$$–$$$ ✕ **Adrian's.** Adrian Cyr's restaurant crowns a high bluff overlooking Pilgrim Lake and all of Provincetown; his cooking also hits the heights. Cayenne-crusted grilled salmon with maple-mustard sauce is one of the well-prepared dishes. Tuscan salad is a constant hit, with tomatoes, olives, fresh basil, plenty of garlic, and balsamic vinegar. Pizzas, too, are standouts, especially one made with cornmeal dough and topped with shrimp and artichokes. The outdoor deck, always enjoyable, bursts at the very popular breakfasts and brunches, served every day in season. ⊠ *Outer Reach Hotel, 535 U.S. 6, North Truro,* ☎ *508/ 487–4360. Reservations not accepted. AE, MC, V. Closed mid-Oct.– Memorial Day.*

$$–$$$ ✕ **Blacksmith Shop.** Here's where Truro locals like to linger at the bar, gossiping about what's going on at town hall while choosing from an eclectic menu with everything from seafood to Mexican items. The restaurant looks like it might have once been a place to bring your horse for a shoeing, but these days it's a nice out-of-the-way spot for company. There are excellent steaks as well as an emphasis on greens and gently cooked vegetables that would keep even a Californian happy. A short bar menu has moved south of the border, listing wraps and bean dishes that could use a little more salsa heat. Local shellfishermen deliver excellent quahogs and oysters, then hang around for the latest gossip. ⊠ *Off Rte. 6A, Truro center,* ☎ *508/349–6554. AE, D, MC, V. Closed weekdays Nov.–May.*

$$–$$$ ✕ **Montano's.** This place looms on the side of U.S. 6, a friendly, cavernous Italian-style restaurant with vaulted ceilings and hanging plants. Old harpoons, fish barrels, and lobster-pot "chandeliers" add the requisite nautical touch, and the ever-smooth Tony Bennett croons in the background. Built to handle a tour bus crowd, Montano's serves comfortable, predictable Italian-American fare with a leaning toward seafood and a solid selection of steaks. You can't go wrong with classics such as linguine and mussels in a red or white sauce or a simple thick, center-cut filet mignon with roasted garlic butter. The 14-inch pizzas are made on fresh dough, and you can taste the difference. Montano's is one of those endangered species that still offer an unlimited salad bar. This is a good place to take a big family. ⊠ *481 U.S. 6,* ☎ *508/487–2026. AE, MC, V. No lunch.*

$$–$$$ ✕ **Terra Luna.** An insider's favorite for a special breakfast, Terra Luna has become a wonderful choice for dinner as well. The dining room may lean toward cramped instead of intimate, but the food is stylish and well presented, with surprising sauces for both fish and meat dishes. The striped bass is grilled but not over-grilled, and spicy stuffed lamb chops are an excellent alternative to the usual fish. Here is a kitchen that never took "nouveau" too seriously, so the servings remained ample. ⊠ *104 Shore Rd. (Rte. 6A), North Truro,* ☎ *508/487–1019. AE, MC, V. Closed late Oct.–May.*

$$–$$$ 🏨 **Shoreline Motel.** Although the motel itself won't win any awards for beauty, the location is majestic. Because it's perched right on the sands of Cape Cod Bay with views of daily sunsets and the glimmering lights of Provincetown beyond, you won't even notice the decor. Plus, the rooms are clean and sufficient, which is really all that matters. There are standard motel rooms, suites, and a few efficiencies from which to choose, and nicely, all come with stunning water views. Efficiencies have full kitchens; suites have kitchenettes. Upstairs rooms have private balconies from which to contemplate the tides. ⊠ *Rte. 6A, Box 761, North Truro 02652,* ☎ *508/487–9109. 24 rooms.Air-conditioning, refrigerators, beach. AE, MC, V. Closed Columbus Day–late Apr.* ✑

$–$$ 🏨 **East Harbour.** This meticulously maintained complex outside Provincetown offers simple accommodations ranged around a manicured lawn and separated from the bay beach by low grasses. The two-bedroom cottages have paneled walls, colonial-style furnishings, and full kitchens. Motel rooms have large picture windows, mini-refrigerators and coffeemakers, light paneling, and '60s motel-style furnishings. A newer apartment is all white and bright, with skylights, Shaker-reproduction furnishings, a modern kitchen, and second-floor views of the harbor from a private deck. All units have individual heat, microwaves, and cable TV. ⊠ *618 Shore Rd. (Rte. 6A), Box 183, North Truro 02652,* ☎ *508/ 487–0505,* 𝔽𝔸𝕏 *508/487–6693. 7 cottages, 9 rooms, 1 apartment. Picnic area, beach, coin laundry. In season, 1-wk minimum for cottages, 2-night minimum for rooms. AE, D, MC, V. Closed Nov.–Mar.* ✑

$–$$ 🏨 **Moorlands Inn.** A proud Victorian beauty, this inn shines both inside and out. Artful touches include the creative works—both visual and musical—of innkeepers Bill and Skipper Evaul, artists and musicians, which fill the walls and rooms with lovely images and sounds. Antiques adorn the bright, uncluttered rooms in the main house, and fresh blues and whites are balanced with natural wood accents. The spacious penthouse provides a full kitchen, two bedrooms, plenty of living space, and a deck. Carriage House guests have their own private outdoor whirlpool, and other guests can gather in the communal hot tub out back. Truro is naturally quiet, and this is a beautiful place from which to enjoy the solitude. ⊠ *11 Hughes Rd., North Truro 02652,* ☎ *508/487–0663. 5 rooms, 1 apartment, 3 cottages. Croquet, outdoor hot tub. MC, V. BP.*

$–$$ 🖼 **Sea Gull Motel.** Right on the beach, this motel's location is the real draw here. Several lodging options are available, including standard motel rooms, motel studios, and beach apartments—the latter two are rented weekly, but you can rent rooms by the night. Because it's been family run for decades, you may feel like you're spending time in someone's living room. Decor is straightforward and simple, with floral comforters; some rooms are paneled in traditional Cape Cod knotty pine, making the place seem quaintly behind the times. No matter; rooms are clean, and most have splendid water views. ⊠ *Rte 6A, Box 126, North Truro, 02652,* ☎ *508/487–9070. 26 rooms. refrigerators. AE, D, MC, V. Closed Oct. 15–May 1.* 🐾

$–$$ 🖼 **Truro Vineyards of Cape Cod Inn.** Set on 5 acres of working vineyard, this 1836 former farmstead has been transformed into an elegant inn. The decor reflects the wine motif: antique casks and presses stand in the corners, and deep greens and burgundies predominate. Guest rooms have four-poster king- and queen-size beds and modern tile baths. The luxury room includes a king-size bed and an extra-large bath with a two-person whirlpool bath. Homegrown berries often garnish dishes at breakfast, which is served in the sunroom or, in nice weather, outside on the patio. A large common sundeck has sweeping views of the vineyard. ⊠ *11 Shore Rd. (Rte. 6A), North Truro 02652,* ☎ *508/487–6200,* FAX *508/487–4248. 5 rooms, 4 with bath. No smoking. MC, V. BP.*

$ 🖼 **Hostelling International–Truro.** In a former Coast Guard station right on the dunes, this handsome, well-placed hostel has kitchen facilities, a common area, and naturalist-led programs. It's also right by the ½-mi-long Cranberry Bog Trail, which takes you by a refurbished cranberry bog and an old bog house. ⊠ *N. Pamet Rd., Box 402, Truro 02666,* ☎ *508/349–3889. 42 beds. MC, V. Closed Labor Day–mid-June.*

Outdoor Activities and Sports
BEACHES

A number of Truro's **town beaches,** including Coast Guard Beach and Ballston Beach on the Atlantic, are reserved for residents and renters in season, although anyone can walk or bicycle in. Ask at the town hall (☎ 508/349–3635) about a seasonal sticker.

Corn Hill Beach (⊠ Corn Hill Rd.), on the bay, has beautiful views of Provincetown. The waters are generally calm and warm, typical of bay beaches. There are rest rooms on site as well. Parking requires a Truro beach sticker or a $5 daily fee.

Truro's other bay beaches, **Cold Storage Beach,** (⊠ Pond Rd. off Rte. 6A [Shore Rd.]), **Fisher Beach** (⊠ Fisher Rd.), **Great Hollow Beach** (⊠ Great Hollow Rd.) and **Ryder Beach** (⊠ Ryder Beach Rd. off Old County Rd.) are all beautiful and are ideal for long, lazy days of watching the boats go by, with views of Provincetown in the distance. These beaches all require the Truro beach sticker to park.

On the ocean side, three spectacular beaches are marked by massive dunes and bracing surf. **Ballston Beach** (⊠ Pamet Rd.), **Coast Guard Beach** (⊠ Coast Guard Rd.), and **Long Nook Beach** (⊠ Long Nook Rd.) all share a sense of wildness and isolation. Truro beach stickers are required for all parking.

Head of the Meadow Beach (⊠ Head of the Meadow Rd. in North Truro, part of Cape Cod National Seashore, is crowded than others in the area. Since the bathhouse burned down, it has only temporary rest-room facilities available in summer and no showers. The daily parking fee is $7 in season, or the beach can be accessed with the purchase of a season pass ($20) good for all National Seashore locations.

BIKING

The **Head of the Meadow Trail** provides 2 mi of easy cycling between dunes and salt marshes from High Head Road, off Route 6A in North Truro, to the Head of the Meadow Beach parking lot. Bird-watchers also love the area.

Bayside Bikes (⊠ 102 Rte. 6A, North Truro, ☎ 508/487–5735) rents bicycles by the hour, day, or week, with easy access to the Head of the Meadow Trail.

Cape Outback Adventures (☎ 508/349–1617) offers friendly instruction and guided tours for kayakers, mountain bikers, and beginning surfers. A mobile operation, times, and location are arranged by phone, and owner Richard Miller and staff will provide equipment. Kayak trips explore areas in both Wellfleet and Truro, while off-road mountain-biking excursions take place in the vast wooded areas within the National Seashore. Surfing instruction is available by the hour. These trips are designed for those of all ages and skill levels.

GOLF

The **Highland Golf Links** (⊠ Lighthouse Rd., North Truro, ☎ 508/487–9201), a nine-hole, par-36 course on a cliff overlooking the Atlantic and Highland Light, is unique for its resemblance to Scottish links instead of to the well-manicured and less-challenging courses that are more typically found in the United States.

SURFING

Longnook Beach (⊠ End of Longnook Rd., off U.S. 6) is good for surfing.

Shopping

Atlantic Spice Co. (⊠ U.S. 6 at Rte. 6A, North Truro, ☎ 508/487–6100) stocks a fragrant array of spices, teas, and potpourris, as well as herbs, dried flowers, locally made soaps, sauces, and kitchenware items.

Whitman House Gift Shop (⊠ County Rd. just off U.S. 6, North Truro, ☎ 508/487–3204) sells Amish quilts and other country items.

Provincetown

❼–⓲ *7 mi northwest of Truro, 27 mi north of Orleans, 62 mi from Sagamore Bridge.*

The Cape's smallest town in area and the second-smallest in year-round population, Provincetown comprises 8 square mi packed with history. The curled fist at the very tip of the Cape, Provincetown has shores that curve protectively around a natural harbor, perfect for visitors from any epoch to anchor. Historical records show that Thorvald, brother of Viking Leif Erikson, came ashore here in AD 1004 to repair the keel of his boat and consequently named the area Kjalarness, or Cape of the Keel. Bartholomew Gosnold came to Provincetown in 1602 and named the area Cape Cod after the abundant codfish he found in the local waters.

The Pilgrims remain Provincetown's most famous visitors. On Monday, November 21, 1620, the *Mayflower* dropped anchor in Province-

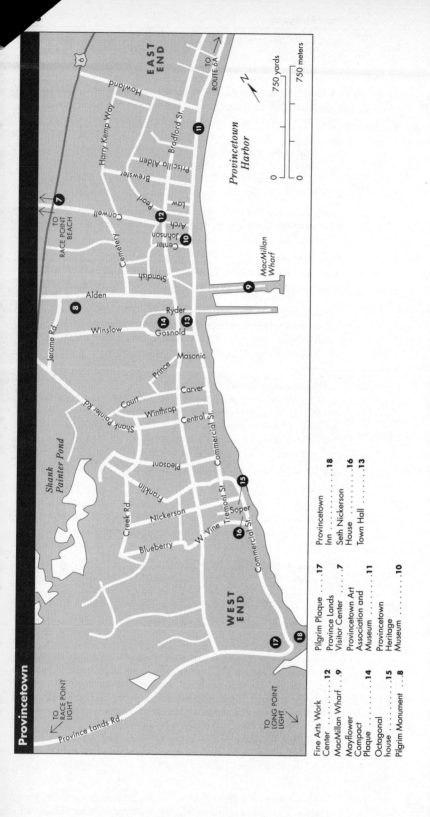

Provincetown

EAST END

WEST END

Provincetown Harbor

MacMillan Wharf

Shank Painter Pond

TO RACE POINT LIGHT

Province Lands Rd.

TO LONG POINT LIGHT

TO ROUTE 6A

TO RACE POINT BEACH

Commercial St.

Streets: Howland, Harry Kemp Way, Bradford St., Priscilla Alden, Brewster, Pearl, Law, Conwell, Center, Johnson, Arch, Cemetery, Standish, Alden, Jerome Rd., Winslow, Ryder, Gosnold, Prince, Masonic, Court, Shank Painter Rd., Winthrop, Carver, Central St., Pleasant, Franklin, Nickerson, Creek Rd., Blueberry, W. Vine, Tremont St., Soper, Commercial St.

0 — 750 yards
0 — 750 meters

Large numbered markers appear on map: 6, 7, 8, 9, 10, 11, 12, 13, 14, 15, 16, 17, 18.

town Harbor after a difficult 63-day voyage from England; while in the harbor they signed the Mayflower Compact, the first document to declare a democratic form of government in America. One of the first things the ever-practical Pilgrims did was to come ashore to wash their clothes, thus starting the ages-old New England tradition of Monday wash day. They stayed in the area for five weeks before moving on to Plymouth. Plaques and parks commemorate the landing throughout town.

During the American Revolution, Provincetown Harbor was controlled by the British, who used it as a port from which to sail to Boston and launch attacks on colonial and French vessels. In November 1778 the 64-gun British frigate *Somerset* ran aground and was wrecked off Provincetown's Race Point. Every 60 years or so, the shifting sands uncover its remains.

Incorporated as a town in 1727, Provincetown was for many decades a bustling seaport, with fishing and whaling as its major industries. In the late 19th century, groups of Portuguese fishermen and whalers began to settle here, lending their expertise and culture to an already cosmopolitan town. Fishing is still an important source of income for many Provincetown locals, but now the town ranks fourth in the world as a whale-watching, rather than -hunting, mecca.

Artists began coming here in 1899 for the unique Cape Cod light—in fact, Provincetown is the nation's oldest continuous art colony. Poets, writers, and actors have also been part of the art scene. Eugene O'Neill's first plays were written and produced here, and the Fine Arts Work Center continues to have in its ranks some of the most important writers of our time.

During the early 1900s, Provincetown became known as Greenwich Village North. Artists from New York and Europe discovered the town's unspoiled beauty, special light, lively community, and colorful Portuguese flavor. By 1916, with five art schools flourishing here, painters' easels were nearly as common as shells on the beach. This bohemian community, along with the availability of inexpensive summer lodgings, attracted young rebels and writers as well, including John Reed (*Ten Days That Shook the World*) and Mary Heaton Vorse (*Footnote to Folly*), who in 1915 began the Cape's first significant theater group, the Provincetown Players. The young, then unknown Eugene O'Neill joined them in 1916, when his *Bound East for Cardiff* premiered in a tiny wharfside East End fish house. After 1916 the Players moved on to New York. Their theater, at present-day 571 Commercial Street, is long since gone, but a model of it and of the old Lewis Wharf on which it stood is on display at the Pilgrim Monument museum.

Provincetown is a place of liberating creativity, startling originality, and significant diversity. In the busy downtown, Portuguese-American fishermen mix with painters, poets, writers, whale-watching families, cruise-ship passengers on brief stopovers, and gay and lesbian residents and visitors. In summer Commercial Street is packed with sightseers and shoppers hunting for treasures in the overwhelming number of galleries and crafts shops. At night raucous music and people spill out of bars, drag shows, and sing-along lounges galore. It's a fun, crazy place, with the extra dimension of the fishing fleet unloading their catch at MacMillan Wharf, in the center of the action.

Near the Provincetown border, **massive dunes** actually meet the road in places, turning U.S. 6 into a sand-swept highway. Scattered among the dunes are primitive cottages called dune shacks, built from flotsam and other found materials, that have provided atmospheric as well as cheap lodgings to a number of famous artists and writers over the years—among them poet Harry Kemp, Eugene O'Neill, e. e. cummings, Jack Kerouac, and Norman Mailer. The few surviving shacks are privately leased from the Cape Cod National Seashore, whose proposal to demolish the shacks was halted by their inclusion on the National Register of Historic Places in 1988. The dunes are fragile and should not be walked on, but there are paths leading through them to the ocean. You can see some of the shacks by van on Art's Dune Tours (☞ Guided Tours *in* The Outer Cape A to Z, *below*).

The **Province Lands** begin at High Head in Truro and stretch to the tip of Provincetown. The area is scattered with ponds, cranberry bogs, and scrub; unfortunately, this terrain provides optimal conditions for the deer tick, which can cause Lyme disease, so use extra caution. Bike and walking trails lace through forests of stunted pines, beech, and oak and across desertlike expanses of rolling dunes. Protected against development, the Province Lands are the "wilds" of the Cape.

A beautiful spot to stop for lunch before biking to the beach, the **Beech Forest picnic area** (⊠ Race Point Rd.) in the National Seashore borders a small pond covered with water lilies. The adjacent bike trails lead to Herring Cove and Race Point beaches, both part of the National Seashore.

❼ Inside the **Province Lands Visitor Center** in the Cape Cod National Seashore you'll find literature and nature-related gifts, frequent short films—on local geology, the U.S. Life Saving Service, and more—and exhibits on the life of the dunes and the shore. You can also pick up information on guided walks, birding trips, lectures, bonfires, and other current programs throughout the seashore, as well as on the Province Lands' own beaches, Race Point and Herring Cove, and the walking, biking, and horse trails. Don't miss the wonderful 360-degree view of the dunes and the surrounding ocean from the observation deck. ⊠ *Race Point Rd.,* ☎ *508/487–1256.* ☉ *Apr.–Nov., daily 9–5.*

Not far from the present Coast Guard station is the **Old Harbor Station,** a U.S. Life Saving Service building towed here by barge from Chatham in 1977 to rescue it from an eroding beach. It is reached by a boardwalk across the sand, and plaques along the way tell about the lifesaving service and the whales seen offshore. Inside are displays of such equipment as Lyle guns, which shot rescue lines out to ships in distress when seas were too violent to launch a surfboat, and breeches buoys, in which passengers were hauled across those lines to safety. At 6:30 on Thursday night in summer there are reenactments of this old-fashioned lifesaving procedure. ⊠ *Race Point Beach, end of Race Point Rd.,* ☎ *no phone.* 🎟 *Donations accepted; Thurs. night $3.* ☉ *July–Aug., daily 10–4.*

Provincetown's main downtown thoroughfare, **Commercial Street,** is 3 mi from end to end. In season, driving from one end of the main street to the other could take forever, so walking is definitely the way to go; you'll see signs for parking lots as you head into town. A casual stroll will allow you to see the many architectural styles (Greek Revival, Victorian, Second Empire, and Gothic, to name a few) used in the design of the impressive houses for wealthy sea captains and merchants. Be on the lookout for blue plaques fastened to housefronts explaining their historical significance—practically the entire town has been designated part of the Provincetown Historic District. The Historical Society puts out a series of walking-tour pamphlets, available for about $1 each at many shops in town, with maps and information on the history of many buildings and the more or less famous folk who have occupied them. You may also want to pick up a free Provincetown gallery guide.

The center of town is where the crowds and most of the touristy shops are. The quiet East End is mostly residential, with some top galleries, and the similarly quiet West End has a number of small inns with neat lawns and elaborate gardens. Narrated trolley sightseeing tours make the downtown circuit throughout the day, or the romantically inclined can hire a **horse-drawn carriage** from the stand in front of the town hall (⊠ 260 Commercial St.).

8 The first thing you'll see in Provincetown is the **Pilgrim Monument** stretching into the sky. This grandiose edifice, which seems somewhat out of proportion to the rest of the low-rise town, commemorates the Pilgrims' first landing in the New World and their signing of the Mayflower Compact (the first colonial-American rules of self-governance) before they set off from Provincetown Harbor to explore the mainland. Climb the 116 steps and 60 ramps of the 252-ft-high tower for a panoramic view—dunes on one side, harbor on the other, and the entire bay side of Cape Cod beyond. On an exceptionally clear day you can see the Boston skyline. At the tower's base is a museum of Lower Cape and Provincetown history, with exhibits on whaling, shipwrecks, and scrimshaw, a diorama of the *Mayflower,* and another of a glass factory.

The tower was erected of granite shipped from Maine, according to a design modeled on a tower in Siena, Italy. President Theodore Roosevelt laid the cornerstone in 1907, and President Taft attended the 1910 dedication. On Thanksgiving Eve, in a ceremony that includes a museum tour and open house, 5,000 white and gold lights that drape the tower are illuminated—a display that can be seen as far away as the Cape Cod Canal. They are lighted nightly into the New Year. ⊠ *High Pole Hill Rd.,* ☎ *508/487–1310.* ⊠ *$5.* ⊙ *Apr.–June and Sept.– Nov., daily 9–5; July–Aug., daily 9–7; last admission 45 mins before closing.*

9 **MacMillan Wharf,** with its large municipal parking facility, is a sensible place to start a tour of town. It is one of the remaining 5 of the 54 wharves that once jutted into the bay. The wharf is the base for P-town whale-watch boats, fishing charters, and party boats. The **Chamber of Commerce** is also here, with all kinds of information and events schedules. Kiosks at the wharf have rest-room and parking-lot locations, bus schedules, and other information for visitors.

The former Provincetown Marina building, on MacMillan Wharf, holds the **Expedition Whydah Sea Lab and Learning Center,** a new home for artifacts recovered from the pirate ship *Whydah,* which sank off the coast of Wellfleet more than 265 years ago. (☞ Close-Up: Cape Cod's Madame Butterfly, *below.*) The *Whydah* is the only pirate shipwreck ever authenticated anywhere in the world, and the museum is entertaining and educational, with one display on the restoration and conservation processes and another on the untold story of the 18th-century pirating life. The curators hope to collect all the recovered pieces eventually; some are on loan to other museums across the country. ⊠ *16 MacMillan Wharf,* ☎ *508/487–8899 or 800/949–3241.* ⊠ *$5.* ⊙ *Memorial Day–Labor Day, daily 10–7; Apr.–Memorial Day and Labor Day–Oct. 15, daily 10–5; Oct. 16–Dec., weekends 10–5.*

10 Housed in an 1860 Methodist church listed on the Register of Historical Places, the **Provincetown Heritage Museum** displays scenes of domestic life and workplaces from centuries past. Exhibits include antique fire-fighting equipment, fishing artifacts, and artwork donated by Provincetown-related artists. There are also antique prints and watercolors of schooners; wax figures; and a half-scale model, 66 ft long, built by a master shipbuilder, of the fishing schooner *Rose Dorothea,* which won the Lipton Cup in 1907. The museum has been closed for

182

Close-Up

CAPE COD'S MADAME BUTTERFLY

AMONG THE GENTLY SWAYING dune grasses, and beneath the waves of the Atlantic, waft the whispers of a legend. It's a classic tale with all the ingredients—true love, pirate treasure and a storm-wrought tragedy—and for nearly three centuries it has inspired fanciful embellishments and lustful searchings. Though she was wrecked in a treacherous storm back in April of 1717, the pirate ship *Whydah*, with cargo, captain, and legacy, still captivates.

As with any great legend, that of the *Whydah* has several versions, some conflicting. Many say the story began with an innocent love, when a dark, ambitious sailor named Sam Bellamy met the beautiful Maria Hallett in Wellfleet. From their brief acquaintance blossomed love, grand promises, and a child (the latter unknown to the wayward Bellamy), and the sailor gave his word that he would return, armed with riches.

He set off for England in hopes of finding fortune in shipping, but he soon realized that piracy was far more lucrative. Black Sam Bellamy, as he became known, and his men were wildly successful, taking over many dozens of ships. On a pirating jaunt in the Caribbean, Bellamy and his men captured a beauty—a slave ship loaded with gold and silver. Wealthy beyond their dreams, the men headed north with Bellamy at the helm of this exciting vessel, called the *Whydah*.

While the sailors grew rich and famous, young Maria Hallett was banished by her family because of her pregnancy. She fled to a small cabin in Eastham, awaiting the birth of her child and the return of her lover. She had a son, but he died in in-fancy, and the discovery of the dead child landed Maria in jail. Reputations were made swiftly in those days: It wasn't long before the townspeople decided Maria was a witch who had made an unholy pact with the devil. She suffered in isolation as Bellamy made his way back to Wellfleet.

Mariners have long feared the dangerous shoals, sand bars, and temperamental weather of the waters off Cape Cod. On the night of April 26, 1717, a sudden fierce storm interrupted Bellamy's homecoming, and the once sleek and swift *Whydah* was no match for the fury of the sea. Blasted by wave and wind, she met her demise in the form of a sturdy sandbar—nearly all hands were lost, and the ship lay broken, exposed to the tides.

At this point the legend sways wildly. The *Whydah* lay a mere 200 yards off the beach, within easy reach of eager treasure hunters. Historical records show that an officer, sent by the king to gather the spoils of the pirate ship, left the scene empty-handed, so the location of the gold, silver, and gems remains a mystery. Perhaps they were hidden by 18th-century scavengers; perhaps they still await discovery in the depths.

In 1984 modern-day pirate Barry Clifford and his crew uncovered some of the *Whydah*'s remains, but the promise of grand treasure has yet to unfold. In Provincetown, at the Expedition Whydah museum, you can see some artifacts from this ship and other historic wrecks.

And what of poor Maria? Some say her ghost still wanders among the dunes, wailing and cursing all sailors. Listen closely, on a foggy and ominous evening, to decide for yourself.

renovations for the past couple years; it is expected to reopen for the 2001 season. ✉ *356 Commercial St.,* ☎ *508/487–7098.* 🎫 *$3.* ☉ *Memorial Day–mid-Oct., daily 10–5:30.*

The **Provincetown Portuguese Bakery** (✉ 299 Commercial St., ☎ 508/487–1803) makes fresh Portuguese breads and pastries and serves breakfast and lunch all day from March to October. Novices should ask the counterperson which pastries to try. It's open until 11 PM in summer.

⑪ Founded in 1914 to collect and show the works of artists with Provincetown connections, the **Provincetown Art Association and Museum** (PAAM) houses a 1,650-piece permanent collection, displayed in changing exhibits that mix up-and-comers with established 20th-century figures. Some of the work hung in the four bright galleries is for sale. The museum store has books by or about local artists, authors, and topics, as well as posters, crafts, cards, and gift items. PAAM-sponsored year-round courses (one day and longer) offer the opportunity to study under such talents as Sal Del Deo, Carol Whorf Westcott, and Tony Vevers. ✉ *460 Commercial St.,* ☎ *508/487–1750.* 🎫 *$3.* ☉ *Nov.–Apr., weekends noon–4 and by appointment; Memorial Day–Labor Day, daily noon–5 and 8–10; May and Sept.–Oct., Fri.–Sun. noon–5.*

⑫ To see or hear the work of up-and-coming artists, visit the gallery or attend a reading at the **Fine Arts Work Center** (FAWC). A nonprofit organization founded in 1968, the FAWC sponsors 10 writers and 10 artists from October through May each year with a place to live and work, a stipend on which to live, and access to artists and teachers. A new summer program has open-enrollment workshops in both writing and the visual arts. The buildings in the complex around the center, which it owns, were formerly part of Day's Lumber Yard Studios, built above a lumberyard by a patron of the arts to provide poor artists with cheap accommodations. Robert Motherwell, Hans Hoffmann, and Helen Frankenthaler have been among the studios' roster of residents over the years. ✉ *24 Pearl St.,* ☎ *508/487–9960.* ☉ *Weekdays 9–5.*

The former studios of two noted artists, Edwin W. Dickinson, at 46 Pearl Street, and Charles W. Hawthorne, at 48 Pearl Street, give an idea of the proliferation of now-famous artists who worked in the area. Hawthorne's **Cape Cod School of Art,** established here in 1899 (now managed by Lois Griffel, a former student of Henry Hensche, one of Hawthorne's disciples), put the town on its path to becoming a major art colony. The school runs weeklong workshops in summer; call ahead to get the catalog. The year 1999 marked the school's centennial, and the town celebrated being home to the nation's oldest continuous art colony. ✉ *22 Brewster St.,* ☎ *508/487–0101.* ☉ *Late May–late Sept.; call for hrs.*

⑬ The **town hall** was used by the Provincetown Art Association as its first exhibit space and still exhibits paintings donated to the town over the years, including Provincetown scenes by Charles Hawthorne and WPA-era murals by Ross Moffett. The Provincetown Repertory Theatre sometimes takes up residence here. ✉ *260 Commercial St.,* ☎ *508/487–7000.* ☉ *Weekdays 8–5.*

⑭ In a little park behind the town hall is the **Mayflower Compact Plaque** (✉ Bradford St.), carved in bas-relief by sculptor Cyrus Dalin and depicting the historic signing.

NEED A
BREAK?

The **Provincetown Fudge Factory** (⌂ 210 Commercial St., ☎ 508/487–2850), across from the post office, makes silky peanut-butter cups, chocolates, saltwater taffy, yard-long licorice whips, custom-flavor frozen yogurt, and the creamiest fudge on the Cape—a must stop for those with a discriminating sweet tooth—and will ship goodies to you, too.

⓯ An **octagonal house** (⌂ 74 Commercial St., between Soper and Nickerson Sts.) built in 1850 is an interesting piece of Provincetown architecture in the West End. The house is not open to the public.

The oldest building in town, dating from 1746, is the small Cape-style
⓰ **Seth Nickerson House** (⌂ 72 Commercial St., at Soper St.), still a private home. It was built by a ship's carpenter, with massive pegged, hand-hewn oak beams and wide-board floors. Renovated in 1998, the house does not offer the glimpse into centuries past that it once did, but it's still impressive.

⓱ The bronze **Pilgrim Plaque** (⌂ West end of Commercial St.), set into a boulder at the center of a little park, commemorates the first footfall of the Pilgrims onto Cape soil—Provincetown's humble equivalent of the Plymouth Rock.

⓲ In the **Provincetown Inn** (⌂ 1 Commercial St., ☎ 508/487–9500) you can see a series of 19 murals, painted in the 1930s from old postcards, depicting life in the 19th-century town. The inn still operates as a hotel; the murals are in the lobby and hallways.

Dining and Lodging

$$$$ ✕ **Chester.** Understated and golden-hued, Chester is the newest, most expensive addition to Provincetown's upscale dining scene. Named for a pet terrier, the single-room restaurant in a Greek Revival sea captain's house has a small, elegant contemporary menu that changes regularly. The owners' philosophy that fresh quality food need not be masked with extraneous ingredients has created a reputation for memorable, beautifully presented food. The menu lists locally procured meats and seafood, and the chef collects tomatoes, herbs, and lettuces from a garden behind the restaurant. Try seasonal choices such as asparagus-and-fiddlehead risotto and lamb with cranberry jus, potatoes, and vegetables. The carefully crafted wine list has 100 selections, all the better to help you create unusual food and wine pairings, as the owners suggest. ⌂ 404 Commercial St., ☎ 508/487–8200. Reservations essential. AE, MC, V. Closed part of Dec.–Mar; call for Dec. dates.

$$$ ✕ **Café Edwige.** Nancy Meads now owns the restaurant she has run
★   for years, which is good news for one and all. Delicious contemporary American food, relaxed and friendly service, and an eclectic, homey upstairs setting—Café Edwige delivers all this night after night. Begin with a Maine crab cake, warm goat cheese on crostini, or a refreshing field-green-and-wild-lettuce salad, and then consider lobster and Wellfleet scallops over pasta with a wild mushroom, Asiago, and tomato broth, or planked local codfish with roasted corn and shiitakes. Don't pass on the wonderful desserts, such as the Cape Cod cranberry crumble served with vanilla ice cream. Breakfast here is a local institution. ⌂ 333 Commercial St., ☎ 508/487–2008. AE, MC, V. Closed Nov.–May.

$$$ ✕ **Front Street.** Front Street is so good, so consistent, and so romantic that many locals consistently rate it a contender for the title of best
★   restaurant in P-town. Chef-owners Donna Aliperti and Kathleen Cotter link classic Italian cooking to offerings from other Mediterranean regions such as Greece and southern France and even North Africa. Duck smoked in Chinese black tea is dense and luscious, served with a different lusty sauce every day; a current favorite is fresh tropical fruit with mixed peppercorns. An aromatic smoked-salmon chowder comes

and goes from the menu (there ought to be a town meeting to put it on permanently). Littleneck clams and calamari with butternut squash in a roast garlic broth is essentially a simple dish, but its unique flavors show off these traditional ingredients in a new light. The wine list is also a winner. Make sure to call well ahead for a reservation, even during the shoulder seasons, when the menu turns purely Italian. ⊠ *230 Commercial St., ☎ 508/487–9715. Reservations essential. AE, D, MC, V. Closed Jan.–mid-May.*

$$$ ✕ **Martin House.** When Provincetown seems an utter zoo, it's a relief
★ to find this island of calm and creative contemporary fare right on crazy Commercial Street. Original 1850s woodwork lends a touch of history, and Provincetown paintings grace the walls. The menu leans toward colonial fare with a sophisticated touch, including unusually flavorful chutneys, risotto, and wild game. Some of the more interesting dishes include Oysters Claudia, which matches native Wellfleets-on-the-half-shell with an Asian dipping sauce, wasabi, and pickled ginger, and pan-roasted lamb rib eye with an exotic mint chutney and quinoa–wild rice tabbouleh. ⊠ *157 Commercial St., ☎ 508/487–1327. AE, D, DC, MC, V. Closed Wed.–Thurs. in Jan.–Mar.*

$$$ ✕ **The Mews.** This town favorite is still going strong, its menu focusing on seafood with a cross-cultural flair. Some popular entrées are rich and spicy scallops, shrimp-and-crab mousse in a wonton on grilled filet mignon, and a decadent French lentil ragout with chipotle aioli sauce. Downstairs, the main dining room opens onto magnificent harbor views. A piano bar upstairs serves lunch (weekdays in summer) and dinner from a light café menu. The view of the bay from the bar is near perfect, and the gentle lighting makes this a romantic spot for a drink. Brunch is also served every day in season. Off-season Monday evenings have featured some of the town's more amusing and raucous entertainment with locally infused open-mike venues. ⊠ *429 Commercial St., ☎ 508/487–1500. Reservations not accepted. AE, D, DC, MC, V. Closed Jan. No lunch weekdays off-season or Sat. between Columbus Day and Memorial Day.*

$$–$$$ ✕ **Dancing Lobster Café Trattoria.** Chef and owner Pepe Berg put in some time at Harry's Bar in Venice and brought back to P-town rich Italian flavors and stylish whimsy. Berg has moved for the third time in four years, this time back to the restaurant where his father held court for years (known then as Pepe's Wharf). This feels like a homecoming, and although the food is tending upscale, it remains among the best prepared in Provincetown. Presentations are innovative and sophisticated, outstanding in every way. Appetizers are pure classics— carpaccio is a favorite—and the *zuppa di pesce* (Italian seafood stew) with couscous is complex and filling. The chef can sometimes be a bit too generous with the olive oil, but think of it as more of a good thing. The lobster may not dance, but the customers will—sometimes joined by Robert the bartender, a great local favorite. ⊠ *371 Commercial St., ☎ 508/487–0900. AE, D, MC, V. Closed mid-Nov.–mid-May.*

$$–$$$ ✕ **Lobster Pot.** Provincetown's Lobster Pot is fit to do battle with all the Lobster Pots anywhere (and everywhere) on the Cape. As you enter, you'll pass through one of the hardest-working kitchens on the Cape, which turns out classic New England cooking: lobsters galore, generous and filling seafood platters, and some of the best chowder around. The upstairs deck overlooks the harbor, and every time you turn around it seems to expand. It now ranks as the best lunch location in town. There's also a take-out lobster market and bakery on the premises. The bad news is that you'll have to wait in line; the good news is that the line is in the center of town, great for people-watching. ⊠ *321 Commercial St., ☎ 508/487–0842. Reservations not accepted. AE, D, DC, MC, V. Closed Jan.*

$$–$$$ ✕ **Lorraine's.** In its new, much bigger location in the East End of town, Lorraine's has an ambience that is more robust than intimate, but the Mexican-inspired menu is as finely prepared as ever. After five successful years Lorraine still keeps her hand in the kitchen—and welcomes her mother to cook alongside her on her trips from California. Specials are always worth a listen. An appetizer of three large shrimp stuffed with cheese and fresh jalapeños packs a punch, and the *mujeres* clams (steamed littlenecks in a cilantro-citrus broth) are addictive. Also wonderful is a dish called simply *carnitas,* slow-cooked pork tenderloin with fresh guacamole, salsa, sour cream, and lots of frilly greens. The vessel-shape bar draws a loyal, lively clientele. ⊠ *463 Commercial St.,* ☎ *508/487–6074. Reservations essential. MC, V. Closed Jan.–Mar.; no lunch.*

$$–$$$ ✕ **The Moors.** Buoys and nets hang everywhere—an authentic testament to the fine Portuguese seafood the Moors has been serving for almost 40 years. If this place looks like it was just tossed up by an errant wave, that's because in a way it was. After a fire destroyed it years ago, locals scoured the outer beaches for driftwood, which was used to rebuild the establishment. Mylan Costa passed the torch to new owners in 1998; patrons are happy to report that they haven't noticed that much of a difference. Specialties include a delicious soup made from *chouriço* (pork sausage) and *linguiça* (garlic-flavored sausage), sea-clam pie, and marinated swordfish steaks. Prix-fixe Portuguese dinners with a choice of three entrées are offered ($16–$20). There's entertainment in the lounge (☞ Nightlife and the Arts, *below*). ⊠ *5 Bradford St. W,* ☎ *508/487–0840. AE, D, DC, MC, V. Closed Nov.–Mar.*

$$–$$$ ✕ **Napi's.** No visit to Provincetown is complete without dinner at Napi's, an excellent Mediterranean-style restaurant. The food and the interior share a penchant for unusual, striking juxtapositions—a classical sculpture in front of an abstract canvas, for instance. On the gustatory front, look for sharp combinations such as shrimp flambé in ouzo and Metaxa, served with a tomato, garlic, and onion sauce. The menu is strong on vegetarian items with an international flair—rice heaped with spicy vegetables is one example. If you arrive early and see a man at the bar drinking, a glass of muscadet in summer and a martini in winter, hunched over the *New York Times* crossword puzzle, introduce yourself: it's Napi himself, with his wife, Helen, soon to appear from the kitchen. ⊠ *7 Freeman St.,* ☎ *508/487–1145. Reservations essential. AE, D, DC, MC, V. No lunch June–mid-Sept.*

$$–$$$ ✕ **Sal's Place.** Tucked away in the peaceful West End, this little waterfront place serves up massive portions of southern Italian specialties. Calamari and linguine, *vongole* (tiny clams) over pasta, and delicious vegetarian spinach lasagna are all longtime favorites. Determined carnivores will want to tackle the steak *pizzaiola*: a massive 25-ounce rib-eye steak served with marinara sauce. Opinions on the decor depend on your commitment to the authenticity of wine bottles in wicker, but the back dining room overlooks the harbor—the best decor there is. ⊠ *99 Commercial St.,* ☎ *508/487–1279. MC, V. Closed Nov.–Apr. and Mon.–Thurs. Oct. 2–mid-June; no lunch.*

$$ ✕ **Bubala's by the Bay.** Personality bubbles up at this funky joint, which once was a staid standby. When owner John Yingling took over in 1993, he and his crew pumped up the funk as well as the quality—the building is painted bright yellow and adorned on top with campy carved birds. The result is an inviting, mellow-delic seaside '60s feel. The kitchen rarely stops, serving breakfast, lunch, and dinner; it's strong on seafood bought directly off local boats and cut in back just hours before it's served. The Cuban cod would surprise any Cuban because it has little to do with that cuisine (except the beans), but it's wonderfully fresh and tasty. The same thing can be said of the Jamaican fish stew. The wine list is priced practically at retail, and the U-shape bar picks up into the evening. Outdoor seating along Commercial Street is a social focal point, while quieter indoor seating reaches right down to the bay. ✉ *183 Commercial St.,* ☎ *508/487–0773. AE, D, MC, V. Closed Halloween–April Fool's Day.*

$–$$ ✗ **Pucci's Harborside.** Here's a friendly, casual standby if you're looking for an easy lunch or dinner way out in the quiet East End. Perched out over the harbor on high tides, Pucci's is a relatively small place with a great water view and airy feel. It blew down several years ago during Hurricane Bob and has been sturdily rebuilt. The house specialties are a big plateful of fiery chicken wings or a wonderful, big stuffed artichoke, gleaming with garlic butter. This is a good place for a solid mushroom-and-blue-cheese burger, a Gorgonzola salad with mixed greens and roasted red peppers, a messy nachos Fiesta, and a decent shrimp scampi. The bartender serves up big, frosty Bloody Marys for steamy summer afternoons. ✉ *539 Commercial St.,* ☎ *508/487–1964. AE, MC, V. Closed mid-Oct.–late Apr.*

$ ✗ **Mojo's.** This is Provincetown's fast-food institution, where anybody who knows anything about food and happens to be in a hurry goes to grab a bite. The tiniest of kitchens turns out one of the most varied and eclectic menus in town, everything from fresh-cut French fries to fried clams with the bellies, steak subs, tacos, tofu burgers (and the regular kind), tacos, hummus, roll-up sandwiches, salads, and the best fried fish. How they crank it out, so fast and so good, is anybody's guess. It's hard to believe Mojo's has been around for 27 years, but it's even harder to believe it hasn't always been a part of Provincetown. There's some seating in the back at colorfully painted picnic tables. ✉ *5 Ryder St. Extension,* ☎ *508/487–3140. Reservations not accepted. No credit cards. Closed mid-Oct.–early May, depending on weather and crowds.*

$ ✗ **Spiritus.** The local bars close at 1 AM, at which point this pizza joint–coffee stand becomes the town's epicenter. The crowd gets so big and flamboyant that Commercial Street virtually shuts down for an hour. It's the ultimate place to see and be seen, pizza slice in hand and witty banter at the ready. In the morning, the same counter serves up restorative coffee and croissants. ✉ *190 Commercial St.,* ☎ *508/487–2808. No credit cards. Closed Nov.–Apr.*

$$–$$$ ✗🏠 **The Commons.** Built as an inn in the 1860s, this combination guest house and bistro had long suffered a reputation for tackiness until Carl Draper and Chuck Rigg took the helm in 1994. The rooms are now comfortable and tasteful, with wide-board floors, antique furnishings, Oriental carpets, and marble-tile baths. Most rooms have a view of the bay; some have private balconies. All have TVs and fans or air-conditioning. The bistro has an innovative, ever-changing Continental menu, with dishes such as seared halibut with lobster risotto. You can relax in the garden or at the deck bar that overlooks the bay. ✉ *386 Commercial St., 02657,* ☎ *508/487–7800 or 800/487–0784,* 🆁🆇 *508/487–0358. 14 rooms. Restaurant, bar. AE, MC, V. Restaurant closed Jan.–mid-Feb.; guest house closed Jan.–Easter. CP.* 🍽

$$$$ 🏠 **Brass Key.** Conveniently close to restaurants, shops, galleries, and
★ nightlife, this complex of buildings is fast becoming Provincetown's most luxurious resort. The main house, originally an 1828 sea captain's home, is beautifully restored, and there are several other carefully groomed buildings and cottages. Rooms include antique furniture with a decidedly Victorian flavor, floral wall-coverings, and ultramodern amenities; all have Bose stereos, mini-refrigerators, and TV/VCRs (there's a videocassette library). Deluxe rooms also have gas fireplaces and whirlpool baths or French doors opening out to wrought-iron balconies. A widow's-walk sundeck has a panoramic view of Cape Cod Bay. Complimentary cocktails are served in the courtyard; in winter, wine is served before a roaring fire in the common room. The Brass

Key has long been favored by a largely gay clientele, but the owners and staff make everyone feel welcome and pampered. ⊠ *67 Bradford St., 02657,* ☎ *508/487–9005 or 800/842–9858,* FAX *508/487–9020. 36 rooms. Air-conditioning, in-room safes, in-room VCRs, pool. No smoking. AE, D, MC, V. CP.* ♿

$$–$$$$ 🏠 **Beaconlight Guesthouse.** It may be Provincetown outside, but within the walls of this inn is the elegance of the English countryside. The casual nature of the place fits in just fine with the designer wallpapers, freshly painted walls, antiques, and luxurious touches such as six pillows per bed and televisions and VCRs. Outside, three different decks offer varied, stunning views of the entire town and the harbor, and an outdoor hot tub invites soaks under the night skies. The guest house is between busy Commercial and Bradford streets, so it's close to everything but still a bit quieter than places on the main thoroughfares. ⊠ *12 Winthrop St., 02657,* ☎ *508/487–9603 or 800/696–9603. 7 rooms, 3 suites. In-room data ports, outdoor hot tub. AE, D, DC, MC, V. CP.* ♿

$$$ 🏠 **Best Western Chateau Motor Inn.** This may be part of a chain, but the personal attention of owners Charlotte and Bill Gordon, whose family has run the place for decades, shows in the landscaped grounds and in the well-maintained modern rooms with wall-to-wall carpeting and tile baths. Atop a hill with expansive views from picture windows of marsh, dunes, and sea, the motel is a longish walk to the center of town. Children under 18 stay free. ⊠ *105 Bradford St. Extension, Box 558, 02657,* ☎ *508/487–1286 or 800/528–1234,* FAX *508/487–3557. 54 rooms. Pool. AE, D, DC, MC, V. CP. Closed Nov.–Apr.* ♿

$$–$$$ 🏠 **Bayshore and Chandler House.** Formerly known as the Hargood
★   House, this apartment complex on the water, ½ mi from the town center, is a great option for longer stays. Many of the individually decorated units have decks and large water-view windows; all have full kitchens, modern baths, and phones. Number 8 is like a light, bright beach house on the water, with three glass walls, cathedral ceilings, private deck, dining table, and chairs. Number 20 has a fireplace and a home-style kitchen. Rental is mostly by the week in season; there's a two-night minimum off-season. Pets are welcome. ⊠ *493 Commercial St., 02657–2413,* ☎ *508/487–9133,* FAX *508/487–0520. 25 apartments. Beach. AE, MC, V.* ♿

$$–$$$ 🏠 **Fairbanks Inn.** This comfortable, nicely decorated inn on the next street over from Commercial Street includes the 1776 main house and auxiliary buildings. Guest rooms have four-poster or canopy beds, Oriental rugs on wide-board floors, and antique furnishings, and some have fireplaces or kitchens. Many original touches remain here, from the 18th-century wallpaper to artifacts from the inn's first residents. The baths are on the small side, but they help preserve the colonial integrity of the home. The wicker-filled sunporch and the garden are good places for afternoon cocktails. ⊠ *90 Bradford St., 02657,* ☎ *508/487–0386 or 800/324–7265,* FAX *508/487–3540. 13 rooms, 1 efficiency. Parking (free). AE, MC, V. CP.* ♿

$–$$$ 🏠 **The Captain and His Ship.** Built in 1887 for a sea captain, this stately mansard-roof Victorian is only a short walk from the center of town and is across the street from Provincetown bay. Jim Baer, who has owned the house since 1980, fills his immaculate, spacious rooms with period antiques and Oriental carpets. Room 3, done in subtle earth tones, has a king-size bed, a gas fireplace, and private access to the garden. Most rooms have water views; all have color TVs, VCRs, mini-refrigerators, and hair dryers. Seven rooms have private baths, while two have hallway baths. Some have private decks. A Continental breakfast is included in July and August. There's a fee for the limited parking. ⊠ *164 Commercial St., 02657,* ☎ *508/487–1850 or 800/400–*

2278. *9 rooms, 7 with bath. Air-conditioning. No smoking. MC, V. Closed Nov.–Apr.* ✎

$–$$$ ☵ **Christopher's by the Bay.** The rooms in this art-inspired inn are named after the greats—Rembrandt, Picasso, Monet, Van Gogh—and elegantly appointed with brass beds and rich fabrics. Many have splendid views of the bay. The building itself is a graceful old Victorian and is surrounded by carefully maintained gardens and brick patios. Rooms on the upper floors share bathrooms. Set back from the bustle, it's still a quick walk to the center of town. Like most other inns in town, there's a minimum stay requirement during holidays in peak season. ⊠ *8 Johnson St.,* ☎ 🖷 *508/487–9263. 10 rooms, 5 with bath. Air-conditioning, in-room data ports. AE, MC, V. BP.* ✎

$–$$$ ☵ **The Masthead.** Hidden away in the quiet west end of Commercial Street, the Masthead is a charming cluster of shingle houses that overlook a lush lawn, a 450-ft-long boardwalk, and a private beach. Spacious rooms, efficiencies, apartments, and fully outfitted cottages offer a wide range of lodging options. The cottages, for instance, which sleep four to seven, are an ideal choice for families or larger groups and for longer stays (children under 12 stay free). The deepwater and in-shore moorings right on the property make this a great choice if you're boating into town. This is classic Provincetown—friendly, unpretentious, and homey. ⊠ *31–41 Commercial St., Box 577, 02657,* ☎ *508/487–0523 or 800/395–5095,* 🖷 *508/487–9251. 7 apartments, 3 cottages, 2 efficiencies, 9 rooms. Beach, dock. AE, D, DC, MC, V.* ✎

$–$$ ☵ **Dexter's Inn.** This inn is so blended into a complex of buildings that you'll hardly realize it's there. Just a block from the action of Commercial Street, the inn offers simple and pretty rooms at some of Provincetown's more reasonable prices. Adorned with colorful quilts or lace bedspreads, beds are backed by wicker or brass headboards. Ceiling fans whir above the decent-size rooms, most of which have views of the Pilgrim Monument. The lowest-price accommodations share a bath, but most have their own. Relax in the keeping room by the warmth of a gas fireplace in winter. ⊠ *6 Conwell St.,* ☎ *508/487–1911 or 888/521–1999. 15 rooms, 12 with bath. Air-conditioning. MC, V. CP.* ✎

$ ☵ **The Meadows.** At the far west end of Bradford Street, between the town center and the beach, these motel-like rooms may not have the convenience of an in-town location, but they do offer a good value, especially for families. Rooms are bright, clean, and comfortable, furnished in standard motel style. All rooms have cable TV and mini-refrigerators. Bicycle rentals and tennis courts are nearby. ⊠ *122 Bradford St. Extension, 02657,* ☎ *508/487–0880 or 888/675–0880,* 🖷 *508/487–4691. 20 rooms. MC, V.*

Nightlife and the Arts

THE ARTS

The **Beach Plum Music Festival,** held in August at the Provincetown Town Hall (⊠ 260 Commercial St., ☎ 508/349–6874), is a series of popular folk and jazz concerts by performers such as Wynton Marsalis, Arlo Guthrie, Queen Ida, and Holly Near.

Provincetown Inn (⊠ 1 Commercial St., ☎ 508/487–9500) hosts several unusual theater productions in summer. Look for shows performed by C.A.P.E. Inc. Theatre and those offered during the Provincetown Fringe Festival. There are also nights of live music.

The year 2000 was only the second annual **Provincetown International Film Festival** (✎), but most of the screenings were sold out. Aside from a full schedule of independent films, it has guest appearances by such notables as director John Waters, Lily Tomlin, and Christine Vachon. The festival is held in mid-June.

The **Provincetown Playhouse Mews Series** (✉ Town Hall, 260 Commercial St., ☎ 508/487–0955) presents classical chamber, folk, ethnic, and jazz concerts in summer.

The **Provincetown Repertory Theatre** (☎ 508/487–0600) stages a summer lineup of classic and modern drama, presenting Equity actors and local talent. The theater held its 2000 season performances in the town hall; call for current performance locations.

The **Provincetown Theatre Company** (☎ 508/487–8673) presents classics, modern drama, and new works by local authors year-round, as well as staged readings and playwriting workshops.

The **Provincetown Reservations System** (✉ 293 Commercial St., ☎ 800/648–0364 or 508/487–2400) offers a quick and painless way to secure theater and show tickets. The system also handles lodging and travel reservations.

NIGHTLIFE

Atlantic House (✉ 6 Masonic Pl., ☎ 508/487–3821), the grandfather of the gay night scene and the only gay bar open year-round, is frequented mostly by men. It has several lounge areas and an outdoor patio.

Boatslip Beach Club (✉ 161 Commercial St., ☎ 508/487–1669) holds a gay and lesbian tea dance daily from 3:30 to 6:30 on the outdoor pool deck. The club has indoor and outdoor dance floors. There is ballroom dancing here, as well, in addition to two-stepping Thursday through Sunday nights.

The **Cape Cod National Seashore** offers summer evening programs, such as slide shows, sunset beach walks, concerts (local groups, military bands), and sing-alongs, at its Province Lands Visitor Center (✉ Race Point Rd., ☎ 508/487–1256), and sunset campfire talks on the beaches in Provincetown.

Club Euro (✉ 258 Commercial St., ☎ 508/487–2505) has weekend concerts by big names in world music, including African music, Jamaican reggae, Chicago blues, and Cajun zydeco. The venue itself is fantastic: the 1843 Congregational church, later a movie theater, is an eerie ocean dreamscape with oceanic sea-green walls with a half-submerged three-dimensional mermaid, spouting fish, and a black ceiling high above. Pool tables and a late-night menu are available.

The **Crown & Anchor Complex** (✉ 247 Commercial St., ☎ 508/487–1430) in the heart of town was ravaged by fire in 1998. The restoration of the building's original facade and its many different venues kept contractors working through most of the 1999 summer season. By summer 2000 the complex was back in action, with several bars, a cabaret with drag shows, and a game room. Next door, **Whalers' Wharf** is also slowly recovering from the fire. The wharf is much like an old European marketplace, with a brick pathway that leads straight to the beach and a rotunda theater alive with street performers and entertainment.

Governor Bradford Restaurant (✉ 312 Commercial St., ☎ 508/487–9618) is perhaps better known as a sometimes-rowdy pool and dance hall. In the afternoon you can play chess or backgammon at the tables by the window. After 8 PM the place revs up with live music or a DJ spinning everything from hip-hop to disco. On weekend nights get set for a raucous evening of drag-hosted karaoke.

The **Moors** (✉ 5 Bradford St. W., ☎ 508/487–0840; ☞ Dining, *above*) has presented Lenny Grandchamp in its lounge for nearly 20 years. Grandchamp tells jokes, plays the piano, sings, and leads sing-alongs up to six nights a week in season.

Napi's (⊠ 7 Freeman St., ☎ 508/487–1145; ☞ Dining, *above*) of-fers easy-listening piano in its upstairs lounge on weekends, nightly in season.

Pied Piper (⊠ 193A Commercial St., ☎ 508/487–1527) draws hordes of gay men to its post–tea dance gathering at 6:30 every evening in July and August and weekends in the shoulder seasons. Later in the evening, though, the crowd is mostly, though not exclusively, women. The club has a deck overlooking the harbor, a small dance floor with a good sound system, and two bars.

Vixen (⊠ 336 Commercial St., ☎ 508/487–6424) is a lively women's club that gets packed with dancers. On most nights, before the dance crowd sets in, there are both national and local women entertainers. Look for live music and comedy. There are also a couple of pool ta-bles in the front room.

Outdoor Activities and Sports

BEACHES

The entire stretch of Commercial Street is backed by the waters of Provincetown Harbor, and most hotels have private beaches. Farther in town there are plenty of places to settle on the sand and take a re-freshing dip. Just be mindful of the busy boat traffic.

Race Point Beach (⊠ Race Point Rd.), one of the Cape Cod National Seashore beaches in Provincetown, has a wide swath of sand stretch-ing far off into the distance around the point and Coast Guard sta-tion. Behind the beach is pure duneland, and bike trails lead off the parking lot. Because of its position, on a point facing north, the beach gets sun all day long, whereas the east-coast beaches get fullest sun early in the day. Parking is available, and lifeguards are stationed in season; the beach has showers and rest rooms. From mid-June through Labor Day, parking costs $7 per day, or $20 for a yearly pass good at all Na-tional Seashore beaches.

Herring Cove Beach, a National Seashore beach, is calmer (and a lit-tle warmer) than Race Point Beach, though it's not as pretty since the parking lot isn't hidden behind dunes. But the parking lot to the right of the bathhouse is a great place to watch the sunset, and there's a hot-dog stand. Lifeguards are on duty in season, and there are showers and rest rooms. For fees, *see* Race Point Beach, *above.*

For a day of fairly private beachcombing and great views, you can walk across the stone jetty at low tide to **Long Point,** a sand spit south of town with two lighthouses and two Civil War bunkers, named Fort Useless and Fort Ridiculous because they were hardly needed. It's a 2-mi walk across soft sand—beware of poison ivy and deer ticks if you detour from the path—or hire a boat at Flyer's (☎ 508/487–0898) to drop you off and pick you up.

BIKING

The **Province Lands Trail** is a 5¼-mi loop off the Beech Forest parking lot on Race Point Road, with spurs to Herring Cove and Race Point beaches and to Bennett Pond. The paths wind up and down hills amid dunes, marshes, woods, and ponds, affording spectacular views. More than 8 mi of bike trails lace through the dunes, cranberry bogs, and scrub pine of the National Seashore, with many access points, includ-ing Herring Cove and Race Point.

The **Beech Forest** bike trail (⊠ Off Race Point Rd.) in the National Seashore offers an especially nice ride through a shady forest to Ben-nett Pond.

Arnold's (⊠ 329 Commercial St., ☎ 508/487–0844) rents all types of bikes, children's included.

Nelson's Bike Shop and Rentals (⊠ 43 Race Point Rd., ☎ 508/487–8849), across from the Beech Forest bike trail, rents a variety of bikes, including trailers, and has a deli with picnic-ready food; parking is free. Nelson's was long known for its horseback-riding trips in the dunes, but, sadly, property disputes have put an end to these grand excursions.

Ptown Bikes (⊠ 42 Bradford St., ☎ 508/487–8735) has Trek and Mongoose mountain bikes at good rates; the shop also provide free locks and maps.

BOATING

Bay Lady II Excursion Schooner (⊠ MacMillan Wharf, ☎ 508/487–9308) is a beautiful 73-ft sailing schooner. Two-hour cruises leave three times daily. Passengers are welcome to bring their own spirits and snacks for this scenic and peaceful sail.

Flyer's Boat Rental (⊠ 131A Commercial St., ☎ 508/487–0898) has kayaks, surfbikes, Sunfish, Hobies, Force 5s, Lightnings, powerboats, and rowboats. Flyer's will also shuttle you to Long Point (☞ Beaches, *above*).

Schooner Hindu (⊠ MacMillan Wharf, ☎ 508/487–3000) offers a graceful sail in the waters around Provincetown; trips leave four times daily.

FISHING

You can go for fluke, bluefish, and striped bass on a walk-on basis from spring through fall with **Cap'n Bill & Cee Jay** (⊠ MacMillan Wharf, ☎ 508/487–4330 or 800/675–6723).

HORSEBACK RIDING

The **Province Lands Horse Trails** lead to the beaches through or past dunes, cranberry bogs, forests, and ponds.

Bayberry Hollow Farm (⊠ 27 W. Vine St. Extension, ☎ 508/487–6584) has pony rides year-round. It's fun for children.

KAYAKING

Kayaking has become increasingly popular on the Cape, and **Off the Coast Kayak Company** (⊠ 3 Freeman St., ☎ 508/487–2692 or 877/785–2925) offers guided kayak tours as well as equipment rentals for those who wish to venture out on their own. Choose a tandem kayak or go solo; all skill levels are welcome. Several tours are offered, including sunset paddles, town harbor tours, clinics, and the special Kayak Clambake tour.

TENNIS

Bissell's Tennis Courts (⊠ 21 Bradford St. Extension, ☎ 508/487–9512) has five clay courts and offers lessons. It's open from Memorial Day to September.

Provincetown Tennis Club (⊠ 286 Bradford St. Extension, ☎ 508/487–9574) has several outdoor clay courts open to nonmembers; you can also take lessons with the resident tennis pro.

TOURS

There are several pleasant options if you choose to leave your car behind and let someone else show you around. Whether it's for an historic tour through town or a wilder excursion into the dunes, you'll be well taken care of.

Art's Dune Tours (⊠ Commercial and Standish Sts., ☎ 508/487–1950 or 800/894–1951) has been taking eager passengers into the dunes of

Province Lands for more than 50 years. Bumpy but controlled rides are peppered with lively tales of legend and history. These popular 1- to 1½-hour tours are offered several times daily; especially mysterious are the sunset and moonlight tours.

King of the Hill Adventures (✉ Standish St., ☎ 508/487–1296 or 877/738–6377) has off-road vehicles that take passengers into the dunes for narrated rides several times daily.

Provincetown Trolley, Inc. (✉ Commercial and Ryder Sts., ☎ 508/487–9483) takes you through the crowded and narrow streets of Provincetown—you'll be glad you're not driving. Tours leave every half hour, from 10 to 4 and then again at 5, 6 and 7. Meet the trolley in front of the town hall.

Willie Air Tours (✉ Provincetown Airport, off Race Point Rd., ☎ 508/487–9989) offers the kind of vistas mostly reserved for birds.

From the water, **Y & C Harbor Tours** (✉ MacMillan Wharf, ☎ 508/487–4330) offers 40-minute narrated cruises around Provincetown Harbor daily on the hour.

WHALE-WATCHING

One of the joys of Cape Cod is spotting whales while they're swimming in and around the feeding grounds at Stellwagen Bank, about 6 mi off the tip of Provincetown. On a sunny day the boat ride out into open ocean is part of the pleasure, but the thrill, of course, is in seeing these great creatures. You might spot minke whales; humpbacks (who put on the best show when they breach); finbacks; or perhaps the most endangered great whale species, the right whale. Dolphins are a welcome sight as well; they play in the boat's bow waves. Many people also come aboard for birding, especially during spring and fall migration. You can see a great variety of birds at sea—gannets, shearwaters, and storm petrels, among many others.

Several boats take whale-watchers out to sea—and bring them back—with morning, afternoon, or sunset trips lasting from three to four hours. All boats have food service, but remember to take sunscreen and a sweater or jacket—the breeze makes it chilly. Some boats stock seasickness pills, but if you're susceptible, come prepared.

The municipal parking area by the harbor in Provincetown fills up by noon in summer. Consider taking a morning boat to avoid crowds and the hottest sun. And although it may be cold in April, it is one of the better months for spotting whales, who at that time have just migrated north after mating and are very hungry. Good food is, after all, what brings the whales to this part of the Atlantic.

The **Cape Cod Whale Watch** is a new addition. Naturalist-narrated trips leave three times daily from MacMillan Wharf. ✉ *Ticket office at MacMillan Wharf or 293 Commercial St.,* ☎ *508/487–4079 or 877/487–4079.* ✆ *$18 (seasonal variations).* ☉ *Tours Apr.–Oct.*

Dolphin Fleet tours are accompanied by scientists from the Center for Coastal Studies in Provincetown who provide commentary while collecting data on the whale population they've been monitoring for years. They know many of the whales by name and will tell you about their habits and histories. Reservations are required. ✉ *Ticket office in Chamber of Commerce building at MacMillan Wharf,* ☎ *508/349–1900 or 800/826–9300.* ✆ *$18 (seasonal variations).* ☉ *Tours Apr.–Oct.*

The **Portuguese Princess** sails with a naturalist on board to narrate. The snack bar offers Portuguese specialties. ✉ *Tickets available at 70 Shank Painter Rd. ticket office or at Whale Watchers General Store,*

309 Commercial St., ☎ *508/487–2651 or 800/442–3188.* 🎫 *$15–$19.* ⊙ *Tours May–Oct.*

Shopping

ART GALLERIES

Albert Merola Gallery (✉ 424 Commercial St., ☎ 508/487–4424) has 20th-century and contemporary master prints and Picasso ceramics and features artists from in and around Provincetown, Boston, and New York, including James Balla and Richard Baker.

Bangs Street Gallery (✉ 432 Commercial St., ☎ 508/487–0743) represents contemporary artists as well those from the 1970s.

Berta Walker Gallery (✉ 208 Bradford St., ☎ 508/487–6411) deals in Provincetown-affiliated artists, including Selina Trieff, Nancy Whorf, and many of the artists who migrated here from the now-defunct Long Point Gallery.

The **DNA Gallery** (✉ 288 Bradford St., ☎ 508/487–7700) represents a wide variety of artists working in various media, including many former fellows from the Fine Arts Work Center. The gallery also hosts readings, films, and concerts.

Julie Heller Gallery (✉ 2 Gosnold St., ☎ 508/487–2169) has a good combination of contemporary artists as well as some Provincetown icons. The gallery has works from the Sol Wilson estate, as well as those from such greats as Robert Motherwell and Blanche Lazzell.

Hilda Neily Art Gallery (✉ 432 Commercial St., ☎ 508/487–6300) is named for its featured artist, who was once a student of Impressionist painter Henry Hensche. Her oil paintings follow the same tradition of magical light and color.

New on the art scene, the **Schoolhouse Center** (✉ 494 Commercial St., ☎ 508/487–4800) has already established itself as a vital addition to the town. Housing both the Driskel Gallery and the Silas Kenyon Gallery, it has changing exhibitions of antiques as well as the works of local and national artists and photographers. A full range of performing- and visual-arts classes is available year-round, and the center has a Summer Reading Series on Thursday evening at 8. A true community organization, the center is open Thursday through Monday.

The **William Scott Gallery** (✉ 439 Commercial St., ☎ 508/487–4040) primarily shows contemporary works such as John Dowd's reflective, realistic Cape 'scapes.

SPECIALTY STORES

Far Side of the Wind (✉ 389 Commercial St., ☎ 508/487–3963) specializes in New Age paraphernalia, including some unique Native American jewelry and artifacts, gifts, books, and music. Psychic readings are also available.

Giardelli Antonelli (✉ 417 Commercial St., ☎ 508/487–3016) specializes in quality handmade clothing by local designers. Hand-knit sweaters are especially popular.

Impulse (✉ 188 Commercial St., ☎ 508/487–1154) has contemporary American crafts, including jewelry and an extraordinary kaleidoscope collection. The Autograph Gallery features framed photographs, letters, and documents signed by celebrities.

Kidstuff (✉ 381 Commercial St., ☎ 508/487–0714) carries unusual, colorful children's wear.

Marine Specialties, Inc. (⊠ 235 Commercial St., ☎ 508/487–1730) is akin to a vast basement full of treasures, knickknacks, and clothing; it even has that same pleasantly musty smell. Here you can purchase some very reasonably priced casual and military-style clothing, as well as sea shells, marine supplies, stained-glass lamps, candles, rubber sharks (you get the idea), and prints of old advertisements.

Moda Fina (⊠ 349 Commercial St., ☎ 508/487–6632) offers an eclectic selection of women's fashions, shoes, and jewelry. Style is the word here, from flowing linen or silk night wear to the funky and casual. Unique Mexican crafts are also for sale.

Remembrances of Things Past (⊠ 376 Commercial St., ☎ 508/487–9443) deals with articles from the 1920s to the 1960s, including Bakelite and other jewelry, telephones, neon items, ephemera, and autographed celebrity photographs.

Silk & Feathers (⊠ 377 Commercial St., ☎ 508/487–2057) carries an assortment of fine lingerie, women's clothing, and jewelry.

Tim's Used Books (⊠ 242 Commercial St., ☎ 508/487–0005) has volumes of volumes—rooms of used-but-in-good-shape books, including some rare and out-of-print texts. It's a great place to browse for that perfect book to read on vacation.

Wa (⊠ 184 Commercial St., ☎ 508/487–6355) is an oasis of peace and Zenlike tranquillity. Unusual and Japanese-inspired items include fountains, home accent pieces, and even a collection of framed and sometimes frightening tropical insects.

West End Antiques (⊠ 146 Commercial St., ☎ 508/487–6723) specializes in variety: $4 postcards, a $3,000 model ship, handmade dolls, and better-quality glassware—Steuben, Orrefors, and Hawkes.

THE OUTER CAPE A TO Z

Arriving and Departing

By Bus
Plymouth & Brockton Street Railway (☎ 508/746–0378) provides bus service to Provincetown from downtown Boston and Logan Airport, with stops en route. The Logan Direct airport express service bypasses downtown Boston and makes stops in Plymouth, Sagamore, Barnstable, and Hyannis.

By Ferry
Ferries shuttle to Provincetown from Boston and Plymouth in season.

TO AND FROM BOSTON

Bay State Cruise Company makes the three-hour trip between Commonwealth Pier in Boston and MacMillan Wharf in Provincetown daily from mid-June to Labor Day, and then weekends only through Columbus Day. The company also runs a two-hour express boat from Boston to Provincetown's Fishermen's Wharf daily from June to Columbus Day. ☎ 617/748–1428 in Boston, 508/487–9284 in Provincetown. *3-hr boat trip $18 one-way, $5 additional for bicycles; same-day round-trip $30, $10 additional for bicycles. 2-hr express boat $39 one-way, $5 additional for bicycles; same-day round-trip $75, $10 additional for bicycles.*

TO AND FROM PLYMOUTH

Capt. John Boats' passenger ferry makes the 1½- to 2-hour trip between Plymouth's State Pier and Provincetown from Memorial Day to mid-June, weekends; mid-June to Labor Day, daily. Schedules allow for day excursions. One-way fares are only available in May, June, and September. ☎ 508/747–2400; 800/242–2469 in MA. ✉ $25 round-trip, $14 one-way, bicycles $2 additional for.

By Car

From the Bourne Bridge to Provincetown, expect to be in your car for a good hour and a half—and that's when traffic is light. During peak driving times (Friday afternoon and Saturday), expect lengthy delays on Route 6 at Exit 9 and then again just before the Wellfleet town line—here Route 6 narrows to one lane. For a more pleasant drive that will avoid aggravating delays (but won't get you there faster), detour on historic Route 6A. From the bridge to Orleans the road ambles alongside some beautiful old sea captains' homes and dozens of antiques and specialty shops.

By Plane

Cape Air serves Boston year-round from **Provincetown Municipal Airport** (✉ Race Point Rd., ☎ 508/487–0241).

CARRIERS
Cape Air/Nantucket Airlines (☎ 508/771–6944 or 800/352–0714) flies direct from Boston to Hyannis and Provincetown year-round and from New Bedford to Martha's Vineyard and Nantucket. Cape Air has joint baggage agreements with eight major U.S. airlines and with KLM.

Getting Around

By Bus

Plymouth & Brockton Street Railway (☎ 508/746–0378) has service between Boston and Provincetown, with stops at many towns in between, including Wellfleet center, Truro, and Provincetown.

The **Shuttle** (☎ 800/352–7155), run by the Cape Cod Regional Transit Authority, provides a desperately needed transportation boost. The shuttle begins its route at Dutra's Market in Truro and continues to Provincetown along Route 6A; it stops wherever a passenger or roadside flagger dictates. Once in Provincetown, the shuttle continues up Bradford Street, with alternating trips to Herring Cove Beach and Pilgrim Park. It runs every 20 minutes and is outfitted to carry bicycles. Immensely popular and reasonably priced ($1), its only trouble seems to be finding parking on the Truro end—plans are in the works to find alternate areas for parking. The shuttle runs from the end of June until mid-September; from then until October 15, service is within Provincetown only.

By Car

Driving to Provincetown from other points on the Cape is mostly a scenic adventure. The wooded surrounds of Truro break into a breathtaking expanse of open water and sand dunes, with the skyline of Provincetown beyond. All of this is spectacular, unless you are caught in horrendous traffic. The busiest time is early morning—especially on days when the sun is reluctant to shine—when it seems that everyone on Cape Cod is determined to make it to Provincetown. Traffic is heaviest around Wellfleet, and since the road is just one lane until North Truro, it can be slow going. Except during the traffic-heavy season, you'll find the drive from Wellfleet to Provincetown beautiful and only 25 minutes in duration.

By Taxi

Cape Cab (✉ Provincetown, ☎ 508/487–2222).

Mercedes Cab Co. (✉ 35 Alden St., ☎ 508/487–3333) offers local and long-distance service in vintage Mercedes sedans.

Provincetown Taxi (✉ Box 277, North Truro, ☎ 508/487–8294).

Contacts and Resources

B&B Reservation Agencies

In summer, lodgings should be booked as far in advance as possible—several months for the most popular cottages and B&Bs. Assistance with last-minute reservations is available at the Cape Cod Chamber of Commerce information booths. Off-season rates are much reduced, and service may be more personalized. Keep in mind that most lodging establishments require a minimum stay of three days during peak season and holiday times.

Provincetown Reservations System (✉ 293 Commercial St., Provincetown 02657, ☎ 508/487–2400 or 800/648–0364, FAX 508/487–6517) makes reservations year-round for accommodations, shows, transportation, and more.

Camping

Coastal Acres Camping Court, Inc. (✉ W. Vine St. Extension, ☎ 508/487–1700), in Provincetown, is within walking distance of the town center. There are numerous tent and RV sites, with showers, rest rooms, and a small general store for supplies. It's open until November.

The only camping permitted on the Cape Cod National Seashore itself is in nonrented, self-contained RVs at Provincetown's **Race Point Beach** (✉ Provincetown, ☎ 508/487–2100).

Car Rentals

Budget rents cars at Provincetown Municipal Airport in season (☎ 508/487–4557).

Children's Activities

The wonderful **Wellfleet Public Library** (✉ 55 W. Main St., ☎ 508/349–0310), in a town visited by numerous authors of children's books, has a story hour at 10:30 on Tuesday and Friday.

Massachusetts Audubon Wellfleet Bay Sanctuary (✉ U.S. 6, Box 236, South Wellfleet 02663, ☎ 508/349–2615) has daily and weekly nature programs and camps for children.

Emergencies

For rescues at sea call the **Coast Guard** (☎ 508/487–0070 in Provincetown). Boaters should use Channel 16 on their radios.

DENTISTS

Provincetown Dental Associates (✉ 86 Harry Kemp Way, ☎ 508/487–9936).

PHARMACIES

Adams Pharmacy, Inc. (✉ 254 Commercial St., Provincetown, ☎ 508/487–0069) is open until 10 PM.

A & P Pharmacy (✉ 28 Shank Painter Rd., Provincetown, ☎ 508/487–3738) offers prescription service until 8 PM.

Wellfleet Pharmacy (✉ Main St., Wellfleet, ☎ 508/349–3774).

MEDICAL CLINICS

Outer Cape Health Services (✉ 3130 U.S. 6, Wellfleet, ☎ 508/349–3131; ✉ 49 Harry Kemp Way, Provincetown, ☎ 508/487–9395).

Guided Tours

CRUISES

The gaff-rigged schooner **Bay Lady II** makes two-hour sails, including a sunset cruise, across Provincetown Harbor into Cape Cod Bay. Private charters are also available. ✉ *MacMillan Wharf, Provincetown,* ☎ *508/487–9308.* 🎫 *$10–$15.*

FLIGHTSEEING

Cape Air (Provincetown Municipal Airport, ✉ Race Point Rd., ☎ 800/352–0714).

TROLLEY TOURS

The **Provincetown Trolley** leaves from the town hall on the hour from 10 to 7 and on the half hour from 10:30 to 4:30; you can also hop on and off at the Provincetown Inn, Province Lands Visitor Center, and Provincetown Art Association. Points of interest on the 40-minute narrated tours include the downtown area and the Cape Cod National Seashore. ☎ 508/487–9483. ✆ $9. ☉ May–Oct.

VAN TOURS

Art's Dune Tours, around for years, are hour-long narrated van tours through the National Seashore and the dunes around Provincetown. ✉ *Standish and Commercial Sts., Provincetown,* ☎ *508/487–1950; 800/894–1951 in MA.* ✆ *$12 daytime, $15 sunset.* ☉ *Tours mid-Apr.– late Oct.; call for schedule*

House Rentals

Rental opportunities are plenty on this quiet part of the Cape, particularly in Wellfleet and Truro.

Compass Vacation Rentals (✉ Main St. Mercantile Unit 19, U.S. 6, Eastham 02642, ☎ 508/240–7600 or 800/724–1307, ℻ 508/240–6943, ✎) is one of many realtors with a listing of available apartments and houses on the Outer Cape.

Roslyn Garfield Associates (✉ 115 Bradford St., Provincetown 02657, ☎ 508/487–1308) lists rentals for Wellfleet, Truro, and Provincetown.

Libraries

The **Wellfleet Public Library** (✉ W. Main St., ☎ 508/349–0310) is particularly nice. The collection of books is impressive, as is the children's section. Also available are videos, books on tape, and Internet access. A full schedule of readings, yoga classes, and lectures is offered year-round.

Outdoor Activities and Sports

CANOEING AND KAYAKING

Off the Coast Kayak Company (☞ Outdoor Activities and Sports *in* Provincetown, *above*) rents kayaks and leads group paddles on the Outer Cape.

Visitor Information

LOCAL CHAMBERS OF COMMERCE

Provincetown (✉ MacMillan Wharf, Box 1017, 02657, ☎ 508/487–3424). It's open from March until New Year's Day.

Provincetown Business Guild (✉ 115 Bradford St., Box 421, 02657, ☎ 508/487–2313) specializes in gay tourism, and the office is open year-round.

Truro (✉ U.S. 6 at Head of the Meadow Rd., Box 26, North Truro 02652, ☎ 508/487–1288). The office is open weekends only in June and September; daily in July and August.

Wellfleet (✉ Box 571, 02667, ☎ 508/349–2510; information center off U.S. 6 in South Wellfleet). It's open from mid-May through Columbus Day.

7 PORTRAITS OF CAPE COD

The Cape's Six Seasons

A Brief History of the Cape

Home, Sweet Rental Home

Cape and Islands Books

THE CAPE'S SIX SEASONS

So MUCH HAS BEEN MADE of the difference between "the season" and "the off-season" that you might think a magic switch flicks Cape Cod on and off. The truth is something more complicated. Far from having only two seasons, much less the traditional four, the Cape really has six identifiable seasons, each distinct and dramatic.

From early April until Memorial Day, it's spring—a season that can be beautiful, bursting with wildflowers and green grass. Locals shake out the kinks and get ready. In the old days you could smell tar and pitch as fishermen prepared their nets for another season at sea. Now, you're likelier to smell paint as bed-and-breakfast owners put on a fresh coat. Provincetown's exotic little gardens, nurturing unusual plants brought home from seaports around the world, are in their glory. And it's a great time to enjoy bird walks, nature hikes, and country drives, along with lower prices and a lack of crowds.

"The season" is generally thought to start on Memorial Day, but, in fact, the holiday is a quick and busy harbinger, nothing more. After the long weekend a lull sets in that lasts until the end of June, when schools finally let out. The weather is still iffy—balmy one minute, freezing the next—but everything is open, and not too many summer people have arrived yet. It's the calm before the rush—more anticipation than real hustle.

Then, all at once, comes the high tide of visitors—from late June through early September, with surges on July 4 and Labor Day. Inns, restaurants, beaches, and roads can be packed; everything is open and bustling, and the weather can be warm and beautiful. It's not a time for people who don't enjoy being in a crowd at least occasionally, although it's always possible to walk a bit farther on the beach and escape everyone.

Some people find the spell between Labor Day and Columbus Day the most intriguing time on the Cape. School's back in session, so families are gone. Yet summer often sticks around. And the ocean, not nearly as fickle as the air, holds on to its warmth. Many people not tied to summer vacations have discovered this so-called shoulder season.

Columbus Day to New Year's becomes a time of slow retraction. Under crisp blue skies in the clear autumn light, the lower Cape's cover of heather, gorse, cranberry, bayberry, box berry, and beach plum resembles, in Thoreau's words, "the richest rug imaginable spread over an uneven surface." Oaks and swamp maples burnish into beautiful, subtle tones, and fields of marsh grass that were green just a few weeks ago become tawny, like a miniature African savanna. Thanksgiving is a particularly evocative moment, when the Cape's Pilgrim history comes to the fore.

And then—winter. The mainland gets much more snow than the Cape, but nonetheless, it's a stark, tough time. The landscape has a desolate, moorish quality, which makes the inns and restaurants that do remain open all the more inviting. Many museums and shops close, although a year-round economy has emerged, especially around Hyannis, Falmouth, and Orleans. The Cape's community-theater network continues throughout the year, and many golf courses remain open, except when it snows (some open their courses to cross-country skiers). Intimate B&Bs and inns make romantic retreats after a day of ice fishing or pond skating.

Still, the farther toward the fringes you get, the quieter life becomes. If you believe that less can be more, this is the time to discover what others never could have found during the hectic high-season months.

Many towns on the Cape celebrate Christmas in an old-fashioned way, with wandering carolers and bands, theatrical performances, crafts sales, and holiday house tours. The Cape's holiday season extends from Thanksgiving to New Year's, with celebratory activities including First Night celebrations in many towns.

— Seth Rolbein

A BRIEF HISTORY OF THE CAPE

THE FORTUNES of Cape Cod have always been linked to the sea. For centuries fishermen in search of a livelihood, explorers in search of new worlds, and pilgrims of one sort or another in search of a new life—down to the beach-bound tourists of today—all have turned to the waters around this narrow peninsula arcing into the Atlantic to fulfill their needs and ambitions.

Although some maintain that Iceland Viking Thorvald broke his keel on the shoals here in 1004, European exploration of Cape Cod most likely dates from 1602, when Bartholomew Gosnold sailed from Falmouth, England, to investigate the American coast for trade opportunities. He first anchored off what is now Provincetown and named the cape for the great quantities of cod his crew managed to catch. He then moved on to Cuttyhunk, in the Elizabeth Islands (which he named for the queen); on leaving after a few weeks, he noted the crew was "much fatter and in better health than when we went out of England." Samuel de Champlain, explorer and geographer for the king of France, visited in 1605 and 1606; his encounter with the resident Wampanoag tribe in the Chatham area resulted in deaths on both sides.

None of these visits, however, led to settlement; that began only with the chance landing of the Pilgrims, some of whom were Separatists rebelling from enforced membership in the Church of England, others merchants looking for economic opportunity. On September 16, 1620, the *Mayflower*, with 101 passengers, set out from Plymouth, England, for an area of land granted them by the Virginia Company (Jamestown had been settled in 1607). After more than two months at sea in the crowded boat, they saw land; it was far north of their intended destination, but after the stormy passage and in light of the approach of winter, they put in at Provincetown Harbor on November 21. Before going ashore they drew up the Mayflower Compact, America's first document establishing self-governance, because they were in an area under no official jurisdiction, and dissension had already begun to surface.

Setting off in a small boat, a party led by Captain Myles Standish made a number of expeditions over several weeks, seeking a suitable site for a settlement in the wilderness of woods and scrub. Finally they chose Plymouth and there established the colony, governed by William Bradford, that is today re-created at Plimoth Plantation.

Over the next 20 years settlers spread north and south from Plymouth. The first parts of Cape Cod to be settled were the bay-side sections of Sandwich, Barnstable, and Yarmouth (all incorporated in 1639), along an old Indian trail that is now Route 6A. Most of the newcomers hunted, farmed, and fished; salt hay from the marshes was used to feed cattle and roof houses.

The first homes built by the English settlers on Cape Cod were wigwams built of twigs, bark, hides, cornstalks, and grasses, which they copied from those of the local Wampanoag people who had lived here for thousands of years before the Europeans arrived. Eventually, the settlers stripped the land of its forests to make farmland, graze sheep, and build more European-style homes, though with a New World look all their own. The steep-roof saltbox and the Cape Cod cottage—still the most popular style of house on the Cape and copied all over the country—were designed to accommodate growing families.

A newly married couple might begin by building a one- or two-room half-Cape, a rather lopsided 1½-story building with a door on one side of the facade and two windows on the other; a single chimney rose up on the wall behind the door. As the family grew, an addition might be built on the other side of the door large enough for a single window, turning the half-Cape into a three-quarter-Cape; a two-window addition would make it a symmetrical full Cape. Additions built onto the sides and back were called warts. An interesting feature of some Cape houses is the graceful bow roof, slightly curved like the bottom of a boat (not surprising, since ships' carpenters did much of the house building as well). More noticeable, often in the older houses, is a profusion of small, irregularly shaped and located windows in the gable ends; Thoreau wrote of one such house that it looked as if each of the various occupants "had punched a hole where his necessities required it." Many ancient houses have been turned into historical museums. In some, docents take you on a tour of the times as you pass from the keeping room—the heart of the house, where meals were cooked at a great hearth before which the family gathered for warmth—to the nearby borning room, in whose warmth babies were born and the sick were tended, to the relatively showy front parlors, where company was entertained. Summer and winter kitchens, backyard pumps, beehive ovens, elaborate raised-wall paneling, wide-board pine flooring, wainscoting, a doll made of corn husks, a spinning wheel, a stereopticon, a hand-stitched sampler or glove—each of these historic remnants gives a glimpse into the daily life of another age.

The Wampanoags taught the settlers what they knew of the land and how to live off it. Early on they showed them how to strip and process blubber from whales that became stranded on the beaches. To coax more whales onto the beach, men would sometimes surround them in small boats and make a commotion in the water with their oars until the whales swam to their doom in the only direction left open to them. By the mid-18th century, as the supply of near-shore whales thinned out, the hunt for the far-flung sperm whale began, growing into a major New England industry and making many a sea captain's fortune. Wellfleet, Truro, and Provincetown were the only ports on the Cape that could support deepwater distance whaling (and these were overtaken by Nantucket and New Bedford), but ports along the bay conducted active trade with packet ships carrying goods and passengers to and from Boston. Cape seamen were in great demand for ships sailing from Boston, New York, and other deepwater ports. In the mid-19th century the Cape saw its most prosperous days, thanks largely to the whaling industry.

The decline in whaling hit the economy hard, and the Cape began cultivating tourism in the 19th century. Whereas previously people traveled from Boston to and along the Cape only by stagecoach or packet boat, in 1848 the first train service from Boston began, reaching to Sandwich; by 1873 it had been extended little by little to Provincetown. In the 1890s President Grover Cleveland made his Bourne residence (now gone) the Cape's first "summer White House" (to be followed in the 1960s by John F. Kennedy). Grand seaside resorts grew up for summering families, and Cape Cod began to court visitors actively.

ARTISTS WERE DRAWN to Provincetown starting in the early part of the 20th century. In 1899 Charles W. Hawthorne opened the Cape Cod School of Art and taught the Impressionist *en plein air* style (outdoors) on the beach. It was the first of several art schools established over the next few years that promoted Provincetown as an art colony. Writers (including John Reed and the young Eugene O'Neill) started the Provincetown Players, which would be the germ of Cape community theater and professional summer-stock companies. The Barnstable Comedy Club, founded in 1922 and still going strong, is the most notable of the area's many amateur groups; novelist Kurt Vonnegut acted in its productions in the 1950s and 1960s and had some of his early plays produced by the group. Professional summer stock began with the still-healthy Cape Playhouse in Dennis in 1927, and its early years featured Bette Davis (who was first an usher), Henry Fonda, Ruth Gordon, Humphrey Bogart, and Gertrude Lawrence. In 1928 the University Players Guild (today called Falmouth Playhouse) opened in Falmouth, attracting the likes of James Cagney, Orson Welles, Josh Logan, Tallulah Bankhead, and Jimmy Stewart (who, while on summer vacation from Princeton, had his first bit part during Falmouth's first season).

The idea of a Cape Cod canal, linking the bay to the sound, was studied as early as the 17th century, but not until 1914 did the privately built canal merge the waters of the two bays. It was not, however, a thunderous success; too narrow and winding, the canal allowed only one-way traffic and created dangerous currents. The federal government bought it in 1928 and had the U.S. Army Corps of Engineers rebuild it. In the 1930s three bridges—two traffic and one railroad—went up, and the rest is the latter-day history of tourism on Cape Cod.

The building of the Mid Cape Highway (U.S. 6) in the 1950s marked the great boom in the Cape's growth, and the presidency of John F. Kennedy, who summered in Hyannis Port, certainly added to the area's allure. In 1961 President Kennedy signed the legislation that established Cape Cod National Seashore. Today the Cape's summer population is more than 500,000, 2½ times the year-round population.

Though tourism, construction, and light industry are the mainstays of the Cape's economy these days, the earliest inhabitants' occupations have not disappeared.

There are still more than 100 farms on the Cape, and the fishing industry—including lobstering, scalloping, and oyster aquaculture, as well as the fruits of fishing fleets such as those in Provincetown and Chatham—brings in $2 million a month.

Visitors are still drawn here by the sea: scientists come to delve into the mysteries of the deep, artists come for the light, and everyone comes for the charm of the beach towns, the beauty of the white sand, the softness of the breezes, and the roaring of the surf.

HOME, SWEET RENTAL HOME

ONE OF THE JOYS of a Cape Cod vacation can be renting a furnished house—one with plenty of space to accommodate extended families or groups of friends, a backyard or deck where you can kick back with a cool drink, and a kitchen where you can boil up some lobsters. If a house rental is in your plans, you must act early. Cape realtors report it's not unusual to get bookings a year in advance, and by January the summer pickings in many prime beachfront areas may already be getting slim.

Most Cape Cod house rentals run weekly, from Saturday to Saturday—you can move in on Saturday afternoon, and you must be out the following Saturday morning. There may be some flexibility outside the peak summer season of July 4 through Labor Day, but otherwise you'll have to cross the bridges with the rest of the week-to-week renters. Two-week minimums for some choicer properties are not uncommon. Note that summer rental prices can vary, even from week to week, depending on the most popular times; mid- to late June and early September prices may be a bit lower.

If you're planning a summer rental, here are some tips on making arrangements:

Decide where you'd like to be. Most Cape realtors deal with a particular town or area (☞ Contacts and Resources *in* the A to Z section of the appropriate Cape chapter), so narrow your search before you start asking about houses. Do you want to be on Cape Cod Bay or Nantucket Sound, or close to the beaches of Cape Cod National Seashore? Will you stay put, or do you want a central location that lets you explore the Cape easily? The towns on the Cape have different personalities, and that will be part of your decision making.

Know what you'll need. How many bedrooms (with how many beds) and how many bathrooms? Is there a washer and dryer? What about a yard or a deck? How close to the beach? Is a water view important? Or a quiet street where the children can play? Do you want to be close to a supermarket and other stores, or are you willing to drive a bit?

Ask what's included. Most Cape rentals do not include linens, so you'll need to bring your own sheets and towels. Most do provide a cleaning service before you arrive and after you leave, but ask whether you're responsible for taking trash to the dump or for handling other cleanup tasks. Inquire about using the phone; some owners restrict their tenants to local calls, while others ask for a deposit to cover your phone bill. If you want anything special—a crib, bicycles, a barbecue grill, air-conditioning—be sure to ask.

Request a photo. If you can't visit properties in person, ask the realtor or owner to send you pictures of the house. What is described as cozy may turn out to be cramped, and old-fashioned may sometimes be run-down, photos will help avoid misunderstandings.

Use the Internet. Some realtors post photos of properties on their Web sites, and a growing number of property owners handle their own rentals via the 'Net.

Before you head for the Cape, ask your realtor or the local chamber of commerce about beach stickers. Many towns with resident-only beaches or ponds will sell you a weekly beach permit if you present a copy of your lease at the town hall or the town recreation department.

Then pack up the family, pick up some lobsters, and relax in that lawn chair. At least for the week, you're home.

—Carolyn Heller

CAPE COD BOOKS

Cape Cod has inspired a vast number of books, from hard-to-find, locally published autobiographical reminiscences to handsomely illustrated coffee-table books from national publishers. You can explore some of these before your trip at your local library, bookstore, or on-line bookseller, but try to make time to visit some of the many excellent bookstores on the Cape. You may well make a special discovery that will illuminate your stay. For information about local newspapers and magazines, *see* Media *in* Smart Travel Tips A to Z.

General

The classic works on Cape Cod are Henry David Thoreau's readable and often entertaining *Cape Cod,* an account of his walking tours in the mid-1800s, and Henry Beston's 1928 *The Outermost House,* which chronicles the seasons during a solitary year in a cabin at ocean's edge. Both reveal the character of Cape Codders and are rich in tales and local lore, as well as observations of nature and its processes. *Cape Cod: Henry David Thoreau's Complete Text with the Journey Recreated in Pictures,* by William F. Robinson, is a handsome New York Graphics Society edition (currently out of print), illustrated with prints from the period and current photographs. *Cape Cod Pilot,* by Josef Berger (alias Jeremiah Digges), is a Works Progress Administration guidebook from 1937 that is filled with "whacking good yarns" about everything from religion to fishing, as well as a lot of still-useful information. *A Place Apart: A Cape Cod Reader* (1993), edited by Robert Finch, includes writings about the Cape from dozens of writers, from Melville to Adam Gopnik.

History

Cape Cod, Its People & Their History, by Henry C. Kittredge (first published in 1930), is the standard history of the area, told with anecdotes and style as well as scholarship. Now out of print, *Sand in Their Shoes,* compiled by Edith and Frank Shay, is a compendium of writings on Cape Cod life throughout history. *Of Plimoth Plantation* is Governor William Bradford's 17th-century description of the Pilgrims' voyage to and early years in the New World. *Art in Narrow Streets,* by Ross Moffett; *Figures in a Landscape,* by Josephine Del Deo; *Provincetown as a Stage,* by Leona Rust Egan; and *Time and the Town: A Provincetown Chronicle,* by Provincetown Playhouse founder Mary Heaton Vorse, paint the social landscape of Provincetown in the first half of the 20th century, concentrating on the lives and contributions of the many writers, artists, and actors that flocked to the town. More recently, Paul Schneider has written *The Enduring Shore: A History of Cape Cod, Martha's Vineyard, and Nantucket,* another look at the region's past. An illustrated history for children, *The Story of Cape Cod,* by Kevin Shortsleeve (available through *Cape Cod Life,* ☎ 800/645–4482), is written in rhyming verse and sure to entertain. *In the Footsteps of Thoreau: 25 Historic and Nature Walks on Cape Cod,* by Adam Gamble, is a useful guide for naturalists and Thoreau admirers. For baseball fans, Christopher Price's *Baseball by the Beach: A History of America's National Pastime on Cape Cod* provides a portrait of the Cape Cod Baseball League and the Cape's version of summer on the sandlots.

Fiction

Herman Melville's *Moby-Dick,* set on a 19th-century Nantucket whaling ship, captures the spirit of the whaling era. *Cape Cod,* by William Martin, is an historical novel and mystery following two families from the *Mayflower* voyage to the present, with lots of Cape history and flavor along the way. Norman Mailer's *Tough Guys Don't Dance* is a murder mystery set in Provincetown and Truro, and several other novels use Provincetown as a setting, including *Resuscitation of a Hanged Man,* by Denis Johnson, and Anne LeClaire's *Grace Point.* Other writers who have set books on the Cape are Margot Arnold, Rick Boyer, Philip A. Craig, Virginia Rich, Marie Lee, Alice Hoffman, Jane Langton, David Osborn, and Phoebe Atwood Taylor. *Cape Cod Stories,* edited by John Miller, is a collection of Cape-related short fiction by such luminaries as Edgar Allen Poe, John Cheever, and Sylvia Plath. *Cape Discovery,* edited by Bruce

Smith and Catherine Gammon, an anthology of poetry and fiction by former fellows of the Fine Arts Work Center in Provincetown, includes the work of noted contemporary American writers such as Louise Glück, Michael Cunningham, Dean Albarelli, and Maria Flook. Many of the poems in *Passing Through,* Pulitzer Prize–winning poet Stanley Kunitz's 1997 collection, evoke the natural beauty of the Cape, and several refer to his garden on Commercial Street in Provincetown.

Memoir

In *Heaven's Coast,* Mark Doty, a Provincetown writer, recounts the death of his lover, Wally Roberts, from complications caused by AIDS. In a similar vein, David Gessner's *A Wild, Rank Place: One Year on Cape Cod* combines insights about the Cape with reminiscence about battling cancer and confronting his father's death. In *The Salt House: A Summer on the Dunes of Cape Cod,* Cynthia Huntington describes a summer during the first year of her marriage spent in a tiny Outer Cape beach shack called Euphoria, while Gladys Taber chronicles her life on the Cape at Still Cove in *My Own Cape Cod.* Journalist Alec Wilkinson portrays a different side of Cape life in *Midnights: A Year With the Wellfleet Police.*

Natural History

Robert Finch, editor of *A Place Apart* (☞ *above*), has also written three lyrical books about natural history: *Outlands: Journeys to the Outer Edges of Cape Cod, Common Ground: A Naturalist's Cape Cod,* and *The Primal Place,* a meditation about life on the Cape, especially its natural rhythms and history. Finch is also the author of *Death of a Hornet and Other Cape Cod Essays* and the attractively illustrated *Cape Cod: Its Natural and Cultural History,* a National Park Service handbook about the National Seashore and the Cape. *In the Company of Light* traces John Hay's journey from Maine to Cape Cod, recounting his observations of light and luminescence—in nature and as revelation. Hay is a wonderful nature writer; his other titles include *The Run,* about the life cycle of alewives, and *Great Beach. A Guide to Nature on Cape Cod and the Islands,* edited by Greg O'Brien, has sections by a variety of experts on the area's flora and fauna.

Photography

A Summer's Day (winner of the 1985 Ansel Adams Award for Best Photography Book) and *Cape Light* present color landscapes, still lifes, and portraits by Provincetown-associated photographer Joel Meyerowitz.

INDEX

NOTES

NOTES

4th Tuesday

Stayed night in Hilton in Dedham. Room service

5th Wednesday

Dunkin Donuts for breakfast + picked up bagels + cream cheese for lunch. Aquarium. Boat trip to Georges Island for picnic + to see Fort Warren. ~~Train back~~ John Hancock Building to watch sunset.

6th Thursday

Breakfast in hotel and set off to Plymouth. Went around Ocean Spray Cranberry Visitors Centre, Mayflower II Plimoth Plantation. Lunch at diner. Friendlies for dinner - Pizza. Arrived at Cranberry Cottage - dirty. Sat in hot tub + had early night with no dinner.

7th Friday

Went back into Plymoth, walked around village, bought binoculars + went on whale watching trip. Saw many Humpbacks + Atlantic White Sided Dolphins. Drove round cape to Eastham to stay in Penny House Inn. Wendys for dinner.

8th Saturday

Gorgeous breakfast then went to Deli to buy lunch. Drove to Salt Water Pond and walked around nature trail. Drove to ~~Nauset Light~~ First Encounter Beach and sunbathed + swam in ~~Atlantic~~ Cape Cod Bay. Played Monopoly + then went to play Crazy Golf + had chinese meal for dinner

O

NOTES

9th   Sunday
Drove to Provincetown and looked
around. Had a smoothie then headed
out to Race Point Beach to relax +
fly kite. Windy but very warm still
Ocean water very cold. Parked in poo

~~10th Monday~~ Crazy Golf then went to
Drive Inn to see 'The Others' +
'American Pie 2'.

10th   Monday
    Went to K-Mart + Shopping Mall.
Friendly's for lunch - Back hosting.
Watched telly.

11   Tuesday
3 Terrorist Attacks on America -
Found out at breakfast about
plane going into World Trade Centre.
Left Perry House Inn. Stopped to
see JFK Memorial + sunbathed
+ swam on Veterans Park Beach
in Hyannis. ~~Chinese take out
when we Got to Palmer House
Inn.~~ Lunch at Deli in Falmouth.
Walked around town + went to
Chamber of Commerce. Checked into
Palmer House Inn. Chinese take out.
No cutlery or chop sticks!

12th   Wed.
   ~~took~~ free shuttle bus to Woods
Hole. Ferry to Marthas Vineyard.
Bought pack lunch stuff.
Trolley tour with 1½ in Edgartown.
Ice cream + caught ferry back
from Oak Bluff. No dinner
- watched film

13th   Thurs.
   Kayaking in Waquoit Bay Estuary

NOTES

Went back to B+B for shower.
Pizza Hut for late lunch Matt!
Went through Sandwich + drove
to Sandy Neck Beach to watch
sunset. Left overs for tea.

14th Friday
Late start. Drove to Salem.
Lunch at Creppy ~~Diner~~ Café
    Creepy

Salem Witch Wax Museum +
Tour. & Drove along coast
to Gloucester. Ate 3 shrimp
+ gave rest to Andy - $50 !!

15th Saturday
Went to flee market. Crazy Golf.
Nacky! Cinema at Mashpee Mall +
watched 'Rock Star'. Packed
Mexican dinner at Iguana's.

16th ~~Sunday~~. DIDN'T REALIE HOW MUCH
I LOVE LIZ UNTIL NOW!

16th SUNDAY
Our last breakfast at Palmer House.
Got up late!! Set off to Stockbridge
and drove across the most beautiful
scenery. - with the leaves having
started to turn. Arrived in
Stockbridge + went to Visitor Centre.
Booked into minging motel for
night. Went to Berkshire Botanical
Gardens + walked around. Drove
north to Mount Greylock + drove
to the summit + sat on wall at
the Veterans Memorial Tower.
We watched the sun go down
hand in hand. Then took
some photos + headed back to

NOTES

motel.
Watched Jaws on TV. Where
they filmed it we've been!
Marthas Vineyard.

NOTES

NOTES

NOTES

NOTES

NOTES

NOTES

NOTES